PUBLIC ART IN SOUTH AFRICA

AFRICAN EXPRESSIVE CULTURES

PUBLIC ART IN SOUTH AFRICA

Bronze Warriors and Plastic Presidents

Edited by
KIM MILLER *and*
BRENDA SCHMAHMANN

INDIANA UNIVERSITY PRESS

This book is a publication of

Indiana University Press
Office of Scholarly Publishing
Herman B Wells Library 350
1320 East 10th Street
Bloomington, Indiana 47405 USA

iupress.indiana.edu

The paper used in this publication meets the minimum requirements of the American National Standard for Information Sciences—Permanence of Paper for Printed Library Materials, ANSI Z39.48–1992.

Manufactured in the United States of America

Library of Congress Cataloging-in-Publication Data

Names: Miller, Kim (Kimberly A.), editor, author. | Schmahmann, Brenda, 1960- editor, author.
Title: Public art in South Africa : bronze warriors and plastic presidents / edited by Kim Miller and Brenda Schmahmann.
Description: Bloomington : Indiana University Press, 2017. | Series: African expressive cultures | Includes bibliographical references and index.
Identifiers: LCCN 2017023154 (print) | LCCN 2017024194 (ebook) | ISBN 9780253030108 (e-book) | ISBN 9780253029591 (cloth : alk. paper) | ISBN 9780253029928 (pbk. : alk. paper)
Subjects: LCSH: Public art—Social aspects—South Africa. | Public art—Political aspects—South Africa. | Public art—South Africa—Public opinion. | Art—Mutilation, defacement, etc.—South Africa. | Public opinion—South Africa. | South Africa—Social conditions—21st century. South Africa—Race relations—21st century.
Classification: LCC N8846.S6 (ebook) | LCC N8846.S6 P83 2017 (print) | DDC 701.03096809051—dc23
LC record available at https://lccn.loc.gov/2017023154

1 2 3 4 5 22 21 20 19 18 17

CONTENTS

INTRODUCTION

Engaging with Public Art in South Africa, 1999–2015

KIM MILLER AND BRENDA SCHMAHMANN

On March 9, 2015, about a dozen protestors gathered in front of a sculpture of mining magnate and politician Cecil John Rhodes on the campus of the University of Cape Town. Among them was a politics student, Chumani Maxwele, who donned a luminous pink protective helmet and adorned himself in sandwich boards with the words "EXHIBIT WHITE ARROGANCE U.C.T." on his front and "EXHIBIT BLACK ASSIMILATION U.C.T." on his back. Calling for the removal of the statue, the protest culminated in Maxwele tossing a bucket of human excrement at it.

The work in question (fig. 0.1), which sculptor Marion Walgate completed in 1934 and which was given as a gift to the University of Cape Town by the Rhodes National South African Memorial Committee, was intended to commemorate the benefactor of the land on which the university's primary campus had been built. Comprising a full figure about one-and-a-half times life size and set on a pedestal six and a half feet in height, it showed Rhodes seated on a bench and contemplating the vista of Cape Town before him. A verse about Cape Town by Rudyard Kipling had been engraved on the sculpture's plinth:

> I DREAM MY DREAM
> BY ROCK AND HEATH AND PINE
> OF EMPIRE TO THE NORTHWARD
> AY, ONE LAND
> FROM LION'S HEAD TO LINE.

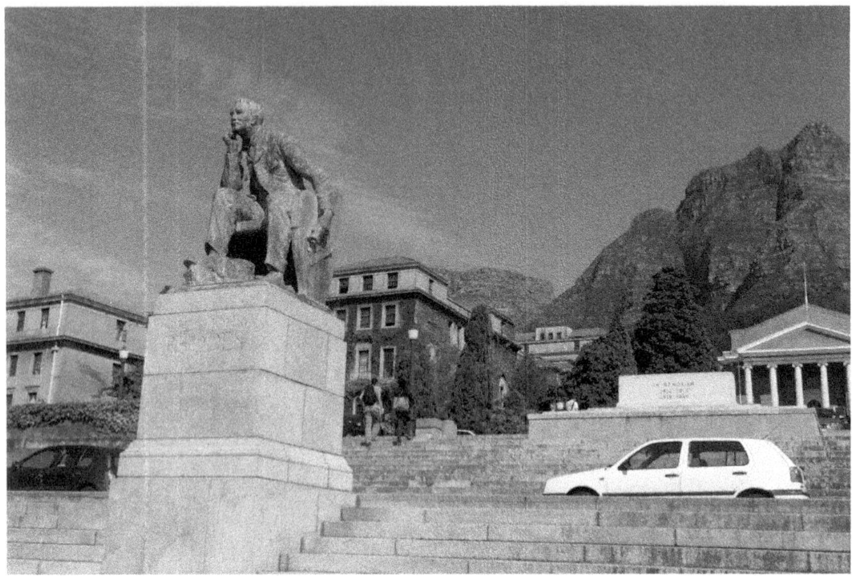

Fig. 0.1 Marion Walgate, *Cecil John Rhodes* (1934), bronze, 160 x 122 x 142 (figure), about 200 cm high pedestal. At the University of Cape Town's upper campus, beneath the steps leading to Jameson Hall, where it was located from 1962 until April 9, 2015. *Photograph by Paul Mills.*

Walgate's figure was initially placed looking over De Waal Drive toward a rose garden on Rhodes's estate. In 1962, when the widening of De Waal Drive necessitated the sculpture being relocated, it was placed in an even more elevated position just above the rugby field and beneath the stairs leading to the institution's Jameson Hall. It was a move that increased its imperialist associations. While Cape Town is often celebrated for its magnificent natural beauty, the words of Kipling suggested that Rhodes's focus as he contemplated the expansive vista before him was less on the landscape itself than on his ambition to build a railway line linking Cape Town to Cairo—one that would enable him to foster and develop British economic interests in Africa.

Concerns about the continued display of Walgate's representation of Rhodes on a central spot on campus had surfaced from time to time in a post-apartheid dispensation,[1] but these had not had particular impact. The 2015 protest was different, however. Despite the fact that the footage posted on YouTube ended up focusing rather more on the endeavors of University of Cape Town security officials to prevent a journalist from a local newspaper from taking photographs of Maxwele's actions, protest against the retention of the statue escalated in scale and impact, achieving national coverage and placing questions about the role of public art as well as issues to do with the negotiation of a visual art inheritance in the spotlight. On March 11, the university's Student Representative Council issued a formal statement that clarified students' perceptions that the retention of the sculpture of Rhodes was symptomatic of the lack of transformative actions being taken by the institution. Arguing that the university "continues to celebrate, in its institutional symbolism, figures in South African history, who are undisputedly white supremacists," the statement questioned how "a colonizer" might "donate land that was never his land in the first place." Drawing attention to Rhodes's introduction of the Grey Act "which allowed for black people to be utilized as cheap exploited labor in the mines owned by him," the letter suggested that the portrait on campus served as "a constant reminder for many black students of the position in society that black people have occupied due to hundreds of years of apartheid, racism, oppression and colonialism."[2] Developing into a campaign titled "Rhodes Must Fall," activities included occupation of the university's administrative building by hordes of students—about a hundred of whom committed to sleeping overnight in the building. Faced with an escalating protest, members of the University of Cape Town's senate were almost unanimous in their vote to permanently remove the sculpture of Cecil Rhodes from campus—a decision that was ratified by the university's council on April 8. On April 9, Walgate's sculpture was placed in safekeeping at an offsite venue.[3]

The campaign had wider impact. Spreading to Rhodes University in the Eastern Cape of South Africa, where focus was placed on the name of the institution, it extended also to the University of KwaZulu-Natal where a sculpture representing George V on the Howard College campus in Durban was discovered on March 26 to have been defaced with white paint and wrapped in a blanket that was inscribed with the words "END WHITE PRIVILEGE." The campaign had additionally in fact spread beyond universities to include art objects in various city centers. Exactly a week prior to the removal of the sculpture, a burning tire was placed on the pinnacle of a monument to the South African War in Uitenhage in the Eastern Cape, thus reiterating the terrifying and cruel act of "necklacing" a perceived collaborator (i.e., placing a tire around the neck of a victim and igniting it) that had been a frequent occurrence during the 1980s. On the evening of April 5, a large monument to Paul Kruger in Church Square in Pretoria was defaced with lime-green paint. On the following day, April 6, the *Horse Memorial* (1905) in Port Elizabeth in the Eastern Cape, a work that commemorated the more than 300,000 horses that the British had lost in the South African War, was vandalized: the figure of a soldier depicted kneeling down and offering a bucket of water to his horse had been toppled. On April 9, the same day as Walgate's sculpture of Rhodes was removed, two men used blue and red paint to deface a sculpture of Afrikaner statesman and the first prime minister following the union of South Africa in 1910, Louis Botha, outside Parliament in Cape Town. And incidents continued thereafter. For example, on the morning of April 10, it was discovered that the sculpture of Queen Victoria outside the public library in Port Elizabeth had been defaced with green paint.[4]

NEGOTIATING DIFFICULT HISTORIES

The reaction against Walgate's sculpture of Cecil Rhodes and the heated response to other works that followed in the wake of the student protest against its retention on campus highlights the first of four key thematic issues or debates tackled in this volume. An important question confronting South Africa is how art objects in the public domain that are associated with ideologies that are out of favor, such as British imperialism or Afrikaner nationalism, be negotiated. And how, by extension, might South Africa manage other kinds of indices or material traces of histories that have involved the terrible subjugation of humankind, such as spaces and places in the Western Cape that are associated with slavery?

Taking place twenty-one years after the end of apartheid, a defacing of objects that celebrate individuals and histories associated with the suppression of local people seemed oddly belated in the sense that South Africa's transition to democracy had in fact seen neither the kind of triumphant toppling of monuments that accompanied the demise of the Soviet Union, for example, nor even a sustained project of removing objects associated with former dispensations. While the visual domain included numerous monuments that attest to the influence of British imperialist or Afrikaner nationalist ideas, only objects with the potential to be highly inflammatory had for the most part been removed.[5] In a context where the focus was on reconciliation and where, for example, hearings held under the auspices of the Truth and Reconciliation Commission were perceived as a way of enabling different parties to overcome divisions and histories of conflict, the overall approach was to enable diverse histories to be commemorated. Consequently, rather than calling for the removal of monuments and public art associated with ideologies that had fallen out of favor, and thus risking alienating groups associated with them, a post-apartheid dispensation mooted that new artworks be built alongside those from former apartheid and colonial dispensations. Setting up the South African Heritage Resources Agency (SAHRA) as a management body and introducing the National Resources Heritage Act (1999) to articulate its policies, the government indicated that memorials and public monuments would require consent of local branches of National Heritage prior to any permanent adjustment to them.[6]

This is not to say that objects and monuments associated with British imperialism and Afrikaner nationalism were necessarily ignored rather than being contextualized or subject to any critical scrutiny. Textual strategies were sometimes deployed to suggest critical responses. The University of Cape Town, for example, deployed an online document devised to introduce monuments on campus to highlight ambivalent feelings about Walgate's sculpture of Cecil Rhodes. While recognizing that "without this section of the Groote Schuur estate which he donated for the founding of a university, U.C.T. would probably not have come into existence in 1918," the unnamed author of the text also acknowledged that "Rhodes' imperialist and racist attitude to Africa causes much controversy and resentment today."[7] More occasionally, such textual strategies might be used on the plaques accompanying monuments. A memorial to the victims of terrorism, constructed in 1988 in Pretoria, was accompanied by a plaque with a biblical verse from Romans 12:19 ("Vengeance is mine: I will repay") as well as a dedication "To our victims of terrorism." Sabine Marschall (2010, 159) notes that the plaque was adjusted shortly after the First Democratic Election: "After heated debate in which Conservative Party councilors voiced their strong objection, it was resolved to re-dedicate the memorial to 'all' instead of 'our' victims of terrorism and to remove the biblical quote."

Another strategy was to build new monuments and objects that served as a decisive and deliberate counterpart to older ones. An example might be found in the juxtaposition of monuments near Dundee in KwaZulu-Natal at the site of the so-called Battle of Blood River—that is, the battle won by the Voortrekkers on December 16, 1838, against amaZulu forces under the leadership of Dingane.[8] A 1970s monument designed by Cobus Esterhuizen and consisting of sixty-four bronzed cast-iron wagons arranged in a laager, the battle formation adopted by Voortrekkers, was provided with a post-apartheid counterpart in 1999—a Wall of Remembrance invoking the horn-like battle formation used by Dingane's army. Discussing this example as well as some others, Marschall (2010, 311) notes how a related principle plays out in the juxtaposition of sculptures of individuals perceived to be counterparts from different groups within the cultural spectrum. Sometimes involving posthumous reconciliations between enemies, such pairings have also in certain instances included those who enjoyed good relationships in their lifetimes. The latter was true of a sculptural arrangement at the corner of Berea Road and Warwick Avenue in Durban, where an existent statue of Louis Botha was paired with a new figure of Dinizulu kaCetshwayo, for example (fig. 0.2). Assisting Dinizulu become paramount chief of the amaZulu in 1884, Botha made it a priority following his appointment as prime minister "to release Dinizulu from prison, where he had begun serving a four-year term for his role as instigator of the Bhambatha Rebellion in 1909" (Marschall 2010, 311).

But faced with instances of vandalism in the wake of the Rhodes Must Fall campaign, the Department of Arts and Culture found itself obliged to reconsider whether its official policy of leaving in place older works remained feasible. On April 17, 2015, the Minister of Arts and Culture, Nathi Mthethwa, convened a discussion of transformation and heritage in Pretoria, and a variety of resolutions were made in the course of the daylong meeting. Determining that dumping unwanted objects in a museum would be impractical, it was instead mooted that "theme parks depicting our history" be developed "at national, provincial and local levels" for such works.[9] Yet this idea was not in fact new. As Marschall (2010, 153) observes, several South African cities had from time to time mooted for "the establishment of designated commemorative spaces where relocated monuments of the past would be joined by new monuments dedicated to the heroes of the present order." The reason that such an initiative has not to date been implemented, however, was because it is essentially unworkable on an ideological level. In the 2015 discussion, as in past endeavors to implement such "theme parks," it was unclear how an agenda to achieve inclusive histories might be reconciled with pressure to remove objects from the public domain that some consider offensive. As Marschall (2010, 156) has observed, "Resistance

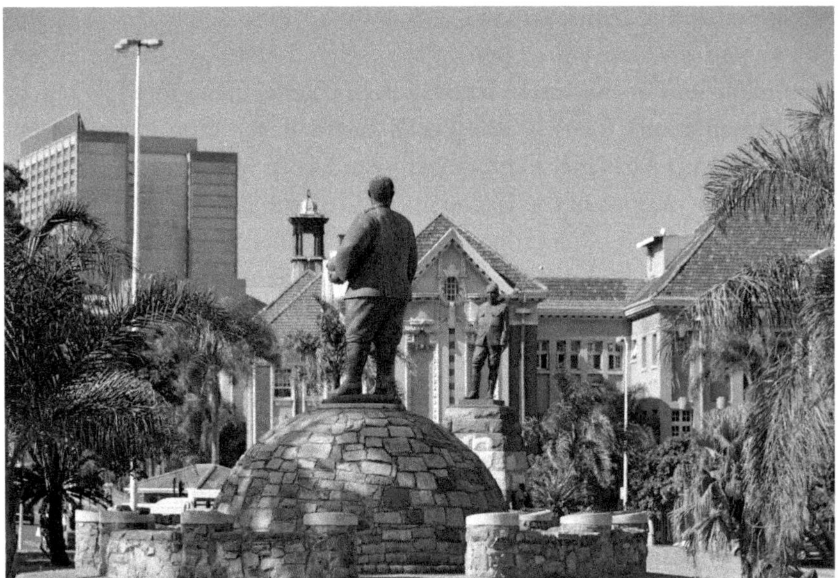

Fig. 0.2 Peter Hall, *Dinuzulu ka Cetshwayo* (2006), bronze, on beehive base designed by Erhard Huizinga. Opposite is Anton van Wouw, *Louis Botha* (1921), bronze. Installation is at the corner of Berea Road and Warwick Avenue, Durban. *Photograph by Gordon Hiles.*

towards a designated, shared place of honour for old and new heroes prevails not only on the part of people who identify with the 'old guard' but also on the part of those who identify with the new order, because the commemoration of their leaders is perceived to be neutralised, rendered ambiguous or even 'contaminated' through the presence of 'enemy' heroes."

These issues are picked up in part 1 of the volume, where three contributors explore ways in which new monuments address fraught histories as well as negotiate older monuments associated with ideologies that have fallen from favor. In chapter 1, titled "A Janus-Like Juncture: Reconciling Past and Present at the Voortrekker Monument and Freedom Park," Elizabeth Rankin explores two interrelated issues. She reveals how the Voortrekker Monument, a structure in Pretoria inaugurated in 1949 and intricately associated with Afrikaner nationalism, has sought to reinvent itself in the years following the demise of apartheid. In parallel to the two monuments near Dundee in KwaZulu-Natal and the sculptural arrangement at the corner of Berea Road and Warwick Avenue in Durban, mentioned above, she also examines how Freedom Park, first officially opened in 2013, has been conceptualized and structured in such a way that it offers both a dialogue with and an alternative discourse to the earlier monument—and explores the implications of this interrelationship. In chapter 2, authored by one of us (Schmahmann), focus is also placed on the negotiation of art objects associated with Afrikaner nationalism—but in this instance, three monuments on the campus of the University of the Free State in Bloemfontein. The chapter offers an exploration of how potential meanings in those monuments are unsettled and their authority questioned through the inclusion of additional works of art on campus—notably by Willem Boshoff's *Thinking Stone,* which was installed in 2011. The university has welcomed discursive engagements with these older monuments through their temporary adjustment, it is also noted, and the implications of an intervention undertaken in 2014 by Australian artist Cigdem Aydemir is explored. In chapter 3, titled "The Mirror and the Square—Old Ideological Conflicts in Motion: *Church Square Slavery Memorial,*" the focus shifts from histories of Afrikaner nationalism and its representation to questions around the memorialization of people who were enslaved in South Africa. Gavin Younge, codesigner with Wilma Cruise of the *Church Square Slavery Memorial,* explains how histories of slavery remain underplayed or obfuscated in the South African commemorative landscape and of the necessity to counter symbol blindness—that is, to address ways in which slave bells and other structures associated with slavery, rather than being linked to repressive and brutal practices, are often treated as picturesque features of the Western Cape. The final form of the *Church Square Slavery Memorial* developed only subsequent to he and Cruise winning the commission, Younge explains, recounting how their decision to memorialize this history through abstract form presented challenges for many stakeholders more accustomed to figuration as well as the debates and concerns that led to the final choice of components and texts.

DEFINING AND REDEFINING HEROES

Questions about identity and nationhood do not, however, arise only in regard to statues associated with colonialism and apartheid and quandaries about how to negotiate them. Public sculpture has also generated robust controversy in regard to questions about how beloved icons are best represented and remembered in the public sphere—a second key theme that is addressed in this volume.

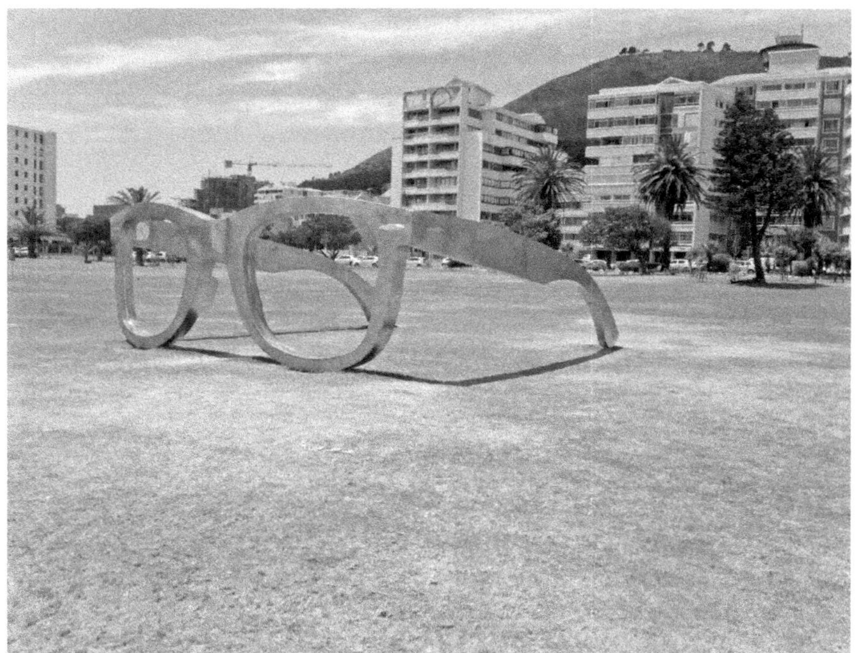

Fig. 0.3 Michael Elion, *Perceiving Freedom* (2014), steel, Sea Point Promenade, Cape Town. (The photograph shows the work without its glass lenses, which required restoration following their defacing in the wake of the controversy the sculpture raised.) *Photograph by Julian Richfield.*

A number of debates and differences have involved the representation of Nelson Mandela, for example. One such controversy erupted in November 2014 in response to Michael Elion's public sculpture—ostensibly a tribute to Mandela—that took the form of a gigantic pair of Ray-Ban Wayfarer sunglasses (fig. 0.3). While the work's title, *Perceiving Freedom*, references the liberation struggle in general, its link to Mandela is made clear through its accompanying plaque, which includes a photograph of Mandela wearing a pair of dark sunglasses (not Ray-Bans). The context of the photograph is critical in understanding public dissatisfaction over this work: the original photograph was taken in 1977 while Mandela was incarcerated on Robben Island. While there, he and other political prisoners spent countless hours engaged in hard labor in the island's limestone quarry, enduring thick dust and blinding sunlight. Although Mandela asked for sunglasses for protection from these conditions, his request was denied for three years, and when he eventually received them, he had sustained permanent injury to his eyes. The artist's willingness to use Mandela's life, and indeed his suffering, for personal and commercial gain was seen by many as opportunistic, as well as deeply insulting to the former president, who had died less than a year before the sculpture's installation.

Furthermore, the location and positioning of *Perceiving Freedom* has further political meanings when considered in the context of the history of apartheid. The gigantic sunglasses are on the busy Sea Point Promenade in Cape Town. The Promenade is along beaches with spectacular views that were available for whites only under the Separate Amenities Act in operation under apartheid—a painful history that is part of the collective memory of that space, as it is in many other locales in South Africa. More immediately, the gigantic sunglasses are positioned in such a way that the lenses face the sea and toward Robben Island in the distance. A UNESCO World Heritage Site, Robben Island is the country's most popular tourist destination, and virtually all world leaders who come to South Africa tour the island and have their photographs taken in the tiny cell that Mandela occupied for nearly two decades. *Perceiving Freedom,* which claims to be a sculptural homage to Robben Island's most famous prisoner, clearly connects the sculpture to the political history of this important space.

Given the above factors, and because the sculpture was both approved of and endorsed by the City of Cape Town and partly financed by Ray-Ban, the work set off an immediate and robust public debate about how liberation history, including individual figures, should be commemorated. Public dissatisfaction, waging primarily in local news media and via social media platforms, included a petition to have the work removed, which circulated on Facebook and received nearly 1,100 signatures. A key issue of contention was the work's reference to Mandela and the use of his name to fuel commercial profit. Elion was accused of exploiting the public art process to create advertising, not art. The work was seen as opportunistic in representing the former president's sacrifice for and vision of democracy via a pair of expensive designer sunglasses, especially in the context of extreme poverty and other inequalities that persist in South Africa today. (The overt commercialism was further communicated through photographs of the artist and accompanying dignitaries at the work's unveiling, which showed them all wearing Ray-Ban sunglasses.) Public discussion about the work also raised

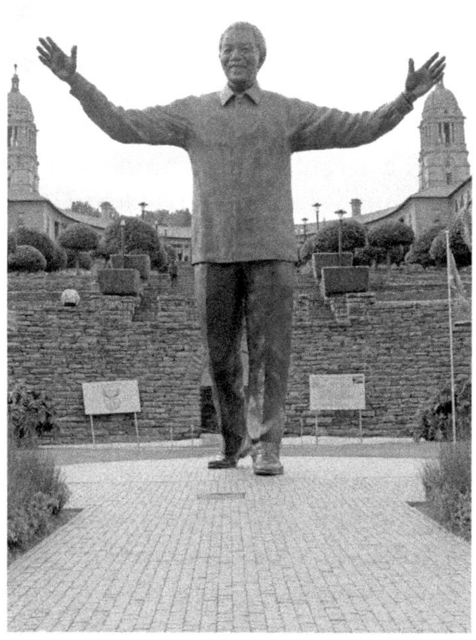

Fig. 0.4 André Prinsloo and Ruhan Janse van Vuuren, *Nelson Mandela* (2013), bronze, 9 meters (about 30 feet) in height, Union Buildings, Pretoria. *Photograph by Paul Mills.*

more general questions about the processes by which public art projects get financed, approved, and built in public spaces.

Another controversy centered on questions about what might be appropriate for a public work representing Nelson Mandela had in fact arisen shortly after his death on December 5, 2013. On December 16, 2013, the Day of Reconciliation, a statue of Mandela that is nine meters (nearly thirty feet) in height was installed at the Union Buildings (fig. 0.4) in a spot that had been formerly occupied by a four-meter (thirteen-feet) sculpture of Afrikaner nationalist James Barry Hertzog, who served as prime minister from 1924 until 1929 (and that was relocated). Commissioned from sculptors André Prinsloo and Ruhan Janse van Vuuren by the National Heritage Council and intended to celebrate the centenary of the Union Buildings, the seat of government in Pretoria, the production of the Mandela sculpture was overseen by Koketso Growth, a company whose chief executive officer is Dali Tambo, the son of struggle heroes Oliver and Adelaide Tambo. The sculptors had received the commission in July 2013 and had completed the work in record time.

Prinsloo and Janse van Vuuren represented Mandela in terms that were wholly uncontroversial and (apart from the unnerving and bizarre scale of the sculpture) conventional—smiling and with outstretched arms and thus, as President Jacob Zuma indicated at the work's unveiling, "embracing the whole nation."[10] But, it emerged in January, the sculptors had included a quirky addition to the work: a tiny bronze rabbit had been inserted in Mandela's right ear. Denied permission to sign their names on the trousers, the artists had sought another trademark reference to themselves as makers. The Afrikaans word *haas* means both "rabbit" and "haste," and the motif thus served as a playful allusion to the fact that the artists were under pressure to meet a tight deadline.

But those involved in organizing the commission were decidedly unamused. Mogomotsi Mogodiri, spokesman for the Department of Arts and Culture, indicated that the sculptors' inclusion of their signature motif was unacceptable "because Nelson Mandela never had a rabbit on [sic] his ear" (Saul 2014). Dali Tambo's objection, while less literal-minded, was also problematic: "That statue isn't just a statue of a man, it's the statue of a struggle, and one of the most noble in human history," he observed, adding, "so it's belittling, in my opinion, if you then take it in a jocular way and start adding rabbits in the ear" (Saul 2014). Whereas those objecting to Elion's image were not suggesting that gigantic Ray Ban sunglasses were undignified but were instead concerned with a crass commercialism underpinning the artist's association of his sculpture with Mandela, Dali's objection to the sculptors' inclusion of a whimsical element was underpinned by a conception that public sculpture must be free of humor if it is to be respectful. But such an argument relies on a narrow conception of the playful. Johan Thom, writing about the works of Angus Taylor, makes reference to the idea of "serious play" by designer and artist Paula Scher, observing that she draws an important distinction between "seriousness" and "solemnity." While "solemnity" "is grave or sober, and seeks to perpetuate the status quo," "'seriousness' is always playful," "capitalizes on opportunities presented by chance," and "does not lead to socially correct results but often generates new discoveries" (Thom 2010, 30). Such a distinction may be instructive in this context. Tambo, it seems, viewed the rabbit motif as an unwelcome departure from the solemnity he thought essential in a representation of Mandela: clearly

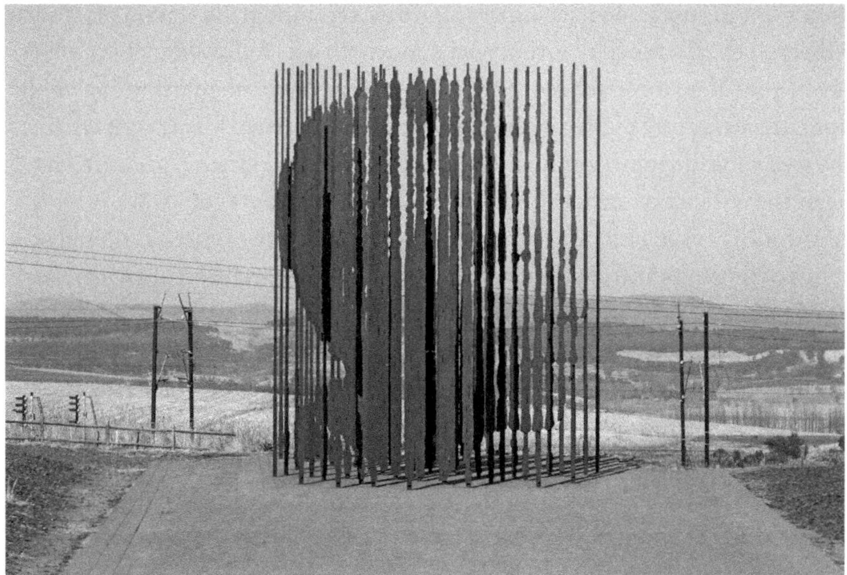

Fig. 0.5 Marco Cianfanelli, *Release* (2012), painted laser-cut mild steel and steel tube construction, 9.48 meters in height x 5.19 meters (width) at the end of a 20.8 meter pathway, Nelson Mandela's Capture Site Monument near Howick, KwaZulu-Natal. *Photograph by Paul Mills.*

unaware that a sculpture on this scale necessarily has an element of the absurd or fantastical, and impervious to its peculiar relation to the Union Buildings, his commentary suggests that he envisaged that the sculpture would inspire sober deference. The sculptors, in contrast, conceived the rabbit in Mandela's ear as a form of "serious play," which might indicate that the work was not a "reflection" of the former president that had been mechanistically enlarged to a massive scale but rather that this ginormous representation had been *constructed*—and at great speed! Nonetheless, the upshot of the controversy was that the artists were obliged to offer an apology for the inclusion of this motif—even though it was only visible with the aid of binoculars—and make arrangements to remove it.

The work by Prinsloo and Janse van Vuuren is not in fact the tallest public image of Mandela. A sculpture by Marco Cianfanelli (fig. 0.5), which is adjacent to the R103 and about three kilometers outside Howick in KwaZulu-Natal, includes some columns that are 9.5 meters (thirty-one feet) in height. Indexing the spot where Mandela had been captured by security police on August 5, 1962, when, disguised as a chauffeur, he was on his way to Albert Luthuli's home in Groutville and which was followed by his twenty-seven-year-long imprisonment and consequent banishment from the public domain, it was unveiled exactly fifty years later, in August 2012. But whereas the two subsequent works by Elion and Prinsloo and Janse van Vuuren have been the subject of criticism or controversy, the Cianfanelli work is widely admired. This success story points to ways in which the artist has managed a series of tensions and challenges that underpin the rendition of an icon such as Mandela. Creating an image that, while respectful, is accessible, Cianfanelli has rendered Mandela recognizable but in a way that circumvents the realms of the literal or traditionalist. And, while enormous in scale, his monument avoids being bombastic.

Comprised of fifty steel columns that are at the end of a paved pathway, these apparently abstract structures bring into focus a portrait of Mandela when one is about thirty-five meters (115 feet) away from the structure. While referring to the fifty years following Mandela's capture, they also suggest, Cianfanelli indicates, "the idea of many making the whole; of solidarity," thus pointing "to an irony as the political act of Mandela's incarceration cemented his status as an icon of struggle, which helped ferment [sic] the groundswell of resistance, solidarity and uprising, bringing about political change and democracy."[11]

Large-scale but nevertheless mimetic figures of Mandela, including the example by Prinsloo and Janse van Vuuren at the Union Buildings, normally encourage viewers to be transfixed by the art object—indeed to lose a sense of their own bodies in temporal time and space. Not simply iconic, such works tend also to represent leaders as somewhat remote and inaccessible even when assuming a welcoming gesture. Norman Bryson suggests that such remoteness is encouraged in works constructed through a transparent illusionism—in other words, that blot out all signs that they are constructed objects by, for example, excluding all traces of the artist's hand.[12] (And in the case of the work by Prinsloo and Janse van Vuuren, this is particularly true in the sense that not only does the surface of the work not carry indices of touch, but the artists were in fact also prevented from adding their signature to the work.) The monument by Cianfanelli, however, is comprehended in and through time and space. One walks up to the steel columns, discerning how these components fuse into an image, and then, as one moves closer and looks at them from different angles, the viewer ceases seeing any reference to a face and instead comprehends only abstract metal stakes—the raw materials, as it were, from which the illusion is constituted. The outcome is that rather than being transfixed by the image and viewing the work as iconic and remote, one comprehends it in terms of what Bryson (1983, 94) calls "the glance"—a form of looking that recognizes "the durational temporality of the viewing subject."

In part 2 of this volume, contributors focus on issues related to those that have been raised in these various representations of Mandela but through the examination of commemorations of a variety of iconic figures. Examining the relationship between public art and heroism, each considers how choices were made as well as the implications of those selections—including disputes that have developed. In chapter 4, Liese van der Watt looks at controversies that have arisen in relation to public projects by Durban-based sculptor Andries Botha, focusing on a depiction of King Shaka, which was critiqued for being insufficiently heroic. The controversies that arose in relation to his work speak to larger debates about Shaka as a disputed symbol of Zulu unity and masculinity and give insight about the challenges facing the commemoration of such an ambiguous figure in a public space. In chapter 5, "Mandela's Walk and Biko's Ghosts: Public Art and the Politics of Memory in Port Elizabeth's City Center," Naomi Roux uses representations in the Port Elizabeth city center to consider how public art contributes to the emphasis of certain heroic narratives in public space and the occlusion of others. She focuses specifically on contrasting the official recognition of Nelson Mandela through permanent representations with ephemeral references to Steve Biko, associated with Black Consciousness, suggesting how the appearance of the latter within the public domain may to some extent be read "as a challenge to a narrative of post-apartheid reconciliation, unity and successful transformation" invoked by the former. In chapter 6, titled "Remembering Solomon Mahlangu: The Making and Unmaking of a 'Struggle' Icon," Gary Baines also contributes to the discussion about figures who are selected and established as heroic. Solomon Mahlangu was a member of Umkhonto we Sizwe (MK), the military wing of the African National Congress (ANC), who was killed by the apartheid state in 1979. While constituted immediately thereafter as a martyr who symbolized the ANC's commitment to remedying the oppression of ordinary people through the armed struggle and consequently being memorialized in, for example, a commemorative stamp and a statue, he has become more latterly, Baines suggests, representative of "an idealism betrayed by a cohort of greedy and corrupt politicians" in the ANC.

ERASURES AND RUINS

The enormous figure of Mandela by Prinsloo and Janse van Vuuren is a work that has heightened visibility. But another post-apartheid work at the Union Buildings suffers from an antithetical problem. In 1998, South Africa's new government announced a competition for the creation of a monument to commemorate the Women's March in 1956, when more than 20,000 women from across South Africa had marched to Pretoria's Union Buildings to protest the apartheid government's proposal to extend its oppressive pass laws to women. Not only was this the first national effort to recognize women's role in the liberation struggle within the public sphere, but it was also the first piece of public art commissioned by the new government at the national level. But despite its crucial significance, the monument has been virtually inaccessible since the moment of its creation because the space where it is located—the site of the occurrence it commemorates—is now permanently closed to the public.[13] The memorial is thus in practice invisible, and not even Wilma Cruise and Marcus Holmes, the two artists who made the work, can glean ready access to it. But inaccessibility is not the only factor underpinning erasure from the commemorative landscape. As is explored in part 3 of this volume, so too is the vandalizing of, or failure to maintain, public art.

The potential significance of this issue becomes evident if one considers questions raised by another significant memorial constructed in the post-apartheid era—that of Sarah Baartman. A Khoisan woman whose birthday is usually estimated to have been in 1789,[14] Baartman had been persuaded by William Dunlop, a medical superintendent at the Slave Lodge in Cape Town, to travel with him to London in April 1810. While promised fame and fortune, she was in fact treated as nothing more than a curiosity in England and, following her relocation there in September 1814, in Paris. Given the name "Hottentot Venus," she was put on display not only during her lifetime but also after her premature death in 1815, when George Cuvier, Napoleon's surgeon general, together with other scientists and anthropologists concluded that she provided clear evidence of the superiority of the white race and proceeded to dissect her body and genitalia. Coupled with a body cast, these remains ended up in the Musée de l'Homme in Paris, where they were on display until 1985.

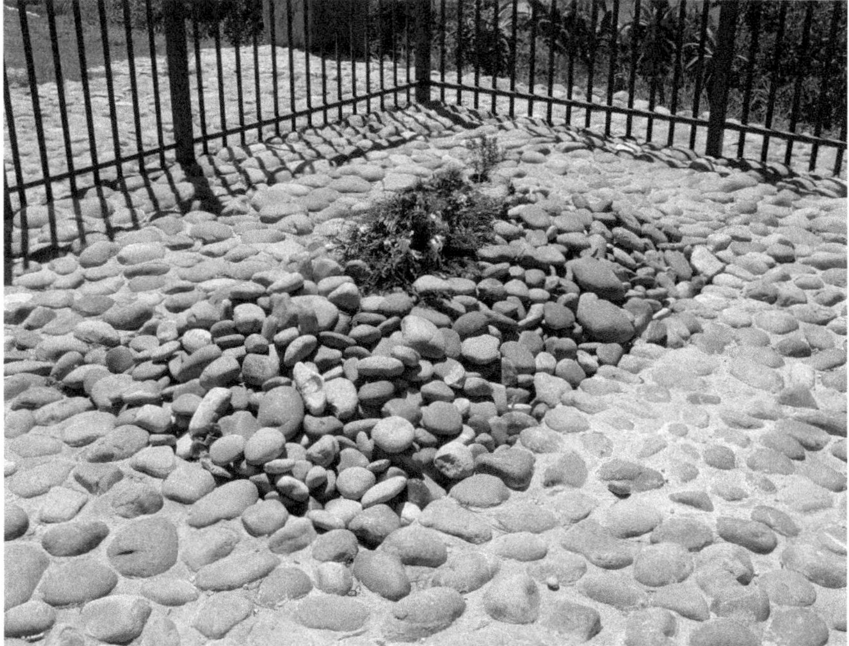

Fig. 0.6 Memorial gravesite of Sarah Baartman on the outskirts of Hankey in the Eastern Cape. The bottom of the memorial stone can be discerned outside the fence around the grave. *Photograph taken in 2007 by Paul Mills.*

In a widely publicized ceremony that took place on National Women's Day (August 9) in 2002 and following a prolonged effort to repatriate her body back to South Africa, Baartman was laid to rest in a memorial site established on a hill on the outskirts of Hankey in the Eastern Cape of South Africa. Overlooking the Gamtoos River Valley, Baartman's presumed place of birth,[15] the site includes her grave itself, which is fenced (fig. 0.6), as well as a large memorial stone in natural form—except for its front, which has been flattened out and displays a plaque with text that speaks to the memorial's purpose and meaning. Here, the primary reference to Baartman comes not through image or representation but rather through text inscribed onto the plaque. Providing a vehicle for acknowledging a history of not only colonial abuses toward indigenous peoples (especially the exploitation of women) but also those who suffered under apartheid, it commemorates an individual life—perhaps even elevating Sarah Baartman to the realm of the heroic—while also affirming symbolically the dignity and history of the marginalized Khoisan peoples in general. As Cecil le Fleur, chairman of the National Khoisan Consultative Conference Council, commented, "Baartman became a symbol of our suffering, and all the misery she went through was a manifestation of how the Khoisan people were treated during that period and beyond" (McGreal 2002).

But, tragically, a disrespect afforded Baartman during her lifetime and the years in which her remains were in a museum in Paris in fact continued following the repatriation of these effects. Established in a site devoid of proper security or protection, the memorial grew increasingly dilapidated, and the fence around Baartman's grave was frequently scratched, seemingly with keys or other sharp implements. On April 25, 2015, a more deliberated and large-scale desecration occurred, when a group of men (whose identities remain unknown) threw white paint onto the memorial stone, covering most of the plaque and rendering its text unreadable. Highlighting the fact that in diametric opposition to that at the Union Buildings, Baartman's grave is *overly* accessible even if in a locale somewhat remote from centers that most tourists visit, this desecration suggests a need to expedite plans currently under way to develop a Sarah Baartman Centre of Remembrance adjacent to her memorial—not exclusively for the purposes of enabling knowledge and memory but also for securing the site.[16]

Coming so soon after the events surrounding the removal of the figure of Rhodes at the University of Cape Town, one cannot but consider this defacement as another moment in the ongoing struggle over memory that is being conducted on the surface of public art sites across South Africa. But what is one to make of the fact that, in this instance, an aggressive defacement has been enacted on a memorial that reacted against colonialist atrocities rather than celebrated imperialist figureheads? Is this an act best understood as grounded in misogyny? Or is this a backlash by right-wingers against those vandalizing memorials associated with British imperialism and Afrikaner nationalism? Alternatively, is this an act by those who, finding themselves without opportunity or agency in a current dispensation, have sought to desecrate its icons? Could these even be individuals who, despite the promise of new jobs during the construction phase of the new Sarah Baartman Centre of Remembrance, have found themselves not benefitting from that initiative? In a context where complex sets of agendas and shifting allegiances underpin responses to public art, the implications of acts of desecration are much more ambiguous than they might once have been.

The two contributors to part 3 of this volume engage with the destruction and vandalism of art objects in the public domain. As with the questions posed in response to the desecration of a plaque at Baartman's memorial site, the authors suggest that acts of vandalism are not simply symptomatic of the lack of sufficient arrangements to ensure the protection of works in the public domain but that they can in fact be interpreted as making reference to the sentiments and attitudes of their viewers. Chapter 7, authored by one of us (Miller), focuses on a single incident—the 2011 theft and dismemberment of a bronze statue depicting Nokuthula Simelane, a female activist who, like Mahlangu, lost her life fighting for the liberation struggle. It is argued that this particular episode is instructive for thinking through the relationship between violence and representation in the public sphere—what W. J. T. Mitchell (1990, 891) calls "the economy of violence encoded in public images"—and that this would seem to be especially true in relation to commemorations of heroic women, whose courageous actions have gone relatively unnoticed in post-apartheid public domain. It is suggested that the relative absence of depictions of heroic women has significant implications for women's political viability and power in public art. In chapter 8, titled "Transgressive Touch: Ruination, Public Feeling and the *Sunday Times* Heritage Project," Duane Jethro addresses public art that has been damaged or destroyed by examining three instances of desecration or neglect of works organized under the auspices of the *Sunday Times* Heritage Project—the *Bruce Fordyce Memorial* in Durban, the *Race Classification Benches Memorial* in Cape Town, and the *Tsietsi Mashinini Memorial* in Soweto. In exploring these case studies, Jethro considers the kinds of public feelings that acts of destruction might express, and what this in turn might tell us about the political orientation and emotional needs of the works' intended audiences.

EPHEMERAL PROJECTS

Most of the examples invoked in this introductory discussion are commissioned works that assume a sculptural form. But South African artists working in the public domain, like those elsewhere, have also undertaken experimental works that trouble conventional understandings of "public art" as a category. Operating in terms of performance, billboards, and other temporal modes of communication rather, expressive culture of this type may sometimes enjoy the same official sanction as commissioned sculptures and other works conceived as permanent additions to the public domain. But this category of imagery also involves genres conventionally outlawed from the public spaces, such as graffiti, as well as enactments and interventions for which no permission is sought. Ephemeral engagements—both licit and unsanctioned—constitute the thematic focus of part 4 of this volume.

Ephemeral art, in contrast with more permanent and tangible public art, may speak to different—often marginalized—audiences. It may also involve interventions to the public domain that, precisely because they are temporary, sometimes assume more provocative, radical, and adventurous form than permanent installations: whereas those commissioning the latter normally ensure that works satisfy a range of stakeholders, instances of the former—even when undertaken with permission rather than being unauthorized—lend themselves to being confrontational and defiant. Also, whereas audiences may become accustomed to permanent public art and thus no longer even really notice sculptures or other kinds of art that might once have seemed unusual, noteworthy or provocative, a temporary disruption of expectations about a milieu, even when discreet, has the advantage of never becoming habitual and thus unremarkable.

One form that temporary work has assumed is through (readily reversible) adjustments to sculptures in the public domain—whether for the purposes of discursive commentary about visual heritage or about the people and incidents that they represent. A notable instance of this strategy being deployed was a project devised specifically for September 24, 1999. Formerly Shaka Day, which was observed by isiZulu speakers alone, September 24 had been renamed Heritage Day and developed by the post-apartheid government as a public holiday that might serve as a forum for different manifestations of culture to be celebrated. For the 1999 public holiday, a newly established company, Public Eye, orchestrated temporary adjustments to public monuments in Cape Town. The title, *P.T.O.* (meaning "please turn over"), invoked the idea of turning over a new leaf, as it were, or perhaps viewing these monuments from a different perspective. One of its contributions was by Beezy Bailey, who transformed the figure of Louis Botha in the sculpture of him on horseback (i.e., the work that would be vandalized on April 9, 2015) into a Xhosa initiate. Another was John Nankin's *Mister*

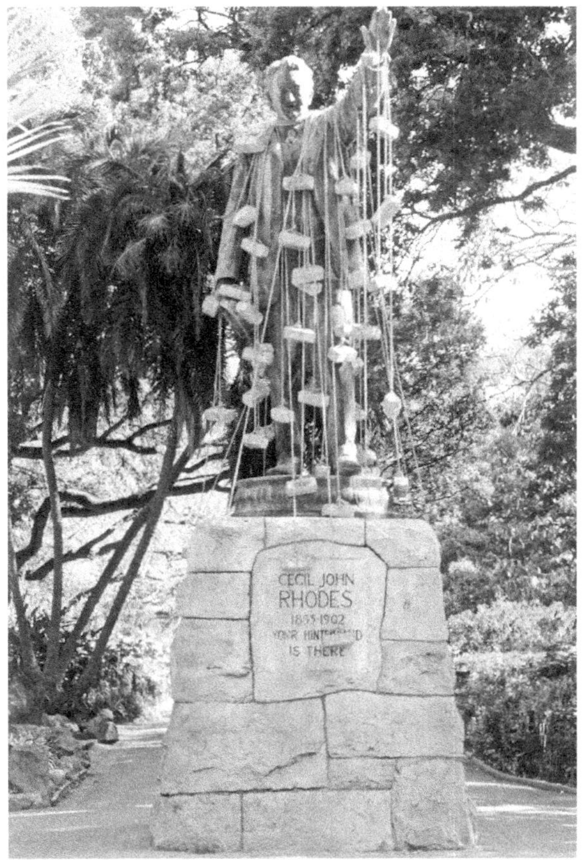

Fig. 0.7 John Nankin, *Mister Rhodes*. 1999. Addition of ropes and bricks to Henry Alfred Pegram's *Cecil John Rhodes*, 1908, bronze, Company Gardens, Cape Town. *Photograph by John Nankin.*

Rhodes (fig. 0.7), an adaptation to a sculpture by Henry Pegram of Cecil Rhodes in the Company Gardens where the figure was represented pointing north and which alluded to the subject's ambition to build a railway from Cape Town to Cairo. Suspended brick-weighted ropes from his arm and shoulder alluded to riggings in mining in Kimberley while simultaneously suggesting gold bars, which served to suggest "a burden or retribution" and thus an "inversion of the idea of accumulation."[17]

There are also examples of unauthorized ephemeral public works that are noteworthy. These include those of the Tokolos Stencil Collective, an anonymous group of activists who have made interventions in the public domain since 2013. ("Tokolos" is the colloquial form for "Tokoloshe." While a type of counterpart to the bogeyman and normally associated with negative forces, the tokoloshe is envisioned by the collective as fighting for good.) The collective is best known for imagery developed to mark the first anniversary of the Marikana massacre, a shocking incident that took place on August 16, 2012, when security forces opened fire on a group of miners and other employees of the Lonmin platinum mine in the town of Marikana, who were protesting over wages, and consequently caused the death of thirty-four strikers and injury to many others. In commemoration of this event and the oppression underpinning it, the Tokolos Stencils, using stencils, spray-painted on various sites the words "Remember Marikana" accompanied by an image of Mgcineni Noki, a strike leader among those who were gunned down. This stencil has appeared in various contexts subsequent to the anniversary. For example, members of the Tokolos Collective responded to Michael Elion's *Perceiving Freedom* (see fig. 0.3) by spray-painting not only "We Broke Your Hearts" in large black lettering across the lenses of the glasses but also coupling it with their "Remember Marikana" stencil. While "We Broke Your Hearts" may be read on one level as a commentary about limitations and problems of the sculpture itself, which we discussed earlier, its juxtaposition with the Marikana stencil served to highlight the need to see clearly, to recognize, the profound disappointment of the population in a government that through its brutal suppression of the demonstrators had betrayed the principles that had underpinned the liberation struggle. Given the placement of *Perceiving Freedom* opposite Robben Island, the additions to the sculpture point to a chilling disregard for the sacrifices of those formerly incarcerated there.

The first two chapters of part 4 of our book focus on large-scale projects that were temporary and that, like *P.T.O.*, were authorized initiatives involving multiple sites. In chapter 9, titled "Troubling Tropes: An Unsettling Intervention in Cape Town," Shannen Hill examines *Returning the Gaze*, a series of public programs and artistic interventions in 2000, which like *P.T.O.*, took place in Cape Town. Organized by the Black Arts Collective (BLAC), the artists included in the program engaged with the ideals and history of Black Consciousness—an approach, Hill indicates, that was often misunderstood and therefore opposed by arts professionals, including a number involved in Public Eye. Revealing how a Black Consciousness focus on relations of power underpinned its imagery, which appeared throughout the city on billboards and murals and circulated via T-shirts and postcards, she indicates how *Returning the Gaze* challenged the notion that South Africa had in fact become unified since the end of apartheid. In chapter 10, titled "Unsettling Ambivalences and Ambiguities in Mary Sibande's *Long Live the Dead Queen* Public Art Project," Leora Farber shifts our focus to Johannesburg where, in 2010, a public art project featuring large-scale photographic images created by artist Mary Sibande transformed the visual landscape of the city. Mounted on billboards and building facades, the photographs depict Sibande herself, posing in character as a fictional domestic worker and in a manner that invokes a range of women's histories and experiences, ranging from Queen Victoria to the artist's mother and grandmother (who were both domestic workers). Farber's discussion explains how the placing of such monumental and unexpected imagery into a familiar urban space works as a kind of invasion that abruptly and creatively inserts seemingly private and concealed experiences in the public domain.

The last three chapters in this volume explore ephemeral interventions to the urban milieu that, like those of the Tokolos Stencils Collective, were undertaken outside of commissioning structures or without official authorization and that offered challenges to values and norms that had social currency. In chapter 11, titled "*Unsanctioned*: The Inner-City Interventions by Julie Lovelace," Karen von Veh explores the implications of three interventions to downtown Johannesburg by British emigrant Julie Lovelace. Combining made and found objects, Lovelace's works, von Veh suggests, engage with liminality in such a way that they point to aspects of the experiences of immigrants—a discussion that is particularly pertinent in light of waves of xenophobic violence that have plagued South Africa, notably in 2008 and once again in early 2015. In chapter 12, titled "Rage against the State: Political Funerals and Queer Visual Activism in Post-Apartheid South Africa," Kylie Thomas explores not only how the public domain presents dangers for LGBT people but also how it serves as a site of visual activism. Examining three responses to the death of a twenty-eight-year-old lesbian, Thembelihle Sokhela, which took the form of performances, she reveals how events such as funerals serve as primary sites for "public art" on the part of queer communities. In chapter 13, the last in the book, Matthew Ryan Smith explores yet another form of visual activism—in this instance, graffiti. In "Telltale Signs: Unsanctioned Graffiti Interventions in Post-Apartheid

Johannesburg," he engages with ways in which illicit graffiti in the Johannesburg milieu expresses oppositional politics, suggesting that is unique because it "constantly negotiates between historical trauma and the promise of renewal."

FROM 1999 TO 2015—SCOPE OF THIS VOLUME

As examples discussed in this introduction indicate, there has been a tremendous amount of activity in the public domain in South Africa since the demise of apartheid. While often motivated by an impetus to reshape the commemorative landscape, such activities may also be linked to efforts at enabling urban regeneration. Focusing on the latter agenda and on Johannesburg specifically, Todd Pitock (2014) suggested in a travel article in the *New York Times* that "public art is helping to revivify urban Johannesburg, a seemingly implausible regeneration in this city of more than four million residents, which not that long ago seemed as though it was about to fall through the widening cracks of crime and dilapidation." According to Pitock, such developments have "made Joburg cool again—and popular."

Although a commentary such as this may imply that ongoing work on art in the public domain is symptomatic of escalating confidence and positivity in South Africa, the truth is in fact more complex. Thabo Mbeki's loss of grassroots support during his presidency, which commenced in 1999, was coupled by diminishing investment confidence through his denial of the mounting HIV crisis in South Africa as well as refusal to condemn the violations of human rights in neighboring Zimbabwe. A sense of unease with ANC governance would, however, become increasingly pronounced following the recall of Mbeki at the ANC's meeting in Polokwane in 2007 and the replacement of him by Kgalema Motlanthe and, in 2009, by Jacob Zuma—the latter accused of (among other charges) rape, corruption during a national arms deal, and illegally using public funds for a lavish upgrade of his Nkandla homestead in KwaZulu-Natal. It should also be noted that South Africa remains one of the most unequal countries in the world and that its level of unemployment reached more than 26 percent in the first three months of 2015.

Diminishing confidence in the country's leadership as well as sentiments of alienation, marginalization, or despondency on the part of many citizens invariably have an impact on public art and its reception. Hardly surprisingly, while much work from the new millennium has continued to celebrate the liberation struggle as well as South Africa's multicultural inheritance, as it did in the years immediately following the first democratic elections, public art in South Africa has also served as a forum in which tensions and uncertainties in regard to race, gender, identity, or nationhood have played out. A key purpose in this volume is to identify and explore examples in which such concerns have been manifest.

Rather than focusing on the immediate post-apartheid period and early public art initiatives in a new dispensation, our study takes as its starting point 1999, the year that saw the appointment of Thabo Mbeki as president. In designating this as the commencement date for the contents of this volume, our intention is not to imply that Mbeki's appointment had in practice marked a distinctive shift in governance from that of Mandela (prior to assuming the presidency and when vice-president, Mbeki had in any case contributed enormously to governance) but rather to highlight that our focus is on examples of public art made after the euphoria following the overthrow of apartheid had passed. The year 1999 may be understood as additionally significant for public art in the sense that, as indicated, it saw the passing of the National Resources Heritage Act.

The closure of the time frame of works explored in this volume is 2015—a choice of date that is not motivated by it coinciding with the completion of the study but rather by important activities that took place in the public domain. The general election of May 2014 was the first to include the vote of the so-called born-free generation. But the fact that economic inequality and prejudicial discrimination continues to limit the opportunities of many, including those born in an era free of legislated discrimination, was in immediate evidence in March 2015, when the "Rhodes Must Fall" campaign was initiated. Involving not simply the removal of Walgate's sculpture of Rhodes but also, as indicated, the desecration of a number of public artworks, such acts suggested that the accommodation of cultural symbols associated with diverse groupings in the public domain had begun to be seen by some South Africans as a marker not of reconciliation but rather the lack of appropriate social and economic transformation in the country. In other words, acts of desecration suggest that for many who experienced themselves as oppressed and denied opportunity, a public art policy grounded in a principle of reconciliation was understood as simply perpetuating discrimination experienced in colonial and apartheid eras and as therefore being untenable. The "Rhodes Must Fall" campaign might thus be understood to mark the end of an era in which official ideas about a spirit of reconciliation informing public art remained largely uncontested.

DEFINING PUBLIC ART

As the discussion of the themes and content of this volume make evident, we have deliberately excluded from in-depth consideration various temporary exhibitions in museums or galleries. Although some such shows do engage with the possibilities of the public museum or gallery as a discursive space and thus reflect critically on histories of display for diverse audiences, others are considerably more focused on the histories of particular artists or subject matter—in other words, on issues with no immediate relevance to developing understanding of "public art" as a category or genre of visual culture. In avoiding including temporary exhibitions as a focus of the volume, we have sought to prevent its scope from being widened in such a way that "public art" would be in danger of becoming a catch-all phrase for any and all art, and our study consequently lacking in coherency and direction.

The field remains nevertheless wide. Cameron Cartiere, referring to a volume on public art he coedited with Shelly Willis (Cartiere and Willis 2008), speaks of "grappling with a definition of public art that could embrace the vast spectrum of activity that falls across a field . . . [that] includes sculpture, performance, activism, social engagement, place-making, monuments and memorials, and a range of other artistic practices that are difficult to categorize but share the common ground of existing in and for the public realm" (Cartiere 2016, 14). Although Cartiere and Willis had come up with a working definition that was more detailed, their suggestion that public art is comprised of visual expressions "existing in and for the public realm" in the above passage would seem sufficiently inclusive but also precise to accommodate the examples of public art that are the focus of this volume.[18]

We would want to note, however, that in speaking of art "in and for the public realm," we are talking only about realms that are *physically* accessible to a diversity of people rather than implying that such art necessarily has broad public *appeal*. While South Africa's complex and fractious history has created controversy in regard to older works of art associated with ideologies such as British imperialism or Afrikaner nationalism, contemporary works of art may also sometimes be experienced as alienating—albeit for different reasons. Malcolm Miles, writing in 1997, observes that "art today privileges individualism and subversion of the previous mainstream position," adding that it may appeal "to a specialist public for whom this self-referential development has meaning, but its re-location to public places does not in itself increase access to it more than incidentally" (Miles 1997, 6–7). This is true in post-apartheid South Africa, too. Indeed, it is important to acknowledge that in addition to responses to public art being affected by race, class, gender, and political allegiance, for example, they are also often shaped by the degree to which viewers are (or are not) versed in debates about public art and its histories. While some works of art located in public spaces may have mainly specialist rather than wide appeal, others use mimetic or illustrative modes of representation that to many art and design professionals may seem trivial or reductive. Works such as Cianfanelli's monument near Howick, which impress people from not only a range of different social strata but who have unlike aesthetic preferences or tastes, are thus comparatively rare.

PRIOR WRITINGS ON PUBLIC ART IN SOUTH AFRICA

Our volume focuses on imagery produced subsequent to what is examined by Annie Coombes in her influential *History after Apartheid: Visual Culture and Public Memory in a Democratic South Africa* (first published in 2003)—a study in which she considers "how various forms of visual and material culture dramatized the tensions involved" in the shift from apartheid to democracy (Coombes 2003, 1). Coombes, it should also be noted, does not engage with "public art," as such, but instead uses the term *new public histories* to encapsulate a broad range of discourses. The considerations in our book thus also differ theoretically and empirically from her work. Additionally, our volume departs in focus from that adopted in *Landscape of Memory: Commemorative Monuments, Memorials and Public Statuary in Post-Apartheid South Africa*, where its author, Sabine Marschall (2010, 10), sought to take up some of the issues identified by Coombes, but, in her words, add to them "concerns specific to the genre of the public monument." While her detailed study is helpful in providing information about heritage policy and its impact on public commissions, its scope is only on "official objects which are either initiated or endorsed by various agencies of the state and addressed to the general public" (Marschall 2010, 18). Consequently, while *Landscape of Memory* engages with the period from 1994 to 2009, thus overlapping with the earlier part of the time frame we are exploring, the vast majority of works that are the focus of examination in our volume—among them the important *Sunday Times* Heritage Project, which resulted in more than thirty works made for public spaces across the country—are outside its framework of consideration.[19]

While other studies may sometimes touch on content related to this study, they also have an overall emphasis that is very different. For example, Oliver Barstow and Bronwyn Law-Viljoen's (2011) *Firewalker,* is centered on a single public sculpture by Gerhard Marx and William Kentridge, which we do not examine. Issues of memory rather than the politics and meaning of public art, as such, are the primary focus in Martin Murray's (2013) *Commemorating and Forgetting: Challenges for the New South Africa.* While including some discussion of memorials, the examples that are given close scrutiny (other than the Voortrekker Monument) are different to those that are the focus of our volume. *Picturing Change: Curating Visual Culture at Post-Apartheid Universities,* authored by one of us (Schmahmann 2013), includes consideration of commissioned works on university campuses in South Africa. But the university-based case study we discuss in this book—new art at the University of the Free State—was not examined in that 2013 volume.

Additionally, there has not to date been a comprehensive edited volume on public art in South Africa that brings together specialist research by a range of contributors. This volume addresses this significant gap. Including the work of established academics as well as some midcareer and younger scholars, and, along with art historians and art theorists, other academics working in the humanities and social sciences, the various chapters are all the product of original research and make an important contribution to furthering understanding of this complex and important aspect of visual practice.

Notes

1. For example, in 2005, a staff member at the nearby University of the Western Cape, Anthony Holiday, argued that images of Rhodes ought to be removed from the city, suggesting that Ndebele, vice-chancellor at the time, might encourage such actions "by abolishing the brooding figure of Rhodes that stares across the Cape Flats from his university's upper campus" (Holiday 2005).

2. Ramabina Mahapa, "Press Release on UCT Student Protest," March 11, 2015. http://www.scribd.com/doc/258502122/UCT-SRC-Press-Release-on-UCT-Student-Protest

3. See Schmahmann (2016) for detailed discussion of the implications of removing Walgate's sculpture of Rhodes.

4. While many of these acts were undertaken by members of the Economic Freedom Fighters (EFF), a party established during the run-up to the election in 2013 and led by former leader of the African National Congress Youth League, Julius Malema, they do not seem to have necessarily been part of an orchestrated strategy.

5. For example, many representations of Hendrik Verwoerd, understood as the architect of apartheid, found their way to the storage sections of monuments associated with Afrikaner histories, such as the Voortrekker Monument and the Taal Monument. See Coombes (2003, 22).

6. Republic of South Africa, "National Heritage Resources Act," 30 (11) (a). http://www.sahra.org.za/sites/default/sahranascptho/website/articledocs/Sahra_Act25_1999.pdf.

7. Heritage@UCT. Accessed May 13, 2015. https://www.uct.ac.za/downloads/uct.ac.za/about/introducing/heritage/heritagetrail.pdf.

8. These were Dutch speakers who left the Cape Colony (then under the control of the British) in the 1830s and 1840s, moving into the interior of South Africa to establish new settlements.

9. Department of Arts and Culture. 2015. "Resolutions of the National Dialogue on Statues and Symbols." *Politicsweb*, April 22. Accessed March 26, 2017. http://www.politicsweb.co.za/politics/resolutions-of-the-national-dialogue-on-statues-an.

10. See http://www.southafrica.info/news/mandela-statue-181213.htm#.VV3YtWeJjct.

11. See http://marcocianfanelli.com/index1c.html.

12. By blotting out of all traces of process and of the presence of "hand" of the artist, the work is inclined to "encourage a synchronic instant of viewing which will eclipse the body, and the glance, in an infinitely extended Gaze of the image as pure idea" (Bryson 1983, 94).

13. For a feminist analysis of the work, see Miller (2011). Miller argues that the monument's very success in making women's political power discernible may well be a factor in its present invisibility.

14. Crais and Scully (2009) believe that she was in fact born in the 1770s.

15. Crais and Scully (2009) suggest that she was probably in fact born in Camdeboo, an area slightly north of Hankey.

16. See http://www.cacadu.co.za/article/77.

17. Personal e-mail communication between Brenda Schmahmann and John Nankin, April 11, 2015. The work is discussed in greater detail in Schmahmann (2016). See Penfold (1999) for discussion of a range of works constituting the P.T.O. initiative.

18. Cartiere and Willis suggest that it is "art outside of museums and galleries and must fit within at least one of the following categories:

1. in a place accessible or visible to the public: in *public*
2. concerned with or affecting the community or individuals: *public* interest
3. maintained for or used by the community or individuals: *public* place
4. paid for by the public: *publicly funded*" (Cartiere and Willis 2008, 10).

19. Notable also is that one key example included in this study that does in fact fall within the narrow category of "public art" as Marschall conceives of it, as well as within the time frame of her study, is excluded by her for no apparent reason: the book makes no mention at all of the important *Church Square Slave Memorial* by Wilma Cruise and Gavin Younge that was commissioned by the Cape Town City Council and unveiled in 2008.

References

Barstow, Oliver, and Bronwyn Law-Viljoen. 2011. *Firewalker.* Johannesburg: Fourthwall Books.

Bryson, Norman. 1983. *Vision and Painting: The Logic of the Gaze.* New Haven, CT: Yale University Press.

Callinicos, Luli. 2009. Personal interview, Johannesburg, July.

Cartiere, Cameron. 2016. "Through the Lens of Social Practice: Considerations on a Public Art History in Progress." In *The Everyday Practice of Public Art,* edited by Cameron Cartiere and Martin Zebracki, 13–26. New York: Routledge.

Cartiere, Cameron, and Shelly Willis, eds. 2008. *The Practice of Public Art.* New York: Routledge.

Coombes, Annie. 2003. *History after Apartheid: Visual Culture and Public Memory in a Democratic South Africa.* Durham, NC: Duke University Press.

Crais, Clifton, and Pamela Scully. 2009. *Sara Baartman and the Hottentot Venus: A Ghost Story and a Biography.* Johannesburg: Wits University Press.

Holiday, Anthony. 2005. "Rhodes Statue Insults the New Order." *Cape Times,* March 14.

Jelin, Elizabeth. 2003. *State Repression and the Labors of Memory.* Minneapolis: University of Minnesota Press.

Marschall, Sabine. 2010. *Landscape of Memory: Commemorative Monuments, Memorials and Public Statuary in Post-Apartheid South Africa.* Leiden, the Netherlands: Brill.

McGreal, Chris. 2002. "Coming Home." *The Guardian,* February 20. http://www.theguardian.com/education/2002/feb/21/internationaleducationnews.highereducation.

Miles, Malcolm. 1997. *Art, Space and the City: Public Art and Urban Futures.* London: Routledge.

Miller, Kim. 2011. "Selective Silence and the Shaping of Memory in Post-Apartheid Visual Culture: The Case of the Monument to the Women of South Africa." *South African Historical Journal* 63, no. 2: 295–317.

Mitchell, W. J. T. 1990. "The Violence of Public Art: Do the Right Thing." *Critical Inquiry* 16, no. 4 (Summer): 880–99.

Murray, Martin. 2013. *Commemorating and Forgetting: Challenges for the New South Africa.* Minnesota: University of Minnesota Press.

Penfold, Denise. 1999. "P. T. O.—Public Monuments Reconsidered." *Artthrob,* no. 26 (October). http://www.artthrob.co.za/99oct/reviews.html.

Pitock, Todd. 2014. "Seeing Johannesburg through Artists' Eyes." *New York Times,* July 11. Accessed March 26, 2017. http://www.nytimes.com/2014/07/13/travel/seeing-johannesburg-through-artists-eyes.html?emc=eta1&_r=1.

Saul, Heather. 2014. "Nelson Mandela Statue: Sculptors Told to Remove Bronze Rabbit Hidden in the Ear." *Independent Online,* May 31. Yeattp://www.independent.co.uk/news/world/africa/nelson-mandela-statue-government-tells-sculptors-to-remove-bronze-rabbit-hidden-in-the-ear-9079130.html.

Schmahmann, Brenda. 2013. *Picturing Change: Curating Visual Culture in Post-Apartheid South Africa.* Johannesburg: Wits University Press.

———. 2016. “The Fall of Rhodes: The Removal of a Sculpture from the University of Cape Town.” *Public Art Dialogue* 6, no. 1 (Spring): 90–115.

Thom, Johan. 2010. “Into the Magic Factory: Serious Play in Angus Taylor’s Disproportion of Inflation.” In *Angus Taylor: New Work* (exhibition catalog), 26–32. Johannesburg: CIRCA on Jellicoe.

ACKNOWLEDGMENTS

THE EDITORS CONVEY SINCERE thanks to Indiana University Press for assisting us to realize this volume. Particular appreciation is owed to Dee Mortensen, editorial director, for her enthusiasm for this project from start to completion as well as Paige Rasmussen, assistant acquisitions editor, for her helpfulness and support.

We thank the many people who kindly made available photographs they had taken previously. And we are very grateful indeed to Paul Mills, Gordon Hiles, and Julian Richfield who, on request, took photographs for us in Pretoria, Durban, and Cape Town without charging us for them.

The number of illustrations we were able to include in this volume would not have been possible without financial support from the National Research Foundation (NRF) in South Africa. It is to be noted, however, that any opinions, findings, conclusions, or recommendations expressed in the course of the volume are those of contributing authors, and the NRF does not accept any liability in regard to them.

PUBLIC ART IN SOUTH AFRICA

PART 1

NEGOTIATING DIFFICULT HISTORIES

CHAPTER 1

A Janus-Like Juncture: Reconciling Past and Present at the Voortrekker Monument and Freedom Park

ELIZABETH RANKIN

The day should not be far off, when we shall have a people's shrine, a Freedom Park, where we shall honor with all the dignity they deserve, those who endured pain so we should experience the joy of freedom.
Nelson Mandela, speech on Freedom Day, April 27, 1999

Freedom Park was planned as an inclusive national monument, reflecting Mandela's concept of a people's shrine and giving visual representation to the liberation of South Africa, honoring all those who had contributed to the country's hard-won democracy, in particular those who had resisted apartheid. Standing on a fifty-two-hectare site on the elevated Salvokop, east of the southern entrance to Pretoria (fig. 1.1), Freedom Park offers vistas that encapsulate something of the diverse history of the administrative capital, named after the Voortrekker hero Andries Pretorius, and erstwhile capital of the nineteenth-century Zuid-Afrikaansche Republiek. Across the city, one can see a distant view of the Union Buildings, erected on Meintjies Kop after Britain defeated Kruger's Afrikaner republic in the Anglo-Boer War and amalgamated the country's four regions into a union in 1910. It was a stately building to signify imperial authority but came to house changing administrative bodies, whether representing a British dominion or a republic and whether dominated by English, Afrikaans, or African leaders.[1] It is an example of how old forms can be adapted for new purposes and, as the

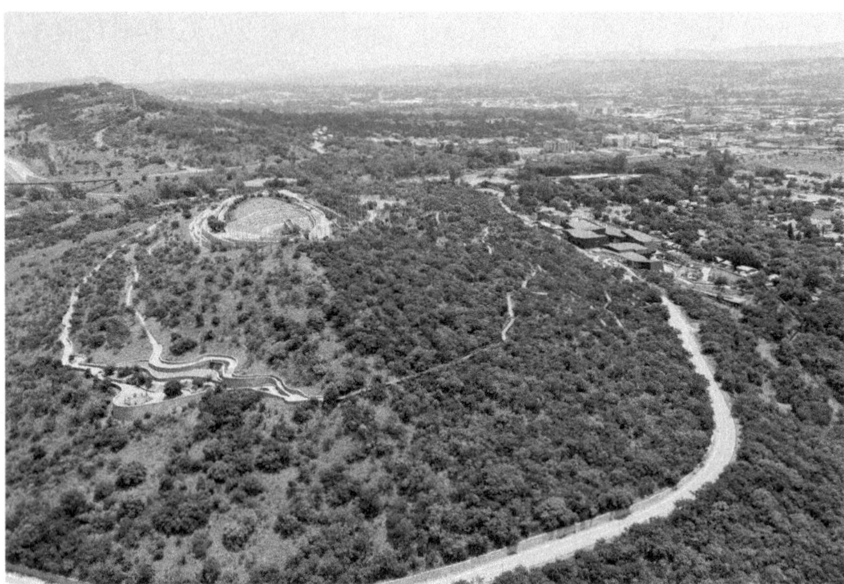

Fig. 1.1 Freedom Park. Aerial photograph showing the Salvokop site. Isivivane is on the lower left, Sikhumbuto with amphitheater, sanctuary and wall of remembrance on the hilltop above, and //hapo on the right, with Pretoria beyond. *Photograph courtesy of OCA Architects.*

home to South Africa's African National Congress (ANC)–led government today, an embodiment of the symbolic appropriation of power.[2]

But another edifice that does not lend itself easily to appropriation is also visible from Freedom Park. Opposite, on a hill to the west, stands the Voortrekker Monument (fig. 1.2), an edifice commemorating what came to be known as the Great Trek, when, from 1835, parties of Dutch speakers left the Cape Colony for the South African interior to escape British rule; their journeys have assumed iconic significance as the foundation myth of Afrikanerdom in nationalist discourses. Redolent with the ideologies of the deposed Afrikaner Nationalist regime, the Monument's persistent presence prompts questions about what the role of such monuments might be in a newly constituted South Africa. Is it possible to reconceptualize them?[3] A novel interpretation of imagery at the Monument offered on a 1996 visit by Tokyo Sexwale, then premier of Gauteng province where Pretoria is located, implies this is possible. He cleverly inverted the meaning of Afrikaner symbols, suggesting, for example, that the Zulu assegais represented on the Monument's gates and in many scenes of confrontation on the historical

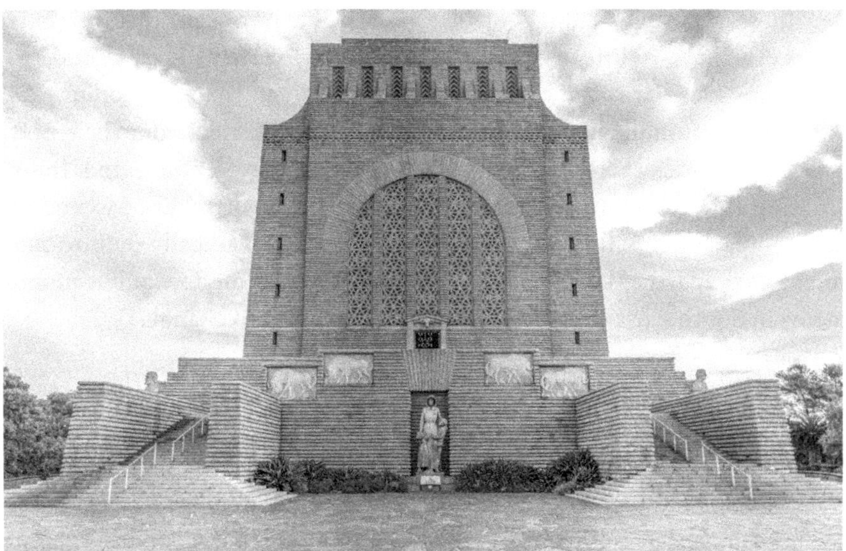

Fig. 1.2 Voortrekker Monument. View from the north, with Van Wouw's *Mother and Children* in the forecourt. *Photograph by Russell Scott.*

frieze of the Hall of Heroes within did not have to be understood as a deterrent in the quest to bring white culture to the interior, as the Voortrekkers would have claimed. Instead, he proposed that the weapons were signifiers of the military wing of the ANC, Umkhonto we Sizwe (Spear of the Nation), which in liberating South Africa had "opened up the path of civilisation" (Coombes 2003, 37).

The Chief Executive Officer (CEO) responsible for the Voortrekker Monument and Nature Reserve, Major-General (Ret.) Gert Opperman, uncoupled the Monument from an Afrikaner Nationalist agenda differently. While not denying the history it represents, he argued in a paper for the African Congress on Peace through Tourism in 2007 in Uganda that the Monument was never intended to represent apartheid (Opperman 2007, 3), and he has also stated that it "had been misused for political purposes during the previous government as it had such a tremendous appeal to the Afrikaner nationalism [sic]" (Opperman 2011). Yet another repositioning to be discussed later—this time in 2011—saw the Monument linked to Freedom Park in a symbolic act of reconciliation, officiated over by President Jacob Zuma. Coupled in a Janus-like juncture, one monument focused on South Africa's past, while the other used the past to look toward the future.

These differing readings of the Monument may seem disingenuous. However, they are informative in highlighting efforts to review outdated ideologies faced with new dispensations—and validate old monuments. While such monuments cannot readily be disassociated from their past, their significance can be rethought, reformed, and even reinvented. In examining the post-apartheid repositioning of the Voortrekker Monument and comparing it with Freedom Park, which was specifically built to represent post-apartheid principles, I aim to throw light on how public monuments in South Africa respond to political and cultural change.

THE GREAT TREK AND AFRIKANER NATIONALISM AT THE VOORTREKKER MONUMENT

When in the mid-1930s the Central People's Monuments Committee (Sentrale Volksmonumentekomittee [SVK]) chose a hill outside Pretoria as the site to memorialize the Voortrekkers of South Africa, it bypassed the claims of locations far more closely associated with the journeys of the early Afrikaner pioneers or Voortrekkers. Instead of Voortrekker battlefields or early settlements, the committee favored a place associated with Kruger's Zuid-Afrikaansche Republiek: the choice embodied a desire to revive an independent Afrikaner state based on white supremacy. It was an aspiration already gaining traction by the time of the Monument's inauguration in 1949, for the National Party had won the South African elections the previous year and was soon to legislate the racist principles of apartheid that branded its more-than-forty continuous years in power. The building of the Monument undoubtedly played a part in the ascendancy of Afrikaner nationalism in the 1930s and 1940s. Opened by the new prime minister D. F. Malan, it was also to be an insistent reminder that the country was under control of the Nationalists, who indeed declared it a republic in 1961 in fulfillment of the Afrikaner dream.[4]

The location of the Monument had pragmatic as well as symbolic implications: situated at the South African capital of the north, it was accessible and highly visible. The design and scale of the edifice, too, was intended to capitalize on its prominent position: it was to be an arresting and powerful emblem, free of associations with British imperial architecture, its monolithic granite form signaling a new nationalism associated with Africa.[5] Yet while the building referenced the grandeur of Great Zimbabwe and Egyptian architecture, it did not venerate the indigenous peoples of Africa but

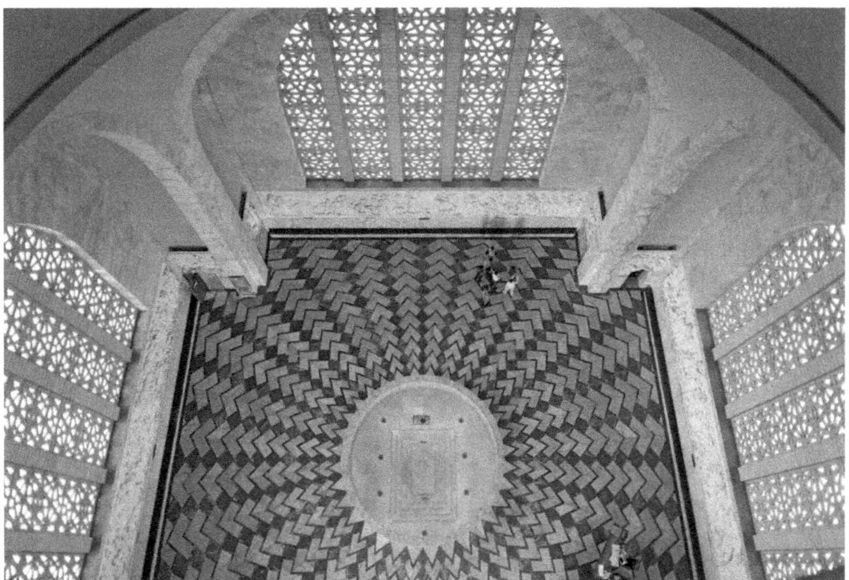

Fig. 1.3 Voortrekker Monument. Interior view looking down on the Hall of Heroes and the marble frieze, with the Cenotaph visible below. *Photograph by Russell Scott.*

instead the white settlers who had imposed their culture on the subcontinent in the wake of the journeys of the Voortrekkers: it was an exhaustive story of settlement that purposefully excluded the British.

The lower hall houses an eternal flame of remembrance and a cenotaph for Piet Retief (fig. 1.3), the hero-martyr who, when trying to negotiate ownership of land in Natal, was put to death with his followers at the decree of the Zulu king Dingane. Retief was seen to personify the courage and steadfastness of all the Voortrekkers who lost their lives in the pursuit of freedom.[6] The Monument particularly commemorated the victory that avenged the death of Retief, when the Zulus were defeated at the Battle of Blood River by a small band of Voortrekkers on December 16, 1838, which they vowed to honor forever if they were successful. To mark this, the oculus in the Monument's overarching dome was designed so that the sun's rays fell on the cenotaph at noon on that day each year. It was on this Day of the Vow that the foundation stone was laid for the centenary in 1938 and the building inaugurated in 1949. The beam of light focused on the cenotaph's simple monolingual inscription, *Ons vir jou Suid-Afrika* (We for thee South Africa), embodying an exclusively Afrikaner patriotism, which barred the British national anthem and the use of English at both the 1938 and 1949 celebrations, despite South Africa being a dominion of the British Commonwealth and the government meeting the bulk of the costs for what was deemed a national monument.[7]

But it is the defeat of African forces rather than the defiance of British rule that is portrayed in the ninety-two-meter historical frieze that surrounds the upper Hall of Heroes, from which visitors can look down on the cenotaph. The carved marble frieze with its life-size figures recounts major episodes of the history of the "Great Trek," as conceived by Afrikaner historians.[8] It portrays not only the challenges of traversing difficult territory but also confrontations with hordes of seminaked Africans depicted as committing acts of treachery and barbarism; against all odds, they are overcome by the resolve of the god-fearing Voortrekkers. The purity of the white marble of the frieze connotes both the superior moral position claimed by the Voortrekkers and the white race whose culture and civilization they carried with them to the hinterland. The belief that the Voortrekkers were a chosen race, predestined to establish a white Christian nation, was summed up by the architect, Gerard Moerdijk, for the *Official Guide* prepared after the inauguration. He compared the Monument to altars set up by Abraham "when he left Ur of the Chaldees to found a new state" (Moerdijk 1970, 32) and wrote of the massive bronze of the *Voortrekker Mother and Children*, commissioned from Anton van Wouw for the entrance to the Monument: "A place of honour has been given to the woman because it was she who ensured the success of the Great Trek and thus brought civilization into the interior of South Africa. She made everything possible by trekking with her husband. Her courage and enterprise founded a white civilization in the interior of the black continent" (Moerdijk 1970, 36).[9] Without women, Moerdijk (1970, 31) wrote, "the Great Trek . . . would have resolved itself into a reconnoitering [sic] expedition which may have established outposts or hunters camps but nothing more permanent."

The underlying agenda of the Monument, and particularly the frieze, was to demonstrate the Afrikaner's right to the country: "A people that have sacrificed so much blood and tears have left their mark on such a country, and therefore spiritually and physically that country belongs to them and their descendants" (Moerdijk 1970, 34).

In Prime Minister Malan's opening address at the 1949 inauguration, Voortrekker history translated into the principles of apartheid: "White

Christian civilisation had to struggle for its existence against the attacks and the influences of an encircling barbarism, and where equality and the consequent forfeiture of white race purity and white supremacy could only have had the most fateful results for both sides" (*Historical Record* [1950], 20).

THE ROLE OF THE VOORTREKKER MONUMENT IN A DEMOCRATIC SOUTH AFRICA

It is hardly surprising then, that after more than forty years of Nationalist rule came to an end in South Africa in the 1990s, it was confidently expected that the Voortrekker Monument—to so many an icon of apartheid oppression—would not survive the change. A History Workshop symposium at the University of the Witwatersrand in July 1992, titled "Myths, Monuments, Museums: New Premises?," chose a Penny Siopis image of a crowd toppling the Monument as its conference logo. Another design she had offered portrayed the Monument as a mere plinth for an enormous figure of a black laborer. In overturning Afrikaner hegemony in a less literal way than demolishing the edifice, this work recalled one of the first proposals for the monument—a mammoth statue of a Voortrekker by sculptor Coert Steynberg—replacing it with an image representing the workers the Nationalists had oppressed, a figure who thus reclaimed the land for his indigenous forebears.

A large charcoal from Diane Victor's *Monuments of Mass Destruction* series (fig. 1.4), *Monument,* also conjured up an early design, in this case a sectional drawing of the architecture by Moerdijk, well known through its publication in the many editions of the Monument's *Official Guide.* Victor's image of the building is not opened up to display the niceties of the architect's hieratic triple-level design, however, but to reveal a devastated building, its structure torn asunder. Isolated in the forecourt from the cascading rubble, Van Wouw's *Voortrekker Mother and Children* that stood for the procreation of white civilization in southern Africa lies in the forecourt overthrown.

Made in 2007, some fifteen years after Siopis's drawings, Victor's image could only have been conceived as symbolic of the nation's degeneration, not of any likely destruction, for by that date it was clear that there would be no implosion of the Voortrekker Monument. In 1993, the year after the History Workshop's logo predicted the fall of the Monument, a preemptive move by a group of Afrikaners had set up a Section 21 nonprofit company to

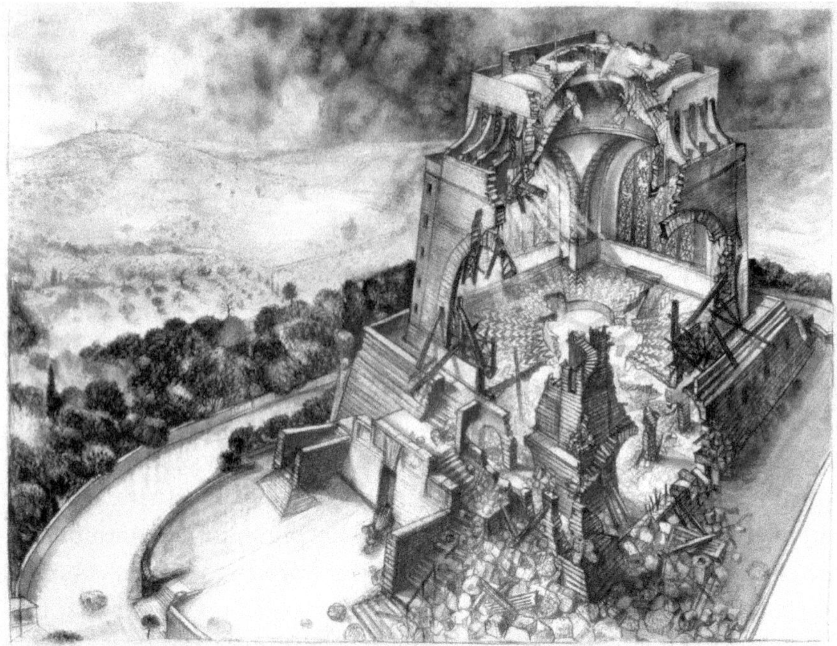

Fig. 1.4 Diane Victor, *Monument*. 2007. Charcoal, 200 x 150 cm. *Photograph courtesy of Diane Victor and David Krut Publishing.*

ensure its survival.[10] As a result, the institution was able to celebrate its half century undeterred in 1999 and, in an ironic twist, has become the refuge for items that have not survived political change. The Monument's storerooms now house images removed from display at venues controlled by the public works department, provincial administrations, parliament, and the defense force, such as portrait busts of historical Afrikaner figures, Verwoerd having the dubious honor of being the most prominent with no fewer than six images.

That the Monument has been perceived as a reliable repository may relate to its well-run administration, reconfigured in 2000 by an effective management team under CEO Opperman, which convinced the Department of Arts and Culture to maintain and increase its financial support.[11] In 2002, a Heritage Foundation was also established, based at the Monument, "with the purpose of looking after endangered heritage objects, specifically those that the Afrikaans-speaking people of the population consider of value."[12] Alongside the new management, the hard work of this nonprofit organization, very active in its fund-raising efforts, has ensured that the Monument remains a prominent feature of the landscape at the entrance to Pretoria. The Africanization of landmarks and city streets, even the renaming of the metropolitan area itself as Tshwane, has not diminished its dominance.

But physical survival alone would not have had significance had the Monument gradually become no more than a vacuous reminder of the past, a past, moreover, that everyone wanted to forget. That this has not happened has been facilitated by what Opperman (2007, 2) termed a policy of "aggressive marketing" that endorses Annie Coombes's (2003, 12) contention "that monuments are animated and reanimated only through performance." Various events have kept the Monument in the public eye through the media as well as through its literal presence. Succeeding in gaining support from Nelson Mandela is a key example. Marc Ross (2007, 246) notes that in 2000, Mandela was persuaded to write to potential donors encouraging support of the Monument. A more overt gesture of support that garnered considerable publicity was Mandela's acceptance of an invitation to speak on March 6, 2002, at the dedication of a statue to one of the heroes of the Anglo-Boer War, Danie Theron, installed at Fort Schanskop, part of the site under the control of the Voortrekker Monument.[13] The organizers must have been jubilant that Mandela contributed so handsomely to their goal of reconciling previously opposed ideological positions. For he spoke admiringly of Theron's patriotism and the contribution of Afrikaners in building South Africa and referred to a "shared experience of fighting for one's freedom" against British colonial rule, which bound African and Afrikaner together "in a manner that is most profound" (Ross 2007, 246). Thus on this occasion, Mandela unexpectedly upheld Afrikaner settlers at the cost of the British and, most unusually, even used Afrikaans in his speech.[14]

A policy of reconciliation has continued beyond Mandela's personal generosity. President Zuma, too, has undertaken conciliatory acts, all the more remarkable when, himself a Zulu, his relationship to the Monument with its focus on the Voortrekker defeat of the Zulus must surely seem more personal and confrontational. On the Day of Reconciliation, December 16, 2011, he opened an access road between Freedom Park and the Voortrekker Monument.[15] The link, presented as a symbol of accord between two very different heritage institutions, was paralleled by the inauguration by Zuma of a bridge of reconciliation at another site under control of the Monument on the Day of Reconciliation in 2014, a year that had the added significance of marking the twentieth anniversary of democracy in South Africa. The bridge was installed between the old Afrikaner monument on the site of the Battle of Blood River (the Ncome River renamed because the waters were said to have run red with the blood of slain Zulu warriors) and the new complex on the other side of the Ncome, which honors Zulu involvement in the event.[16]

From a more cynical viewpoint, these acts of reconciliation can be interpreted as ways of defusing the potency of earlier monuments, rendering them less effective as iconic markers of Afrikaner nationalism without destroying them. Similarly, it could be suggested that the reconstitution of the Day of the Vow as the Day of Reconciliation was a way of neutralizing an almost-sacred date on the Afrikaner calendar without removing it. While the Day of the Vow (popularly known as Dingane's Day) does not seem to have been kept in the decades immediately following the 1838 battle,[17] it gained prominence under President Paul Kruger, and came to signify Afrikaner solidarity. Chosen for the inauguration of many Afrikaner monuments, it is particularly telling that it was selected for the induction of the Vrouemonument (Women's Monument) in Bloemfontein in 1913, although it memorialized not the Voortrekkers but those who died in Anglo-Boer War concentration camps: the date defied Afrikaner defeat in that war with the memory of past victory. The day's significance was also noted by African leaders who chose Dingane's Day for early protests and most notably selected the date for the founding of Umkhonto we Sizwe in 1961, countering the symbolic potency of the Blood River battle and its implication in the subsequent oppression of black people.[18] The divergent histories associated with the day made it a particularly appropriate, if somewhat ironic, choice for the Day of Reconciliation.

On the occasion of opening the road between Freedom Park and the Voortrekker Monument, Zuma also affirmed that the two institutions had signed a memorandum of understanding and would strive to work together on certain projects. Related to this was the announcement by the ANC government that the Monument was to become a national heritage site.[19] At a ceremony at the Monument in 2012, the then Minister of Arts and Culture defined the declaration as "one of the most significant milestones in our journey to build a South African nation that is truly united in its diversity" (Mashatile 2012). Examining the text of his speech, it is evident that one assertion lent itself to radically different interpretations: "We are making a bold statement to uphold the ideals of the founding fathers of our democratic nation." While Minister Mashatile went on to qualify this, saying, "These are the ideals of one country, one people, one democratic state and a non-racial destiny for all who live in it, black and white," he did not explicitly define who the founding fathers were. Making the statement in the context of the Voortrekker Monument, from a podium placed in front of the marble relief representing the Battle of Blood River, surely left it open for at least some of his audience to assume that he was referring to the Voortrekkers. It seems unlikely that Mashatile was unaware of the possibility and its potential to win over reactionary right-wing opinion. The comfortable elision of historical detail is also evident in his reference to "a new and inclusive narrative for our country . . . to tell the true and complete story of where we come from as a people," and his claim that "while our struggle for national liberation could easily have been conducted as one against a racial group, it rose above this category to embrace the principle of non-racialism; to see humanity as one and diversity as a source of strength" (Mashatile 2012). His position may be conciliatory, but it also signals that Afrikaner history has lost its potency.

EXPANDING MEANING AT THE POST-APARTHEID VOORTREKKER MONUMENT

The depoliticization of the Voortrekker Monument is not, however, something that is being imposed entirely from without. It has been part of the internal agenda driven by CEO Opperman as well, albeit without any intention of reducing the historical significance of the Monument. In some respects this has been the outcome of changing attitudes among Afrikaners themselves. Opperman describes a period of decline for the Monument in the 1990s, attributing it at least in part to these changes: "Deprived of substantial government support, and suffering the effect of a traditional support base that were [sic] increasingly withdrawing from public life and deliberately distancing themselves from what was considered to be politically incorrect, the Voortrekker Monument entered a period of gradual but consistent recession" (Opperman 2007, 2).

But changes in white Afrikaner attitudes were discernible long before the ANC won the 1994 elections, with interest in Voortrekker history dwindling after the heady years of the 1950s and 1960s when the Nationalists were first in power. Grundlingh and Sapire (1989, 34) point out the increased "pragmatism and diminished interest in the past" among the growing number of middle-class "white-collar" Afrikaners, who became increasingly aware of the flaws in apartheid policy; they note in particular the embarrassingly tepid response to the Great Trek celebrations in 1988. They suggest that while "most would still feel the need to show due respect to events such as the 150th anniversary of the Great Trek, . . . such events no longer have the capacity to raise markedly the cultural and emotional temperature."

Yet the Monument did become an iconic rallying point for extremely heated Afrikaner groups of the far right, such as the paramilitary Afrikaner Weerstandsbeweging that aggressively opposed change in the country's policies, and held protest meetings there. Opperman understandably wanted to distance the Monument from such radical positions: his various statements and many of the changes he and his team have instituted stress that the Monument's value lies in its representation of an important episode in South Africa's history, but they try to separate it from any ideological stance. It is notable that the museum exhibits in the lower halls of the Monument focus on the Voortrekkers' way of life, rather than recounting their military achievements. It also seems relevant that tapestries depicting the Great Trek, made by Afrikaner women in the 1950s, which do not minimize the tribulations of the journeys but give greater emphasis to daily life than battles, are today installed in the lower hall, although they were initially deemed inappropriate for display alongside the cenotaph.[20] Today's focus on cultural history at the Monument may be seen as a way of underplaying the confrontational aspects of the treks, which invariably pitted whites against blacks, even if little can be done to modify the presentations of the historical frieze.

Associated with these changes are various strategies to diversify the meaning of the Monument by widening its scope. For example, the 341 hectares around the building were declared a nature reserve in 1993, and this aspect has been promoted, with the introduction of zebra, wildebeest, and buck species.[21] Wild life is an entrenched trope of South African life, admittedly associated more with whites but generally free of obvious political implications. So, too, are outdoor pursuits, part of the lifestyle of suburban as well as rural South Africans, with an emphasis on fitness. The Monument grounds offer picnic spots and cycling trails, also bird watching and horse riding; an athletics club meets twice weekly on the site, and there are also "fun runs." Other popular events are open-air concerts and monthly country markets selling plants, homemade produce, and craft items, as well as an antique and collectables fair on certain public holidays. Many of these activities are privatized, as are the gift shop and restaurants, as well as facilities for conferences and other events, such as school dances and weddings. In addition to the museum in the Monument, there is a modern building housing exhibition galleries and a research facility, and an energetic education program has been established. While events associated with the specific heritage of the site continue, other aspects of South African culture have also been drawn into the program.

Alongside their undoubted importance in generating funds, these developments signal what could be understood as a concerted effort to depoliticize the site—and, it could be said, to secularize it. While there is still an annual church service on December 16, one might note that a beer festival had been scheduled three days before on December 13, 2014, albeit by organizations renting venues in the grounds.[22] But while there is undoubtedly an effort to broaden the base of Monument support, most events seem designed to appeal particularly to the Afrikaans-speaking sector, for this remains key to the continued relevance of the Monument. It is notable that the organization Friends of the Voortrekker Monument includes Blood River, which has not been party to this widened agenda.[23] And there is a further development on the Monument site that seems particularly directed at Afrikaners, in this case with religious overtones—a *Gedenktuin* (Garden of Remembrance) planted around a fishpond and enclosed by stone walls. Playing on anxieties about the desecration of cemeteries, it offers a secure, secluded place to remember loved ones, in what the website calls a culture-friendly environment, with niches for purchase in the columbarium to house ashes or simply for commemoration.[24] In the grounds, there is also a chapel that can be hired for funerals or weddings. While the garden and the chapel are nondenominational, rather than under the auspices of the Dutch Reformed Churches associated historically with Afrikaner nationalism, it seems unlikely that South Africans other than those associated with the Monument and white Afrikaners of a conservative persuasion would choose the grounds of the Voortrekker Monument for such events or for their family memorials.

Yet Afrikaners today represent only a relatively limited proportion of those who visit the Monument. Its role as a tourist attraction has been of great importance in its survival, with annual visitor numbers in excess of 150,000, and some 60 to 70 percent being foreign, headed by Chinese and then German tourists;[25] the construction of an "authentic" Zulu beehive dwelling in the grounds seems directed at this audience.[26] Being a standard stop on tours of Pretoria not only provides the Monument with much-needed income but also shifts perceptions away from the singular concept of an Afrikaner stronghold.[27] Tourism packages and neutralizes contested pasts and, as Barbara Kirshenblatt-Gimblett (1998, 136) has remarked, provides a "safe haven" for "troubled history that glorifies colonial adventure." Guidebooks on sale today are available in Chinese, German, French, Spanish, Italian, and Portuguese, suggesting international interest, as well as English and Afrikaans (and braille). The lack of availability of guidebooks in any of the other official languages of South Africa is conspicuous, but the Monument has included North Sotho in some of its wall texts, and tours are offered in Setswana, Sesotho, and Tshivenda as well as English and Afrikaans. Black visitor numbers are on the increase, probably chiefly due to organized school visits, making up 30 to 40 percent of visitors, importantly no longer limited to white and predominantly Afrikaans schools but including many black pupils.[28]

It is intriguing to speculate how black schoolchildren might interpret the stories of the frieze—do they understand them merely as one chapter in South Africa's history, or do they seek out African meaning?[29] Although he meets an ignominious end in the panel depicting his death, Dingane is presented as a powerful figure, whether negotiating with Voortrekkers or decreeing their death, and he might well be thought of as an African hero in his resistance to the incursions of Europeans. And it is notable that Mpande is celebrated as the new Zulu king in one of the panels, which might also be seen as a positive portrayal to be weighed against the many black figures shown as assailants or victims. On the other hand, for those less inclined to discover positive African values in the frieze, it could be understood—as could the Monument as a whole—to represent what black South Africans had to overcome to win freedom in their own land.[30]

COMMEMORATING THE STRUGGLE AT FREEDOM PARK

The celebration of liberation is not best served by a reinterpretation of the Voortrekker Monument, however, but by the new memorial erected on the adjacent Salvokop, a presidential legacy project, conceived in the wake of the Truth and Reconciliation Commission and its revelations regarding so many victims of the liberation struggle. The Freedom Park Trust was established at the end of 2001, and the project was launched by President Thabo Mbeki on Youth Day, June 16, 2002, when he planted an olive tree and unveiled a plaque inscribed *Motho ke motho ka batho* (I am because we are). The official opening was held in 2013 after the completion of //hapo Museum, a name intended to reflect, as Deputy President Kgalema Motlanthe put it, "the ancient wisdom of the San and Khoi that 'a dream is not a dream until it is shared by the entire community'" (Oliphant, Raman, and Serote 2014, 29). Taking account of the origins of humankind in Africa, the museum encompasses 3.9 million years of the history of southern Africa, the more recent centuries recast with an emphasis on a black perspective that notably gives little attention to the story of the Voortrekkers. Yet the story told at Freedom Park is fundamentally an inclusive one: it recognizes the place of all South Africans, not only indigenous people but also those who came as settlers from other continents to play their part in the country. The Voortrekker Monument is in stark contrast. While its architect was at pains to affirm in the *Official Guide* that figures other than Afrikaners had played a part in the Trek (the Grahamstown settlers' support in presenting a bible to the Voortrekkers, for example, and the death of the English translator Halstead alongside Retief and his men, both represented in the frieze, as is the Italian heroine, Teresa Viglioni), these seem tokenist additions to an exclusively Afrikaner story. And it is notable that they are Europeans: in this history, with the single exception of the chief Moroka, who sent aid to Potgieter's laager after the Vegkop defeat of the Ndebele, Africans are represented primarily as impediments in the development of South Africa.

While Freedom Park may not have been designed specifically to counter Afrikaner claims embodied in the Voortrekker Monument, the choice of an adjacent location suggests this was part of the agenda. Intriguingly, consultation about the site for Freedom Park is reminiscent of debates about the Voortrekker Monument site, not only because of the contiguous outcome, with its position convenient for use by the government in power, but because of anxieties that local heroes and events would be eclipsed by the centralizing of the memorial (Marschall 2010, 217–18). Like the Monument, too, the Freedom Park project grew more ambitious as it developed and took more than a decade to come to fruition. Funding, which came from the government, has also considerably exceeded the initial budget, in this case reaching more than R900 million (Oliphant, Raman, and Serote 2014, 68), as opposed to the Monument's topping R700,000, which seemed startlingly extravagant at the time.

In commemorating those who fought for freedom in opposition to the apartheid precepts of Afrikaner nationalism, Freedom Park represents a very different view of South African history. And it has chosen to do so in a way that is the converse of the Voortrekker Monument's block-like monumental form, which dominates its elevated site, enclosed by a laager wall of ox wagons sculptured in relief, recalling the Voortrekker's favored military strategy, and symbolically protecting the Monument from outside dangers that might defile the purity of the white *volk*. Despite recent efforts to make the Monument more welcoming, such as its recreational aspects and nature reserve setting, it remains fundamentally monolithic. Freedom Park, on the other hand, was conceived as a sprawling indigenous garden, open in form, and organic as opposed to rectilinear. According to Jeremy Rose, a member of the appointed consortium of Mashabane Rose Architects, GAPP Architects and Urban Designers, and MMA Architects:[31]

> The team of architects were encouraged to encompass ideas that arose from rural architecture, traditional homestead design and IKS [indigenous knowledge systems], to consider the unique southern African architectural structures and urban formations from sites across southern Africa, Mapangubwe, Great Zimbabwe and the mountains in the Free State where traditional healers reside. . . . The conversation challenged the architectural team to search for essential and universal qualities in architecture to answer the complex process of a large client body with a range of opinions. (Oliphant, Raman, and Serote 2014, 59)

In some ways, this seems curiously reminiscent of the approach at the Voortrekker Monument, where Moerdijk attempted to create an architecture that was African in spirit. Both sites make use of local stone, with forms reminiscent of Great Zimbabwe, but at Freedom Park, the forms deployed are earth hugging rather than assertive, with structures of stacked stone, not ashlar granite. Although there are monumental elements at Freedom Park, they are integrated into the site, which, with its emphasis on winding walks, water features, and indigenous planting, creates an eco-friendly impression. The park is encircled by two hundred tall stainless-steel poles, representing reeds which connote birth, the most visible part of Freedom Park from a distance. At night, they are picked out by lights on their tips, white to signify

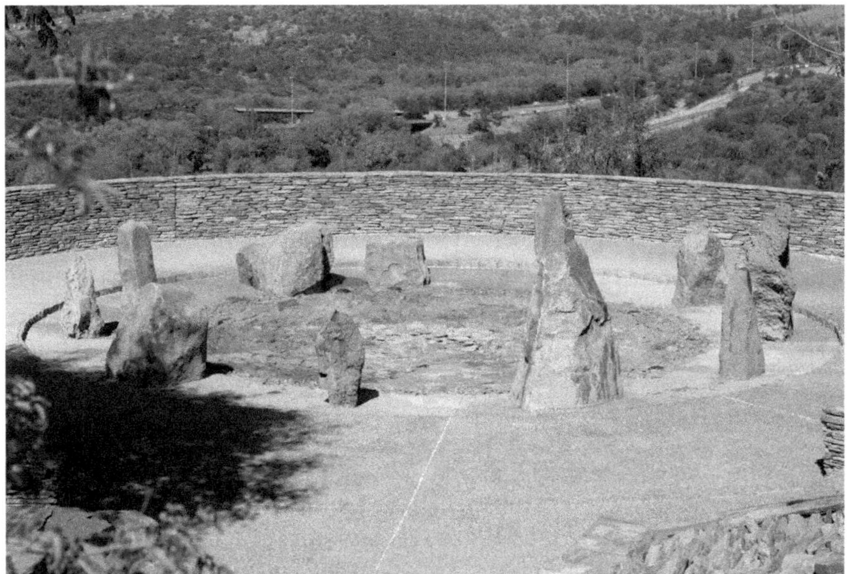

Fig. 1.5 Freedom Park. *Isivivane* showing the *Lesaka* (resting place) with nine boulders adjacent to the *Lekgotla* (meeting place). *Photograph by Paul Mills.*

peace replacing the original red, their delicate luminosity in contrast to the floodlit mass of the nearby Voortrekker Monument.

While it was a goal to develop the project on the basis of indigenous knowledge systems as opposed to Western traditions, Freedom Park is intended to be welcoming to all and representative of South African society at large. The various parts are named in the different official languages of the country, and the ceremonies associated with them have been inclusive, representing South Africa's diverse belief systems, albeit with a strongly African emphasis. The first element to be completed was named with the isiZulu word for "collective effort," *Isivivane*, which is centered on a circular *Lesaka*, a symbolic burial place, surrounded by boulders from the nine provinces, plus two representing the national and international communities (fig. 1.5). A mist of steam from the surface suggests the sanctity of this spiritual resting place, while a nearby waterfall invokes cleansing. Return of the spirits ceremonies were held across the country, with soil and plants from each site introduced into *Isivivane*.

At *Isivivane's* inauguration in 2004, marking a decade of democracy, traditional healers and interdenominational representatives, on behalf of immigrant peoples as much as indigenes, performed rituals of cleansing and regeneration to heal the wounds of the past, mirrored in miniature on an everyday basis when respectful visitors remove their shoes on arrival and wash their hands at a fountain as they leave. Those commemorated here remain unnamed, so visitors who sit in contemplation or join in discussions in the *Legotla* area are at liberty to think of the departed who are meaningful to them. *Isivivane* is "not conceived as a Western-style memorial or shrine, but rather is intended as a performative site of embodied memory, ritual and spirituality, and is infused with a wealth of over-determined symbolic references" (Noble 2011, 234). Just as the symbolism of the Voortrekker Monument and its frieze needed the architect to elucidate them, so the complex meanings of *Isivivane* require explanation for most audiences.

A more recent National Heritage Monument established nearby provides a simpler alternative to the metaphoric approach of Freedom Park. A grassy slope at Groenkloof Nature Reserve has been populated with a crowd of life-size bronzes, some fifty at present but ultimately to be more than four hundred, commemorating figures who took part in South Africa's "Long March to Freedom." How the individuals were selected for representation remains obscure, but the official claim is that they are intended to "create a substantial sculptural narrative that engages the complexities of South African history" and "generate national pride and search for and address the absent voices that were substantive in the shaping of the South Africa of today" (Gamedze 2015). The grandeur of the idea may be matched by the use of bronze, long associated with timeless monuments, and by the costliness of the project but is hardly met by the lack of a coherent concept to guide the many artists involved and by the somewhat anecdotal treatment of the sculptures, whose accessible realism has been further emphasized by the polychromy that was added without consulting the sculptors. There is undoubtedly popular appeal in a smiling Walter and Albertina Sisulu hand in hand, stout Olive Schreiner with a friendly small dog, and Sol Plaatje mounting the bicycle he used to travel South Africa, to mention just a few. But the ensemble seems more directed at creating a tourist attraction with multiple photo opportunities than memorializing historical South Africans with suitable gravitas, and banality is hardly overcome by the lengthy didactic plaques identifying each figure. Promoting tourism was indeed the intention of Dali Tambo who initiated the project; he proclaims, "Heritage tourism is a massively growing aspect of international tourism, with the educated middle classes seeking otherness. . . . Heritage is the show business of history . . ." (Gamedze 2015).[32] Its economic potential is supported by Tshwane mayor Kgosientso Ramokgopa, but he also claims grandly that the new project completes the city's "political quadrant," together with the Union Buildings, Voortrekker Monument, and Freedom Park.[33]

Considered in this company, the populism of the Groenkloof project is pronounced. The Voortrekker Monument and Freedom Park may also rely on tourism for income, but this was not their primary motivation, and their memorializing forms are fundamentally symbolic. While symbolism might circumvent a trivialization of history at Freedom Park, however, there is a danger that it could become overly enigmatic. At the time of its inauguration with *Isivivane*, it was felt that some more explicit record of commemoration was needed, and a different approach was introduced in the next phase of development, recording names in a way reminiscent of Western war memorials, particularly the Vietnam Memorial in Washington, DC. In excess of 75,000 names have been inscribed on narrow stone blocks making up the 697-meter Wall of Names (see figs. 6.2 and 6.3) wrapped around the high ground of the area called *S'khumbuto,* a SiSwati word meaning *memorial* (fig. 1.6). Here, we find the sanctuary with its eternal flame, another symbol shared with the monument, and the amphitheater, which accommodates gatherings.

There is an open invitation for the nomination of individuals who took part in the liberation struggle to achieve all-inclusiveness for the Wall of Names. The recorded names are in no particular order, avoiding hierarchy and permitting additions as they are verified.[34] Each vertical stack of names has a reference number that will make it possible to find individuals more easily once a database with the information related to each has been completed. Following the inclusive precepts of the ANC, the names recorded are not limited to those who died in the struggle—even if they predominate in their positioning on the largest and highest wall of remembrance—but has been extended to all those who died in conflict that contributed to the shaping of South Africa, a holistic view of the country's history rather than the narrow focus on the Voortrekker Monument. A series of lower memorial walls relate to precolonial wars, genocide, slavery, wars of resistance, the Anglo-Boer War, and World Wars I and II, a wide-ranging listing that, for example, records the dead on both sides in the Anglo-Boer War and those who died in British concentration camps. But this well-intentioned attempt

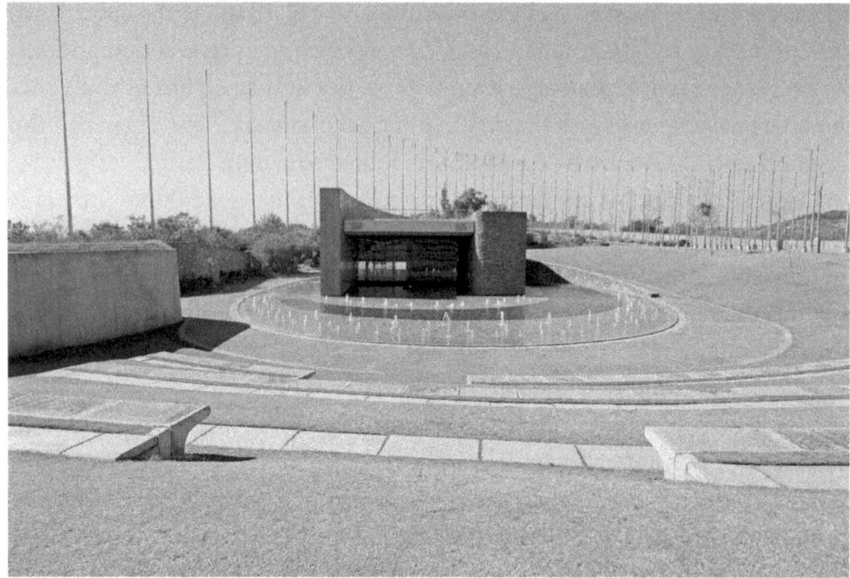

Fig. 1.6 Freedom Park. *S'khumbuto* from the amphitheater in the foreground toward the sanctuary and sacred flame. The reeds (stainless steel poles), the tallest of which are 32 meters in height, can be seen in the background. *Photograph by Paul Mills.*

to create reconciliatory comprehensiveness has proved contentious, particularly the decision to exclude soldiers of the South African Defence Force (SADF), all the more so when Cubans fighting against them in the Angola border wars were included. While it was understandable to decide that the SADF had been upholding apartheid rather than fighting for freedom and human rights, in the face of the inclusiveness of other lists, this resolution caused deep offense. Although in 2008, the Freedom Park Trust made the conciliatory gesture of hosting the families of SADF soldiers who died on duty and launching a memorial book to record their names, it continues to resist representations from veterans seeking to have them added to the Wall of Names.[35]

In the face of this, the Voortrekker Monument raised private funding to erect an SADF Memorial Wall in its grounds in 2009 and hosts commemorative services there. The wall records 2,521 names of those who died between 1961 and 1994, with more added since its unveiling. While the SADF dead were not exclusively Afrikaner, and in view of conscription no doubt included servicemen who did not feel supportive of apartheid policies, this action on the part of the Voortrekker Monument tends to homogenize all who died into a standardized group representing a particular brand of patriotism. Moreover, it underlines the persistence of ideological differences between those associated with the old and new regimes.

CONCLUSION

Notwithstanding gestures of reconciliation and astute attempts to co-opt the Monument into a new cultural dispensation, it seems that the intensity of opposing perspectives has not wholly dissipated. From an Afrikaner viewpoint, there might seem to be an element of provocation in Freedom Park launching *S'khumbuto* on the Day of Reconciliation 2006 and holding annual events on that date just as the neighboring Voortrekker Monument does. But the reverse is equally true. As Noble (2011, 218) comments of the two sites, "Explicit ideological differences parallel . . . aesthetic contrast." Yet the coexistence of both is perhaps necessary for the constructed landscape to encompass South Africa's history. Pattabi Raman writes:

> The location of Freedom Park at Salvokop adjacent to the hill on which the Voortrekker Monument stands is in itself a type of insurrection and therefore a meaningful proposition. Viewed together, the heritage sites constitute a metaphor for what the physical, social, political and cultural landscape of South Africa [has been] in the past and in the present as well as what it may become in future as cultures interact and change. (Oliphant, Raman, and Serote 2014, 47)

From a more matter-of-fact angle, Grundlingh (2009, 168) points out that the installation of a black government gave black people "the freedom to ignore or display indifference to that which they might have found offensive in the past." And the Voortrekker Monument's own policy of repackaging itself as heritage for tourist consumption has defused its potential to offend. But the very fact that an alternative edifice was built on a site adjacent to the Voortrekker Monument and that yet another is under way with Groenkloof's National Heritage Monument seems to represent an ongoing need to counter the ideology that held sway in South Africa for more than forty years. It could be construed as an acknowledgment that ideology persists and that it cannot be changed overnight or simply legislated out of existence, any more than the ongoing effects of apartheid can. And however much the Monument seeks to diversify its meaning, it cannot control visitor response: like all cultural institutions, it is multivalent, its meaning constituted by the viewer. It no doubt continues to serve old ideologies alongside the new.

ACKNOWLEDGMENTS

I wish to record my appreciation for assistance with this chapter and related research from staff at the Monument, particularly Etta Judson, manager of museum services at the Voortrekker Monument and Nature Reserve, Cecilia Kruger, senior manager of the Heritage Foundation, and Zabeth Botha, archivist, who have generously supplied data on the collection, visitor figures, legislation, and many other details. I am also grateful for grants from the Faculty Research Development Fund at the University of Auckland that enabled me to undertake my research in South Africa. And I must record my debt to my co-researcher, Professor Rolf Schneider, with whom I have enjoyed so many fruitful exchanges about the Voortrekker Monument.

ELIZABETH RANKIN is Emeritus Professor of Art History at the University of Auckland, New Zealand. Most recent among her publications are *Listening to Distant Thunder: The Art of Peter Clarke* with Philippa Hobbs, and an edited digital book, *Neil Pardington: The Order of Things*.

NOTES

1. Stephen Dubin (2009, 293) records that architect Herbert Baker "purposely built alcoves into his design so that different governments could decorate them with what they considered appropriate symbols," although this has not happened.

2. The closure of the Union Buildings to the public for security reasons makes it seem even more an enclave of power than in the past. It means that new installations, such as the Women's Memorial, cannot be visited and equally shrouds the fate of its many statues of the old regime.

3. Among various frivolous suggestions to adapt the Monument to the new dispensation, including converting it to a pink-painted gay nightclub, a more serious proposal was rumored: that the Cenotaph Hall be used to mount an exhibition on the struggle against white minority rule (Kruger 2002, 90).

4. This despite the very narrow majority of 52.29 percent in favor of a republic in the referendum of 1960, even though it was restricted to white voters.

5. For discussion of the anti-imperial design intentions, see Rankin and Schneider (2017).

6. The flame, lit from a torch carried by a relay of runners from Cape Town to Pretoria for the centenary, was kept alight at the University of Pretoria until the Monument was complete. Ritual acts like this and the reenactment of the trek with replica ox wagons in 1938 played a key role in igniting a sense of pride in Afrikaner identity across the country.

7. As a small concession, E. G. Jansen, chair of the SVK (and somewhat ironically Minister of Native Affairs at the time), welcomed foreign delegates to the inauguration in English, but even Newton-Thompson, representing the English settlers of Grahamstown who presented a bible to the departing Voortrekkers, delivered his speech in Afrikaans.

8. The SVK appointed a special committee to advise on the frieze, including well-known Afrikaner historians Professor "Fanie" Engelbrecht and Gustav Preller.

9. The racist implications are even more overt in Moerdijk's speeches for the Day of the Vow: "If you want to know to whom the honor goes, look at numerous other lands. At South America, for example. There too the whites tried to establish themselves. Cortez took the land and tried to keep it, and what remained? Only a slightly lighter color on the cheeks of the native. . . . And here where the Afrikaner came? He brought his gun and his Bible, yes, but alongside him was his wife, and his children with her, and we became a nation" (Vermeulen 1999, 130, my translation).

10. Voortrekker Monument and Nature Reserve, Memorandum of Association of a Non-Profit Company (Section 54(1), regulation 17(1) and 17(3), 1993–11–01) (Kruger 2002, 107).

11. Unexpectedly discontinued in late 2014.

12. "Die Erfenisstigting." Accessed January 24, 2015. http://www.erfenisstigting.org.za/?id=174.

13. The invitation to Mandela caused outrage among right-wing Afrikaners, who felt it inappropriate to honor an Afrikaner hero in this way. The monument was a refurbishment of a sculpture from the now defunct Danie Theron Combat School in Kimberley, transferred to the care of the Heritage Foundation by the South African National Defence Force.

14. Mandela, an isiXhosa speaker, customarily made public statements in English.

15. Reported, for example, in the *Mail and Guardian*: http://m.mg.co.za/article/2011–12–16-zuma-cuts-reconciliation-road-ribbon-linking-monuments.

16. The bridge was an earlier concept, and the metal construction was already complete in 2010 when I visited the site but not installed for some years—a potent reminder of the difficulties of reconciling opposing positions.

17. In 1866, the site of the Blood River laager was identified by Voortrekkers who had fought there.

18. South African History Online (www.sahistory.org.za) records pass burning on this day in 1919 and protests in 1929, as well as ANC conferences regularly planned on dates on or near December 16.

19. Gazetted on July 8, 2011, this was the outcome of submissions since 2006 to the South African Heritage Resources Agency by Monument staff.

20. The tapestries, so-called although they are stitched not woven, were designed by W. H. Coetzer (1980, 61), who made the preliminary drawings for the Monument's

frieze but sought a more feminine emphasis for the tapestries. Initially displayed in the museum area under the Monument, they were moved to the separate museum building because of problems with damp.

21. Administrator's Notice 270, Nature Conservation Ordinance (No. 12 of 1993) (Kruger 2002, 107).

22. See http://www.vtm.org.za/annual-events/. Accessed January 24, 2015.

23. Membership allows free entry to the Voortrekker Monument site to those who pay the R250 annual fee but is possibly undertaken more in the spirit of supporting Afrikaner heritage than achieving personal benefits.

24. For further details, see http://www.vtm.org.za/garden-of-remembrance/. Accessed January 28, 2015.

25. The Chinese are the fastest growing tourist group in the world. App tags for the panels of the frieze were prepared in Chinese, English, and Afrikaans. I was told when visiting the Monument in January 2015, however, that there had been an 80 percent drop in Chinese visitors since the Ebola epidemic.

26. The choice of a Zulu structure suggests a link with the history depicted in the Voortrekker frieze, as Zulu did not inhabit this part of the country historically. See Witz, Rassool, and Minkley (2005, 309) for discussion of cultural villages as representing the "real Africa," celebrating "a South Africa at last freed from bondage," particularly popular with domestic leisure tourism (310).

27. Opperman (2011) estimated that tourism generated 56 to 60 percent of the Monument's income.

28. When the Monument was declared a National Heritage Site, Tshwane mayor Kgosientso Ramokgopa promised R2.5 million toward tours for impoverished school children (South African Government News Agency 2012).

29. Christo Rabie, the Monument's educational services manager, reports on the program's reaching out to township educators and its acknowledgment of different interpretations, challenging stereotypes from different political perspectives.

30. This interpretation is suggested by Grundlingh (2009, 169). He also suggests the Monument could be seen as "a tribute to black labor," quoting Councilor Donsie Khumalo: "our black people provided all the labor for building the thing." But this is mistaken: exclusively white builders were used for the Monument, and black workers only in the grounds. Labor shortages during the war ultimately necessitated a limited amount of black assistance in building operations, however.

31. In recognition of the contribution of the international community to South Africa's liberation, a worldwide competition was held for the design of Freedom Park in 2002, garnering 138 entries from 37 countries, but none was deemed suitable and only "second place" prizes awarded (Oliphant, Raman, and Serote 2014, 71). Work had already commenced on site infrastructure and the construction of *Isivivane* in order for it to be ready for Freedom Day, April 27, 2004, and it was decided to continue with local designers working in collaboration with the Freedom Park Trust, taking account of ideas arising from wide consultation—again, echoing procedures for the Voortrekker Monument, although that consultation had a very narrow base.

32. Gamedze points out the irony of the bronzes drawing on "colonialist depictions of heroism, an image of democracy that attempts to build on colonialist visual language, and therefore ideology."

33. See http://www.southafrica.info/about/history/heritage-monument-160915.htm#.Vqs-HFInJMS, September 2015. Accessed January 29, 2016. Others had a different idea of economic potential: two of the bronzes have been stolen, and as a countermeasure, it is planned to insert tracing chips in the sculptures.

34. The task of assembling and checking names for the inauguration in 2006 was onerous, and the process is ongoing as the public submit proposals of further names, and each has to be verified. A similar system of checking has been instituted for nominations for incumbents for the Gallery of Leaders; as yet, at the time of writing, only nine banners record deceased men and women deemed to have made significant contributions to human rights causes, with Mandela not yet one of them—O. R. Tambo, Robert Sebukwe, Lilian Ngoyi, Helen Joseph, Steve Biko, Julius Nyerere, Kwame Nkruhma, Agostinho Neto, and Che Guevara.

35. See Baines 2014, 162–70.

References

Baines, Gary. 2014. *South Africa's "Border War": Contested Narratives and Conflicting Memories*. London: Bloomsbury.

Coetzer, Willem Hermanus. 1980. *W. H. Coetzer 80*. Roodepoort, South Africa: CUM Boeke.

Coombes, Annie. 2003. *History after Apartheid: Visual Culture and Public Memory in a Democratic South Africa*. Durham, NC: Duke University Press.

Dubin, Steven. 2009. *Mounting Queen Victoria: Curating Cultural Change*. Johannesburg: Jacana Media.

Gamedze, Thuli. 2015. "Heritage for Sale: Bronze Casting and the Colonial Imagination." *Artthrob* November 20. Accessed January 29, 2016. http://artthrob.co.za/2015/11/20/heritage-for-sale-bronze-casting-and-the-colonial-imagination/.

Grundlingh, Albert. 2009. "A Cultural Conundrum? Old Monuments and New Regimes." In *Contested Histories in Public Space: Memory, Race, and Nation*, edited by Daniel Walkowitz and Lisa Knauer, 157–77. Durham, NC: Duke University Press.

Grundlingh, Albert, and Hilary Sapire. 1989. "From Feverish Festival to Repetitive Ritual? The Changing Fortunes of Great Trek Mythology in an Industrializing South Africa, 1938–1988." *South African Historical Journal* 21: 19–37.

Historical Record of the Opening of Voortrekker Monument, Pretoria, December 16th 1949. [1950]. Johannesburg: Insercor.

Kirshenblatt-Gimblett, Barbara. 1998. *Destination Culture: Tourism, Museums, and Heritage*. Berkeley: University of California Press.

Kruger, Cecilia. 2002. Heritage Resource Management in South Africa: A Case Study of the Voortrekker Monument Heritage Site, Pretoria." MA thesis, University of Pretoria.

Marschall, Sabine. 2010. *Landscape of Memory: Commemorative Monuments, Memorials and Public Statuary in Post-Apartheid South Africa*. Leiden, the Netherlands: Brill.

Mashatile, Paul. 2012. "Address by Minister Paul Mashatile on the Occasion to Commemorate the Declaration of the Voortrekker Monument as a National Heritage." Department of Arts and Culture, March 28. Accessed January 27, 2015. http://

www.dac.gov.za/address-minister-paul-mashatile-occasion-commemorate-declaration-voortrekker-monument-national.

Moerdijk, Gerard. 1970. "Design and Symbolism of the Voortrekker Monument." In *The Voortrekker Monument Pretoria: Official Guide*, 7th ed., 29–37. Pretoria: Voortrekker Monument Board of Control.

Noble, Jonathan. 2011. *African Identity in Post-Apartheid Public Architecture: White Skin, Black Masks*. Farnham, UK: Ashgate.

Oliphant, Andries Walter, Pattabi Ganapathi Raman, and Mongane Wally Serote, eds. 2014. *Freedom Park—A Place of Emancipation and Meaning*. Pretoria: Freedom Park Publishers.

Opperman, Gerrit. 2007. "Healing the Wounds of Conflict." 4th African Congress on Peace through Tourism, Kampala, Uganda, May 20–25.

———. 2011. Presentation to the Parliamentary Monitoring Group, South African Heritage Resources Agency Arts and Culture Committee, November 1.

Rankin, Elizabeth, and Rolf Schneider. 2017. "Copy Nothing: Classical Ideals and Afrikaner Ideologies at the Voortrekker Monument." In *South Africa, Greece, Rome: Classical Confrontations*, edited by Grant Parker. Cambridge, UK: Cambridge University Press.

Ross, Marc Howard. 2007. *Cultural Contestations in Ethnic Conflict*. Cambridge, UK: Cambridge University Press.

South African Government News Agency. 2012. "Voortrekker Monument Now a National Heritage Site." *SANews*. Accessed January 28, 2015. http://www.sanews.gov.za/south-africa/voortrekker-monument-now-national-heritage-site.

Vermeulen, Irma. 1999. *Man En Monument: Die Lewe En Werk Van Gerhard Moerdijk*. Pretoria: J. L. van Schaik.

Witz, Leslie, Ciraj Rassool, and Gary Minkley. 2005. "Repackaging the Past for South African Tourism." In *Heritage, Museums and Galleries*, edited by Gerard Corsane, 308–19. London: Routledge.

CHAPTER 2

A Thinking Stone and Some Pink Presidents: Negotiating Afrikaner Nationalist Monuments at the University of the Free State

BRENDA SCHMAHMANN

IN SEPTEMBER 2009, THE University of the Free State learned it was to be the recipient of a grant of 3.4 million rand (about US$340,000 at that time) from the National Lottery Development Trust Fund, enabling the institution to acquire and install a series of contemporary artworks on its campus. The impetus for the initiative was not simply to transform the aesthetics of the campus or to provide staff, students, and visitors with access to creative and imaginative art objects in key spaces but also, more crucially, to make available to the university "diverse and site-specific sculptures that promote a greater understanding, respect and appreciation of cultural differences" and enable "a sense of belonging for all."[1] The focus here was in fact on remedying and transforming the university's "institutional culture"—a term that, while somewhat inexact, tends to refer to established customs, practices, and discourses that construct some as enjoying a sense of "belonging" to the organization while implicitly marginalizing others. In acquiring new works of art that create "a sense of belonging for all," the implication was that the University of the Free State might potentially redress ways in which its visual culture—conceptualized as an aspect of its institutional culture—was perceived as exclusionary.

Concern about biases underpinning the art on campus was not misplaced. Prior to the installation of the new works, prominent public imagery on the campus tended to not only speak of white Afrikaner histories but also to affirm values and ideals associated with Afrikaner nationalism. A sculpture by Anton van Wouw (fig. 2.1), unveiled in 1929 and located in front of the entrance to the university's Main Building, represented Marthinus Theunis Steyn, sixth president of the Orange Free State and a founding member of the National Party which came to power under the leadership of the staunch Afrikaner nationalist James Barry Hertzog, in 1924. Also in the immediate vicinity of the Main Building (fig. 2.2) was a memorial commissioned to commemorate the 1938 celebrations of the centenary of the Great Trek, the journey of Boers from the Cape to the hinterland of South Africa, which assumed centrality in Afrikaner nationalist discourses. And just a few meters away from that memorial was a third object—a sculpture by Johann Moolman (fig. 2.3) that was unveiled in 1991 and that depicts C. R. Swart. The first state president in the Republic of South Africa in 1961, and the person after whom the law building immediately adjacent to the statue is named, Swart served as chancellor of the university from 1950 to 1976. A member of the secret organization the Broederbond, he played an active role in various other bodies with Afrikaner nationalist agendas.

A dilemma confronting many public organizations and institutions in South Africa is what to do with objects they possess that were commissioned in response to the influence of ideologies that have fallen out of favor—a question that becomes especially tricky to address when it concerns works installed permanently in prominent places or central sections of the campus, as is the case with these three monuments. Although such objects may venerate individuals whose acts were unworthy or commemorate events that compromised some groups, the act of placing them in storage or giving them away can exacerbate rather than remedy divisiveness. Sabine Marschall (2010, 142) writes that white South Africans are often "defensive about and emotionally attached to the symbolic makers of their past" even though they do not necessarily identify "with the role models, values and intended 'message' each of these monuments conveys," suggesting that such sentiments tend to stem from "an increasing sense of alienation, and anxieties over black domination and perceived threats to their sense of cultural identity and their future in the country." More crucially, however, moving objects may in fact encourage amnesia or even denial about difficult histories. Indeed, as I have argued elsewhere, placing objects associated with nationalist or imperialist interests out of immediate access, while seeming

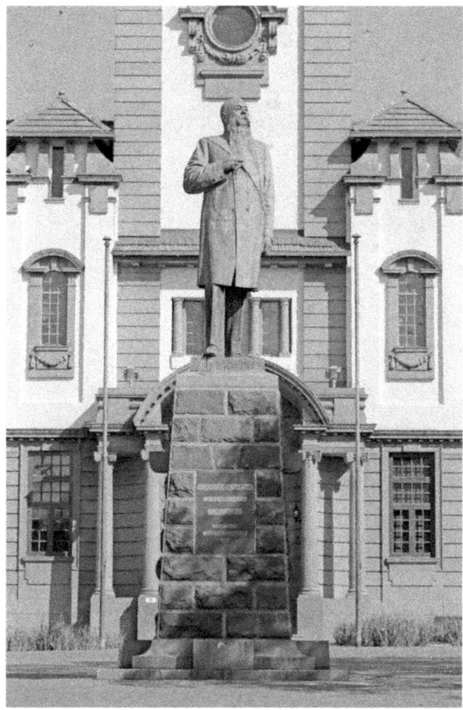

Fig. 2.1 Anton van Wouw, *Marthinus Theunis Steyn* (1929), bronze. *Photograph by Paul Mills.*

to be motivated by transformative sentiments, has on some occasions been prompted in fact by right-wing interests. Sometimes underpinned by assumptions that objects need to be secured against retributive acts of vandalism,[2] removal has been used to curtail debates that have the potential to result in transformative actions.[3] Yet simply leaving such objects where they are, and without any steps being taken to enable them to be seen in light of the histories that informed their production and placement, may be misinterpreted as suggesting ongoing allegiance to the ideologies with which they are associated.

As I will reveal, the application to the National Lottery stemmed to a large extent from debates about how to negotiate existent works on campus, particularly the prominently placed sculpture of Steyn. Although there were sixteen works that were obtained and all contributed to enabling a greater sense of belonging on the part of a changed student body, I focus specifically on only one of these—thus allowing my discussion to be in relative depth.[4]

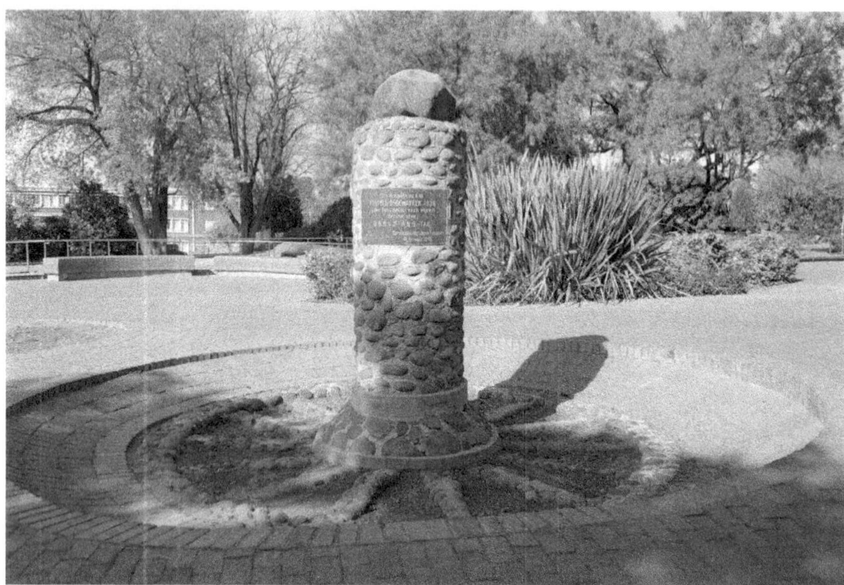

Fig. 2.2 Memorial to the centenary of the Great Trek in 1938 (installed in 1940), stone, gravel, and concrete. *Photograph by Paul Mills.*

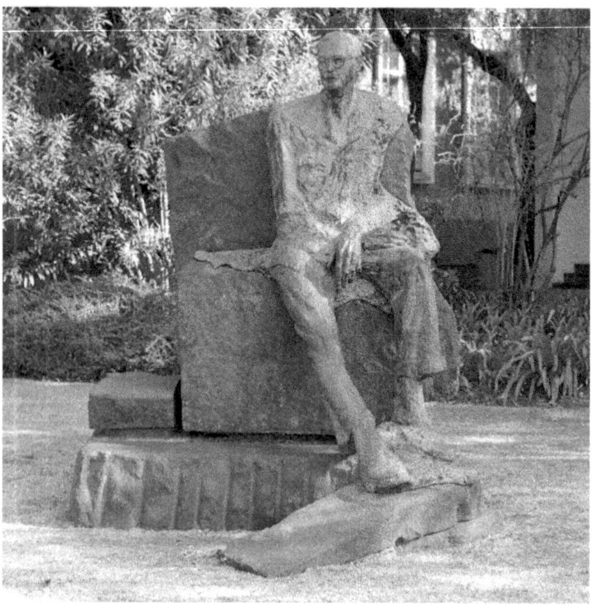

Fig. 2.3 Johann Moolman, *C. R. Swart* (1991), bronze. *Photograph by Paul Mills.*

Through examination of Willem Boshoff's *Thinking Stone,* a key work acquired with funds from the Lotto grant, I suggest how a new art object may introduce discourse that shifts the efficacy and impact of monuments associated with ideals that are out of favor. While not involving any kind of physical alteration to the sculptures of Steyn or Swart or to the memorial to the centenary of the Great Trek, the Boshoff work undermines their authority by offering an alternative narrative about South African histories, subverting tropes associated with Afrikaner nationalism as well as assuming a physical form that is accessible and that promotes dialogue and interchange. A work such as this might indeed be understood in light of what James E. Young (1993, 17–38) would term a countermonument—that is, a monument that engages self-critically with the monument as a form while also offering an alternative perspective on historical events.

Another potentially effective strategy is to engage critically with existent monuments via their temporary adjustment and to prompt dialogue about the possible meanings and significance of these modifications. During the 2014 Vryfees, a performing and visual arts festival that takes place annually in Bloemfontein in the second week of July, Cigdem Aydemir (2014, 7)—who describes herself as a "Sydney based artist of Turkish Muslim heritage"—undertook such an engagement via a project on campus titled *Plastic Histories.* As I indicate, her interventions, like Boshoff's *Thinking Stone,* complicated Afrikaner nationalist tropes. Prompting thoughts about the kinds of histories monuments on campus and the city may preserve as well as the gender politics underpinning them, Aydemir's critical engagement was effected additionally through a process of "queering" the Afrikaner nationalist sculptures.

Prior to engaging with the works by Boshoff and Aydemir, I indicate how the University of the Free State came to acquire works associated with Afrikaner nationalism as well as the ways in which it shaped itself as a campus for white Afrikaans speakers alone. I also provide an immediate context for the examination of the works by Boshoff and Aydemir by revealing how the institution has sought to adjust the effect of its monuments on campus in response to changed circumstances, as well as shifts in its demographics in the twenty-first century.[5]

THE UNIVERSITY OF THE FREE STATE IN THE TWENTIETH CENTURY

The University of the Free State—originally Grey University College—was founded in 1904, shortly after the South African War (1899–1902), and this conflict would shape thinking at the institution as it did elsewhere in South Africa. As Saul Dubow (1995, 248) observes, the "traumatic experience" of the South African War (or Anglo-Boer War) "is generally regarded as having provided the vital stimulus for the development of Afrikaner nationalism as a mass movement. Confused and insecure in defeat, leading Afrikaner nationalist theoreticians sought above all to confront the power of British imperialism." The desire for language rights, especially, would feature in the history of the university from its outset. In a context where the institution's role was to prepare candidates for examinations that would be conducted under the auspices of the University of the Cape of Good Hope and where the first professors were British, it was not feasible for instruction to be in Dutch (Afrikaans), but in 1918 the institution was granted permission to use Afrikaans as a medium of instruction, and in the second half of the 1940s the principle of offering courses in either English or Afrikaans was phased out in favor of tuition in Afrikaans alone (see Barnard 2004, 128).

Unlike the University of Cape Town, the University of the Witwatersrand, and the University of Natal that were to some extent "open" to all, Grey University College[6] established itself as a campus for white students alone well before the apartheid government passed the Extension of University Education Act of 1959 which prohibited black students from registering at them.[7] As is observed in a volume the institution produced to commemorate its centenary, this marginalization of black people had its origins in the constitution of the Orange Free State Republic which was operative from 1854 to 1902 and which indicated that "*slegs blankes burgers van den Orangjeverijstaat zijn*" (only white people are citizens of the Orange Free State). "Coloureds" and the "people of Paulus Mopeli" (the Basotho) were not entitled to participate in the government of the day, or to any other privileges" (Barnard 2006, 5), and these attitudes would be perpetuated at the university for decades. In 1977, the institution agreed to admit three students applying for graduate studies in areas not available at "black universities"—qualifications that could be undertaken without making available accommodation in residences and without necessitating a mixing of races in the classroom. While a year later, in 1978, the university admitted a black student who was also allowed to attend classes, thus paving the way for a small number of people from excluded groups to be admitted to the university in the 1980s, it was only in May 1990 that black students were given access to residence accommodation.[8]

An increasing influence of Afrikaner nationalist ideas on the campus provided the context for the installation of the sculpture of Steyn on the twenty-fifth anniversary of the founding of the institution. Commissioned from Anton van Wouw, a prominent sculptor of Afrikaner statesmen, the work was paid for through the fund-raising efforts of the Afrikaner Studentebond (Afrikaner Student Union), an organization with an Afrikaner nationalist agenda, and it was unveiled by the newly installed rector, Professor Daniël Francois Malherbe, who was committed to orientating the institution in favor of Christian nationalism (see Schmahmann 2013, 26). Afrikaner nationalist ideas reached fever pitch a decade later, in 1938, at the time of the centenary of the Great Trek. Among those who organized symbolic treks to Pretoria, where they met at the site of the future Voortrekker Monument, was a group of eleven students from the university who traveled in their own ox wagon named after its donor, Anna Meyer. Two years later, the centenary of the Great Trek would be permanently commemorated through a memorial comprised of a concrete, gravel, and brick base in the shape of the radial spokes of a wagon week encircling a stone-encrusted plinth supporting a boulder. Commissioned on the initiative of the Afrikaanse Nationale Studentebond (Afrikaans National Student Union), which had replaced the Afrikaner Studentebond in 1934, the younger organization shared the Afrikaner nationalist ideals of its predecessor (see Schmahmann 2013, 28–30).

But if the installation of these two monuments is readily explicable in terms of sentiments that enjoyed currency at the university and in Bloemfontein more generally, the acquisition of the sculpture of C. R. Swart by Moolman might seem somewhat anomalous. Unveiled in June 1991, a few months ahead of the first plenary session of the Convention for a Democratic South Africa (CODESA), which would signal the end of an era dominated by the National Party and its principles of apartheid, Moolman's sculpture was in fact placed on the campus at a time when it was clear to many that the values and ideals held by the person it represented were not destined to be those that would be endorsed by government in the near future. Yet an examination of institutional demographics from the early 1990s suggests that, despite the university endeavoring to dispense with regulations that restricted the access of black students, its primary student body tended in fact to be the same as it had been historically. In 1990, 95.8 percent of students were white, and this figure had shifted only to 85.17 percent in 1994 (see Institute for Reconciliation and Social Justice 2014, 16).

In 1993, two years after the arrival of the sculpture of Swart on campus, the university sought to enable success on the part of black students by introducing a policy of teaching courses in both Afrikaans and English, and, largely because of this as well as the focus on transformation by Stef Coetzee, who became rector in 1997 (see Bryson 2014, 53–64), there was a significant increase in the numbers of black students on campus by the late 1990s. But the most dramatic shift in institutional demographics would occur in the new millennium.

RESPONSES TO CHANGING DEMOGRAPHICS

The National Plan for Higher Education, announced in 2001, aimed to reduce the number of institutions in South Africa through a series of mergers, and it resulted in the University of the Free State inheriting the Qwaqwa campus of the former University of the North in January 2003 and the Bloemfontein campus of the former Vista University in January 2004. These additions to the institution considerably changed the demographics of the student body. By 1998, nearly 45 percent of students were black and by 2004 this percentage had increased to nearly 65 percent. A further crucial change was in terms of the overall number of students, which grew from just over 10 000 in 1998 to more than 25 000 in 2004 (see Institute for Reconciliation and Social Justice 2014, 15–16).

The merger necessitated replanning the campus, and in the course of these discussions, the centrality and impact of Van Wouw's sculpture of Steyn began to be a focus of concern. Frederick Fourie, who became rector in 2003, initiated discussion with Dirk van den Berg, Professor of Art History, and Ben Botma, Professor of Fine Art, about the possibility of adjusting its placement. The idea, Van den Berg indicates, was "not to so much react against" the representation of Steyn and other objects associated with Afrikaner nationalist histories as "to change the atmosphere" of the space, part of which would involve steps to "tone them down or at least to give another voice" to the campus.[9] Fourie thought of incorporating on to campus an image of Moshoeshoe (c.1786–1870), celebrated as the founder of the Sotho "nation" as well as for his military skills and diplomacy, envisaging that he might serve "as a kind of model figure, an icon figure almost, especially for the incoming black students."[10] Mooting initially for a large sculpture of Moshoeshoe to be placed on the same axis as the sculpture of Steyn, the rector subsequently envisaged the two statues placed on either side of the entrance of the Main Building but facing each other, as if conversing.[11] Ultimately, however, a decision was made to change the kinds of messages and meanings invoked by existent monuments on campus not through the introduction of new statuary that was traditionalist in type but rather through motivating to the National Lottery Development Trust Fund for monies to commission or acquire a series of artworks that were more up to date in terms of their visual language as well as articulating very different kinds of messages and meanings to existing monuments on campus. Van den Berg and Botma, working with the marketing and development bodies of the university, began to devise an application to the National Lottery.

Changes in demographics at the University of the Free State did not unfortunately mean that staff (who continued to be mostly white) as well as white students and their parents necessarily all welcomed diversity. When the institution was audited in 2006, the panel organizing the assessment questioned whether steps being taken by the university to enable transformation were "effective in the face of resistance to change on the part of some students, staff and parents" as well as a lack of racial integration evident at the institution's residences (Institute for Reconciliation and Social Justice 2014, 51). The legitimacy of these concerns would be demonstrated horrifyingly some two years later, in February 2008, when a group of white male students at the Reitz residence on campus articulated their opposition to policies to integrate the residences by producing a scurrilous video representing middle-aged black female workers participating in a mock initiation ritual and apparently consuming food that had been urinated on by the students. Posted on YouTube, where it afforded the institution unwelcome international attention, it resulted ultimately in "Reitz" becoming, as the university acknowledges, "a reference point for framing a need for transformation in higher education" in South Africa (Institute for Reconciliation and Social Justice 2014, 6). Frederick Fourie, who was exhausted and suffering from ill health in the wake of the scandal, stepped down from the position of rector in September 2008.[12]

Jonathan Jansen, the University of the Free State's first black rector and the individual tasked with mending an institution whose reputation and standing had been badly damaged, assumed his position in July 2009, when the application to Lotto had already been made. At his inaugural address on October 16, 2009, about a month after the university had been notified that it was to receive this Lotto award, he announced that the University of the Free State would not be pursuing action against the students who had made the racist video. Rather than seeing the video "as a product of four bad apples," he felt focus should be placed on the institutional culture that had enabled it—or, as he expressed it, "What was it within the institution that made it possible for such an atrocity to be committed in the first place?" He also spoke about addressing what he termed "the problem of knowledge," suggesting that the "often troubled knowledge the student comes to university with—the knowledge of the past, the knowledge of black and white and, especially, the knowledge of the future" presented a crucial challenge. Proposing "a fundamental curriculum overhaul," he sought to ensure "that no student graduates from this university without engaging basic human questions such as who we are and where we come from; without learning how to live and learn together in ways that prepare our youth for leadership in the workplace."[13] Hardly surprisingly, the project to acquire new art for campus, set in motion at exactly this time, would be informed by heightened alertness to ways in which imagery on campus can shape understandings of identity, and how it can play a role in informing how people from different backgrounds relate to one another as well as have a significant bearing on feelings of either belonging or exclusion.

Angela de Jesus, who joined the university as curator in September 2009, indicates that, immediately following the award, the institution set up a Sculpture-on-Campus Committee to make arrangements for its implementation. Besides herself, it included Van den Berg, Botma, the late Bannie Brits who was the former Professor of Architecture, people in senior management, as well as individuals responsible for physical planning.[14] Placing particular focus on the reconceptualization of the Red Square, where the Steyn statue is located, the group reached agreement that it should become a space of reconciliation. The possibility of introducing the figure of Moshoeshoe that Fourie had initially mooted was once again considered but ultimately rejected. The committee then considered moving Steyn in such a way that the figure would no longer block the entrance to the main building and, placed on a low base, would have a less overbearing presence, and Van den Berg set about commissioning digital images illustrating some possibilities for relocating the work. But complications ensued when, in a letter on March 8, 2010, Jansen asked the university community for their opinions about removing the Steyn sculpture and whether, as an alternative possibility, "it should be lowered and stand in conversation with a statue of equal size, that of the great King Moshoeshoe of the region." The letter attracted the attention of the local newspaper *Volksblad*, as well as Steyn's descendants, and it became evident that any endeavors to adjust the placement of the sculpture, rather than enabling reconciliation, would likely be interpreted by some sectors of the Bloemfontein community as an act of provocation. The plan was, however, finally abandoned when it was ascertained that the cost of making such an adjustment was in excess of what the university could afford.

A transformative agenda remained nevertheless in the foreground. Botma indicates that Jansen "asked us to consider the whole idea of reconciliation and so on in the process of selecting artists" to produce works. While he did not instruct those involved in organizing the initiative to "do this or that," Botma observes, he inferred that it would be a good idea that "we should think along those lines."[15] Explaining how a transformative agenda was ultimately taken up, De Jesus indicates that there was a feeling that the motif of the *lekgotla* could be explored as a governing idea. Referring to a meeting place in Sesotho or Setswana, it invokes also the idea of a community council or law court where people are each given an opportunity to speak and where decisions are arrived at by consensus. Two strategies were deployed toward this end. One was to create what De Jesus terms actual "meeting places"—that is, artworks that offered seating in a physical sense and that did so in such a way that they implied equal status among individuals being accommodated. Another was to create "conversation pieces"—that is, individual works "that people immediately look at and are amused by or maybe think is a little controversial or just interesting. I've noticed that the immediate response is for people to say, 'Look at that thing!' Now, if somebody says, 'Look at that thing,' somebody else says, "'What do you think it means?'" And then there's a conversation that happens."[16] In such a conception, achieving a healthy accord involves confronting what might be difficult, unsettling, or potentially shocking, as well as recognizing the multiplicity of potential ways an image or object might be interpreted.[17]

WILLEM BOSHOFF'S *THINKING STONE*

Although his complex piece would be completed and installed only in 2011, negotiations with Willem Boshoff for a key work for Red Square began early in the process—toward the end of 2009. Discussions about invoking reference to Moshoeshoe were still under consideration when he was approached, Van den Berg indicates, and the committee wondered whether

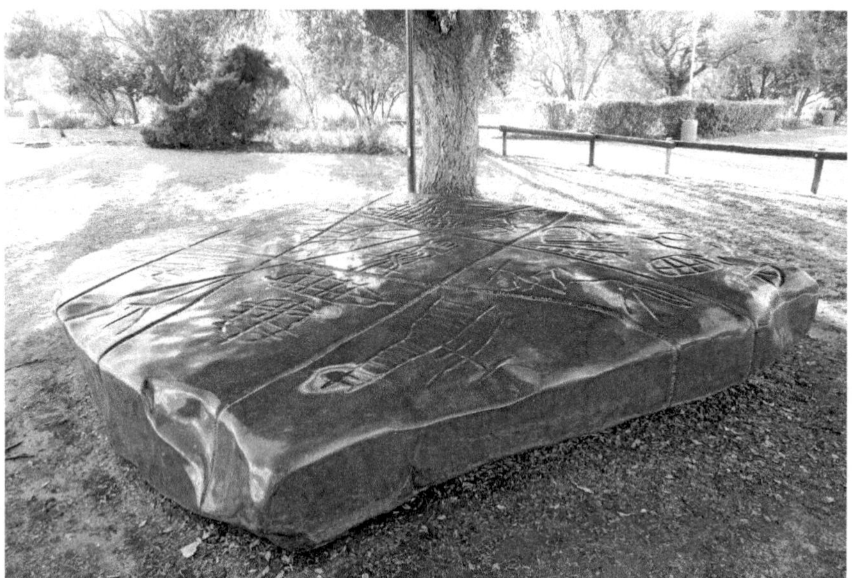

Fig. 2.4 Willem Boshoff, *Thinking Stone* (2011), granite, University of the Free State, Bloemfontein. *Photograph by Paul Mills.*

Boshoff (whose works have often explored the implications of forgiveness and reconciliation) might be interested in referring to a story about Moshoeshoe's response to cannibals who had devoured his grandfather and some other members of his group when they were traveling from Butha Buthe to Thaba Bosiu in 1824. In the absence of a grave and unable therefore to perform ritual functions that were required, it is believed that Moshoeshoe elected not to execute the culprits but instead performed purification rituals on their persons—almost as if they were living tombs—and thus in fact spared their lives (see, e.g., Eldredge 2007, 28).[18]

Boshoff did not, however, elect to develop this idea. Rather, his *Thinking Stone* (fig. 2.4) invokes reference to Driekops Eiland (Afrikaans for "Three Heads Island"), a prehistoric site near Kimberley in the Northern Cape of South Africa, which includes more than 3,000 engravings, or petroglyphs, that are mostly geometric in type and have been worked on the glaciated rock forming a bed within the Riet River. Producing his work from a large rock of Belfast granite, which he polished in such a way that it imitated the wetness of the bedrock, Boshoff sandblasted the boulder to invoke reference to the cracks as well as many of the petroglyphs found on the site.

Instead of focusing on a heritage that had seen the University of Free State framing its identity in terms of Afrikaner nationalist resistance to British imperialism, Boshoff turned his attention to indigenous knowledge systems that had long predated the arrival of both Dutch and English speakers in South Africa. As he observed during a visit to Driekops Eiland that was recorded in a short film:

> I would like to be so bold as to say that I think these few rock beds that we are sitting on here . . . are perhaps the oldest collection of . . . instruments of thought. And because they are such, I think they are the leftover of a once-upon-a-time "university." There was a collection of, call them "scribes" maybe, [or] intellectuals, people with direction, people with focus, people with intellectual acumen, sharpness. Those people who made these things are to me the lecturers, the professors and students of 2000 years ago. This is probably the oldest university that we can have evidence of in this country. And for me it is wonderful that we are sitting on a 2000-year old university, a campus. The word "campus" means "field." . . . In the old days the teachers used to teach under the trees and in the open. (Boshoff 2011)

Functioning as a type of homage to the Driekops Eiland "university," the rock from which *Thinking Stone* is constituted serves as a literal seat as well as locus for interchange and reflection under the trees on a modern-day campus.

While making reference to prehistoric designs, Boshoff also sandblasted onto the boulder various idioms, proverbs, and quotes that have more recent origin. Pertaining to rocks and stones, each is written in a language used in the Bloemfontein area—whether English, Sesotho, Afrikaans, isiXhosa, isiZulu, or Setswana. All appear on sections of the boulder that invoke the idea of a crack—a metaphor perhaps for a social rupture or difference of opinion, or perhaps even a blind spot. Some, such as the following, speak about negotiating conflict and disagreement:

> "The drops of rain make a hole in the stone, not by violence, but by oft falling." (Lucretius)
>
> "Anger is a stone cast into a wasp's nest." (Pope Paul VI)
>
> "Civilization began the first time an angry person cast a word instead of a rock." (Sigmund Freud)

This incorporation of various modern South African languages is important, complementing the work's inclusion of designs derived from ancient petroglyphs that have meanings that are no longer understood. In keeping with the intention of the Lotto Sculpture on Campus project, these devices prompt conversations to figure out their possible meanings. But they also prompt intellectual reflection, as De Jesus explains: "I think what's great about this piece as well is it's called *Thinking Stone*: so it's a place where these conversations can happen, but it's also a place where you can come to contemplate and try to decipher what these marks [i.e., the designs based on the petroglyphs] mean or don't mean."[19]

Rocks and stones were not new to Boshoff's iconography, and other works provided the origin for some of his ideas at play in *Thinking Stone*. His *Writing in the Sand* (2000–1) would seem to be particularly significant. Comprised of words and their definitions that were written in sand in the exhibition venue and swept away when the show was over, one aspect of its inspiration was a passage from the Gospel of John in the New Testament that speaks of the scribes and Pharisees looking for sanction to stone to death a woman for adultery:

> But Jesus stooped down, and with his finger wrote on the ground, as though he heard them not. So when they continued asking him, he lifted up himself, and said unto them, "He that is without sin among you, let him first cast a stone at her." And again he stooped down, and wrote on the ground. And they which heard it, being convicted by their own conscience, went out one by one, beginning at the eldest, even unto the last: and Jesus was left alone, and the woman standing in the midst. When Jesus had lifted up himself, and saw none but the woman, he said unto her, "Woman, where are those thine accusers? Hath no man condemned thee?" She said, "No man, Lord." And Jesus said unto her, "Neither do I condemn thee: go, and sin no more." (John 8:6–11 KJV)

The idea implicit in this passage is that blame should be resisted. Likewise, *Writing in the Sand* suggests that instead of enacting retribution, what one should instead do is write one's thoughts in the sand so that, as Boshoff explains, they "can be blown away by the wind."[20] This concept was also taken up in the contemporaneous *Circle of Knowledge*, which he made for the former Rand Afrikaans University (now part of the University of Johannesburg) and which is comprised of eleven granite boulders, each inscribed with explanations of the definitions of obscure words in one of South

Africa's eleven languages. As I have noted previously in an engagement with that work, Boshoff deployed "the motif of the stone as a signifier of an imperative to exact retribution. But Boshoff's stones are large granite boulders, far too weighty to throw" (Schmahmann 2013, 11). In *Thinking Stone,* which the University of the Free State estimated to weigh as much as thirty tons when they arranged for trucks and cranes to move it to the campus, Boshoff once again uses this idea. A rock that cannot possibly be thrown, it points implicitly to the futility of violent acts of conflict. Indeed its title, *Thinking Stone,* suggests the value of intellectual reflection rather than stone throwing as a way to negotiate difference.

But the rock also establishes an ironic relationship between *Thinking Stone* and two other works on campus where this motif featured. The plinth at the center of the memorial to the centenary of the Great Trek supports a rock and is encrusted with stones and, relatedly, Moolman's sculpture depicts C. R. Swart seated on roughly hewn boulders—as if he were a pioneer in an unfamiliar terrain. Both objects draw immediately on a language in which the rugged South African terrain is conceptualized as a fatherland and the natural inheritance of the Afrikaner. "Central to the mythology of the Great Trek" and a primary trope within Afrikaner nationalist discourse more generally, Jennifer Beningfield (2006, 35) indicates, "was the idea that a new nation had been able to discover itself in the isolated and empty interior. The 'platteland' (literally 'flatland') was depicted as being without history, ripe for inscription." This conception, celebrated in the Great Trek memorial and in the image of Swart, is inverted in Boshoff's work where, rather than alluding to the South African terrain as unoccupied territory awaiting inscription, the boulder becomes the vehicle for revealing and celebrating sophisticated representations that were marked onto the land many years prior to any Europeans arriving on southern African soil. In other words, it makes evident that the Voortrekkers were heading not into vacant terrain but, on the contrary, land that had long since been occupied as well as shaped by the sophisticated cultural understandings of its inhabitants.

The work, however, contrasts to those on campus articulating Afrikaner nationalist sentiments through not only its iconography but also implicitly its visual form. Maya Lin's Vietnam Veterans Memorial is probably the most well-known monument that breaks with the convention of the vertical, phallic monument, developing instead a horizontally oriented structure that has frequently been termed "feminine" and that, from a Jungian point of view, could be viewed in terms of the "mother archetype" (see Haines 1989, 206). Much like the contrast between the Vietnam Veterans Memorial and other monuments on the Mall in Washington, DC, notably the Washington Monument, *Thinking Stone* is in diametric opposition to the image of Steyn on its story-high plinth as well as the phallic monument to the centenary of the Great Trek in the sense that it is low, horizontal, and invites people on campus to sit on it in the manner of a bench, to touch it, or even to climb on it.

CIGDEM AYDEMIR'S *PLASTIC HISTORIES*

While, through its horizontality, *Thinking Stone* is the antithesis of the phallocentric Afrikaner nationalist works on campus, its reference to the gender politics underpinning monuments at the University of the Free State is implicit rather than overt. A more immediate and explicit critique of the gender politics of monuments at the institution was in play when Cigdem Aydemir transformed two of these—the figures of Steyn and Swart—in a project that formed part of the 2014 Vryfees.

In *Plastic Histories*, Aydemir shrink-wrapped and sprayed pink the two sculptures (fig. 2.5). She had hoped the statues of President Brand, General De Wet, and General Hertzog in Bloemfontein could be given the same treatment. But, while the University of the Free State welcomed her engagement with the Steyn and Swart works, and Jansen in fact contributed a piece of writing to Aydemir's catalog, she was not able to secure permission to modify works that were off campus. Consequently, working with another Australian, Warren Armstrong, Aydemir used digital processes to instead create the impression that these three additional monuments had been shrink-wrapped—effects that a viewer was able to access on his or her cell phone or tablet if an appropriate application was loaded. Simultaneous with this initiative, Aydemir held a one-person exhibition in the Johannes Stegmann Gallery on campus that included photographs of monuments that had been digitally manipulated in such a way that they made those objects appear to be vacuum-packed in pink plastic. The projects included walking tours of the various monuments—ones intended to introduce viewers to their histories and the politics that had underpinned them.

The artist explains that her idea for the project developed from an interest in monuments from the nineteenth and twentieth centuries. Directing her thinking "at the people and purposes they serve, and their relevance to the communities they exist in today," she deduced from research that

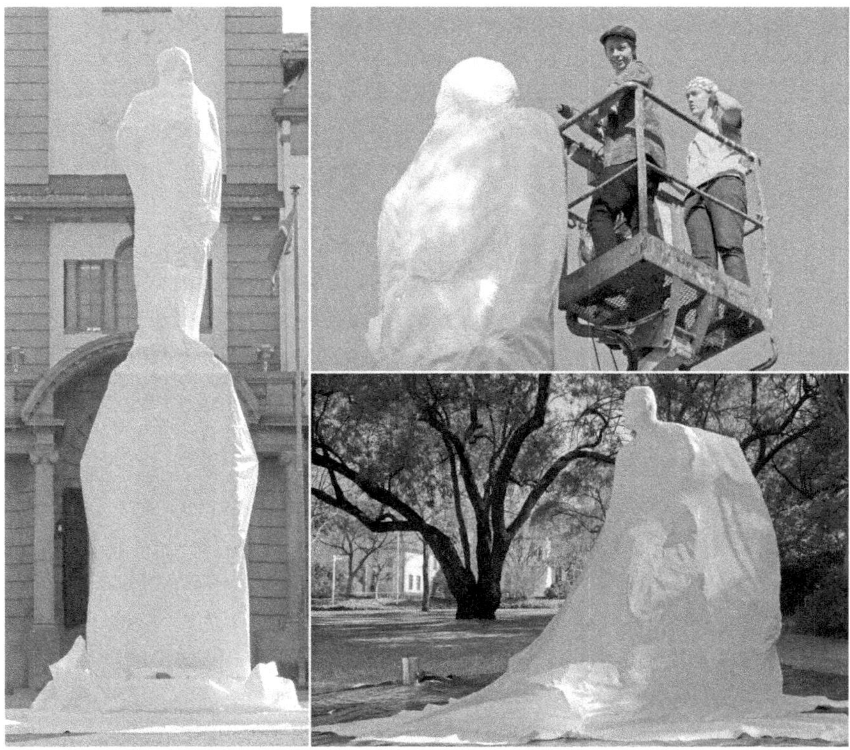

Fig. 2.5 The preparation of works for Cigdem Aydemir's *Plastic Histories* (2014): Left: Anton van Wouw's *Marthinus Theunis Steyn* shrink-wrapped in plastic and prior to it being spray-painted pink; Top right: Cigdem Aydemir (front) organizing the shrink-wrapping of Van Wouw's *Marthinus Theunis Steyn*; Bottom right: Moolman's *C. R. Swart* in the process of being spray-painted pink. *Photographs by Paul Mills.*

"monuments generally serve to shape collective memory in public spaces and ensure against the failure of individual memory."[21] But she also recognized that memory does not simply fix history in immutable ways and that it is in fact "plastic in the sense that it is constantly shaped and molded by our new knowledge of the past."[22] Shrink-wrapping the sculptures extended this idea metaphorically in the sense that it alluded to vacuum-packing as a process used for preservation. Understood in this light, the act of shrink-wrapping the monuments may prompt critical thought about the degree to which values that may have informed the commissioning, making, and installation of these historical objects have (or have not) been conserved on the campus as well as in Bloemfontein more generally.

Crucial to *Plastic Histories* was the decision to not simply vacuum-pack the sculptures but also spray them pink. Perhaps invoking the concept of "pinko" (i.e., an individual with a cowardly disposition), such a reading would obviously be somewhat subversive in the context of sculptures that deploy a language of the heroic. But more crucially, pink is popularly associated with femininity, and through its imposition on male figures, it encourages alertness to a politics of gender at play in the two campus sculptures.

The kind of masculinity that the figures of Steyn and Swart glorify might be described as stalwart. And in both sculptures there is the suggestion that their subjects have agency: the upward tilt of his head and raised right arm of Steyn suggest that he is in the process of speaking, while Swart—tall and broad shouldered—is clearly resting on this pile of rocks for only a short while. Representations of women in sculptures imbued with Afrikaner nationalist ideals tend to be of a very different order, however. For example, Anton van Wouw's sculpture of two adult females and a dying female child at the Women's Memorial just outside of Bloemfontein, constructed to acknowledge the torment inflicted on Boer women and children during the South African War, is emblematic of not only suffering but incapacity. Anne McClintock (1995, 378), writing about the image of the *volksmoeder* (mother of the nation) in its early incarnation, such as in the sculpture at the Women's Memorial, observes how, in its celebration of self-sacrificing femininity, Afrikaner nationalists found a trope for invoking reference to Boer defeat without showing male passivity.[23] Through the representation of the Afrikaner *volk* as a tearful female, "the mighty male embarrassment of military defeat could be overlooked and the memory of women's vital efforts during the war washed away in images of feminine tears and maternal loss."[24]

While the university currently often organizes activities that foreground the need for gender equality and is mindful of the fact that its "much larger growth in the enrolment of female students compared to male students" necessitates that it "provide appropriate role models at all levels for these young women," such a focus on challenging discrimination against women is a relatively recent phenomenon at the university (Institute for Reconciliation and Social Justice 2014, 17–18). Benito Khotseng, who became one of the first black managers on campus in 1993, two years after Moolman's sculpture of Swart was acquired, described to the writer Donna Bryson how he immediately sought allies among white women "who felt undervalued in tradition-bound, patriarchal Afrikaner society" that often denied them leadership opportunities. Aydemir's "feminization" of the two figures may perhaps be understood to prompt awareness of histories of gendered discrimination and to be mindful of the ways in which these underpin different discourses, including a language of memorialization.

Along with raising questions about the kind of gendering that may underpin memorials and other discourses, the use of pink might be interpreted in light of Aydemir's intention to use this as a device for "queering the monuments." As David Halperin (1995, 62) sees it, queer is "by definition whatever is at odds with the normal, the legitimate, the dominant," and as Giffney (2009, 3) suggests, it involves a championing of "those who refuse to be defined in the terms of, and by the (moral) codes of behavior and identification set down by, the dominant society." Thus while drawing attention to a heteronormativity in public art discourse, a queering of these monuments by spraying them an exuberant and shrill pink also involves a disruption to their normalcy in a wider sense, rendering them peculiar and anomalous.

Furthermore, as a mode of analysis indebted to poststructuralism, the process of queering tends to involve an identification of silences and blind spots that underpin discourse (see Giffney 2009, 7)—an orientation that in this instance involves prompting viewers to think about not simply those whom these monuments celebrate but also those whom they marginalize or exclude. In the words of Aydemir, the color pink might be seen as "an opportunity to empower and commemorate the unacknowledged and equally deserving rather than those simply in power."[25] In addition to invoking ideas about the exclusion of LGBT people from commemorative language as well as their reductive imaging of women, this focus on exclusions invites questions about the marginalization of narratives about black communities and individuals in public art discourse on the campus and in Bloemfontein more generally. In other words, the intervention prompts critical alertness to the fact that while some histories are acknowledged in the context of this post-apartheid campus and city, others are left out.

CONCLUSION

By 2014, and twenty years after the first democratic election in South Africa, about 72 percent of the approximately 33,000 students enrolled at the University of the Free State were black (see Institute for Reconciliation and Social Justice 2014, 17). In a social context very different to what had shaped much of the university's history, some might perceive objects such as Van

Wouw's sculpture of Steyn, Moolman's sculpture of C. R. Swart, and the monument to the centenary of the Great Trek as, simply, tired remnants of a problematic past that remain on display only because of the political fallout or legal constraints that would be involved in removing them. Yet one might argue that no matter how problematic the ideologies that had a bearing on their making, it is more potentially productive to enable such objects to serve as prompts that enable enriched and critical understandings of ideas and debates that have shaped not simply the past but also current circumstances. In other words, it makes sense to regard the visibility of such works not as hampering institutional change but instead—through interventions such as those of Boshoff and Aydemir—as potentially enabling understandings to shape a different kind of future.

POSTSCRIPT

But if the approach mooted in this chapter is to be successful, there does need to be popular understanding that the retention of works from prior eras is not a sign that the institution is seeking to perpetuate the values with which they are associated. In a situation where equanimity between different racial groups is tenuous or where the purpose of retention is not widely understood or accepted, such an approach can go awry. This unfortunately turned out to be the case at the University of the Free State early in 2016. National protests at universities that had emerged under the ambit of the @FeesMustFall movement in late 2015 included resistance against the outsourcing of support staff such as cleaners. When a group of (black) students protesting against outsourcing disrupted a rugby match (traditionally a "white" sport) at the University of the Free State on the afternoon of February 22, 2016, the players and their supporters retaliated by assaulting the demonstrators, and a riot broke out that involved damage being done to campus. Targeting Moolman's sculpture of C. R. Swart, the protestors first attempted to set fire to the work but, finding that ineffectual, then used hammers and rocks to dislodge the figure which ended up in a nearby pond. During the turmoil, campus security forces were obliged to blockade the Steyn sculpture to prevent it also being targeted. The sculpture of Swart was then placed in storage, and the University of the Free State began a process of consultation with the Provincial Heritage Council and other stakeholders about its future location. By the time that this chapter was finalized in April 2017, a solution had been found. It was agreed that the sculpture be relocated to the heritage site of the Voortrekker, Sarel Cilliers, on Doornkloof farm in the Kroonstad district of the Free State province.

ACKNOWLEDGMENTS

My sincere thanks to Angela de Jesus, Dirk van den Berg, Ben Botma, and Cigdem Aydemir who set aside time to speak to me about factors surrounding the sculpture award from the National Lottery Development Trust Fund on the part of the University of the Free State. Thank you also to Paul Mills for undertaking photography for me. Research for this chapter was undertaken with funding granted to me by the National Research Foundation (NRF) in South Africa. Please note, however, that any opinions, findings, conclusions, or recommendations expressed in this chapter are those of the author, and the NRF does not accept any liability in regard to them.

BRENDA SCHMAHMANN is Professor and the South African Research Chair in South African Art and Visual Culture at the University of Johannesburg. She has written, edited, or coedited a number of volumes on South African art, the most recent of which are *Picturing Change: Curating Visual Culture at Post-Apartheid Universities* and *The Keiskamma Art Project: Restoring Hope and Livelihoods.*

NOTES

1. See http://www.ufs.ac.za/adhoc-pages/front-page/lotto-sculpture-on-campus-project. Accessed December 27, 2014.

2. In Schmahmann (2013, 36) I suggest that the University of Pretoria's return of an ox wagon from the centenary celebrations to the Afrikaanse Taal-en Kultuurvereniging (Afrikaans Language and Culture Association) in 1994 was likely linked to fears about what would happen to such objects in a new South Africa.

3. In Schmahmann (2013, 42–53) I explore the removal of a bust of Cecil John Rhodes from the entrance of Rhodes University in Grahamstown. As I reveal, this was a response to a call for the university to change its name. By removing the portrait, those resisting this change were better placed to claim that the name was merely a "brand" rather than making reference to a particular individual.

4. Along with Willem Boshoff's *Thinking Stone,* the Lotto-funded works include Brett Murray's *Seeds,* Noria Mabasa's *Unity Is Power: Let Us Be United,* Thomas Kubayi's *Walking Fish,* a work by Jaco Spies done in collaboration with Dina Grobler and the Tshiamo Arts and Crafts Project titled *Philosopher's Circle,* Willie Bester's *Bull Rider,* Strijdom van der Merwe's *Tree of Knowledge,* Angus Taylor's *Van hier tot daar* ("From

Here to There"), Pat Mautloa's *Melodi ya matsha* ("Birth of Rhythm"), and seven sculptures by Azwifarwi Ragimana titled *Baboon, Flying Fish, Fish Bench, Adam & Eve, Olive Bench, Natural Flare 1*, and *Natural Flare 2*.

5. It should be noted that while I discussed the Van Wouw sculpture of Steyn and the memorial to the centenary of the Great Trek in my study of visual culture on post-apartheid campuses, I observed that "new outdoor works at the University of the Free State arrived only after I had completed fieldwork at that institution" (Schmahmann 2013, 244). Thus in discussing Boshoff's *Thinking Stone* and Aydemir's later *Plastic Histories*, as well as the circumstances surrounding their showing on the University of the Free State campus in this chapter, I develop a topic I did not examine in that earlier study. The topic has also not been explored previously. While *Thinking Stone* has been the theme of a short film (Boshoff 2011) and *Plastic Histories* has been examined in a small online catalog (see Aydemir 2014), both of which are informative and insightful, neither initiative has previously been interpreted in relation to the other or in light of the overall history of the university as well as steps it has taken to negotiate its memorials that are related to the impact of Afrikaner nationalism.

6. Grey University College changed its name to the University College of the Orange Free State in the 1940s, then to the University of the Orange Free State when it became an independent university in 1950 and finally to the University of the Free State in 2001.

7. Depending on his or her (supposed) ethnicity, a black individual who wished for a tertiary education was instead directed to institutions that, in 1970, became the Universities of Fort Hare, the North, Zululand, Durban-Westville, and the Western Cape but that, in 1959, were all university colleges and, with the exception of Fort Hare, newly established.

8. See Barnard et al. (2004, 263–65) for an overview of these events.

9. Interview with Dirk van den Berg at the University of the Free State on July 2, 2014.

10. Ibid.

11. It is unclear what precedents Fourie knew about. Possibly he was aware of the pairing of Dinuzulu ka Cetshwayo with the figure by Louis Botha by Van Wouw in Durban (see fig. 0.2), mentioned in the introduction to this volume: although only unveiled in September 2008, the sculpture of Dinuzulu was installed in October 2006 (see Marschall 2010, 311). He may also have known of a competition mounted by the Tatham Gallery in Pietermaritzburg in 2002 for a portrait of Cetshwayo kaMpande (Dinuzulu ka Cetshwayo's father) in traditional dress to be paired with the institution's large *State Coronation Portrait of Queen Victoria* (copied by Charles van Havermaet between 1901 and 1904) that was hanging in its main stairwell. Certainly his sentiments seem to have been similar to those of the Tatham director, Brendan Bell (2003, 36), who described the idea behind that initiative as follows: "Placing portraits of Queen Victoria and King Cetshwayo adjacent to one another reinforces the Gallery's current policy that its collection and displays attempt to reflect the histories and cultural production of different, interdependent peoples."

12. See Bryson (2014, 64–77) for an account of Fourie's endeavors to transform the institution and the controversy of the Reitz video.

13. Jansen's inaugural address can be found at http://blogs.timeslive.co.za/hartley/2009/10/20/jonathan-jansens-inaugural-speech-as-vice-chancellor-of-ufs-full-text/. Accessed December 27, 2014.

14. Britz, who died in 2013, had designed many of the walkways introduced to make the campus more pedestrian friendly.

15. Interview with Ben Botma at the University of the Free State on July 3, 2014.

16. Interview with Angela de Jesus at the University of the Free State on July 2, 2014.

17. Works were acquired through a variety of processes. The committee began in the first instance to identify artists, and those who were interested were each invited to the campus to examine potential sites and meet people with whom they needed to engage. There was some purchasing of works that had already been completed or were in production. The university also put out an open call for works midway through 2011.

18. Interview with Van den Berg, July 2, 2014.

19. Commentary by Angela de Jesus during a guided tour of the University of Free State campus, July 3, 2014.

20. Interview with Willem Boshoff in Johannesburg on February 4, 2010.

21. Video commentary by Cigdem Aydemir on June 17, 2014 posted on "Situate: Art in Festivals" website: http://www.situate.org.au/artwork/plastic-histories-by-cigdem-aydemir/.

22. Video commentary by Aydemir, June 17, 2014.

23. It should be noted, however, that images of the *volksmoeder* made between 1914 and 1948, such as the example from the Voortrekker Monument that Elizabeth Rankin discusses in this volume, associate the figure with resilience. See Van der Watt (2005) for a more detailed discussion of the *volksmoeder* trope.

24. Indeed, this gendering might be understood in light of what Jackie Grobler suggests is a commonality between representations of the South African War and lost cause discourses in the southern states of the United States where the suggestion is of valiant resistance on the part of the losing side defending their way of life as well as the implication that submission was forced through unfair tactics. Representations of a suffering femininity (as in the Women's Monument) combined with a steadfast masculinity (as in Van Wouw's sculpture of Steyn) constituted part of a message that the Boers lost out to the British only "because of the enemy's massive numerical preponderance of about 20 to 1 by the end of the war, and because the British were targeting their women and children by placing them in concentration camps, where large numbers had died. The British had not beaten the Boers—the latter had merely decided to accept a negotiated peace treaty because the British were using barbaric methods against which they were powerless" (Grobler 2006, 206).

25. Video commentary by Aydemir, June 17, 2014.

References

Aydemir, Cigdem. 2014. "Introduction to *Plastic Histories: Public Art Project by Cigdem Aydemir*, 7. July 14–August 1, 2014." Accessed December 27, 2014. http://issuu.com/joh_designs/docs/plastic_histories_catalogue2014.

Barnard, Leo (Project Leader). 2006. *From Grey to Gold: The First 100 Years of the University of the Free State.* Bloemfontein, South Africa: University of the Free State.

Bell, Brendan. 2003. "One Hundred Years: The Fortunes (and Misfortunes) of the Tatham Art Gallery Collection." *Natalia* 33: 32–44.

Beningfield, Jennifer. 2006. *The Frightened Land: Land, Landscape and Politics in South Africa in the Twentieth Century.* New York: Routledge.

Boshoff, Willem. 2011. Commentary in *Thinking Stone: A Commission by Willem Boshoff.* Directed by Guy Spiller. Produced by Helene Smuts. Accessed December 27, 2014. https://www.youtube.com/watch?v=ncuOs25Dp-8.

Bryson, Donna. 2014. *It's a Black/White Thing.* Cape Town: Tafelberg.

Dubow, Saul. 1995. *Scientific Racism in Modern South Africa.* Cambridge, UK: Cambridge University Press.

Eldredge, Elizabeth. 2007. *Power in Colonial Africa: Conflict and Discourses in Lesotho, 1870–1960.* Madison: University of Wisconsin Press.

Giffney, Noreen. 2009. "The 'Q' Word." In *The Ashgate Research Companion to Queer Theory,* edited by Noreen Giffney and Michael O'Rourke, 1–13. Aldershot, UK: Ashgate.

Haines, Harry. 1989. "The Vietnam Veterans Memorial: Authority and Gender in Cultural Representation." In *Vietnam Images: War and Representation,* edited by Jeffrey Walsh and James Aulich, 205–10. New York: St. Martin's.

Halperin, D. M. 1995. *Saint Foucault: Towards a Gay Hagiography.* New York: Oxford University Press.

Institute for Reconciliation and Social Justice. 2014. *Transformation Report 2004–2014.* Bloemfontein, South Africa: University of the Free State. Accessed December 27, 2014. http://institute.ufs.ac.za/dl/Userfiles/Documents/00000/74_eng.pdf.

Jansen, Jonathan J. 2014. "Waiting to Exhale." In *Plastic Histories: Public Art Project by Cigdem Aydemir,* 12–13. July 14–August 1, 2014. Accessed December 27, 2014. http://issuu.com/joh_designs/docs/plastic_histories_catalogue2014.

Marschall, Sabine. 2010. *Landscape of Memory: Commemorative Monuments, Memorials and Public Statuary in Post-Apartheid South Africa.* Leiden, the Netherlands: Brill.

McClintock, Anne. 1995. *Imperial Leather: Race, Gender, and Sexuality in the Colonial Contest.* New York: Routledge.

Schmahmann, Brenda. 2013. *Picturing Change: Curating Visual Culture at Post-Apartheid Universities.* Johannesburg: Wits University Press.

Van der Watt, Liese. 2005. "Art, Gender Ideology and Afrikaner Nationalism—A Case Study." In *Between Union and Liberation: Women Artists in South Africa, 1910–1994,* edited by Marion Arnold and Brenda Schmahmann, 94–110. Aldershot, UK: Ashgate.

Young, James E. 2015. *The Texture of Memory: Holocaust Memorials and Meaning.* New Haven, CT: Yale University Press.

CHAPTER 3

The Mirror and the Square–Old Ideological Conflicts in Motion: Church Square Slavery Memorial

GAVIN YOUNGE

Visitors to Cape Town often remark on the vineyards stretching up to beautiful Cape Dutch manor houses from the seventeenth century. Low white-painted walls surround these buildings and each ensemble seems to follow the same pattern—an H-shaped manor house featuring gables, a *jonkmanshuis* (Afrikaans and Dutch for "young man's house"), a former slave lodge, and a slave bell. Elsewhere and most often out of sight, will be a row of workers' cottages. In the case of Groot Constantia, one of the most celebrated of these historic farmhouses, the former slave lodge is now given over to wine tastings and the *jonkmanshuis* is a now a restaurant.[1]

Often overlooked by visitors and omitted from marketing and publicity narratives is the fact that more than 60,000 women, children, and men were brought to the Cape to be sold into chattel slavery during 1652–1807. These were the people who built much of Cape Town: they built the Castle of Good Hope, they built jetties, and they dug furrows to grow vegetables for the Dutch East India Company or Vereenigde Oost-Indische Compagnie (VOC) and for the so-called *vrye burgers* (literally "free citizens," the Dutch name for officials who had left the employ of the VOC and started farming on their own account). *Vrye burgers* were also permitted to keep their own slaves.[2]

In late 2007, Cape Town announced a competition for the creation of a memorial, one that would symbolize the indomitable spirit of the enslaved and the contributions that they made to the economic and cultural development of the city.[3] The new memorial would be located on Church Square, a large open space where settlers outspanned their oxen and that is bounded on three sides by important buildings: the Slave Lodge which housed VOC slaves (now a museum that forms part of the Iziko Museums of Cape Town), the Groote Kerk where VOC slaves were baptized, and Spin Street, site of a former silk factory in which slave children kept at the lodge were required to work. Spin Street also includes the Slave Tree Plaque, a rather inconspicuous metal plaque placed in the median traffic island and that marked the spot where slaves were auctioned off to the highest bidder.

Wilma Cruise and I entered the competition and were awarded the commission unanimously, although the adjudicating panel did express some concerns. Central to these was the number of blocks of granite that we proposed including in our memorial—seventeen. While this was the number of slaves in Jan van Riebeeck's household, the panel felt that it could mistakenly be read as a tribute to the Heeren XVII, the seventeen directors of the Dutch East India Company (VOC). There was also the unstated concern that the general public would have difficulty in accepting an abstract approach. Contestants for the commission were drawn from all parts of South Africa, and judging by some of the unsuccessful proposals, a highly figurative approach had been favored by most.[4] Such works were in the tradition of Karl Broodhagen's *Bussa Emancipation Statue* (1985) in Barbados, which features a large man on a high pedestal, legs astride, and with broken chains hanging from his manacles. Another, perhaps more evocative memorial, can be found in Zanzibar. For her *Memory for the Slaves* (1998), Clara Sörnäs created a cement pit containing five cast-concrete figures, three of which are chained by the neck to the walls of their den.

Pain, suffering, or personal loss poses huge problems for representation. Jill Bennett, an Australian academic who has written extensively on transnational trauma, suggests that "the traumatic event is beyond comprehension," that it is "inimical to description within normal language."[5] Bennett addressed aspects of my artwork for the 1997 *Memorias Intimas Marcas* project,[6] stating that she focused on my work because I was less concerned with recording verbal testimony than with processes of inhabitation—of what one might call "remaking the world."[7] The work in question is called *Forces Favourites* and is a video installation comprising ten vellum-clad bicycles carrying ten video screens. Playing simultaneously on the screens is a video I made on the killing fields of Cuito Cuanavale in southern Angola. In this sense, she noted that I had entered what the anthropologist Veena Das calls a "scene of devastation"—on one level a "real" space that permits of an outsider's visit, but also a psychic space in which memory, guilt, and pain is worked through.

Some ten years later, I had to revisit his psychic space and work through memory, guilt, and pain in preparing our proposal for the memorial. Wilma and I recognized the complexity and elusiveness of our subject. We could never grasp the fullness of suffering experienced by captured people, either on the Middle Passage, or after being sold into slavery on the farms at the Cape. We had to guard against attempting to contain, or fully represent, this suffering.

Pierre de Vos, a constitutional law expert and frequent blogger, commented on the parole of apartheid assassin Eugene de Kock on January 30, 2015. De Vos writes that if De Kock and his Vlakplaas death squad had not existed, white South Africans would have had to invent him to absolve us of our complicity in the system of apartheid. In thinking through his own possible complicity, De Vos suspects "that it is exactly when you contemplate the possibility that you too—given different circumstances—might have been capable of doing something unthinkably horrible, that you may be best placed to ward off the inhumanity that stalks the world."[8]

It is tempting to think that wider atrocities, the concentration camps, ethnic cleansing, slavery—lie beyond "normal" language. Clifford Chanin, the initiator of the Legacy Project in New York, remembers Theodor Adorno's statement that "to write poetry after Auschwitz is barbaric."[9] He argues that artistic representation of the death camps was not simply misguided; it was a barbaric reversal in which the aesthetic takes precedence over the moral. He writes, "in this reversal there would be faint echoes of the crime itself."[10] Brenda Schmahmann follows this line of thought:

> When I was teaching public art memorials on the Holocaust, a question I would always focus on—and which I think is pertinent—is how do you represent something so enormously terrible that it is almost beyond representation? Some writers argue that you can only understand the horror of the Holocaust by showing it mimetically. "Hitler did not kill in the abstract" is the type of argument forwarded by people coming from this position. The opposite argument is that when one is dealing with something so huge, it belittles the scope and scale of the horror to show one dead or suffering individual or even ten, one hundred or a thousand such individuals. Following such an argument, only

> abstraction is appropriate. Only abstraction can potentially heal. And only abstraction avoids showing bodies in states of degradation—and thus in some sense avoids repeating a trauma.[11]

The attack on the World Trade Center in New York in September 2001 killed 2,996 people including the nineteen suicide bombers. It is a "red letter day" in modern history and has led a number of artists to wrest meaning from a politically inspired atrocity that targeted civilians. The artist Stephen Deo is represented on the Legacy Project, and he used photographs of his hands as "the healing part of the art, intended to shield the viewer from the event and rebuild the towers—to push them back into the sky."[12]

The composer Karlheinz Stockhausen's infamous statement to a group of journalists that the bombings were "*das größte Kunstwerk, das es je gegeben hat*" ("the greatest work of art there has ever been") provoked an outcry and a boycott of some of his performances. In a so-called clarifying press release, Stockhausen claimed that his original statement revolved around Lucifer as "the cosmic spirit of rebellion, of anarchy. He uses a high degree of intelligence to destroy creation. He does not know love."[13] Robert Hilferty, who writes on classical music and who penned an article titled "The Greatest Work of Art in the Entire Cosmos (without a Question Mark)," defended Stockhausen by saying that he was not in fact legitimating the bombings and wondered what the fuss was about given that others (the playwright Dario Fo) are on record as saying "regardless of who carried out the massacre, this violence is the legitimate daughter of the culture of violence, hunger and inhumane exploitation." In conclusion, Hilferty goes on to say that "the magnitude of the catastrophe, an artful work of non-art, has rendered much so-called 'art' irrelevant, worthless, silly or tasteless."[14]

But has it? At a lecture presented at the University of California in Los Angeles on October 2, 2003, Karina Eileraas asked what it meant to think about lesbian participation in AIDS activism in New York alongside the "bigger" issues of slavery, the Holocaust, political violence in Syria, and the event I have just been discussing, 9/11. She answered by saying that personal or private feelings do matter in global contexts and that they do so without "presuming to equate them[selves] with other instances of geopolitical trauma." She argued that she had had to grapple with "the ways sexual trauma and queer trauma can be relegated to invisibility by distinctions between private and public trauma . . . and by structures of homophobia."[15]

In this chapter, I indicate how Cruise and I endeavored to engage with a loaded and complex topic in our memorial. We indicate how changes were effected from the initial proposal to address concerns that were raised with our design, on the one hand, but also how our solutions were arrived at through sustained engagement and research on the topic of slavery. Prior to engaging with these details, I provide further background about slavery in Cape Town, thus suggesting how our memorial has additional importance in the sense that it takes cognizance of a history that, even in the new millennium, is often underplayed or overlooked.

CAPE TOWN AS A SLAVE SITE

The largest, most prominent memorial bearing testimony to the indomitable spirit of slaves is the city of Cape Town itself. This is borne out by the scholarly writings of many respected historians (e.g., Robert Ross, Vivian Bickford-Smith, and the late Robert Shell). Shell (2007, 17) notes that for at least 180 years, enslaved people outnumbered free people in Cape Town.

The first Dutchman to set up a "station" at the Cape, Jan van Riebeeck, needed people to grow vegetables for the passing ships of the Dutch East India Company for which he was employed for ten years because the local people (called Khoi or Quena) refused to work for him. (There were many Quena "tribes"—whom the Dutch called Hottentots because they did not appear to be typically "African"—who fought among themselves, and some fought on the side of the Dutch against the British when Britain decided to invade the Cape at the Battle of Blaauberg in 1805–6.) By 1653, Van Riebeeck kept seventeen slaves for this purpose, most of whom were from Angola and Guinea. In 1657, there was a dramatic increase in the number of slaves imported to work for *vrye burgers*. The VOC established a "slave lodge" to keep control over their slaves and their progeny (children born to enslaved women were also enslaved).

For the next 175 years, about 63,000 slaves were captured on the high seas, or obtained from Indonesia, India, Ceylon, Zanzibar, Madagascar, Angola, and Mozambique and brought by sailing vessel to Cape Town where they were sold at public auction. The growing Cape farming community, especially, sought out young, able-bodied men and women to perform myriad manual tasks, from construction, farming, and furniture making to drawing water, cooking, and tailoring.

In addition to Church Square, there are a number of sites and spaces throughout the city of Cape Town that are part of the city's slave-owning history. For example, almost all of the Bo-Kaap, the Parade, the Slave Lodge, the Slave Tree Plaque, Spin Street, the Company's Garden, Leeuwenhof, Platteklip stream on Table Mountain, the Old Slave Church, St. Andrews Presbyterian Church, St. Stephen's Church, the Auwal Mosque, and the Palm Tree Mosque contain vestiges of Cape Town's slave-owning past. The Auwal Mosque in Dorp Street—the oldest mosque in South Africa—was built in 1794 and was originally owned by a freed slave, Salie Coridon of Ceylon. A recent slave memorial—Prestwich Memorial—exists on the one side of what was the old city center, where it acts as an ossuary for the many skeletal remains of those buried outside the official, church-sanctioned graveyards.[16] All of these sites are important in that they form part of a historical imprint that reaches into almost every facet of life, architecture, and culture at the Cape.

Some sites are places of terrible suffering. A "whipping post" once stood at the corner of Darling and Buitenkant Streets near the Castle of Good Hope—an area known as Justitie Plaats (Justice Square). This was once a place of torture and execution. The Dutch authorities had hoped that bringing these floggings into public view would exert a restraining influence on their captives who, quite naturally, hoped to escape bondage.

Today, one can take a "slave walk" and see the Slave Lodge, the Castle of Good Hope, and the first slave churches. But efforts to draw emphasis to early histories of slavery in South Africa through sites such as these are complicated by tensions between English and Afrikaner inheritances. Martinus van Bart (2012), author of *Kaap van Slawe,* is incensed by the recent "slave walk" pamphlets because, he claims, undue emphasis has been placed on the Dutch period (prior to 1806) and little on the period under British rule. He argues that the audiovisual presentation dealing with the *Meermin* mutiny, which features prominently at the Iziko Slave Museum, together with the posters and models on display, depicts the Dutch as slavers and the British as liberators (Van Bart 2012, 17).[17] Van Bart chronicles the adventures of British royalty in capturing slaves for profit. He (Van Bart 2012, 46) writes that in 1585, Elizabeth I of England fronted for the Barbary Company, which supplied weapons to Moorish factions on the Barbary Coast (now Morocco). James I and Charles I were associated with the Guinea Company of Adventurers of London Trading to Africa and the Association of English Slave

Traders, respectively. The industrially minded British called their slaving ports in West Africa "factories" (Van Bart 2012, 54).

South Africa, like the United States, is a nation founded on slavery. However, while a country in Africa, South Africa never exported slaves—as was the case in Guinea, Angola, Mozambique, and many other African countries, where local rulers on occasion "sold" Africans to *caboceers* (slave traders). The conditions under which these people were hunted and herded into *barracoons* (slave pens) to await the arrival of a slave ship were unspeakable. But, while South Africa did not have these, its importation of slaves renders the country culpable in perpetuating such brutality.

A difficulty surrounding the history of slavery in South Africa, and that Cruise and I felt made our project especially necessary, is a pervasive symbol blindness. For example, visitors to the Cape will be struck by the omnipresent "slave bells" that were used formerly to call slaves to work or to sound the alarm if a slave had absconded. But instead of these edifices being destroyed by slave descendants, they are lovingly given a fresh coat of lime wash every year. Not only do many of the old wine farms still display their slave bells (e.g., Vergelegen, a wine estate founded in 1700, proudly displays its bell and slave lodge as if its slave past was somehow admirable), but some newly built security estates even provide a replica slave bell to authenticate the Cape vernacular architecture—white walls, small shuttered windows, and a thatched roof.

"Symbol blindness" is most evident in the Slave Lodge, built to accommodate VOC slaves. It was small, overcrowded, and badly ventilated. Apart from a useful place for keeping company-owned slaves locked up at night, under the watchful eyes of *mandoors* (a Dutch name for a slave entrusted with keeping watch over other slaves), it was used as a brothel and asylum. Thus, the late Anthony Holiday (2007, 45) was moved to write that "it fused the conceptual themes of servitude, sex and insanity and let them trickle like a polluted stream into almost every facet of [South African] life." He also observed that after the displacement of the VOC slaves in 1811, the building was transformed into the seat of law making and law giving at the Cape—that is, it housed the Cape Supreme Court between 1815 and 1914 and the Legislative Council between 1827 and 1844. He (Holiday 2007, 45) wrote that "if legislators and learned judges were content to situate the ancient edifices of Roman Dutch law in such a setting, it must surely have been because they had so thoroughly absorbed the concepts associated with slavery and its degradations into their own lives and modes of judgment that the significance of what they were doing . . . altogether escaped them."

It is difficult to cast one's mind back to those times. Slavery was legal. Slaves and their master lived in close proximity in the same *werf* (yard). Slave owners had a duty to care for their human possessions: if a slave fell ill or was pregnant, for example, the master was compelled to provide assistance. Infanticide was strictly forbidden, as the young child represented future free labor. When slaves were manumitted through marriage, they too bought slaves. When the church needed restoration work or new buildings, they took on slaves to do the work. Slaves were auctioned every week at the "slave tree."

There was a smallpox epidemic in 1713, and many people died. Of course this affected the slave population as well, and the VOC and the free burghers took revenge on their surviving slaves. Owners were allowed to flog their slaves for "laziness"; minor disobedience could be met by, among other punishments, flaying, crucifixion, and breaking on the wheel. These punishments were meted out in public.

The British banned the import of new slaves in 1807, and slavery was abolished worldwide in 1834. But slave owners in the Cape were allowed to keep their slaves for another four years after 1834 to compensate them for the money they had spent on buying and feeding them.

A PROPOSED CHURCH SQUARE MEMORIAL TO SLAVERY

Our winning proposal envisaged seventeen granite blocks laid out in a grid across Church Square. Each block would carry textual and pictorial information relating to the history of slavery at the Cape. We thought of telling this history through stories. For instance, one of the granite blocks would convey the strong spirit of resistance through the story of a runaway slave called Lena. Another block would tell the story of rebellion by recounting the story of the 1808 Slave Revolt. In this well-planned but overambitious plot, Louis of Mauritius and Abraham van de Kaab led a band of more than 300 barefoot and unarmed runaway slaves on a "long walk to freedom" from Malmesbury (several days away from Cape Town by ox wagon) to the Amsterdam Battery in Mouille Point. They planned to turn the cannons of the Amsterdam Battery on the Cape Town Castle and, in so doing, establish a free state. The leaders of this uprising were found guilty of treason, and two were executed.

Overall, our proposal was marked by five precepts:

Silence. Silence in the face of the abomination that was slavery evoked by the deeply reflective surface of the stone's weighty presences that elicit the memory of the slaves that were sold, tortured, and suffered at Church Square.

Soebat. The plea of the Slave is echoed in this monument with its silent imploration to respect the rights of all humankind.

Sacred. A sacred site. The arrangement of the 17 blocks of granite enhances the sense of contemplation and calm.

A map. A map as well as a presence. The interconnecting lines linking Church Square to other slave sites are spiritual, historical and geographical.

Words. Slave histories are recovered by evoking the lexicon bequeathed to us by slave society.

Because the Slave Lodge is adjacent to the memorial site, and it has an almost-permanent exhibition of objects, documents, and displays that index South Africa's slave-owning period, we were able to adopt a more evocative and less descriptive approach to our project. This gives meaning to the title of this chapter, the "Mirror and the Square."[18] The "mirror" stands for a descriptive approach, and the "square" stands for that arc of modernity initiated by Kazimir Malevich and more commonly known as geometric abstraction. Josef Albers also comes to mind as an artist who has used geometric elements in his paintings. More pertinently to this discussion is the work of the American architect Peter Eisenman who won the commission to design the Berlin Holocaust Memorial, which was completed in December 2004. His winning entry comprises row upon row of unadorned, concrete pillars of different heights.

Cruise and I ascertained from one of the public participation presentations called for by Heritage Western Cape (to which we had to present a Heritage Impact Statement) that our concept fell short of some people's expectations that we take a more documentary approach to the project. For example, some individuals wanted to see a powerful image of a slave throwing off his chains. Indeed, a public intellectual and blogger Patric Mellet suggested as much when we visited him. He spent a good two hours telling us about the "red letter dates" such as the smallpox epidemic in 1713 and the mutiny on board the *Meermin* between Madagascar and the Cape in 1766. He suggested that we concentrate on the loss of the slave ship *San Jose* on the rocks south of Cape Town in 1794. The crew made it to shore, but the entire human cargo drowned. Later, after the ship's timbers had rotted away and the shackles loosened, 250 bodies washed up onto the beaches.

The terms of the competition were, as is usual, fairly specific. The overall budget was set at R350,000 (about US$23,000). Also, we were required to leave the statue of Jan Hendrik Hofmeyr in place on the square. This statue commemorating parliamentarian Hofmeyr's efforts to place Afrikaans and Dutch on an equal footing with English was unveiled in 1920 and, according to Alan Crump and Raymond van Niekerk (1988, 32), it was made by Anton van Wouw. It is set on a four-meter high stone pedestal similar to what supports Van Wouw's figure of President Steyn at the University of the Free State, unveiled nine years later and that Brenda Schmahmann discusses in chapter 2 in this volume (fig. 2.1). We also had to appoint a heritage consultant (at our expense) to draw up a Heritage Impact Statement for presentation to, and approval by, the Cape Institute of Architects and Heritage Western Cape (HWC). Failing their approval (via a highly venerated certificate called a Record of Decision), the commission would fall away, and we would be reimbursed only for any direct expenses incurred. HWC stipulated that we had to enter a public participation process in the form of a public meeting at which our ideas would be presented for comment.

For this public meeting, we prepared full-size color prints of three of our proposed blocks to present to the audience. One block dealt with the 1808 Slave Uprising, a second with resistance and the mutiny on board the *Meermin*, and the third dealt with slavery and the burgeoning wine industry. In each case, a single word was associated with the theme of the block. Thus, the block detailing the *Meermin* incident was associated with the Dutch word *Armazoen* (Dutch term describing a ship with a slave cargo).[19] Other themes (not presented at the public presentation meeting) included the Galant Uprising of 1825, *droster* (Dutch name for a community formed by runaway slaves) communities, a map showing the major slave routes, the Slave Lodge, slave labor, and *Stamouers* (Afrikaans for "ancestors").

A colleague from the School of Architecture, Planning, and Geomatics at the University of Cape Town who attended this public participation meeting commented negatively on the presence of the Hofmeyr statue "lording it over" the proposed slave memorial, clearly not recognizing that the retention of the older work was non-negotiable in the competition brief.

Another person commented on the accessibility of the images and their educational potential. The young reporter who covered the meeting for the daily newspaper, the *Argus*, described our proposal simply as "messages and inscriptions about slavery" (Davids 2008).

In July 2008, we received a "bullet in a letter" from Basil Tommy, our liaison person with the City of Cape Town. His specialist committee was of the opinion that, "apart from one or two instances our words would have little or no meaning for the general public." Most crushingly, the committee felt that our choice of stories and events did not all "symbolize the indomitable spirit of slaves and the contributions that slaves made to the economic and cultural development of the City."[20] Central to the problem was the granite block that Wilma and I called the "Lena block." This section of the memorial was meant to portray slave resistance by telling the story of Lena, a slave who escaped to a *droster* community at Hangklip. The block was also to narrate Lena's expulsion following a lover's spat and her journeys wandering the outlying farms and pilfering goods off the wagon trains making their way over the mountains to the east. The committee did not see this honoring "the contributions that slaves made to the economic and cultural development of the City" nor as a particularly apt example of slave resistance—Lena was recaptured, flogged, branded with a hot iron, and forced to live the rest of her short life in shackles.

Because of these critiques, we then decided to abandon any form of narrative and rely solely on the recovery of memory through the lexicon. Stephen Wright has drawn up a lexicon of usership in which concepts are either due for retirement, useful as modes of usership, or emergent. Imperformativity ranks as "emergent, and underpinning usership." The one I like best is Lexicon—a user-repurposed wordscape.[21]

THE SLAVE MONUMENT IN ITS FINAL FORM

Our final proposal, after seven months of collaboration, negotiation, and fruitful input from two highly respected slave historians, Nigel Worden and Robert Shell, comprised eleven blocks (fig. 3.1). Two of these carried the names of slaves (fig. 3.2), the other nine carried thematic inscriptions (fig. 3.3). These themes are meant to act as touchstones or pointers to a larger reality—that is, that slavery at the Cape suffused all of Cape Town and, by extension, all of South Africa. It is a harsh reality—a reality unsuccessfully concealed in picturesque slave bells on privileged wine estates, in laws in our

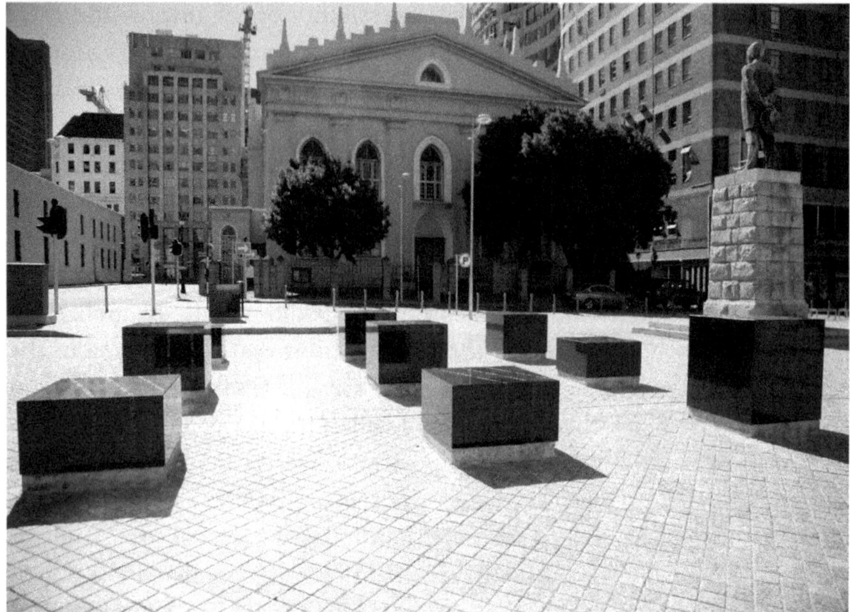

Fig. 3.1 Wilma Cruise and Gavin Younge, *Church Square Memorial to Slavery* (2008). View of blocks B3–B11. *Photograph by Gavin Younge.*

statute books, and in our flat-roofed architecture which developed around the concept of master and slave living in close proximity to each other.

The theme for block 5 is "Enslavement." Here, we chose the following words as indexical markers:

> CAPTURE · BONDAGE · SLAVE TREE · CHATTEL · SHACKLE · GORE-ES · LIBAMBO · BRAND · MARK · COFFEL · BARRACOON · PLAKAAT · SOEBAT · RIXDOLLARS · STATUTES OF INDIA 1642 · BAAREN · CURFEW · CAFFRES · SLAVE CODE 1754 · SLAVE BELL

These words are opaque and most likely do not mean much to the general public. This is intentional. We wanted to provoke further research on the part of those who were interested. Perhaps passers-by would be surprised to discover that the Afrikaans word for a man's jacket, *baadjie,* is of slave origin. The Dutch word for a jacket is *jas.*

Another theme is "Slave Contributions," and here, we engraved the following words on the top and sides of one of the blocks:

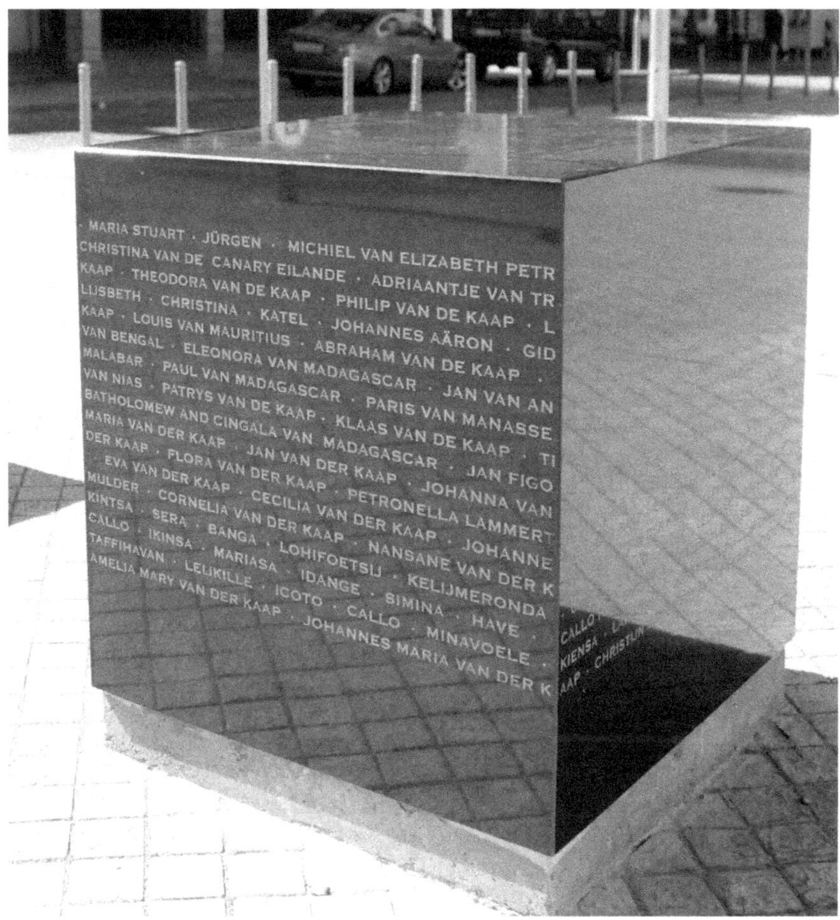

Fig. 3.2 Wilma Cruise and Gavin Younge, *Church Square Memorial to Slavery*, showing block B2 (Slave names). *Photograph by Gavin Younge.*

> GOEMALIEDJIES · RAMKIE · OLD TOWN HOUSE · POPULATION · STAMMOEDER · GABLE · LANGUAGE · CUISINE · COMPANY'S GARDEN · KITAAB · AFRIKAANS · STAMOUERS · PIERING · ARCHITECTURE · WORDS · BAADJIE · BLATJANG · PIESANG · ROTANG · BAIE · TARENTAAL · SOSATIE · KOEKSUSTER · BAADJIE · TAMALETJIE

Of the eleven granite blocks comprising the final memorial, two are placed on a raised plinth on the southwest corner of Church Square close to the Iziko Slave Lodge. A further nine are grouped in a tight grid close to the Slave Tree Plaque. Each block is 80 centimeters (31½ inches) square. Three

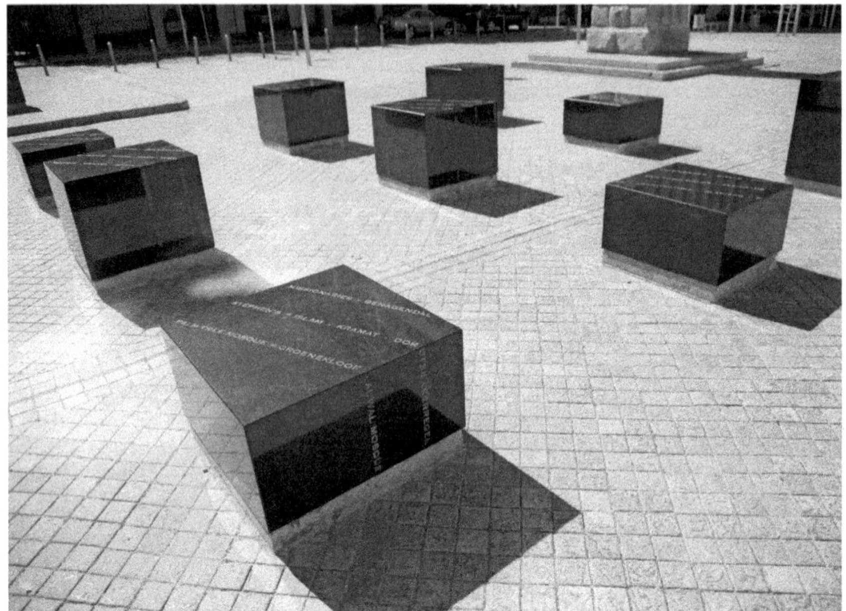

Fig. 3.3 Wilma Cruise and Gavin Younge, *Church Square Memorial to Slavery*, with block B11 (Religion) in the foreground. *Photograph by Gavin Younge.*

are 30 centimeters (about a foot) high, four are 60 centimeters (about 2 feet) high, and four are 40 centimeters (15¾ inches) high. Their common "footprint" represents our common humanity, their different heights represent growth, and the importance we attach to the youth of South Africa—they, too, need to be able to read the texts engraved on the surface of the blocks. Plain, jet-black Zimbabwe granite is used throughout.

The two blocks on the raised plinth are both 80 centimeters high. These are the two that are engraved on their sides with the names of the enslaved. In this task, we were guided by the comprehensive research of many historians and activists. Their research has revealed these forgotten names. By engraving them on the sides of these two blocks, we hope to remember them for what they suffered and for what they contributed to the building of the South African nation.

The other nine blocks are engraved with words from the slave period in South Africa, 1652–1834, the words embrace elements of resistance, rebellion, suffering on the slave ships and on the Middle Passage, the provenance of slaves, religion, slave life, manumission, punishment, and the slave lodge;

the words are engraved in concentric circles, with the Slave Tree Plaque as the center. The words run up the sides of the blocks, across the tops in shallow arcs, and down the other sides. On occasion, the words are truncated—almost as if they run under the surface of the paving.

Thus the memorial is characterized by silence—silence in the face of the abomination that was slavery. This is evoked by the solemn arrangement on Church Square. Their weighty presence elicits the memory of the slaves that were sold, tortured, and suffered at Church Square.

The memorial was unveiled on September 24, 2008. At the event, Cape Town mayor at the time, Helen Zille, praised it, noting that the memorial was "not about the perpetrators. Instead, it is intended to preserve the memory of those who were enslaved, to prevent their history from being lost. It is intended to draw attention to the under-acknowledged contribution that enslaved individuals made to the physical, cultural and economic development of Cape Town. This is one of the reasons we chose to unveil it on Heritage Day."[22]

Since then, the memorial has been accepted into urban nature. It has become a mecca for parkour practitioners, office workers sit on the lower blocks in order to eat their lunch, and they have become handy tables for camera gear when the square is leased out to film companies for film shoots. On February 5, 2015, the square was taken over by Open City 6, a free event about taking ownership of public urban space. It is in the nature of cities that they entertain a robust experiential quality, and as artists and authors of the memorial, we are happy that the site and this instance of public art is being used, as opposed to being boycotted or vandalized.

CONCLUSION

While slavery was apparently finally abolished in 1909, the Global Slavery Index for 2014 indicates that 4 percent of Mauritania's population is held in modern-day slavery, closely followed by Uzbekistan at a shade under 4 percent. The Democratic Republic of Congo holds seventh place at 1.13 percent, Namibia ranks seventeenth, and Botswana is eighteenth on this scale of human ignominy. South Africa, by contrast, ranks 126th (narrowly easing out Japan)[23]—a figure that may seem insignificant but in fact translates into 106,000 people and 0.2 percent of the population.[24]

In such a context, it seems, our memorial is relevant not simply in terms of its insistence on recognizing a history that tends to be overlooked by visitors to Cape Town but also—more worryingly—because slavery remains in fact an international and local concern in the twenty-first century. Our hope is that the memorial might play a role in not only countering symbol blindness but also in stressing the need to be vigilant against human trafficking and other forms of modern-day slavery.

ACKNOWLEDGMENTS

The author wishes to thank Wilma Cruise for our shared months of research and close collaboration; Nigel Worden and the late Robert Shell for their willingness to comment on the project as it developed; Patric Mellet for sharing his thoughts with us; and Glenda Younge for support throughout the project. I thank the Cape Town University Research Committee and the National Research Foundation for continuing to support my research efforts post retirement. I also thank my editors, Brenda Schmahmann and Kim Miller, for dreaming up such an exciting publishing endeavor and for inviting me to participate.

GAVIN YOUNGE is Emeritus Professor and a former director of the Michaelis School of Fine Art at the University of Cape Town. He works internationally as an artist and has completed ten large-scale, publicly sited sculptures in cities throughout South Africa. He is the author of *Art of the South African Townships*.

NOTES

Part of this text dealing with the Legacy Project in New York is drawn from my Keynote Address to the Twentieth Meeting of the South African Art & Architectural Association (now renamed the South African Visual Arts Historians), University of Natal, September 23–25, 2004. "Representing Global Conflict and Transnational Trauma—The Case of the Legacy Project and Its Visual Arts Archive."

1. The Groot Constantia homestead was built soon after 1685 when the land was granted to Simon van der Stel, the commander of the Dutch East India Company, the Vereenigde Oost-Indische Compagnie (VOC). The farm had several owners and eventually passed into the hands of Anna de Koningh, herself a former slave. De Koningh was born into slavery in Batavia (present day Java), one of three children born to Maai Ansiela (Angela van Bengale). The whole family was brought to the Cape by a farmer, Peter Kemp, and sold to Jan van Riebeeck, who in turn sold the family to Abraham Gabbema in 1662. On his transfer back to Batavia in 1666, he set Angela and her three children free. Anna de Koningh married a VOC commander, Olaf Bergh, in 1679. He

acquired Groot Constantia in 1716, and his wife inherited the farm and twenty-seven slaves on his death in 1724. See http://www.wikitree.com/wiki/De_Koningh-1 and http://www.iziko.org.za/sh/resources/slavery/constantia.html.

2. The keeping of slaves was outlawed in Holland. VOC officials, or free burghers, were obliged to sell any slaves they might have possessed, prior to returning to Europe.

3. Another slave memorial exists on the other side of what was the old city center—Prestwich Memorial. This memorial acts as an ossuary for the many skeletal remains of those buried outside the official, church-sanctioned graveyards. The skeletons were unearthed in the 1990s during a phase of urban redevelopment.

4. I had passing sight of some of these when collecting our submission from City Council offices in January 2008.

5. Jill Bennett, 2002, "Material Encounters: Approaching the Trauma of Others through the Visual Arts," unpublished draft, 1.

6. See https://fernandoalvim.wordpress.com/memorias-intimas-marcas/.

7. Bennett, "Material Encounters," 2.

8. "Time to Confront the Evil of Apartheid, Not Only of De Kock who Defended It," accessed February 8, 2015, http://constitutionallyspeaking.co.za/.

9. A web-based Visual Archive of the work of some 579 artists (of which currently only five are South African—chosen by Salah Hassan of Cornell University), the site provides a scholarly, literary, and creative archive covering twenty topics from apartheid in South Africa to the Vietnam War. Also included are entries on the Balkan War, slavery, and the Holocaust.

10. See http://www.legacy-project.org/.

11. Personal communication, February 6, 2015.

12. See http://www.legacy-project.org/arts/display.html?ID=1032.

13. Robert Hilferty, "The Greatest Work of Art in the Entire Cosmos," accessed September 14, 2004, http://www.andante.com/article. I am grateful to Lorraine Khoury for drawing this debate to my attention.

14. Hilferty, 'The Greatest Work of Art in the Entire Cosmos."

15. Karina Eileraas, "Wounding Images: Colonial Photography, Sexual Violence, and Feminist Resistance in North African Literature," accessed September 10, 2004, http://www.women.ucla.edu/csw/fall03calendar.html.

16. The remains were unearthed in the 1990s during a phase of urban redevelopment.

17. While en route from Madagascar to the Cape, the ship's human cargo rose up and seized control of the bridge and forced the captain to return to Madagascar. However, they were outwitted; the vessel was beached and the slaves recaptured.

18. The title is drawn from the author's MAFA dissertation titled, "The Mirror and the Square" (1987). This thesis reflects on the ideology associated with abstraction and realism with special reference to the American avant-garde in the period 1933–1953. The demise of the left-leaning Artists International Association is linked to the loss of prestige suffered by realism because of the stigma attached to socialist realism demanded by Stalin, and the National Socialism demanded by Wilhelm Frick in Germany after 1933. Gavin Younge, 1987, "The Mirror and the Square," MA dissertation, University of Cape Town, 114–17.

19. Ships carrying cargo were known as *cargazoen*.

20. E-mail correspondence from Basil Tommy to Wilma Cruise, July 18, 2008. Author's archive.

21. See http://museumarteutil.net/wp-content/uploads/2013/12/Toward-a-lexicon-of-usership.pdf, accessed January 22, 2015.

22. Speech by Helen Zille, mayor of Cape Town. Unveiling of Church Square Slavery Memorial. Church Square 10h00, September 24, 2008. Author's archive.

23. Ireland and Iceland feature last on the list of nations practicing modern day slavery with a figure of 300 slaves held in Ireland against a mere 23 in Iceland. The Global Slavery Index for 2014 reveals that 60,000 people are currently held captive in the United States.

24. See http://www.globalslaveryindex.org/country/south-africa, accessed February 8, 2015.

References

Crump, Alan, and Raymond Van Niekerk. 1988. *Public Sculptures & Reliefs: Cape Town.* Cape Town: Clifton Publications.

Davids, Niémah. 2008. "Slavery Monument" *Cape Argus,* March 14.

Eliëns, Titus M., ed. 2003. *Domestic Interiors at the Cape and in Batavia 1652–1795.* Cape Town: Fernwood.

Elphick, Richard, and Hermann Giliomee, eds. 1979. *The Shaping of South African Society, 1652–1820.* Cape Town: Longmans.

Ferrari, Teresa, and Simon Bloch. 2014. "Landmark Sentence in Human Trafficking Case." *News 24,* November 22.

Holliday, Anthony. 2007. "Preface." In *From Diaspora to Diorama: The Old Slave Lodge in Cape Town.* E-publication (DVD-ROM). Cape Town: Ancestry24.

Ross, Robert. 1979. "The Occupations of Slaves in Eighteenth Century Cape Town." *Studies in the History of Cape Town* 11: 2–4.

———. 1983. *Cape of Torments: Slavery and Resistance in South Africa.* London: Routledge.

Shell, Robert. 1994. *Children of Bondage: A Social History of Slavery at the Cape of Good Hope, 1652–1838.* Johannesburg: Witwatersrand University Press.

Shell, Robert, ed. 2007. *From Diaspora to Diorama: The Old Slave Lodge in Cape Town.* E-publication (DVD-ROM). Cape Town: Ancestry24.

Van Bart, Martinus. 2012. *Kaap van Slawe: Die Britse slawebedryf van 1562 tot 1910.* Cape Town: Historical Media.

Worden, Nigel. 1985. *Slavery in Dutch South Africa.* E-publication (CD-ROM). Cambridge, UK: Cambridge University Press.

Worden, Nigel, Elizabeth Van Heyningen, and Vivian Bickford-Smith. 1998. *Cape Town: The Making of a City.* Cape Town: David Philip.

Younge, Gavin. 1987. "The Mirror and the Square—A Study of Ideology within Contemporary Art Systems with Special Reference to the American Avant-Garde in the Period 1933–1953." Unpublished MA dissertation, University of Cape Town.

PART 2

DEFINING AND REDEFINING HEROES

CHAPTER 4

Public Art as Political Crucible: Andries Botha's *Shaka* and Contested Symbols of Zulu Masculinity and Culture in Kwazulu-Natal

LIESE VAN DER WATT

If you think about it, that represents 60 houses.
Jo Ann Downs of the African Christian Democratic Party, quoted in the *Sunday Tribune* (Durban), September 4, 2011

THESE WORDS SUCCINCTLY SUMMARIZE what lies at the heart of an almost absurd incident: in a country plagued by fiscal problems—housing deficits, health cuts, poverty, and a struggling education system—a bronze sculpture is commissioned and erected at huge cost, criticized, removed, and another quite similar one recommissioned at double the cost, both representing the historic and legendary Zulu king Shaka kaSenzangakhona. The statement above—uttered by one of the many politicians who entered the fray in disbelief at such flagrant wastefulness displayed by a provincial administration—is not simply a pragmatic response to a political situation but also inadvertently flags the many challenges faced by public art in a young and unsteady democracy such as South Africa. For at the heart of the controversy around sculptor Andries Botha's 2010 interpretation of Shaka for the new King Shaka International Airport outside Durban in Kwazulu-Natal (figs. 4.1 and 4.2) is a question not simply about the politics of representation but also about the priority, function, relevance of, and justification for public art.[1]

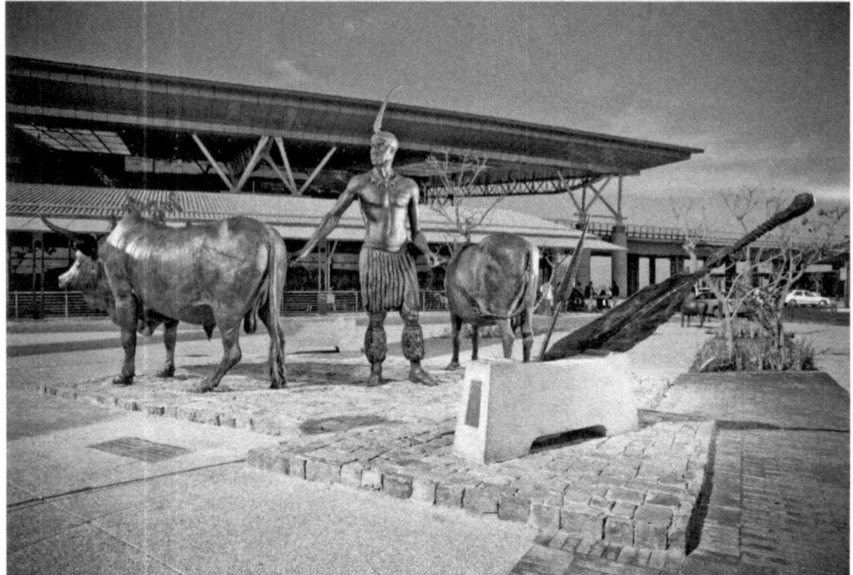

Fig. 4.1 Andries Botha, *King Shaka kaSenzangakhona* (2010), at King Shaka International Airport. *Photograph by Sean Laurénz.*

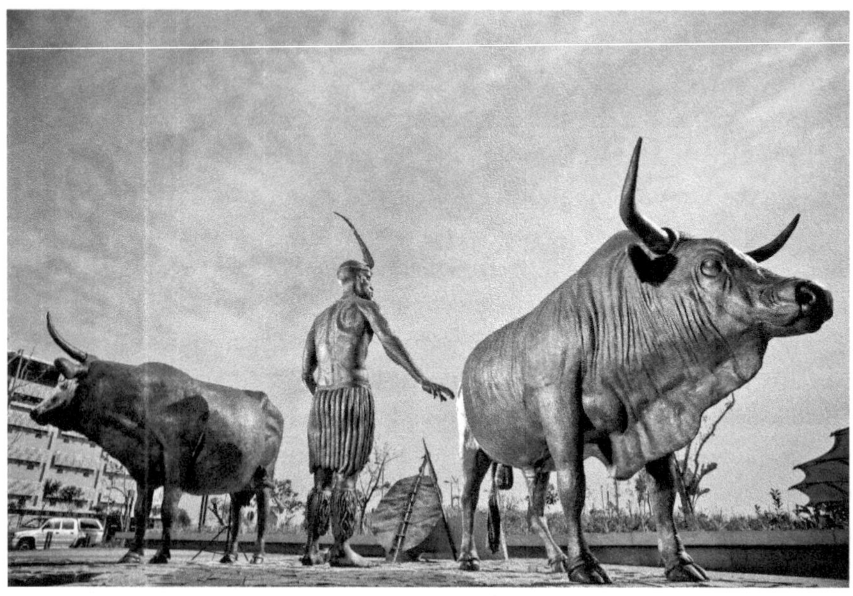

Fig. 4.2 Andries Botha, *King Shaka kaSenzangakhona* (2010), at King Shaka International Airport. *Photograph by Sean Laurénz.*

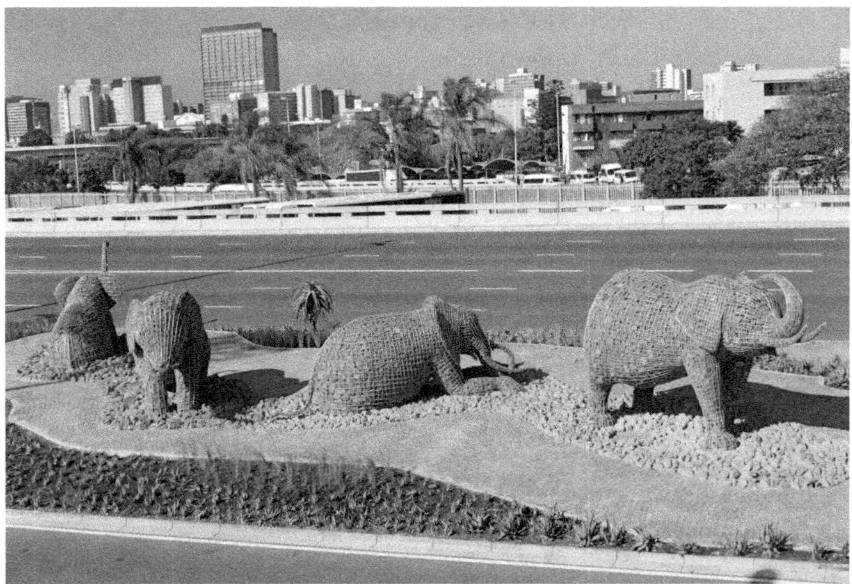

Fig. 4.3 Andries Botha, *Stone Elephants* (2009–2014), Warwick Triangle, Durban. *Photograph by Gordon Hiles.*

These questions were uncomfortably raised by a previous incident that also involved the work of Andries Botha. In 2009, before the 2010 World Cup, Botha was commissioned by the African National Congress (ANC)-led eThekwini Municipality to make three life-size stone-and-wire elephants for a dead piece of land at the Warwick Triangle Viaduct at the entrance to Durban's central business district (fig. 4.3). Although Botha had initially proposed to do seven elephants, to create the impression of a herd, the council could afford only three, and Botha scaled down his initial proposal.[2] Two weeks before completion, he was ordered to stop because an ANC politician complained that the three elephants looked too much like the logo of its rival Inkatha Freedom Party (IFP). This was ironic given the fact that the elephants were specifically commissioned to communicate apolitical ideas about human-nature ecologies and "the forgotten conversation between man and nature."[3] Work had to stop immediately, the almost-completed elephants were left unguarded, and soon they were vandalized—the wire casings removed, no doubt meant to be sold on the city's scrap metal markets.[4]

The "elephant saga," as it became known, raised many issues: the need for education at grassroots levels about the importance and relevance of art in the public space; the extent to which "public space" is experienced, owned, shared, or not; the responsibility of the city in protecting aesthetic assets paid for by ratepayers; and last but not least, the question of political interference and censorship in the creative process and cultural production. The elephant saga is not the focus of this chapter, but suffice to say here that followed in short order by the "Shaka saga," serious questions about the autonomy of art and the freedom of artists in South Africa needed to be asked.[5]

In addition, what both these incidents underscored is that public art is never innocent; it always excludes in the process of including. Indeed, the intervention around the representation of Shaka reveals the many ways in which public art and public space is political for, as Rosalyn Deutsch (1998, xiv) reminds us in her work on the politics of public art, "space is . . . political, inseparable from the conflictual and uneven social relations that structure specific societies at specific historical moments."

As I will demonstrate here, first, the remembrance and commemoration of Shaka has always been subject to the reigning political discourses, as will become clear from the brief overview I give of the formation of Shaka's image. Second, the latest installment in the debate about the representation of Shaka—as petitioned for by King Zwelithini—reveals as many rifts, particularly in relation to contemporary masculinity, as Zwelithini's preferred depiction of Shaka probably meant to conceal.

BACKGROUND

When Andries Botha was commissioned by Dube TradePort to do a commemorative sculpture of Shaka in 2008, he was no doubt chosen for his established international reputation as a sculptor but also for his deep connection with KwaZulu-Natal from where he hails. He has become known for monumental sculptures often made from materials significant to his local context—driftwood, wattle, thatching, rubber tire—and likes to collaborate with local weavers and thatchers in his practice. The sculpture of Shaka was to be done in bronze, and Botha, with assistants George Holloway, Ernest Ngcobo, and Mondli Mdanda, were paid R3 million from ratepayers' pockets. In preparation for the sculpture, Botha says he spent much time "developing a narrative in conjunction with an eminent historian [because] we wanted to depict King Shaka's parallel roles as extraordinary warrior, thinker and general. My sculpture is indicative of heterogeneity rather than homogeneity and presents a more complex definition than the stereotypical image of King Shaka."[6] Botha also spent hours talking to the poet laureate Mazisi Kunene on his epic "Shaka the Great" because, Botha said, "I fully acknowledged my limitations and moved accordingly,"[7] and "as a white Afrikaans boy I was nervous of interpreting the [king's] body, so I engaged the service of a respected historian."[8] Asked why he didn't speak to the Zulu Royal House about their views on their most illustrious ancestor, Botha says his patron Dube TradePort said it was "too complex" and they would handle that relationship—a protocol that was never followed, as it turns out. Botha was however assured that his sculpture was approved "at the highest level."[9]

After Botha's sculpture was presented to and approved by Dube TradePort (but with no input from the Royal House), it was cast in bronze, representing a 3.2 meter tall Shaka, next to a 2.8 meter shield and spear, surrounded by a Nguni bull, a cow, two calves, and two oversized traditional Zulu headrests that would also be used as seats for the public.[10] Positioned at the airport, Shaka would gaze out toward the Valley of the Kings, his right hand touching the Nguni bull, his left hand pointing toward his shield and sword, ready to be taken up in battle. Botha admits to feeling somewhat nervous about the commission but explains that he was not interested in repeating conventional images of "Shaka the warrior" or "Shaka the military leader" because "the thing is, no one really knows what he looked like."[11] Rather, Botha was interested to delve into the "inner landscape and the extraordinary life of a person who in 18 years welded a nation together." In his sculpture, "[Shaka] has put his spear and shield down to contemplate, but they are in an ever-ready position. I decided he would be in among his cattle. It was important to register the cattle as a major form of currency which it still is."[12]

At the unveiling of the sculpture and the inauguration of the airport in May 2010 with the Zulu royal family in attendance, President Jacob Zuma praised the sculpture for its inclusive narrative and its more complex definition of history. However, a few weeks after, King Goodwill Zwelithini expressed significant reservations about the location of the sculpture at the airport and the fact that Shaka was unarmed. Apparently, the royal family felt that Botha's statue of Shaka with spear at his feet betrayed the image of the great "warrior king," and in addition, Kwazulu-Natal premier Zweli Mkhize said that "some people had difficulty with the image of an unarmed Shaka and others felt that the King should be depicted with wild animals as he was known for hunting elephants."[13] ANC councilor Nomvuso Tshabalala even gave the debate a racial spin when she said, "What is offensive is that he [Botha] changed the king to a herdboy. . . . Maybe that's what they all want for us, to be herdboys."[14]

A task team was set up by Mkhize, made up of stakeholders, researchers, academics, and the royal household, to debate how the statue could be modified following suggestions that it should be more elevated and its features defined more clearly.[15] Apparently, the royal family brought to this meeting a drawing from 1825, made by Lt. James King, a British trader who purportedly befriended Shaka in 1824. Academic Jabulani Maphala reported that "the royal household indicated to us that this is the image of Shaka preferred by the King and the Royal House. It is the image of King Shaka with a spear and long shield, is used in all traditional and cultural ceremonies and is the one generally known and accepted by amaZulu."[16]

Barely a month after it was unveiled, the ANC-led municipal council ordered the removal of Botha's Shaka and put it into storage, leaving the Nguni cattle to graze at the entrance to the airport unherded. At the time of writing, almost five years later, Shaka is still in storage after various alternative locations were suggested and refused by Botha who insists, reasonably, that his sculpture is site specific, made for a hub of trade and tourism. The rest of the sculpture group is still in situ at the airport, now supplemented by a craft stall that is operated by local tradesmen. Needless to say, as Botha points out, this has impacted both the moral authority and the intellectual property right of his work.

Shortly after the removal, a new call for submissions went out. Botha, understandably reluctant to get involved in the new round, did attend the first briefing where he says that "it emerged the principal client was now the Zulu Royal household": "The King is asserting cultural ownership over the statue. It would appear the ANC did not take sufficient cognizance of the multi-layered sentiments attached to the legacy of King Shaka. The Zulu Royals have expressed a defined, clear mandate regarding the depiction of King Shaka. Any interpretation that differs from that will be seen as an affront."[17] Peter Hall, an accomplished KwaZulu-Natal–based sculptor known for his naturalistic and meticulous depictions of historical scenes—such as a huge 2007 sculpture of Zulu king Dinuzulu ka Cetshwayo (fig. 0.2)—was awarded the commission to redo a sculpture of Shaka, this time at a cost of R3.5 million. Initial sketches and a striking maquette made by Hall depicting Shaka leading his forces into battle (fig. 4.4) were rejected by the Zulu royal family and Hall was steered toward a sculpture that seems almost exactly like the 1825 drawing

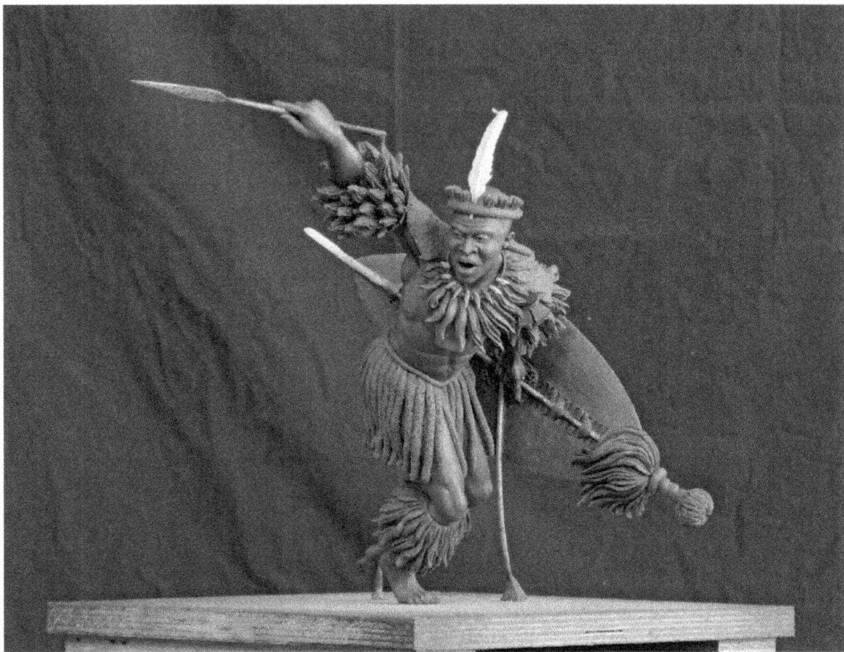

Fig. 4.4 Peter Hall, Maquette for *Warrior King* (2012), rejected by the Zulu Royal House. *Photograph courtesy of Peter Hall.*

they preferred in the first place. The new bronze sculpture, almost 6 meters high—which is in production—shows Shaka triumphantly on a raised platform of shields, holding a long spear in one hand and a shield in the other.

The irony of this is not lost on the viewer. To understand why King Zwelithini should prefer an unreliable colonial image of Shaka as "the one generally known and accepted by amaZulu" as Jabulani Maphala put it above, it is useful to trace the process by which the image of Shaka has been molded and articulated since his reign to the present day. As I will show in the next section, the contestation over Shaka's image is nothing new. Shaka's reputation has waxed and waned over time, and King Zwelithini and the royal house's latest attempt to maintain control over Shaka's story seems like the last installment in this history.

THE MANY FACES OF SHAKA

"We know almost nothing for certain about Shaka. We do not know when he was born, or what he looked like, or exactly when he died," writes Dan

Wylie (2008, 82) in what he refers to as an "antibiography" of Shaka, so called because very little is known about the warrior king. And yet, despite this, Shaka has attained legendary status in South African history, to the point where he is probably one of the most famous historical African figures.

How and why did this happen? In the last twenty to thirty years, many historians have revisited the historiography of Shaka and have reconstructed the many political and social processes that have given rise to particular images of Shaka.[18] Although he is generally celebrated as a great warrior, a heroic statesman and a unifier of the Zulu nation, his star status is by no means self-explanatory as his reputation waxed and waned ever since his short reign from 1816 to 1828, until today.

Dan Wylie (2008, 82), in a study that focused on white accounts of Shaka, writes that

> what has come down to us through the literature is an extraordinary palimpsest of half-understood rumors, speculations and plain old lies. The collage of inventions is more than mere fiction: it is a myth. A myth in the sense is more than just an untrue tale. It is a narrative imbued with the core values of a culture: it embodies and expresses widely held mental patterns of time and space, colour and creed. Shaka—the figure, largely propagated by white writers, familiar through novels, history textbooks and films—is a myth that has historically expressed and served the social psychological and political needs of the white community in southern Africa.

However, as Carolyn Hamilton (1998, 53–56) has pointed out in her landmark work on Shaka, black *and* white people were responsible for the construction of the image of Shaka—indeed, imaging Shaka has been the product of interaction between black and white people, and their views have not been predictably positive or negative. Hamilton writes that at the same time as an early image of a violent Shaka was being constructed by white colonial writers, he was also being demonized in black oral histories, by enemies of the Zulu kingdom.[19] This mutable depiction of Shaka thus started during his own lifetime, before his death, but continued under the reign of his brother and assassin Dingane and has in fact continued to the present day.

John Wright (2006, 139–53) has very usefully periodized this history of Shaka's image by identifying different "kinds" of Shakas that relate broadly to changing political contexts. I give a short outline of Wright's periodization here, but a detailed discussion of the particular political conflicts lies beyond the scope of this article.

Shaka is first established as "Shaka the Mighty" during his reign when, soon after the arrival of British hunters and traders at Port Natal in 1824, reports appeared in Cape Town newspapers in 1825 and 1826 and in printed books by 1827 that the area around the bay was empty of population because they had been driven out by Shaka and his amaZulu (Wright 2008, 71). This notion of Shaka's "devastation"—since the 1960s referred to as the *mfecane*—came to explain the upheavals that transformed the territories south of the Thukela, and as Wright (2008, 69–70) explains, they "are seen as part of a series of wars and migrations, allegedly set in motion by the explosive expansion of the Zulu kingdom, which disrupted life over a much wider area of southeast Africa." The notion of the *mfecane* has subsequently been fiercely critiqued and debated, but the point is that Shaka's image as warmonger dates essentially to this time.[20]

The earliest written references to Shaka emerge at this time in a book called *Travels and Adventures in Eastern Africa*, probably ghost written for an almost-illiterate early trader called Nathaniel Isaacs, published in 1836. The image that King Zwelithini preferred is taken from this book. As Wylie (2011) writes, this image was supposedly "taken from life" by Isaac's companion James Saunders King, but it presents Shaka according to reigning art historical conventions, as a man standing in contrapposto, arm outstretched, on a rocky outcrop. This rather noble image—totally at odds with Isaacs's description of a cruel and despotic Shaka—is clearly inaccurate, probably distorted in the process of etching and publication. "Combine this convention with the inaccurate skirt, assegai and shield, and we can be sure that what we have here is nothing like the real Shaka, but a mere collage of Eurocentric conventions and inventions" (Wylie 2011, 12).

However, these inaccurate references were consolidated by writers afterward and have survived in various forms to the present day even if, as Wright points out, few of these early colonial writers had actually set foot in Port Natal, and none of them had been eyewitnesses of the destruction they purported to convey. The information on which their stories were based was most probably gained from the community that the traders encountered in Post Natal—a place that had been overrun by Zulu forces and therefore the depictions of Shaka and his Zulus was a very particular one, told from the perspective of the defeated. South of the Thukela, not the heart of the Zulu kingdom, black people also viewed Shaka with ambivalence, seeing him primarily as a destroyer of the old, pre-Zulu order (Wright 2008, 71).

Against the alleged devastation and destruction that Shaka brought, Shaka's own people saw his reign as one of order and civilization, in opposition to the general chaos that ruled in Port Natal. Early black reports of Shaka from within the Zulu kingdom were constructed in response to black anxieties over white, specifically Boer, incursions into the interior in the 1830s and 1840s and drew a picture of Shaka as a unifier and a founding figure of firm and stable government. Missionaries and others in colonial administration were also slightly more sympathetic toward him and appreciated the order he brought over his subjects. As Carolyn Hamilton shows in some detail, indigenous ideas about Shaka intertwined with colonial society and even shaped the policies of the native administration so that Theophilus Shepstone as Secretary for Native Affairs from 1845 to 1876, rooted his system of indirect rule in the practices of African rulers like Shaka (Wright 2006, 142 paraphrasing Hamilton 1998, 47–69, 72–104).

Even if early reports of Shaka were variable, by the end of the nineteenth century, Shaka was well on his way, as Hamilton puts it, to be established as a "political metaphor"—open to different interpretations but based on a consensus formed around a narrow set of stereotypes (Wright 2006, 142 paraphrasing Hamilton 1998, 32–25). While detailed individual memories of the era of Shaka continued until the early twentieth century in black rural communities, by the 1920s and 1930s, 100 years after his death, accounts relied more heavily on repetition of stereotypical notions of Shaka. This gave rise to what Wright terms the "black Shakas." As he explains:

> The black authors who were beginning to write histories, novels and plays about Shaka from the 1920s onward all saw him as a great conqueror but were divided about his status as a heroic figure. Writers sympathetic to the emerging Zulu nationalist movement tended to see him as a great founding figure and ruler. Others, influenced at least in part by ideas about "civilisation" imparted by a mission school education, saw him as a destructive despot. . . . Through the 1940s and 1950s and after, in the period of rising nationalist resistance to white domination, black writers generally sought to cast Shaka in a positive light as one of an emerging pantheon of African heroes. (Wright 2006, 144)

In the academy, from at least the 1960s onward, the history of Shaka was receiving more focus against a background of militant African nationalism and decolonization in the rest of Africa. New histories of Africans, rather than of Europeans in Africa, were being written, and Shaka was portrayed less as a bloody tyrant than a great statesman who started a process of "state formation" and "nation building" among African people. By the 1970s and early 1980s, these often uncritical histories were receiving ever more attention and a much more closely historicized periodization of the Zulu kingdom was being written. While this led to a revision of many of the stereotypical ideas about Shaka, at least in the academy, many black writers held firm to stereotypical notions of Shaka, which as Wright (2006, 147–48) shows, were mostly based on early and largely inaccurate colonial texts.

This uncritical celebration of Shaka's legacy that began in the 1950s and 1960s in the context of African postcolonial independence coincided with a new nationalism that started to emerge in KwaZulu and reached its zenith in the 1980s and early 1990s under the leadership of Chief Mangosuthu Buthelezi and his IFP. At this time, we see what Wright (2006,148) calls "the raising of Shaka to an unprecedented pitch of Mightiness in the ideologies of a new Zulu nationalism." In his many public addresses often articulated on KwaZulu's most important holiday, Shaka Day (September 24), Buthelezi constructed a version of Zulu history built seamlessly on the great successes of Shaka in the nineteenth century, positioning the KwaZulu Bantustan—despite it being delineated by apartheid policy—as the successor of the precolonial Zulu kingdom, which therefore gave the Zulu people the right to seek the power and influence they once had (Wright 2006, 148). In this discourse, "Shaka the Mighty" became the central icon of Zulu culture and unity—in Buthelezi's words: "We are immensely proud to be Zulus, descendants of our great King Shaka who conquered to incorporate, who conquered to establish Zulu justice and Zulu social order, who longed to produce stability and equality of all people before their king" (Harries 1995, 118 quoting Buthelezi at King Shaka Day, Stanger, September 24, 1985).

However, after the 1994 elections, when Buthelezi joined Mandela's Government of National Unity and Zulu nationalism as figured by Inkatha started to lose some of its appeal, Shaka the Mighty suddenly disappears from public discourse. It is at this point, writes John Wright (2006, 151), that Shaka becomes a pawn in the now-growing heritage trade:

> From the mid 1990s, as the number of tourists both local and international, visiting [Kwazulu-Natal] multiplied, and as the importance of suitably packaged

> samples of heritage as saleable commodities increased, the making of the region's public history more and more came to be influenced by business interests, large and small. This resulted in a further narrowing of its focus to produce the sort of marketable history-bites that tourists were prepared to spend money on. Much of the most important products of this kind were made up of carefully selected elements of "Zulu history" and "Zulu traditional culture" in which the figure of Shaka was an important feature.

Of course, Shaka and Zulu history have long been recognized as a salable commodity ever since the 1950s when the first draft of the book *Shaka Zulu* was published and by film makers ever since. But since the 1990s, with the opening of tourist attractions such as the holiday resort Shakaland, uShaka Marine World, and various other "Zulu cultural villages," it would seem that Shaka's latest "face" is, as John Wright (2006, 153) puts it, the "Patron of profit-making" in a climate where neither the province's political elites, nor the traders who make a living off heritage, want "the kind of public history that disturbs, [but rather] the expansion of tourism as the basis of a potentially important growth industry."

Indeed, as John Wright (2006, 153) concludes, his history on the faces of Shaka, "the image of Shaka the Mighty . . . was a product of the politics of the colonial era; in post-colonial KwaZulu-Natal, it is in the process of becoming safely domesticated."

"SHAKA THE MIGHTY" IS DEAD, LONG LIVE "SHAKA THE MIGHTY"

Shaka safely domesticated? These words seem somewhat premature given the debacle around Andries Botha's statue. Clearly, the opposite must be true if a Zulu king's complaint is made in such earnest, and taken up so seriously, that a statue of Shaka is removed at enormous cost and planned to be replaced by another statue of Shaka, differing only in pose and the image it projects. It would seem that what King Zwelithini is desiring by protesting Botha's depiction of Shaka is that Shaka should precisely *not* be domesticated but should be preserved as the fighter and warrior he was traditionally perceived to be.

Writing at a time when Zulu nationalism was a major factor in the violence and unrest that preceded the 1994 elections, Hamilton (1995, 4) argues that "appeals to the Shakan legacy are, above all else, expressions of a desire and need for social order, where social order is understood as the alternative to anarchy and violence. . . . Supporters of Zuluist politics (that is, a politics which emphasizes the relevance of the Shakan legacy . . .) prefer its authoritarianism to the freedoms of liberal democratic politics . . . because they perceive it to be a necessary and effective bulwark against current conditions of violence and anarchy." If this is so, if an invocation of the Shakan legacy expressed a desire for order and stability at a time of social upheaval, then King Zwelithini's recent demand for a more heroic and fierce Shaka should be read not simply as a statement of cultural ownership over cultural icons, nor as desire for another more traditional version of Zulu masculinity but also as an admission—albeit unintentionally—of the many fault lines that have come to plague Zulu masculinities, especially in recent years.

Much has been written on the crisis of masculinity among especially working-class African men, owing to the many social changes that characterized the life of rural men in the late nineteenth and especially the twentieth century.[21] In the mid-twentieth century, the increasing demands of migrant labor brought an unraveling of family life, but as Hylton White (2012, 406) writes, at least the lives of these migrant workers were "structured by the goal of posting tight connections between a life of labor and the act of 'building a home' in the Bantustan countryside." By the 1970s, however, with the steady collapse of migrant labor and indeed of waged labor itself, the "temporal links between the rhythms of labor and the rhythms of domestic and personal life in the parts of the country that have historically depended on labor migrancy" (White 2012, 406)—such as KwaZulu—have all but dissolved, leading to a situation where "freedom of a political sort has been compromised by states of arrested development in personal life, occasioned above all by joblessness" (White 2012, 406).

The resulting instability of masculinity—all firm codes erased by the inability of men to provide and by their absence from the homestead[22]—in addition to continuing ethnic loyalties—prepares the stage around 2009 for the entry of Zulu-speaking Jacob Zuma who brings with him not only the political hope embodied by the ANC but also a very decisive and unambiguous gender politics—a performance of traditional Zulu masculinities that steps into the vacuum left not only by various social upheavals but also by the end of Inkatha's political discourse that tied masculinity firmly to ethnicity. With Buthelezi increasingly out of the picture by the late 1990s, and therefore the absence of his rousing oratory, the narratives that bolstered Zulu masculinity came to an end. As Thembisa Waetjen (1991, 661) indicates in her work on Inkatha and gender politics, Inkatha's discourse of Zulu nationalism and masculinity "was directed to the edge of the national fabric where it was most in danger of fraying"—in other words, a fragile masculinity caused by the alienation of migrant life and the erosion of traditional customs was fortified by the marriage of ethnicity to robust masculinity (embodied by Shaka and other Zulu warriors) as promoted by Inkatha in the 1980s and early 1990s. When they effectively exit the political stage, a void is left, and as Hylton White (2012, 407) suggests "personal insecurity [is] the backdrop . . . for the potent mix of authoritarian sentiment and ethnic attachment that drove support for Zuma's campaign in Zululand."

Zuma's mode of masculinity first came to widespread public attention during the rape charges leveled against him in December 2005. Then vice-president, he was charged and eventually acquitted of raping a family friend's daughter, insisting that it was consensual sex. During the trial, Zuma reportedly told the judge that "the very charge of rape was a result of having acted in accordance with what he had been taught as a youngster growing up in Nkandla, in northern KwaZulu-Natal," thereby highlighting the patriarchy of his "Zulu ways" as well as firmly cementing the very troubled relationship between Zulu masculinity and patriarchy.[23] The "100% Zulu boy" slogan that was worn by supporters during the trial later stood central to his successful presidential campaign in 2009.

In the run-up to the 2009 election, journalist Christi van der Westhuizen commented:

> The dogged insistence that Zuma leads the ANC, despite facing charges of fraud, money laundering, racketeering and tax evasion, has strongly depended on the portrayal of Zuma as victim. . . . This [was] the crafting of a victimized masculinity, an identity explicitly gendered by the rape trial where he projected himself as an embattled "real man," "100% Zulu boy," defending his "right" to fulfill his sexual duties as his "cultural tradition" demanded of him. Among others he referred to the alleged victim's genitals as "her father's kraal." His response is a militarized masculinity, as symbolized by his signature song.[24]

Zuma's signature song is namely, "*Umshini wami*," translated as "Bring Me My Machine (Gun)"—a song dating back to the years of the anti-apartheid struggle but resurrected by Zuma for his political rallies. This is important: Zuma's masculinity is signaled not by the usual Zulu symbols of the spear, shield, and traditional weapon but by a machine gun—an articulation of a gendered identity that makes him at once recognizably male in its association with power but also promises something new in place of Inkatha's celebration of spear and shield.

Traditional weapons have stood central to the negotiation of Zulu identity for many years. In the violence that preceded the 1994 elections, President F. W. de Klerk outlawed the carrying of "dangerous weapons" and was pressured by the ANC to extend the ban to so-called cultural or traditional weapons. In response, Chief Buthelezi organized an *imbizo* in Johannesburg where 40,000 Zulu men carrying knobkerries, assegais, and shields showed up. King Zwelithini, addressing the crowd, said that "the call to ban the bearing of cultural weapons was an insult to the manhood of every Zulu,"[25] thereby, as Sandra Klopper (1996, 63) has pointed out, "establishing a link between the ideas of physical prowess and sexual performance and virility." In the lengthy debate and court case that followed this ban, KwaZulu Legislative Assembly Member of Parliament for Elandskop, David Ntombela, reaffirmed the "natural" right of Zulus to carry weapons by stating that "[no one] can say that shields, knobkerries and spears cannot be carried when the *amakhosi* (chiefs) call an *imbizo* (meeting) or if the Chief Minister calls an imbizo. That's the same as saying that the Zulus mustn't have their own king."[26] This perceived primordial link between Zulu men and their traditional weapons is echoed by a young man remarking in the same period: "The Zulu nation is born out of Shaka's spear. When you say 'Go and fight,' it just happens."[27]

However, by the time of the election in 2009, things seem to have changed radically. Hylton White observes in his accounts of visits to the north of Kwazulu-Natal around this time that he was struck by the support for the ANC in what used to be an Inkatha stronghold, and he found this shift in allegiances often articulated around traditional symbols. For instance, a young friend of his, brandishing an imaginary AK-47, remarks, "We're coming for Inkatha. They have spears but we have guns" (White 2012, 407). White (2012, 409) warns us not to be too literal—of course all kinds of people carry guns in South Africa—but throughout the election campaign, he was struck "by the level of open contempt that people—young people in particular—had started to show not just for Inkatha as such but for the whole apparatus of offices and emblems that had previously afforded public representation of Zuluness." This "scorn for the spear," as White (2012, 410–11) calls it, suggests an impatience with traditional structures that "emblems of chiefship itself [were] being made into objects of ridicule" as young people were seeking out the help of state and police above the usual local structures.

It is in the context of this changed social landscape, a year later, that King Zwelithini insists on an *armed* Shaka, appealing for continuity with a tradition not only with regard to how Shaka is usually depicted but also, by implication, reminding Zulu men of their "real" roots and heritage. For the Zulu royal house, this is a decisive claim to cultural ownership over Zulu symbols, in a battle that has primarily been played out between the ANC and the IFP over who owns Zulu culture—with the institution of the king itself used as a pawn in this battle.

In an article that examines these preelection clashes in 1994 between the ANC and the IFP over Zulu cultural ownership, Sandra Klopper (1996, 57) demonstrates how the figure of the king was especially important to symbolize cultural ownership through his continuity with history. As Patrick Harries (1995, 115) also points out, "the outstanding symbol of the Zulu nation is the King himself." Speaking in 1986, Buthelezi proclaimed King Goodwill Zwelithini as "the living symbol of the unity of the people" who "assumes the total unity of the Zulu people in his very being."[28] On other occasions he has indicated, "His majesty and I share a platform and symbolize the unity of our people. His Majesty symbolizes the deep spirit of unity for the Zulu people and I symbolize the political determination to pursue time-honored values which have always been important in the struggle for liberty. Together His Majesty and I share the load which is placed on the Zulu nation. We will never be torn apart."[29]

Of course in the years that followed, they were torn apart. Zwelithini increasingly severed his ties with the IFP and moved toward the ANC, while the IFP in turn tried to curtail Zwelithini's power.[30] The ANC for their part strategically challenged Inkatha's claim to Zulu history. In 1993, for instance, they arranged a *Sonke* (meaning "all of us") in the KwaZulu –Natal region where, as Klopper (1996, 56) points out, it was very clear by the number of Zulu speakers in traditional gear in attendance, that the IFP was not the exclusive custodians of Zulu culture and traditions. At this occasion and at various other rallies leading up to the elections, the ANC made sure that King Goodwill Zwelithini and other notable Zulu supporters were present, often dressed in "traditional" regalia with a "spectacular array of furs and feathers" (Klopper 1996, 54).

Klopper traces this recognition of the political potential of Zulu cultural symbols to the unveiling of the Shaka Memorial in Stanger in September 1954. I refer to it briefly here because it sets a precedent for King Zwelethini's intervention. At this occasion in 1954, the then king Cyprian, Zwelithini's father, situated himself almost literally as a bridge between the past and the future, communicated through the dress he chose to wear, the focus of Klopper's investigation. During the two-day ceremony, King Cyprian arrived first in a blue serge uniform with leopard trimmings, similar to what his father, Solomon kaDinuzulu, had worn, and on the next day, he wore what the newspapers called "tribal dress." Buthelezi, who also attended the unveiling, claims that this was the first time he or King Cyprian ever wore "traditional dress"—which, ironically, had to be newly made for the occasion. Whereas Cyprian's father, King Solomon kaDinuzulu, rejected "traditional dress" and preferred military uniform and riding breeches, "no doubt sharing the widespread conviction that Western forms were synonymous with civilised values," by 1954, the Zulu royal house recognized the importance of cultural symbols in claiming continuity and ethnic pride (Klopper 1996, 58). As Klopper demonstrates, this symbolical gesture is a strategic one at a time when the king hoped to be recognized as an independent ruler and so, as Klopper (1996, 61) explains, "the king's 'traditional' regalia may be taken as indicative of a renewed if totally misplaced optimism in the potential for autonomous political action symbolized by the reign of the first Zulu King." The invocation of Shaka at this event and the king's proclamation to be his official descendent, as signified by the clothes he wore, was a powerful statement about ownership and continuity at the time.

Klopper (1996, 57) writes that "successive twentieth century Zulu kings have played a significant role in bridging the gap between a seemingly glorious past and an increasingly uncertain future." It is in this capacity that Zwelithini's contemporary intervention into the depiction of Shaka's masculinity must surely also be read: a recognition that cultural symbols—Shaka, his shield, his spear—are crucial in communicating and influencing perceptions about oneself, especially at a time when those perceptions are somewhat unstable. His demands for a more masculine, active Shaka is as strategic as King Cyprian's wearing of traditional dress was: when Zwelithini insists on an armed Shaka, who carries his shield and his spear according to familiar Zulu mythology, he is harking back to a past when masculinity was less ambiguous, clearly defined, in order to secure an uncertain future.

The commemoration of Shaka has to protect the past in hopes of forging a better future.

CONCLUSION

As is so often the case with public art, the controversy over the King Shaka statue exposed many fault lines in the very history it was supposed to commemorate. The way Andries Botha originally envisaged it, Shaka would have been less myth, more normal man—an attempt by the artist to humanize Shaka by making the statue respond to a contemporary context of trade and commerce. In Botha's interpretation, Shaka would be surrounded by the historic currency of his day but placed so that he also becomes part of contemporary viewers' experience, an attempt to make history relevant in a shared public space. But instead of embracing the relative humanity of Shaka, King Zwelithini and the Zulu royal house rejected any attempt to share Shaka, reclaiming him as a militant and distant icon in their insistence that Botha's Shaka be removed and replaced with an overfamiliar, clichéd image.

As W. J. T. Mitchell (1992, 4) reminds us, "the pulling down of public art, is as important to its function as its putting up" because it reveals the marginality and limitations of public art. One can't help but think that perhaps if the commission itself had been different—if there had been a recognition that the "public" in public art is diverse and complex; if the commissioning body realized that public art doesn't need to be the proverbial "hero on a horse anymore" (Mitchell 1992, 2 quoting Raven 1989, 1), which presumes a homogeneous—or what Mitchell (1992, 3) calls a "utopian"—public space; if the commission did not ask for the commemoration of yet another man, then the potential for this art piece to engage the entire public for which it was made would not have been wasted in this way.

Hijacked as it was by the Zulu king, the Shaka debacle may have foregrounded some of the rifts that exist in the public sphere, but the opportunity was missed for public art to make itself relevant by disrupting, exposing, and challenging these contradictions in a creative way. Andries Botha recognizes something of this missed opportunity when he concludes, "I look at the debate and I wonder if it's a sign of our complexity and cultural promise, or if it's an index of our collective stupidity. Of course, I will continue doing what I'm doing. It may not always be a comfortable space. It's a combustible space, I've felt humiliated by what has happened, but I'm up for this. Shouldn't all South Africans be?"[31]

ACKNOWLEDGMENTS

Many thanks to artist Andries Botha who shared generously his time.

Liese van der Watt is an independent art historian based in London and a research associate in the University of Johannesburg's Visual Identities in Art and Design (VIAD) research center. She is an associate editor of the art magazine *Contemporary &* and contributes regularly to catalogues and a variety of publications with a focus on African art.

Notes

1. This is an important question, in itself worthy of an article. Sabine Marschall (2010, 12) notes in her work on heritage and commemoration in South Africa and particularly in KwaZulu-Natal where she teaches, that repeatedly her students do not care "in the least about commemorative markers. . . . Many consider such symbols an unnecessary luxury as long as the basic needs of marginalized communities are far from met."

2. Reported in *The Mercury*, November 11, 2010.

3. Reported in *Mail and Guardian*, February 20, 2013.

4. In November 2014, Andries Botha announced on his website that work on the elephants have recommenced. Botha has added a fourth elephant, and upon completion, it will be handed over to the eThekwini municipality and CCTV cameras will be put up to monitor the work's safety. See http://andriesbotha.net/public-commissions/2006–2010/three-elephants/.

5. The case of the "elephant saga" has featured in many debates and workshops on censorship in the arts in South Africa such as at the National Arts Festival public lecture series in 2013. See https://thinkfest.wordpress.com/2013/07/05/arts-censorship-re-emerges-in-south-africa/.

6. "Botha: Over My Dead Body," *Sunday Tribune*, February 27, 2011.

7. Reported in *Sunday Tribune*, June 6, 2010.

8. Botha quoted in Bubu Mbonambi, "Sculptor Botha Tells of 'Nerves,'" *The Mercury*, November 11, 2010.

9. Interview with Andries Botha, Durban, February 24, 2015.

10. Kim Goodwin, the foundry man who cast both Botha and now Hall's sculptures of Shaka, has commented in a telephonic conversation that the whole process of the making of the initial Shaka was "too rushed" and did not follow the correct protocol. According to Goodwin, the process from inception to the casting of Botha's Shaka took four to five months and did not recognize the important role of the royal house in the depiction of a Zulu king.

11. Botha quoted in Barbara Cole, "Shaka Statue to Be Airport Centerpiece; President to Unveil 3.5 Meter Bronze Image of Zulu King," May 2010.

12. Ibid.

13. Sharlene Packree, "King Shaka Statue Removed," *The Witness*, June 3, 2010.

14. Quoted in "Shaka Statue Bungling Rapped; Zulu Royals to Have Say in New Depiction," *Daily News*, June 4, 2010.

15. Sopho Kumalo from *The Mercury* newspaper reports that the team included Jabulani Maphalala (University of Kwazulu-Natal); history lecturer Jabulani Sithole; Vusi Shongwe (head of the heritage directorate in the premier's office) and his colleague Brian; heritage consultant Musa Xulu; Reverend Vikinduku Nculwane; princes Mbonisi Zulu, Thulani Zulu, and Zeblon Zulu; and praise singer Buzetsheni Mdletshe. The team was given a month to finish its consultation process (*The Mercury*, August 19, 2010. Accessed January 19, 2015).

16. Reported by Sipho Kumalo in *The Mercury*, August 19, 2010.

17. Ibid.

18. For instance, Golan (1994), Hamilton, (1998), and Wylie (2000).

19. See Buthelezi (2008) for a discussion of oral histories that tell an alternative, less celebratory history of Shaka's reign.

20. A discussion of the *mfecane* lies beyond the scope of this chapter. John Wright (2008, 70) discusses Julian Cobbing's (1988) controversial critique of the *mfecane* where the latter suggested, as paraphrased by Wright, that the violent role attributed to the amaZulu in the literature "is not based on historical evidence: rather it is a product of the search made by imperialist and settler ideologues for a plausible alibi for the colonial- and imperial-based interests whose aggressions were ultimately responsible for the violence and social disruptions of the period." The empty interior had much more to do with "a continuation of conflicts that had begun long before the 1810s, conflicts whose primary causes are to be sought not in the expansion of the Zulu kingdom but in the intersection of forces emanating from two other epicenters of upheaval. These were the Eastern Cape, where first Dutch then British settlers and imperialists were engaged in persistent attempts to seize land and labor power from neighboring African societies from at least the 1760s onwards and the Delagoa Bay region, where an export trade in ivory, cattle and slaves was developing at around much the same time" (Wright 2008, 70).

21. See especially the writings of Waetjen (1999), Mare and Waetjen (1999), Campbell (1992), and White (2012).

22. On the importance of the home in Zulu constructions of masculinity, see especially Waetjen (1999).

23. See http://mg.co.za/article/2006-04-06-100-zuluboy, accessed January 2015.

24. Van der Westhuizen (2014).

25. *Weekly Mail*, May 30–June 6, 1991, p. 16, quoted in Klopper (1996, 63).

26. *Sunday Tribune*, December 15, 1991, quoted by Klopper (1996, 63).

27. *Weekly Mail*, August 30–September 5, 1991, quoted in Laband (2008, 170).

28. Buthelezi on Shaka Day in Ulundi on September 27, 1986, October 11, 1986. Quoted in Harries (1995, 115).

29. Buthelezi at Shaka Day celebration, Stanger, December 24, 1985. Buthelezi at Shaka Day celebration, Eshowe, September 24, 1991. Quoted in Harries (1995, 115).

30. As Klopper remarks, loyalty to the Zulu king has increasingly been tested by Buthelezi's control over the House of Traditional Leaders, an advisory council composed of Zulu chiefs loyal to the IFP.

31. *Sunday Tribune*, June 6, 2010.

References

Buthelezi, Mbongiseni. 2008. "The Empire Talks Back: Re-Examining the Legacies of Shaka and Zulu Power in Post-Apartheid South Africa." In *Zulu Identities: Being Zulu, Past and Present,* edited by Benedict Carton, John Laband, and Jabulani Sithole, 23–34. Scottsville, South Africa: University of Kwazulu-Natal Press.

Campbell, Catherine. 1992. "Learning to Kill? Masculinity, the Family and Violence in Natal." *Journal of Southern African Studies* 18, no. 3: 614–28.

Carton, Benedict, John Laband, and Jabulani Sithole, eds. 2008. *Zulu Identities: Being Zulu, Past and Present.* Scottsville, South Africa: University of Kwazulu-Natal Press.

Cobbing, Julian. 1988. "The *Mfecane* as Alibi: Thoughts on Dithakong and Mbolompo." *Journal of Africa History* 29: 487–519.

Deutsche, Rosalyn. 1998. *Evictions: Art and Spatial Politics.* Cambridge, MA: MIT Press.

Golan, Daphna. 1994. *Inventing Shaka: Using History in Construction of Zulu Nationalism.* Boulder: Lynne Rienner.

Hamilton, Carolyn. 1995. "'Zoolacraticism' and 'Cannibalism': A Discussion of Historical Disposition toward the 'Shakan' Model of Social Order and Political Rights." *Social Dynamics* 21, no. 2: 1–22.

———. 1998. *Terrific Majesty: The Powers of Shaka Zulu and the Limits of Historical Invention.* Cape Town: David Philip.

Harries, Patrick. 1995. "Imagery, Symbolism and Tradition in a South African Bantustan: Mangosuthu Buthelezi, Inkatha and Zulu History." *History and Theory* 32, no 4: 105–25.

Klopper, Sandra. 1996. "'He Is My King, but He Is Also My Child': Inkatha, the African National Congress and the Struggle for Control over Zulu Cultural Symbols." *Oxford Art Journal* 19, no. 1: 63–66.

Laband, John. 2008. "'Bloodstained Grandeur': Colonial and Imperial Stereotypes of Zulu Warriors and Zulu Warfare." In *Zulu Identities: Being Zulu, Past and Present,* edited by Benedict Carton, John Laband, and Jabulani Sithole, 168–76. Scottsville, South Africa: University of Kwazulu-Natal Press.

Mare, Gerhard, and Thembisa Waetjen. 1999. "Workers and Warriors: Inkatha's Politics of Masculinity in the 1980s." *Journal of Contemporary African Studies* 17, no. 2: 197–216.

Marschall, Sabine. 2010. *Landscape of Memory: Commemorative Monuments, Memorials and Public Statuary in Post-Apartheid South Africa.* Leiden, the Netherlands: Brill.

Mitchell, W. J. T., ed. 1992. *Art and the Public Sphere.* Chicago: University of Chicago Press.

Raven, Arlene, ed. 1989. *Art in the Public Interest.* Ann Arbor: University of Michigan Press.

van der Westhuizen, Christi. 2014. "'100% Zulu Boy': Jacob Zuma and the Use of Gender in the Run-Up to South Africa's Election—Publications." *Heinrich Böll Stiftung Southern Africa.* Published February 3, 2014. Accessed January 2015. https://za.boell.org/2014/02/03/100-zulu-boy-jacob-zuma-and-use-gender-run-south-africas-2009-election-publications.

Waetjen, Thembisa. 1999. "The 'Home' in Homeland: Gender, National Space and Inkatha's Politics of Ethnicity." *Ethnic and Racial Studies* 22, no. 4: 653–78.

White, Hylton. 2012. "A Post-Fordist Ethnicity: Insecurity, Authority, and Identity in South Africa." *Anthropological Quarterly* 85, no. 2: 397–428.

Wright, John. 2006. "Reconstituting Shaka Zulu for the Twenty-First Century." *Southern African Humanities* 18: 139–53.

———. 2008. "Revisiting the Stereotype of Shaka's Devastation." In *Zulu Identities: Being Zulu, Past and Present,* edited by Benedict Carton, John Laband, and Jabulani Sithole, 69–81. Scottsville, South Africa: University of KwaZulu-Natal Press, 2008.

Wylie, Dan. 2000. *Savage Delight: White Myths of Shaka.* Pietermaritzburg, South Africa: University of Natal Press.

———. 2008. "White Myths of Shaka." In *Zulu Identities: Being Zulu, Past and Present,* edited by Benedict Carton, John Laband, and Jabulani Sithole, 82–86. Scottsville, South Africa: University of Kwazulu-Natal Press.

———. 2011. *Shaka.* Johannesburg: Jacana.

CHAPTER 5

Mandela's Walk and Biko's Ghosts: Public Art and the Politics of Memory in Port Elizabeth's City Center

NAOMI ROUX

INTRODUCTION: BIKO'S GHOSTS

IN THE CENTER OF Port Elizabeth in South Africa's Eastern Cape, an easily overlooked graffiti piece is stenciled onto one of the concrete pillars supporting the M4 highway. The highway travels past the third and fourth floors of the office blocks and student accommodation occupying this part of the city, separating the city from the sea and leaving the street in semi-permanent shadow. Sprayed onto the pillar is the figure of Steven Bantu Biko, the Black Consciousness leader who died in police custody in Pretoria Central Prison in 1977. Biko stands with arms folded, facing away from the harbor toward the nondescript 1950s buildings and small ground-level shops (fig. 5.1).

Biko's gaze directs the viewer's gaze toward the entrance of the seemingly abandoned but otherwise unremarkable six-story office block across the road. Formerly known as the Sanlam Building, this building, 44 Strand Street, was the headquarters of the Eastern Cape branch of the South African security police in the late 1970s and early 1980s. Many activists were held here: some never emerged. Police invariably evaded responsibility for these deaths, although partial details of some of these came to light during the Truth and Reconciliation Commission (TRC) process of the 1990s.

Biko was held in this building following his arrest with Peter Jones, an executive member of the Black People's Convention, on August 18, 1977, while returning from a meeting in Cape Town. At the time, following the

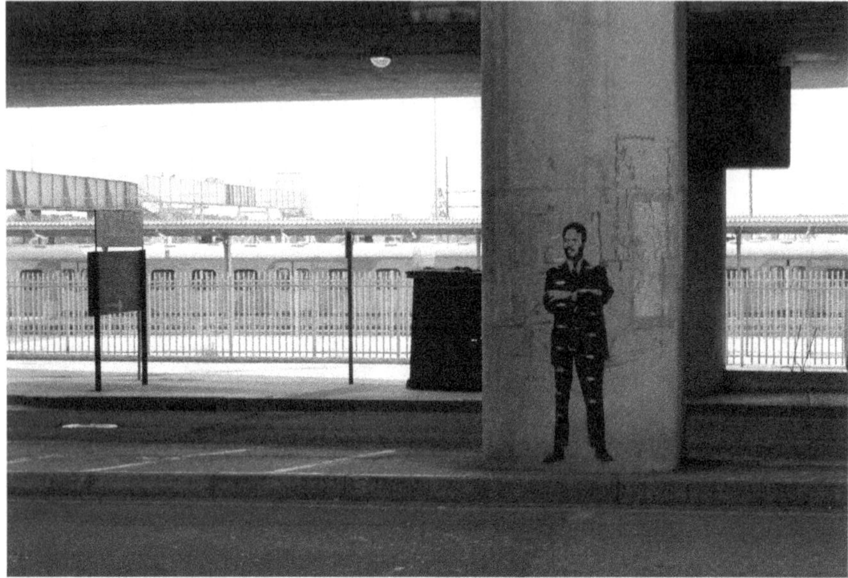

Fig. 5.1 Graffiti piece depicting Biko looking toward the entrance of the Sanlam Building, Port Elizabeth city center. *Photograph by Naomi Roux in 2013.*

explosion of resistance on the heels of the 1976 student uprisings, Biko had been banned to the King William's Town district 250 kilometers from Port Elizabeth. The two men were held overnight in Grahamstown, then transferred to the Walmer Police Station in Port Elizabeth, the last time they would see each other. Biko was held in isolation at Walmer for twenty days before being moved to the Sanlam Building on September 6. It was here, under interrogation, that he sustained the head injuries that would cause his death. He was moved back to Walmer, where a warder found him unconscious and foaming at the mouth on the evening of September 11. He was driven overnight in the back of a Land Rover to the Pretoria Central Prison hospital where he died of a brain hemorrhage on the night of September 12 (Mangcu 2012, 262–63). At the TRC, the police present at his interrogation testified that there had been a "scuffle" during which Biko had accidentally hit his head on the wall: all four were denied amnesty (TRC 1998a, 66–67).

Although Biko is perhaps the building's most famous former occupant, others include George Botha, a high school teacher and activist detained in December 1976. Police alleged that he "fell" down the building's six-floor stairwell. In July 1978, nineteen-year-old Lungile Tabalaza died on the same day of his arrest after falling from a sixth-floor window (TRC 1998a, 65–68; Bilbija et al. 2005, 54).[1] Others, such as Pan Africanist Congress (PAC) activist Moki Cekisani, survived detentions in the building but suffered lasting effects of the torture and interrogation that took place here.[2] Yet, despite the symbolic space the Sanlam Building occupies in the city's past, these histories are in no way publicly marked except by the visual intervention on the pillar. The building's chained-up doors are flanked by shops selling curtains, cloth, mobile phones, and household odds and ends. The interior is in bad repair: loose tiles, broken glass, and other debris crunches underfoot, while the staircase banister threatens to come away from its moorings. Abandoned furniture, old mattresses, and broken cupboards are piled up in the empty rooms, blocking what little light filters through the dusty windows.

A short walk away through the city center, at the apex of the scenic Donkin Reserve, is a very differently positioned and rendered public art piece representing another well-known South African historical figure. The recently redesigned reserve, an open green space at the city's heart, is traversed by winding uphill pathways (fig. 5.2). At the summit, a set of cut-out steel figures drawn from images of the emblematic voting queues of the 1994 elections curve around the base of a flagpole bearing the South African flag, leading toward a silhouetted figure of Nelson Mandela, raising an iconic fist toward the sky (fig. 5.3). A mosaic walkway connects the flag to the nineteenth-century Donkin Pyramid and a lighthouse, now converted into a tourism office and coffee shop. This work, *Voting Line* (2010/2011), by Port Elizabeth–based artists Anthony Harris and Konrad Geel, was one of the first artworks installed by the city as part of a public art route titled Route 67. The route was launched with six initial artworks in 2010 and subsequently extended to include sixty-seven artworks and sites of historical importance throughout Nelson Mandela Bay.

Insofar as this representation of Mandela came into being after a city-driven process of public commission, linked to an urban regeneration and tourist branding strategy, it forms a stark contrast with the image of Biko, which appeared anonymously, illegally, and under the cover of night in the shadow of the highway, outside an unmarked space of trauma. In the introduction to a 2007 edited collection on memory and urban space in South Africa, Nick Shepherd and Noëleen Murray (2007, 1) have used the metaphor of "desire lines" (a planning term describing pedestrian-made pathways

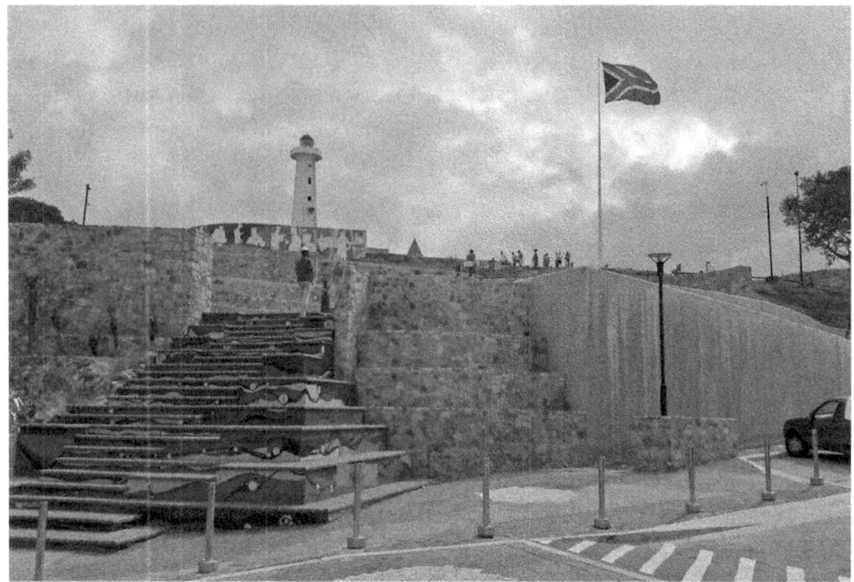

Fig. 5.2 View toward the apex of the Donkin Reserve, with pathways, new public art, lighthouse, Donkin Pyramid, and South African flag. *Photograph by Naomi Roux in 2012.*

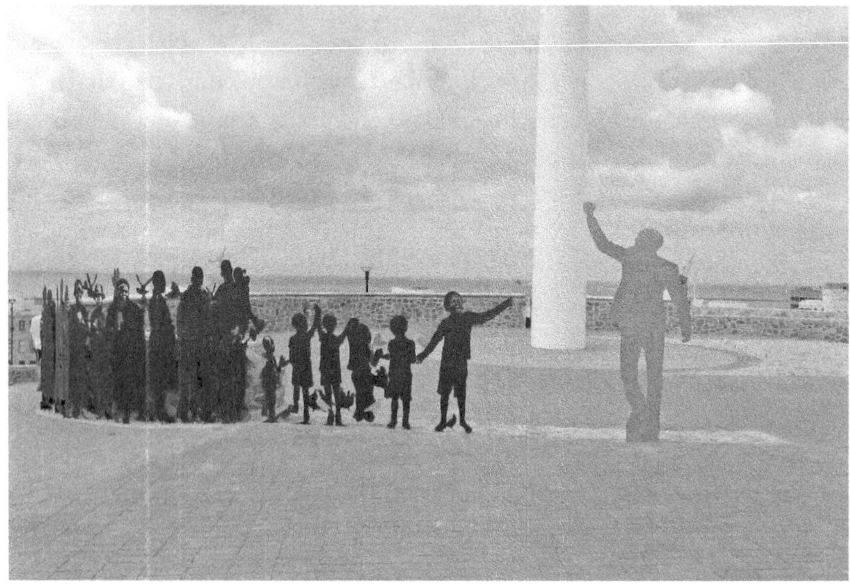

Fig. 5.3 *Voting Line* (2010/2011), Anthony Harris and Konrad Geel. Laser-cut steel figures, wrapped around base of South African flagpole. *Photograph by Naomi Roux in 2013.*

that diverge from pavements and planned walkways) to reflect on "the space between the planned and the providential, the engineered and the 'lived,' and between official projects of capture and containment and the popular energies which subvert, bypass, supersede, and evade them."

In this chapter, I consider the ephemeral, "unofficial" images of Biko in Port Elizabeth's public spaces as a type of "desire line." Viewed through this lens, these images of Biko illuminate the slippages between the city's officially sanctioned images of Mandela and their concomitant notions of transformation and national identity and the subversive or transgressive "popular energies" that call these representations into question. The trajectories of Biko's and Mandela's images through the city's public spaces are related to Rosalyn Deutsche's argument for an understanding of public art as part of a democratized public sphere: for Deutsche (1996), the political value of public art is not its ability to foster or reflect consensus but rather its potential as a site of contestation, productive conflict, and multiplicity. Urban theorists Ash Amin and Nigel Thrift (2002) draw on a similar conception of the radically democratic potential of the city as a space of "spirited adversarial confrontation." As a space of difference and inequality, they ask, "What better place than the city as a site of contested practices and aspirations, a zone of agonistic engagement, a place of experimentation with democracy as practice?" (Amin and Thrift 2002, 140).

The divergent representations of Mandela and Biko in both "official" and "unofficial" public artworks in Port Elizabeth, in this regard, are interesting not only as comparable aesthetic representations of prominent South African political leaders but also as sites through which to read contestations over South African public culture and post-apartheid identity. Biko and Mandela are both highly recognizable, iconic figures in South African resistance history, and representations of both men are ubiquitous in South African public culture. Yet during the transitional period of the 1990s, there was a great deal of contestation regarding the emphasis placed on public histories of the African National Congress (ANC) at the expense of other political parties and liberation movements such as the PAC and the Black Consciousness–inspired Azanian People's Organisation (AZAPO)—contestations that continue to play out today.[3] Biko's image, while iconic as a martyr of the struggle, is also an emblem of a political history that has not been afforded a prominent place in contemporary inscriptions of South African public history.

In this regard, its appearance in Port Elizabeth's public spaces can be read as a reinscription of this history into the contemporary city and to some extent as a challenge to a narrative of post-apartheid reconciliation, unity, and successful transformation represented by the image of Mandela. This challenge is becoming increasingly relevant to contemporary South African politics and public culture, as the cracks in the "rainbow nation" ideal and the failures of the reconciliatory project become increasingly evident. This had been made clear, for example, through interventions such as the student-led Rhodes Must Fall and Fees Must Fall movements of 2015–2016, which dramatically called into question the continued legacies of colonialism and apartheid and the post-apartheid state's perceived inadequacy insofar as addressing these legacies was concerned. As the "desire lines" created by pedestrians may illuminate the shortcomings of planned urban space, Biko's appearance in a city that has so strongly reconstructed its public identity around the Mandela name functions as a symbolic desire line, revealing the slippages and occlusions of the emblems of national identity through which the Donkin Reserve and the city center have been remade.

MANDELA'S WALK: ROUTE 67

The Route 67 project was initiated by the city's development arm, the Mandela Bay Development Agency (MBDA). The MBDA's broad mandate is to drive municipally supported urban regeneration projects in the Nelson Mandela Bay region so as to encourage further public and private investment, in a process summarized by MBDA chief executive officer Pierre Voges (2013) as "dynamic place-making." Interventions to date include city center street upgrades, the refurbishment and reactivation of the nineteenth-century Athenaeum Theatre, the redevelopment of King's Beach, the redesign of the Donkin Reserve, street and public space redesigns in New Brighton township to the north of the city center, and several public art installations.

The Donkin Reserve was both an "upgrading" project and a symbolic remaking of post-apartheid public space. At the center of the Reserve is a stone pyramid, commissioned in 1820 by Port Elizabeth's first governor in memory of his wife, who died in India in 1818 and after whom the city of Port Elizabeth is named. Rufane Donkin declared the space around the pyramid open public land gifted to the "people of Port Elizabeth" in perpetuity. While the reserve and pyramid can be read as intimate memorials or sites of personal grief, they are also intrinsically colonial spaces, read through a long history of displacement, violence, and successive waves of forced removals. The "people of Port Elizabeth" to whom this space was "gifted" did not include all the city's inhabitants: Donkin's claiming and naming of this space and the city as a whole was undoubtedly an act of colonial appropriation.

Thus, while "urban renewal" was one element of the MBDA project's mandate, the reimagining of the Donkin Reserve was also an attempt to reconfigure a historic site of exclusion as a contemporary space of belonging. The nongovernmental organization (NGO) Cultures in Regeneration, run by community arts practitioner Peter Stark, was brought on board to develop the conceptual framework for the project. In a concept document written by Stark with Peggy Calata, a somewhat tenuous temporal link is made between colonial histories and contemporary histories of resistance:

> In 1918, in a small rural settlement at Mvezo . . . Rolihlala Mandela was born. 100 years earlier, Elizabeth Donkin died in India at Meerut. On arrival at Algoa Bay to superintend the arrival of the British Settlers in 1820 [Rufane Donkin] named the settlement after his wife and allocated land around his monument to her "in perpetuity" as public open space. In 1918, the leaders of the white community of the City—unaware of the importance to their future of the birth at Mvezo—were planning another monument—the Campanile—to mark the centenary of the arrival of the British settlers. . . . By [2018] the City Centre has to be re-settled by the mixed population of the new country, at ease with each other in a place they all feel they own and in which they all feel a collective pride. (Calata and Stark 2009)

Based on this "centennial" framework, the Donkin's redesign is anchored both by Mandela's biography and the narrative of a national "journey" toward democracy. From the Campanile monument near the harbor, the symbolic route traverses the city center, past the Victorian architecture of Vuyisile Mini Square and up St. Mary's Steps toward the Donkin Reserve: "A walk from [Mandela's] birth to the crowning achievement of his long life for all to follow" (Calata and Stark 2009). Climbing the Reserve's winding pathways somatically echoes the experience of the long voting queues of 1994, intended to give visitors the experience of a symbolic journey through adversity to the establishment of democracy, represented by Mandela's figure and the new South African flag at the apex.[4]

The first six artworks on the route were commissions given to fairly established artists, while the second phase aimed to develop sixty-seven artworks and sites of historical memory throughout the metropolitan area. Besides *Voting Line,* other works in the first phase include Duncan Stewart's *River Memory,* which follows the path of a no-longer existent stream reclaimed by the city, as well as Dolla Sapeta's *Fish Bird,* evoking a mythic animal figure. Many of the commissions in the second phase were given to emerging artists and to collectives of art students, partly to foster a sense of belonging and ownership over the city for young artists, according to Mary Duker, Principal Lecturer in the Faculty of Arts at Nelson Mandela Metropolitan University (NMMU).[5] The second phase includes works such as Mkhonto Gwazela's *Wall of Texts,* a relief panel placed alongside the Campanile monument, which reflects on histories of creativity and cultural production in the Eastern Cape from the precolonial era to the present, and an installation along Saint Mary's Steps in which metal sheets resembling sheets of newspaper appear to be blown up the steps by the wind, inscribed with images by Port Elizabeth-based artist Michael Barry related to the June 1976 uprisings.

The route is marked by a set of "wayfinders," metal sheets similar to those of the *June 1976* installation, each inscribed with a date from 1942 to 2008 and a quotation from Mandela's writings and speeches. These are mounted on poles alongside the various points on the route. The first wayfinder, 1942, is located next to Gwazela's *Wall of Texts* and the Campanile, while the final one appears outside the renovated Athenaeum Theatre building, bearing the words *It is time for new hands to lift the burdens. It is in your hands now.* The selection of the years 1942–2008, and indeed the title "Route 67," draws on the concept of Mandela's "67 years of public service" between the year in which he moved to Johannesburg, and 2008, his ninetieth birthday.[6] In this sense, while the artworks on the route are not necessarily directly related to Mandela's biography, his life trajectory provides the narrative framework for the route as it traverses the city.

The harnessing of the Mandela name and symbolism has been commensurate with the amalgamation of three formerly separate city councils—Port Elizabeth, Uitenhage, and Despatch—into one metropolitan region, renamed Nelson Mandela Bay in 2001. Following this amalgamation, several public institutions in Port Elizabeth have drawn on the Mandela name: the University of Port Elizabeth, Port Elizabeth Technikon, and Vista University merged to become NMMU, while the King George VI Art Gallery became the Nelson Mandela Metropolitan Art Museum.

The use of Mandela's biography within the Donkin Reserve and the associated citywide public art project is thus linked to broader inscriptions of the Mandela name into Port Elizabeth's identity and representation of itself, although Mandela actually had relatively few historical links to the city.

The Route 67 sculpture was not the first planned representation of Mandela in the city's public spaces. Between 2001 and 2005, there were various iterations of a municipal- and provincially backed plan for a sixty-five-meter statue of Mandela in the city's harbor. A decade later, the Nelson Mandela Bay Business Chamber (2013) reported renewed discussions concerning the best site for the proposed statue amid plans for the drastic redevelopment of the harbor. In 2015, the MBDA was mandated to raise funds for the project. While discussion regarding its location remained ongoing, suggestions on the table at the time of writing included the Motherwell Peace Park or a site closer to the city center such as the Donkin Reserve.

Mandela's visual image as it is used in Route 67 draws on the tropes of "New South African" nationalism and the reconciliatory rhetoric of the 1990s in which a great deal of public discourse around post-apartheid South African identity was premised on the notion of the diverse but unified "rainbow nation." The "New South African" mythology that emerged during the transitional period under the Mandela government, Verne Harris (2010, 116) has argued,

> was always a construct, a vision, embraced first in public discourses in South Africa and then quickly adopted globally as shorthand for the ambitious project of democratisation rising from the wreckage of over four decades of apartheid rule. . . . Public discourse in and about South Africa was emblazoned by the concepts of noble struggle against apartheid, of post-apartheid reconciliation, and of nation-building. Central to this energy was the life and work of Nelson Mandela, the living symbol of Archbishop Desmond Tutu's "rainbow nation."

"RECOLONIZING" THE CITY

Route 67 was partly intended to rehabilitate a colonial urban landscape, in which the "debris" of empire and of apartheid remains deeply embedded (Stoler 2013). Dorelle Sapere, the MBDA's planning and development manager who has been at the helm of the Route 67 project since its inception, notes that among its intentions was "transforming the inner city to be owned by everyone, and recolonizing it to have access by those who didn't have it in the past," while simultaneously developing a "tourism product" in the form of "a journey . . . linking the past history and the new history."[7] The notions of "recolonizing" the city suggests a possible reading of Route 67 within the framework of "symbolic reparations": Route 67 is not only an aesthetic project but also fits into a conception of public art as a social good, intended to intertwine contemporary and resistance narratives with colonial histories already embedded in the city's public spaces and, in so doing, acknowledge these as intrinsic to the city's history. Part of its purpose was certainly to develop the city's aesthetic and tourism appeal, but as Sapere points out, it was also intended to symbolically mitigate the presence of colonial histories in the urban fabric.

While some of the Route 67 artworks have been placed in proximity to colonial monuments such as the Donkin Pyramid and the Campanile, they do not overtly engage with these monuments or significantly recast their meanings. In this regard, the insertion of the Mandela biography into the landscape does not trouble the complexities of the city or the Donkin Reserve's colonial history. Rather, it domesticates them by placing them alongside the reconciliatory, benign figure of Mandela and the unificatory symbolism of the South African flag, rendering the meanings of these older monuments politically neutralized rather than openly acknowledged as sites of contestation or of historic trauma.

One proposed but unrealized artwork on the route did intend to directly intervene in the colonial landscape. This was a piece titled *Conversations with the Queen,* which was to be associated with the 1902 statue of Queen Victoria in Vuyisile Mini Square. *Conversations with the Queen* was thus somewhat unique among the Route 67 pieces in that it would directly incorporate an existing monument into the work. The piece, made by a collective of NMMU fine art students under the supervision of David Jones, consisted of a set of life-size human figures representing well-known resistance leaders: Oliver Tambo, Steve Biko, Mahatma Gandhi, Robert Sobukwe, and Lillian Ngoyi, as well as a generic seated "everyman" figure and a figure of a begging child. The intention was for these to be placed around a human-scale version of the Queen Victoria statue, while the original would be placed in storage, in this way representing a conversation or confrontation between the queen and these figures. In the context of debates regarding what should be done about the presence of colonial statues and symbols in the postcolonial city, this piece would not remove the Victoria statue or attempt to erase the history of domination that it represents but would place the queen on an equal footing with resistance leaders who came after her and with figures representing the ordinary inhabitants of the city. However, the installation has been delayed by a planned renovation of the square and the figures are currently installed in the lobby and courtyard of the Athenaeum Theatre, while the queen continues to reign over the square.[8]

Victoria's statue is significant as a site of intervention in light of existing controversies and debates around the statue's right to remain in the city's central public space. In 2004, prior to the April national elections, Mike Xego, then regional ANC deputy chairperson, called for the statue's removal. In support of Xego, Xolela Mangcu (2004), at the time the director of the Steve Biko Foundation, asked, "What reconciliation is it that demands a people to deny their own history, and instead glorify murderers. . . . What kind of people glorify their conquerors?" For Mangcu, as for Xego, the need to remove colonial iconography was seen as a necessary step toward reconstructing an "African" public history and public culture; what was at stake was no less than a "war of memory."[9]

In March 2010, a few months prior to the start of the FIFA Soccer World Cup, the statue was covered with graffiti overnight. Victoria's eyes were blacked out, and the plinth was sprayed with the phrases "Goduka Victoria" ("Go home, Victoria") and "Hamba" ("Go"). These mobilizations and interventions suggest that the statue retains a measure of symbolic power, raising necessary questions regarding the potential role of new public art projects such as Route 67 in mitigating the continuing presence and symbolism of colonial histories and their aftermaths. The insistence that Victoria "go home" can be read as a demand for the symbolism of empire to be removed from this position of prominence in the city's main public square, as well as an angry comment on the persistence of historic inequality in a city with long histories of colonial violence and displacement. The traumatic histories that Victoria symbolizes remain deeply felt in the physical and social fabric of the city, and this graffiti intervention was a blunt but effective means of rejecting their persistent presence.

The question of dealing with colonial remnants is not unique to Nelson Mandela Bay. For the most part, South African colonial objects have not been discarded, although they may have been recast in new ways. The Voortrekker Monument in Pretoria is a pertinent example of this kind of "translation" (Coombes 2003). Zayd Minty (2006) has similarly argued for the need to "recontextualize" such monuments rather than destroying or erasing them.

Considering the role of public art as a form of "symbolic reparation" in the segregated landscape of Cape Town, Minty (2006, 432) argues that "since the built environment in Cape Town reflects almost exclusively the histories of those with power and/or capital, the opportunities to critique or insert new narratives come either with a recontextualisation of the old or the creation of the new. There have been very few developments that are new and which reflect 'hidden histories' in the city. In this context, public art engagements with the old become important." Minty points to Beezy Bailey's *Abakwetha* (1999) in which Bailey altered an equestrian statue of Louis Botha, the first South African prime minister, transforming him into a representation of a Xhosa initiate returning home. Botha's face was painted white, and he was adorned with a blanket and a hat. The title "Abakwetha" was temporarily added to the work's plinth. As indicated in the introduction to this volume, the intervention was part of a project called *P. T. O.* ("please turn over") by artists collective Public Eye that entailed creative engagements with several Cape Town monuments as a reclamation of colonial space and symbolism.

Minty discusses these works in the context of a consideration of public art as a potential form of "symbolic reparations," one of the elements of post-apartheid reparations recommended by the TRC (1998b, 175) in the commission's final report. Route 67 has not explicitly been framed in this way by the MBDA, although it is presented as a project intended to foster the sense that the city's new public spaces belong to all its residents, including those formerly excluded from them. In a historical context of displacement and exclusion, therefore, this social function of public art can be read as a potential form of reparations, linked to the process of transforming and developing the post-apartheid city. Yet, as many cases of new monuments, public spaces, and public artworks in the Eastern Cape and elsewhere in the country suggest, there is little clear strategy in place for precisely how such developments are intended to achieve these effects.[10]

Hall and Robertson (2001) have offered a critique of the arguments for public art as a potential contributor to urban regeneration, social cohesion, and other social benefits. As they point out, it is difficult to develop critical frameworks to evaluate such claims despite "a widespread and uncritical acceptance, particularly among its main commissioners, that putting art in the public realm is inherently a good thing," a view that "posits public art either as an essential component of the cultural stock of cities, contributing to the enhancement of city-center environments and the externally projected images of cities, or as a panacea for a range of social problems" (Hall and Robertson 2001, 18). In the case of the MBDA's work in Nelson Mandela Bay, the "social use" of Route 67 is related to the organization's broader mandate in the city in the form of urban regeneration and Voges's notion of "dynamic place-making." In this regard, the arts are given a heavy task in terms of not only "upgrading" the city but also fostering a more just and inclusive space. At the same time, through its conceptualization as a symbolic biographical narrative and its claims of rehabilitating colonial landscapes and public spaces, Route 67 needs to be read as a work not only of design-based urban upgrade but also as a project of memory and the creation of new forms of urban identities and senses of belonging. While the MBDA's interventions have begun to transform the appearance of the city, it is worth asking what is occluded from this work.

EPHEMERAL BIOGRAPHIES: LOCATING BIKO

In the 1990s, the Sanlam Building was purchased by a private developer and converted into student accommodation. In the process, traces of its former history as a site of detention and interrogation were removed, including door numbers and fittings. The infamous room 619 became an ordinary residence room. In 2002, the building was bought by Irish developer Ken Denton, a controversial figure who had purchased large swathes of property in Port Elizabeth in the 2000s (including the Baakens Street Post Office, another former site of incarceration) and was often accused of allowing these to lapse into decay.[11] The students moved out, and in the intervening years, the building has fallen increasingly into disrepair.

44 Strand is an ordinary building in a busy city center thoroughfare. Simultaneously, this ordinary space is a site of deeply traumatic memory. For many who were held here, it retains the aura of this past, although there is little to mark it as such. The building's presence as a site of the sedimentation of a violent history, whether "officially" acknowledged or not, calls to mind James Holston's (1998, 37) characterization of cities as places where narratives and stories accrue and collide:

> Cities . . . condense and conduct the currents of social time. Their layered surfaces, their coats of painted stucco, their wraps of concrete register the force of these currents both as wear and as narrative. That is, city surfaces tell time and

> stories. Cities are full of stories in time, some sedimented and catalogued; others spoorlike, vestigial, and dispersed. . . . Yet, although obvious, their registry is never wholly legible because each foray into the palimpsest of city surfaces reveals only the trace of these relations.

Like many such sites and in particular spaces of trauma or violence, the "vestigial" history of this site is only accessible by means of translation or interlocution. In the absence of narrative or visual intervention, the Sanlam Building remains an untranslatable ruin.

There have been few direct or permanent memorial interventions at the Sanlam Building or at the Walmer Police Station where Biko was held before and after his interrogation. There was a spike in commemorative activity in 2002, the twenty-fifth anniversary of Biko's death, when then AZAPO president Mosibudi Mangena delivered a commemorative lecture at the Lillian Ngoyi Sports Centre in Kwazakhele and a cleansing ceremony was held in the Walmer Police Station cells (Anonymous 2002, 3; Matavire 2002, 8; 2004, 2). In 2005, a tire company that sponsored a community center located at the Walmer Police Station commissioned an illustrator, Nathan Millar, to install a mural of Biko in the cell as part of the company's corporate social investment program.[12] The cell remains in day-to-day use, creating a rather surreal juxtaposition in which the most regular audience for this artwork are detainees who sit on the concrete floor underneath Biko's image.

In 2006, in the run-up to the thirtieth anniversary of Biko's death the following year, a second cleansing ceremony was held at the Walmer station. This was driven by the provincial Department of Safety and Security, with no mention of the similar ceremony initiated by AZAPO four years previously. This was a distinctly government-driven event: Eastern Cape premiere Nosima Balindlela was in attendance, as was the Nelson Mandela Bay mayor and various Members of the Executive Council and provincial and metropolitan politicians. Methodist bishop Ziphozihle Siwa sprinkled holy water in the cell and incense was burned, while Siwa incanted a prayer invoking the "shame in this cell of darkness we are entering," asking God to "cleanse this place and drive away our painful memories" (Masondo 2006, 3).

These ceremonies of opening and cleansing sites of torture and atrocity are reminiscent of several other examples in the African continent, including that of Nairobi's Nyayo House, a state building constructed in the early 1980s. Under Daniel Arap Moi's presidency, cells in the basement were used as a clandestine torture center, specifically constructed for the purpose (ICSC 2010; Citizens for Justice 2003). These secret cells were opened in 2003 by a ministerial delegation under newly elected president Mwai Kibaki in an emotive ceremony:

> Shem Ogola stood in the middle of the small crowd that had gathered to witness the opening of the basement of perhaps the most well-known building in Kenya. And in the glare of world television cameras, he broke down in a flood of tears. His body shook. . . . Through Ogola, a torture survivor, Nyayo House torture chambers gained a human face. . . . The occasion became a revelation into the past, a window through which Kenyans glimpsed into their country's dark history. (Citizens for Justice 2003, ix)

Both Nyayo House and the Sanlam Building were sites of everyday bureaucracy that appeared entirely banal from the outside. Similarly to the Sanlam Building, while there have been performative interventions at Nyayo House such as the ceremonial opening of the cells and revisiting by former prisoners, it has never been formally identified as a site of memory despite its prominent place in the city's physical and symbolic fabric.

In 2007, marking the thirtieth anniversary of Biko's death, the Steve Biko Foundation (SBF) submitted an application to have the Biko family home in Ginsburg declared a heritage site, part of an envisaged heritage trail in and around King William's Town. Neither the Sanlam Building nor the Walmer police cell in Port Elizabeth were included in the list, which was centered on the new Steve Biko Education Centre in Ginsburg for which planning was under way at the time. Nonetheless, much of the commemorative activity in Port Elizabeth in 2007 was driven by the SBF, under the brand "Biko 30:30." For these events, an exhibition on deaths in detention was installed in room 619 in the empty Sanlam Building, making reference not only to Biko but also to others who had died in police custody in Port Elizabeth and elsewhere, while film screenings, seminars, and other events were held in the week leading up to the anniversary of Biko's death. This was the last public memorial activity to take place inside the building.

Since 2011, the Centre for the Advancement of Non-Racialism and Democracy (CANRAD) at NMMU has organized an annual program of commemorative events in September in conjunction with student groups. These take the form of annual lectures, discussion groups, informal seminars, and various arts-based interventions. Walmer resident Simphiwe Msizi, through his NGO Ezingcanjini African Heritage (meaning "from the roots"), has worked closely with CANRAD to establish a series of "Biko conversations," inviting students and young people to participate in informal seminars connected to Black Consciousness histories and philosophies, and is also engaged in campaigning for the Walmer Police Station to be declared a national heritage site.

The various representations and memorial interventions related to Biko's histories in Port Elizabeth have been, almost without exception, ephemeral, performative, or temporary. There is a significant difference between the permanent, city-sanctioned representation of Mandela and the sculptural representations of democracy's achievements that appear at the apex of the Donkin Reserve, reaching upward toward the South African flag as a symbol of nationhood, and the small, momentary, informal images of Biko that appear at particular moments scattered throughout the city, including the graffiti image on Strand Street and the Biko mural in the Walmer Police Station.

PUBLIC ART AND SPATIAL POLITICS

Unlike the figure of Mandela, fixed at the culmination of Route 67, Biko's image travels throughout the city, ephemeral and ghostlike. The graffiti, painted murals, and poster art bearing Biko's images are changeable: they appear and disappear, rather than acting as fixed or monumental works of public art. In late 2013, for example, images of Biko's face appeared pasted onto walls, poles, and electricity boxes, in a set of posters advertising a play by young Port Elizabeth playwright Xolisa Ngubelanga titled *Dinner with Bantu* (fig. 5.4). In the play, the character Nelson lays on a daily feast for the character Bantu, constantly awaiting his return. When Bantu arrives, it is to chastise Nelson for his naïveté: "I am never coming back Nelson," he declares. "Do you really think I want to return to a house I left 33 years ago to find it looking the exact same way?" (Ngubelanga 2010). The piece, which has also been staged at the National Arts Festival, places the prelapsarian figure of Biko in opposition to Mandela as the emblem of the achievement of democracy. The incursion of Biko in the play's narrative suggests a need to engage seriously with the alternative political imaginaries opened up by Black Consciousness histories and philosophies that remain sidelined in public and political discourse. As Ngubelanga explains, "It's very hard to

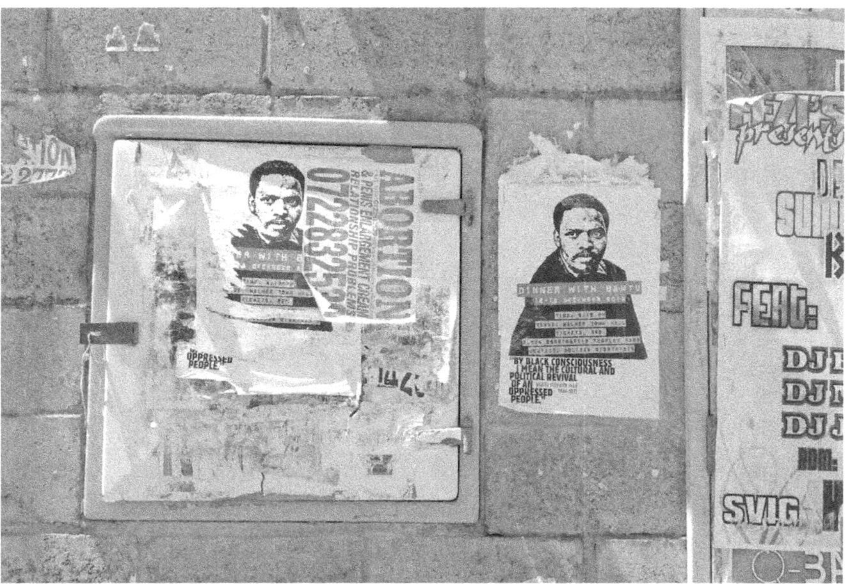

Fig. 5.4 Posters for the production of *Dinner with Bantu* by Xolisa Ngubelanga, pasted on an electricity box along with other advertisements, Walmer Township, Port Elizabeth. *Photograph by Naomi Roux in 2014.*

understand [these silences] because here in PE Biko's history is very loud when it comes to infrastructure: Sanlam Building, the Walmer Police Station—it's tangible. So [my opinion is] the only way it can be silenced is if there's a deliberate attempt to silence it."[13]

The transgressive occupation of public space with these poster, mural, and graffiti images is also a form of symbolic political occupation. By making Biko's image visible in public space in this way, the artists and makers of these images also make the ideas, histories, and political philosophies they represent visible in the political landscape. At the same time, this is a performative inscription of memory into public space: for example, almost all of the memorial interventions that have taken place in or around the Walmer police cell and the Sanlam Building have been ephemeral in the sense that they are events that take place and then disappear, activating these sites temporarily in a way that is based on practice rather than the permanence of monumentality or on the kinds of built structures and forms that dominate Route 67.

These ephemeral engagements have included CANRAD's annual Steve Biko Memorial Lectures, which have often been accompanied by visits and symbolic openings of the Walmer cell, or by gatherings and performances outside the Sanlam Building.[14] At times, this performative claiming of Black Consciousness philosophy and political alternatives, particularly by young artists, poets, and activists, is unmoored entirely from physical structures or sites: for example, a group of NMMU students have established a group called the Cultural Consciousness Society (CCS), drawing on Biko's writings on culture as a political practice and using performance, visual arts, and spoken word as a means of engaging with Black Consciousness philosophy in a contemporary milieu.[15] The CCS's most regular activity is a gathering of hip-hop and spoken-word artists that takes place weekly in Njoli Square in Kwazakhele, suggesting a very different pathway for engagement with the past and its meanings than the bricks-and-mortar approach of traditional monuments and standard forms of public art such that appear in the city center and elsewhere.[16] As architectural "desire lines" are made collectively through the practice of walking, these ephemeral interventions are made collectively in the moment: they may lack the monumental permanence of traditional memorial architecture but have the potential to work as sites of memory that are inclusive, alive, and multivocal.

A small number of well-known images of Biko's face have circulated since the 1970s in the form of posters, graffiti, T-shirts, flyers, and badges, ranging from protest posters of the late 1970s to contemporary book covers and designer T-shirts.[17] In the Port Elizabeth representations, the portrait used as source material in the Walmer Police Station mural and the Strand Street graffiti piece first appeared in news reports in the East London *Daily Dispatch* newspaper and has been circulating widely since it was first used in the 1970s. The image that appears on Ngubelanga's posters, similarly, has been in circulation since the 1970s, originally in the contexts of memorial and political posters at the time of Biko's detention and death, and more recently ranging from book covers, to commercial enterprises such as T-shirts and coffee mugs.[18] In this process, these images become a form of traveling signifier, accruing new meanings in new contexts. For the graffiti artists intervening in the space outside the Sanlam Building, as for young playwrights such as Ngubelanga or for many of the young artists linked to the CCS, these appropriations of Biko and the placement of his figure in public space are a means of making visible a set of histories that are seen to offer alternative political possibilities in the present.

Where the image of Mandela as it has been used in Route 67 represents past achievement in the form of the triumph of democracy and the hopeful imagery of the 1994 voting lines, the image of Biko represents as-yet unrealized future possibilities and the desire to write these possibilities into a contemporary political landscape. In *Dinner with Bantu*, Ngubelanga (2010) issues a call for a dramatic move away from the status quo and the opening of new future possibilities, when the character Bantu insists, "If this house be where my spirit ought to be homed then may this house be brought to the ground, may its foundation collapse and walls explode. I never asked for a temple or a statue, stone and marble my only identity." The rejection of the concept of monumentality and of monumental histories is also a rejection of a political status quo and, ultimately, a statement of a search for alternative futures.

At the same time, Mandela's and Biko's images both speak to heroic, masculine biography that is pervasive in South African post-apartheid representations of heritage, including in the framing of testimony at the TRC and in later representations of this testimony (Coombes 2011). In this sense, representations of the two figures are not that drastically different: although the kinds of representations of Biko in the city appear in different contexts and forms to those of Mandela, they replicate similar narrative trajectories, focusing on well-known male activists who were prominently at the forefront of the struggle. Yet, the ephemerality (and in some cases illegality, such as the Strand Street graffiti) of the Biko images render them powerful interventions in a heritage landscape predicated on celebratory urban branding and an overarching narrative of post-apartheid reconciliation, pointing toward the incompleteness of these constructions.

Sitas and Pieterse (2013) have made a case for the possibilities of public art as part of a democratic imaginary, underpinned by participation and space for multiple voices, including those that are contradictory or conflictual. In this view, public art practices hold powerful potentialities in a context where "no group or coalition can elevate itself to the status of arbiter about what counts as [transformative] political action and what does not. . . . There must be a fundamental acceptance that a cast plurality of actions, interventions, gestures and speculations are a necessary part of an agonistic left democratic sensibility" (Sitas and Pieterse 2013, 341). In the case of Nelson Mandela Bay, reading the city's public art practices and interventions through the lens of the ephemeral and dispersed appearances and mobilizations of Biko's image suggests potential pathways toward this type of plurality.

These possibilities are not, perhaps, as easily traced as the linear walk up the winding pathways of the Donkin Reserve toward the celebratory flag and the raised fist of Mandela. In the manner of "desire lines," they appear and disappear, intervene and are painted over, manifesting as momentary interventions rather than fixed structures, and are difficult to pin down or to readily identify within the rubric of "public art" at all. Yet, this flickering, changeable quality points powerfully toward the continuing presence of echoes and reverberations of the past, and toward unrealized possibilities for the future that are not easily captured in the structures and landscapes that characterize Route 67 as well as many other post-apartheid public visual and memorial interventions.

ACKNOWLEDGMENTS

I am grateful to the many people in Port Elizabeth who made the research for this chapter possible and who gave their time for interviews, conversations, and site visits, especially Moki Cekisani, Janet Cherry, Mark Dawson, Craig Duffield, Anthony Harris, Brett Jackman, Simphiwe Msizi, Xolisa Ngubelanga, Dorelle Sapere, Amy Shelver, Pierre Voges, Allan Zinn, and many others. Thanks also to Annie Coombes for advice, insight, and support. This work was partially funded by grants from the Oppenheimer Memorial Trust, the Birkbeck School of Arts, and the French Institute of South Africa. Valuable space and time for writing was provided by fellowships at LSE Cities, funded by the Andrew W. Mellon Foundation, and at UCT's African Centre for Cities, funded by the Foundation for Urban and Regional Studies.

Naomi Roux is a postdoctoral fellow at the African Centre for Cities at the University of Cape Town. Her current work focuses on heritage, the politics of memory, and public space.

Notes

1. Botha, who had been active in student politics at the University of the Western Cape in the late 1960s, was arrested during the 1976 uprisings as a result of his vocal support for student activists at Paterson High, where he was teaching at the time. Tabalaza was arrested on suspicion of arson and robbery, although his mother testified at the

Truth and Reconciliation Commission (TRC) that to her knowledge, he was not politically active.

2. Cekisani was arrested shortly before Biko and Jones on August 3, 1977, under section 6 of the Terrorism Act and suffered permanent hearing loss as a result of electric shock torture (Cherry and Gibbs 2006, 590).

3. Annie Coombes (2003) has discussed these contestations in detail in relation to the development of Robben Island from political prison to heritage site.

4. Anthony Harris, interviewed by Naomi Roux, ART Gallery, Port Elizabeth, January 31, 2014; Peter Stark, interviewed by Naomi Roux, Richmond Hill, Port Elizabeth, March 9, 2012.

5. Mary Duker, interviewed by Naomi Roux, Athenaeum Theatre, Port Elizabeth, February 1, 2014.

6. The concept of "67 years of public service" was developed by the Nelson Mandela Foundation in a campaign that has been running since 2010, encouraging South Africans to commit sixty-seven minutes of community service annually on July 18, Mandela's birthday.

7. Dorelle Sapere, interviewed by Naomi Roux, Athenaeum Building, Port Elizabeth, March 27, 2012.

8. Mary Duker, interviewed by Naomi Roux, Athenaeum Theatre, Port Elizabeth, February 1, 2014.

9. For further discussion of the politics of colonial statuary in the post-apartheid South African context, see Schmahmann (2013), Dubin (2006), and Coombes (2003).

10. For a discussion of the failure of a public space and heritage project in Johannesburg developed with these kinds of intentions, for example, see Judin, Roux, and Zack 2014.

11. See, for example, Hayward (2009).

12. Nathan Millar, e-mail communication with Naomi Roux, August 24, 2014.

13. Xolisa Ngubelanga, interviewed by Naomi Roux, KwaDwesi, Port Elizabeth, January 18, 2014.

14. Allan Zinn, interviewed by Naomi Roux, CANRAD, Port Elizabeth, February 4, 2014.

15. Monwabisi Soxuza, interviewed by Naomi Roux, Port Elizabeth, January 14, 2014. Soxuza is one of the founding members of the CCS.

16. The potential for performance to activate public space is especially compelling when considered against many existing Nelson Mandela Bay memorials, many of which—including the Emlotheni Heroes' Acre in New Brighton and the Cradock Four memorial near Motherwell—have been fenced off to prevent vandalism, rendering them entirely inaccessible.

17. Not all these contexts are necessarily transgressive, and these images of Biko have also been commercialized. For discussions of the use of Biko's image on designer T-shirts, for example, popularized by the Johannesburg-based fashion label Stoned Cherrie, see Nuttall (2008) and Vincent (2007).

18. Judy Seidman (2007) has traced the use of posters as political representations in South Africa, identifying the resistance posters made in South Africa and in exile by groups such as the MEDU Art Ensemble as part of a South African "Poster Movement," which she dates to approximately 1975–2000.

References

Amin, Ash, and Nigel Thrift. 2002. *Cities: Reimagining the Urban*. Cambridge, UK: Polity.

Anonymous. 2002. "Biko to Be Remembered." *The Herald*, September 6.

Bilbija, Ksenija, Jo Ellen Fair, Cynthia E. Milton, and Leigh A. Payne. 2005. *The Art of Truth-Telling about Authoritarian Rule*. Madison: University of Wisconsin Press.

Calata, Peggy, and Peter Stark. 2009. "Conceptual Framework for the 'Century Walk': Nelson Mandela and the 100 Year Journey to a New Settlement at Ibhayi."

Cherry, Janet, and Pat Gibbs. 2006. "The Liberation Struggle in the Eastern Cape." In *The Road to Democracy in South Africa*, edited by the South African Democracy Educational Trust (SADET), 569–614. Pretoria: Unisa Press.

Citizens for Justice. 2003. "We Lived to Tell: The Nyayo House Story." http://library.fes.de/pdf-files/bueros/kenia/01828.pdf.

Coombes, Annie E. 2003. *History after Apartheid: Visual Culture and Public Memory in a Democratic South Africa*. Durham, NC: Duke University Press.

Deutsche, Rosalyn. 1996. *Evictions: Art and Spatial Politics*. Boston: MIT Press.

Dubin, Steven. 2006. *Transforming Museums: Mounting Queen Victoria in a Democratic South Africa*. New York: Palgrave.

Hall, Tim, and Iain Robertson. 2001. "Public Art and Urban Regeneration: Advocacy, Claims and Critical Debates." *Landscape Research* 26: 5–26.

Harris, Verne. 2010. "Jacques Derrida Meets Nelson Mandela: Archival Ethics at the Endgame." *Archival Science* 11, no. 1–2 (February 25): 113–24.

Hayward, Brian. 2009. "Outraged Group Plans 'Slumlord' Class Action." *The Weekend Post*, November 28, p. 1.

Holston, James. 1998. "Spaces of Insurgent Citizenship." In *Making the Invisible Visible: A Multicultural Planning History*, edited by Leonie Sandercock. Berkeley: University of California Press.

International Coalition of Sites of Conscience (ICSC). 2010. "From Nyayo House to Godown Center: A Needs Assessment of Memorialisation Initiatives in Kenya." http://www.sitesofconscience.org/wp-content/uploads/2013/01/Kenya-Needs-Assessment.pdf.

Judin, Hilton, Naomi Roux, and Tanya Zack. 2014. "Kliptown: Resilience and Despair in the Face of a Hundred Years of Planning." In *Changing Space, Changing City: Johannesburg after Apartheid*, edited by Philip Harrison, Graeme Gotz, Alison Todes, and Chris Wray, ••–••. Johannesburg: Wits University Press.

Mangcu, Xolela. 2004. "Eastern Cape Losing War of Memory." *Daily Dispatch*, April 29.

———. 2012. *Biko: A Life*. Cape Town: Tafelberg.

Masondo, Sipho. 2006. "Ceremonial Cleansing for Cell Where Biko Was Tortured." *The Herald*, June 19.

Matavire, Max. 2002. "Biko Police Cell 'Cleansed' as Part of Commemoration Events." *The Herald*, September 9.

———. 2004. "Azapo Organising Tributes for Biko." *The Herald*, September 6.

Minty, Zayd. 2006. "Post-Apartheid Public Art in Cape Town: Symbolic Reparations and Public Space." *Urban Studies* 43, no. 2: 421–40.

Nelson Mandela Bay Business Chamber, "Investigation into Which Site Best for Statue of Liberation," 2012, accessed August 23, 2014, http://www.nmbbusinesschamber.co.za/blog/posts/investigation-into-which-site-best-for-statue-of-liberation.

Ngubelanga, Xolisa. 2010. *Dinner with Bantu*. Unpublished script.

Nuttall, Sarah. 2008. "Stylizing the Self." In *Johannesburg: The Elusive Metropolis*, edited by Achille Mbembe and Sarah Nuttall, 91–118. Durham, NC: Duke University Press.

Schmahmann, Brenda. 2013. *Picturing Change: Curating Visual Culture at Post-Apartheid Universities*. Johannesburg: Wits University Press.

Seidman, Judy. 2007. *Red on Black: The Story of the South African Poster Movement*. Johannesburg: STE Publishers and South African History Archives.

Shepherd, Nick, and Noëleen Murray. 2007. "Introduction: Space, Memory and Identity in the Post-Apartheid City." In *Desire Lines: Space, Memory and Identity in the Post-Apartheid City*, edited by Noeleen Murray, Nick Shepherd, and Martin Hall. Abingdon, UK: Routledge.

Sitas, Rike, and Edgar Pieterse. 2013. "Democratic Renovations and Affective Political Imaginaries." *Third Text* 27, no. 3: 327–42.

Stoler, Ann Laura, ed. 2013. *Imperial Debris: On Ruins and Ruination*. Durham, NC: Duke University Press.

Truth and Reconciliation Commission of South Africa (TRC). 1998a. *Truth and Reconciliation Commission of South Africa Report*, vol. 3. Cape Town: TRC.

———. 1998b. *Truth and Reconciliation Commission of South Africa Report*, vol. 5. Cape Town: TRC.

———. 1999. "Amnesty Decision on Death of Steve Biko." February 16.

Vincent, Louise. 2007. "Steve Biko and Stoned Cherrie: Refashioning the Body Politic in Democratic South Africa." *African Sociological Review* 11, no. 2: 80–93.

Voges, Pierre. 2013. "Competitive Local Economic Development through Urban Renewal in the City of Port Elizabeth, South Africa." University of Pretoria.

CHAPTER 6

Commemorating Solomon Mahlangu: The Making and Unmaking of a "Struggle" Icon

GARY BAINES

ARTIST BRETT MURRAY'S EXHIBITION "Hail to the Thief II" caused a furor when it was mounted at the Goodman Gallery in 2012. The focus of attention was a painting called *The Spear*, which depicted President Jacob Zuma, modeled on a Soviet propaganda poster of Lenin, with exposed genitalia. Zuma supporters defaced the work and took to the streets where they toyi-toyed and sang Zuma's signature song "Wami Mashini" ("Bring Me My Machine Gun") threatening violence against all and sundry while brandishing imitation AK-47s. Amid the ensuing political ruckus, the media and the public fixated on *The Spear* rather than other works that were equally controversial. One of these was a poster titled *The Struggle* (fig. 6.1).

The Struggle is a revision of an image originally designed by Judy Seidman for Medu,[1] a collective of exiled South African artists and cultural workers living in Gaborone, Botswana, during the 1980s. The poster depicts the silhouette of an Umkhonto we Sizwe (MK) cadre holding an AK-47 rifle with the words attributed to Solomon Mahlangu, who was sent to the gallows in 1979. In his work, Murray used the same image as Seidman but altered her text. The first part of the sentence "Tell my people that I love them and that they must continue the struggle" is the same as on the original poster. But Murray has added "for Chivas Regal, Mercs and Kick-Backs," an alteration that *Sunday Independent* commentator Mary Corrigall (2012, 5) observed was an excoriating critique of the African National Congress's (ANC's) loss of its mooring from the values that it embodied during the liberation struggle. But this begs the questions, why did Murray choose to lampoon the message associated with Mahlangu's memory?

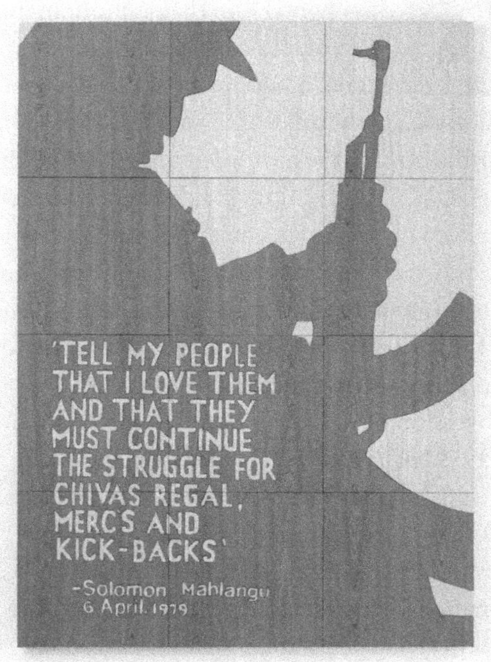

Fig. 6.1 Brett Murray, *The Struggle* (2010), wood and wood veneer, 152 x 113 x 2 cm. *Photograph courtesy of Goodman Gallery.*

Murray's choice of title for the poster is telling. "The Struggle" is shorthand for "a teleological narrative, implying coherence and unity, a more or less concerted effort towards liberation led by the ANC and supported by its armed wing uMkhonto weSizwe (MK), [which translates as] 'Spear of the Nation'" (Marschall 2010, 14). Underpinning the narrative of the nation in the making is the story of "The Struggle"—with a capital *S*; an attempt by the ANC government to eulogize the achievements of MK in defeating the apartheid regime. Although MK had a degree of success with sabotage and what it called armed propaganda, it could not even remotely lay claim to defeating the South African Defence Force in any engagement (Suttner 2008, 164). Nor was it able to claim more than a few minor victories against other branches of the security forces. In the absence of a credible military record, MK has sought to nurture a legitimizing or usable past. This has been termed the myth of the armed struggle (Ellis 2012, 296, 300–1, 309). Mahlangu is a key figure in the myth.[2] Given the shortage of stories about feats of military bravado by "freedom fighters" in the public domain, Mahlangu has been elevated to the pantheon of fallen heroes of "The Struggle."

All nation-states have need of heroes as national icons. South Africa is no exception. Since 1994, memories of the apartheid past and the elevation of certain figures to heroic status have been marshaled by the ANC government for the purpose of nation building and identity construction. By commemorating new heroes, we create what Sabine Marschall (2006, 176–93) calls a genealogy or chosen ancestry that serves—in an ideological sense—as a foundation for our preferred identity. By establishing a new canon of heroes, political elites create a carefully selected genealogy for themselves—and, by extension, the new nation-state.

Murray's subversion of struggle art and heroism did not go unnoticed by the ruling party. ANC spokesperson, Jackson Mthembu, was apparently appalled by this (mis)appropriation of the words attributed to Mahlangu (Mthembu 2010). But there is something of an irony here. For, as I reveal in this chapter, Mahlangu himself appropriated the words of nineteenth-century Italian nationalist leader Giuseppe Mazzini. The fact that Murray subverted the words of Mahlangu who mimicked Mazzini was lost on Mthembu.

Murray did not pioneer the subversion of struggle art. For instance, the iconic image of Hector Pieterson by photographer Sam Nzima has been satirized in order to deride the ANC's performance in government by the country's leading graphic artists and cartoonists (Simbao 2008, 78). Indeed, Murray has joined a chorus of critics who have suggested that the ANC has betrayed its principles and, thereby, undermined its standing as the leader of the liberation struggle. In this chapter, I will not attempt to ascertain whether there is evidence to substantiate this perception. Instead, I have a much less ambitious agenda: to establish the credentials of Mahlangu as an icon and to ask why he enjoys such status in "The Struggle" narrative that constitutes the founding myth of the nation. Then I will attempt to explain why Mahlangu, who has been used to bolster the ANC's legitimation, is now a casualty of the ruling party's waning credibility.

THE POST-APARTHEID STATE IN SEARCH OF A NATION

Nation and state are not synonymous. Indeed, as Benedict Anderson (1991 [1983]) has shown, nations are made by states more often than the other way around, and "official nationalism" promoted by the state plays a significant role in this process. In the case of South Africa, a postcolonial state has been constructed on the edifice of the old order, while the ANC government's nation-building project has undergone a sequence of reimaginings in the post-apartheid era. Initially, it was envisioned by way of the ubiquitous metaphor of the Rainbow Nation during the Mandela presidency (Baines 1998). Then, during the Mbeki era, this inclusive vision of a nonracial national identity was challenged by a more exclusive Africanist one whereby Mbeki promoted his notion of the African Renaissance. And under Zuma, there have been contradictory manifestations of the national idea: an African populism coexisting with an exclusive and, at times, xenophobic nationalism.

Anderson's apt definition of the nation as an "imagined political community" has come close to being accepted as conventional wisdom in the social sciences and ancillary disciplines. However, only in the second edition of his by-now-classical text did he explore the implications of the expression "imagine"—that is, what it meant to create a sense of belonging through political discourse and communication. According to Anderson (1991, 133), "the most important thing about languages . . . is their capacity for generating imagined communities, building particular solidarities." Apart from language, this imagining may be undertaken through an array of signs and symbols, including pictures or references to persons or objects, such as flags, maps, and monuments. However, Anderson made no more than passing mention of some other examples of visual culture such as posters and postage stamps that may sometimes have a particularly wide reach. In this chapter, I will suggest that these forms of public and official art are deserving of more attention in understanding the construction of the national imaginary than has hitherto been the case.

Legal tender such as banknotes and coins, as well as postage stamps, invariably portrays images of national leaders or symbols. Van den Muijzenberg argues that with stamps, the ruling elite of the state possess an eminent medium whereby they convey *their* representations of the nation. He holds that this is one of the few areas where the state exercises a monopoly over the issue of these symbolic currencies of exchange (Van den Muijzenberg 2000, 270). The elite attempt to legitimate its views of the nation and the state through representations on postage stamps. Few governments admit using stamps for propagandistic purposes. Both democratic and authoritarian societies regard the practice as an expression of the "common good"—in other words, a politically and ethically neutral practice. A more informed sociological analysis would suggest that we can read the dominant views of society and culture, or what Leclerc (1993: 15–48 [1973]) calls an "official imaginary" in the iconography of stamps, as opposed to perspectives of those outside of the hegemonic power structure.

If stamps have been relatively neglected in discussions of symbolic markers that attest to the legitimacy of the regime, sites of memory have not. There is considerable consensus that memorials and monuments are key elements in the symbolic repertoire available to the nation-state to promote processes of collective national identification (Marschall 2010, 7). Anderson's (1991, 174) definition of a monument as a construction that is nonutilitarian, "that is those in which iconography prevails over functionality," is useful for the purposes of this chapter. It allows us to make a connection between monuments and postage stamps. Commemorative stamps have long had little utilitarian value and have been issued largely with collectors and philatelists in mind. And with the advent of the postal franking machines and the internet, definitive stamps too have little use value.[3] Following Murray (2013) and McEachern (2002), I will argue that commemorative practices such as the issue of stamps and the erection of monuments can serve to institutionalize and legitimize the elite's state-sanctioned version of history. I will illustrate my argument with reference to post-apartheid representations of the armed struggle and, specifically, the mythicization of the martyr-hero Solomon Mahlangu.

(Mis)REPRESENTING AND (Dis)REMEMBERING THE ARMED STRUGGLE

If the reproduction of the nation-state depends on a dialectic of remembering and forgetting (Billig 1995, 10), then South Africa's new ruling elites have been very arbitrary in what they have chosen to remember or deliberately forget. There has been considerable emphasis on the ANC's struggle narrative within the metanarrative of new nationhood (Meskell and Scheermeyer 2008, 154, 155, 158; Popescu 2013, 190–205). And yet the liberation movement's armed wing, MK, enjoys a rather ambiguous position in this narrative and the politics of post-apartheid South Africa (Davis 2010).

The ANC was a revolutionary organization during its years of exile, yet it always posited the primacy of the political over the military struggle. And although it recruited thousands into the ranks of MK and trained many as guerrillas and saboteurs, few actually infiltrated South Africa to engage with the security forces. If they were deployed at all, it was more likely that they fought against the Rhodesian armed forces or the National Union for the Total Independence of Angola (UNITA) in Angola. Most cadres wiled away many years in camps in Angola, Tanzania, and Zambia. Indeed, MK was characterized by its restraint and ineffectiveness (Cherry 2011, 130). Although the ANC benefitted by projecting itself as a militant organization, the armed struggle did not play a significant role in bringing about the demise of the apartheid state. Thus MK was never able to march triumphant into Pretoria as it was not a victorious liberation army. But the myth that apartheid was overthrown largely through the armed struggle has been perpetuated by political elites (Ellis 2012, 301).

MK members were demoralized when romantic notions of returning as conquering heroes were dashed by the anticlimactic negotiations with the erstwhile enemy. Some were demobilized and opted for gratuities or pension payouts. Others were integrated into the South African National Defence Force (SANDF), but relatively few became professional soldiers. Some from the officer corps attained prominent positions in the party and government. But rank and file MK members did not fare as well. Exile created a culture of dependency, and this, combined with a lack of experience of the market economy, meant that those with only military skills to offer found it difficult to find employment or set up a business. Indeed, some veterans expected the state to take care of their needs. When the financially wasteful vocational programs failed to teach marketable skills, many swelled the ranks of the under- and unemployed. For the most part, the reintegration of MK veterans into civilian society was unsuccessful, and they remained a somewhat stigmatized group. Thus, some resorted to criminal activities to make ends meet and others to substance abuse rather than seeking counseling for posttraumatic stress and other disorders (Mashike 2007, 351–78). In short, aggrieved MK veterans believe they were the sacrificial victims of the negotiated settlement. Like ex-combatants or soldiers from many other wars, many of those who felt betrayed embraced a discourse of victimhood (Baines and Gear 2013, 263–73).

Given the factionalism, internal dissensions, leadership disputes, and corruption in the organization, the MK Military Veterans Association (MKMVA) was unable to promote the interests of its members in the early years of the democratic dispensation. The fortunes of some MK veterans have changed for the better since Zuma was elected ANC president and subsequently became head of state. Their treatment under Zuma's predecessors had been inconsistent and opportunistic. MK veterans had been used as a "political football" by the ANC leadership, sometimes courted as a political asset and other times disowned as a liability or embarrassment. Ensuring the political loyalty of MK veterans so as to avert serious social disruption comes at a cost. Indeed, the political capital to be gained or the cost of placating MK veterans has increased significantly (Baines and Gear 2013).

The Zuma administration has recognized (former nonstatutory) military veterans as a special interest group. The MKMVA has come to comprise an influential lobby group as it has insisted on benefits and access to resources as the coffers of the state have been systematically plundered. The ANC determined to make the MKMVA a voting bloc in the election of its national executive committee at its Polokwane Conference in 2007. Then, in 2009, Military Veterans became a separate ministry within the Department of Defence. The ministry was tasked with addressing the plight of military veterans by introducing new legislation to create a comprehensive framework for dealing with their specific interests and needs. Following considerable controversy as to who qualified as a veteran,[4] the Military Veterans Bill was passed as Act No. 18 of 2011. According to the deputy minister, the bill was designed to enhance the well-being and quality of life of veterans through an incremental realization of socioeconomic opportunities. But the means to fund the provisions of the Military Veterans Act still have to be found by a treasury that has to meet a range of demands from bona fide stakeholders and Zuma's patrons.

The creation of a ministry dedicated to veterans affairs means that the Zuma government has followed the lead of South Africa's neighboring states (notably, Namibia and Zimbabwe) in seeking to address the needs of a group that regards itself as marginalized and neglected by the very liberation movement that it helped bring to power. But unlike these states that have honored their ex-combatants as victors in the armed struggles by way of the erection of monumental Heroes' Acres outside of Windhoek and Harare, respectively, the ANC has accorded only limited recognition to the sacrifices of MK cadres. This is on account of the negligible role that MK and the armed struggle played in the country's liberation, as well as how its contribution to the struggle is perceived in the present.

Stephen Davis poses the problem in the following terms: "How does a ruling party claim legitimacy from a purportedly victorious liberation struggle that included a less than victorious army? How do you deploy the image of MK but not 'let slip the dogs of war?'" In other words, how does the ANC invoke the militant spirit of the armed struggle without promoting violence? Davis (2010, 307–8) adds that these questions address "more than who is, and who is not, a part of the South African nation." It is about claims of belonging to the nation, of rights of citizenship, and of how nationalism is constituted through state-sanctioned national monuments. And it is also about how the armed struggle has been represented in other state-funded projects such as school textbooks, official histories, and so on. Equally, it is about how the people constitute their own recollections through counter-memorials and public art.

The ANC government has attempted to revive the image of MK by according it victories that it never won on the battlefield. Thus at its aforementioned Polokwane Conference, the party resolved to celebrate the twentieth anniversary of the battle of Cuito Cuanavale, which it described as "a decisive defeat of South African racist forces and their UNITA surrogates." The delegates further resolved that in consultation with Angola, Namibia, Cuba, and Russia to arrange countrywide celebrations to cultivate public awareness of the "sacrifices of the revolutionary forces" in winning a crucial battle in South Africa's liberation struggle (ANC NEC 2008). This sentiment was endorsed by the ANC's National Executive Committee at its March 2008 meeting, although its statement toned down the rhetoric of the original resolution. It "paid tribute to many thousands of Angolans, Cubans, Namibians and South Africans for their sacrifices in the fight against the forces of apartheid and imperialism in the protracted Angolan war" (ANC NEC 2008). This was followed by a media briefing where a program to commemorate the battle of Cuito Cuanavale was announced.

The commemorative activities were sponsored by Parliament's Millennium Project (PMP), the legislature's primary nation-building and heritage agency. The PMP's mission was to ensure that the younger generation be made aware of the battle of Cuito Cuanavale. According to Themba Wakashe, the then director-general of the Department of Arts and Culture, "the commemoration should deal with issues of memory and legacy of this liberation struggle. And it is important to invest in the minds of the younger generation a sense of history, heritage and identity" (Parliament of the Republic of South Africa 2008, 4). ANC Member of Parliament Zoliswa Kota added that it was imperative to "ensure that this famed battle is not relegated to the obsolete depths of history [and stressed the need] to bring Cuito

Cuanavale into our school history and to the public consciousness . . . it's events like these that can act as catalysts to the rewriting of our history" (Parliament of the Republic of South Africa 2008, 5). Such "revisionism" was regarded by critics as a government ploy to foist the ANC's version of events on the public. Acrimonious exchanges followed in the columns of the national press and in numerous blogs in cyberspace (Addison 2008).

The flagship PMP-sponsored event was a Heritage Journey that involved a party of "stakeholders" undertaking a trip from Freedom Park in Pretoria to Cuito Cuanavale in March 2008.[5] The party included military veterans, as well as representatives from government and civil society. At the battle site, the party was joined by ANC president Zuma, representatives of the Angolan government, and other dignitaries. A commemorative ceremony to honor those who died during the battle was held. Wreaths were laid at the monument although it was (mistakenly) reported that they were placed on the graves of MK veterans who had purportedly died during the battle of Cuito Cuanavale (ANC 2008). The South African Broadcasting Corporation (SABC) threw its weight behind the project when it commissioned and screened a documentary film called *The End of the World* about the journey on its Special Assignment program. The broadcast occasioned a storm of controversy. Most of the objections were to the reiteration of the ANC's narrative of the battle of Cuito Cuanavale as a SADF defeat and catalyst of transformation in South Africa (SABC News 2008).

As an MK veteran, Zuma made a number of undertakings to his former comrades in arms. One of these was the erection of a monument in honor of fallen MK members who died in the battle of Cuito Cuanavale. He vowed to reinter the remains of fallen MK soldiers and place memorials on their graves. Notwithstanding an absence of any corroboration of the story that MK members had participated in the battle of Cuito Cuanavale, Zuma was convinced that "there had to be existing evidence that there were South Africans buried there" (Anonymous 2008). Zuma has persisted in making the unsubstantiated claim that MK soldiers had died as heroes and heroines at Cuito Cuanavale. In a speech delivered in 2010, he reiterated this theme (Barnard n.d., 9). MK combatants based in camps in Angola were actually involved in assisting the People's Armed Forces of Liberation of Angola (FAPLA) to destroy UNITA because Savimbi was allied with the apartheid regime. But they were deployed mostly on the eastern and northeastern fronts and not in the southeast of the country. Still, Zuma has desperately attempted to lay claim to a share of Cuba's victory so that it would redound to MK's glory. But he has omitted to remind his supporters of the disconcerting fact that the governments of both Angola and Cuba consented to the expulsion of MK from Angola as part of the agreement negotiated with the apartheid regime in 1988 (Cherry 2011, 97). This selective remembrance and self-serving revision of the historical record reveals the lengths that the ANC has gone to bolster the image of its armed wing as "victors." Yet, it has not been an unqualified success.

Stephen Davis (2010, 354) has reflected on the ambiguous legacy of MK and the armed struggle as follows: "No one has figured how to address the Janus-faced nature of MK; the victory for the heroes, those who made it after the transition, and the hard reality of the anti-heroes, those who did not make it after the transition. The national idea gives no reasons why some should be remembered and others should be forgotten." Davis reckons that the ambiguous place of MK in the country's history is reflected in the public sphere. He observes that "the handful of MK monuments and collections that now exist bear a few marks of this indecision. Most collections are notable for the way they are not marked. Several museums decontextualized their displayed collections of MK weapons, uniforms, and printed propaganda" (Davis 2010, 314).

This state of affairs might have as much to do with the limited amount of knowledge about the MK in the public domain and the financial and other constraints under which archivists, curators, librarians, and other state functionaries have to operate. Whereas the ruling party has committed considerable resources to commemorating "The Struggle," in heritage projects such as Freedom Park and Robben Island, it has not seen fit to prioritize the preservation of archives and artefacts.[6] With the profusion of struggle (auto)biographies that "assert a heroic self-identity" (Murray 2013, 183), narratives by luminaries in the liberation movement might be exemplary but are far from typical. The swashbuckling, romantic adventure story of an MK commander like Ronnie Kasrils was far removed from the experience of rank and file members (Murray 2013, 184). Neither they nor their struggle narratives occupy a prominent place in the public imaginary or monumental art forms. This is exemplified by Freedom Park.

In her chapter in this volume, Elizabeth Rankin describes the conceptualization and composite design of Freedom Park, as well as its phased construction. It is in part a place of propitiation, part peace sanctuary, and

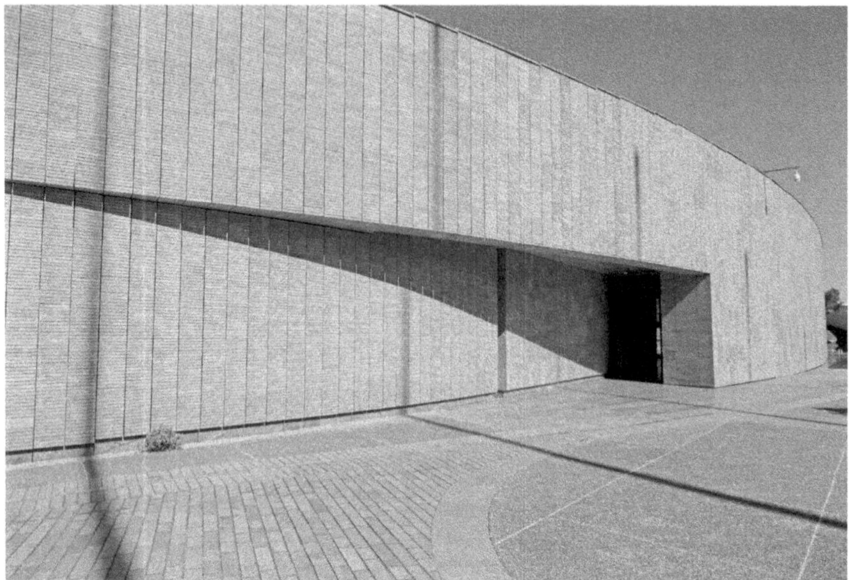

Fig. 6.2 Freedom Park. Wall of Names on the building included in *S'khumbuto. Photograph by Paul Mills.*

part war memorial. The last-mentioned site includes a series of walls that pay tribute to casualties of the country's earlier colonial wars of dispossession and resistance, the South African War, and the World Wars. The largest and tallest of these walls is *S'khumbuto,* which honors those "who died for liberation" (fig. 6.2). The names of struggle heroes are arranged in no particular order thereby avoiding creating a hierarchy. It includes clusters of names comprising victims of state violence (e.g., the Sharpeville massacre) but not of MK operations or acts of resistance. All those complicit in the apartheid system, whether SADF soldiers or uniformed policemen, state functionaries, collaborators, and all those deemed to have been villains of the piece (or peace) are excluded. The many anomalies evident in the selection of names suggest that the criteria used to determine who merits inclusion have been inconsistently applied and the verification process is flawed. Still, Davis (2010, 326) chooses to read the walls as "a text that contains an ideological codex drawn from the national idea." He elaborates: "Who gets on these walls and the reasons why underpin the logic of the national idea. For the liberation struggle the ends justified the means, for the apartheid state the means did not justify the ends, nor did the ends justify the means. Like it or not, this is the Manichaen black and white world of the national idea" (Davis 2010, 329). In other words, there are no shades of gray; one either supported or opposed apartheid in this binary version of the liberation struggle.

Davis holds that the confusion in conceptualization and design of Freedom Park obfuscates what the site has to say about MK's place in South African history. The names of MK members are not grouped together. Davis (2010, 331) points out that

> the names of struggle heroes who were members of MK are interspersed among the names of struggle heroes who were not members of MK. There is no way of telling one affiliation from another other, unless you already know who to look for and what affiliation they had. Thus they avoid the trap of Heroes Acre, and fall into a stranger predicament, that MK is dispersed within the national idea and, in some sense, anonymized by it. Sikhumbuto, siSwati for "We Remember" is actually a place where we "disremember" MK.

It is worth noting another anomaly: whereas the names of deceased MK cadres appear on Wall of Names in their individual capacities, there is a discrete section of the wall devoted to the Cuban soldiers who died in Angola during tours of duty fighting the SADF or the "apartheid army." Thus, the Cubans have been accorded a collective identity by the park's curators but MK cadres have not.

Solomon Mahlangu's name appears on the Wall of Names (fig. 6.3) under "Executions/Hangings" and without any specific attempt to identify him as a "freedom fighter." But through other forms of public art, he has been singled out by the ruling party and government for mythicization and canonization.

THE MYTHICIZATION OF SOLOMON MAHLANGU

In November 2009, the South African Post Office issued a standard postage stamp to commemorate the thirtieth anniversary of the death of Solomon Kalushi Mahlangu. The stamp (fig. 6.4) reproduces a portrait of Mahlangu superimposed on a replica of a document of the Rand Supreme Court that outlines the charges brought against the defendant. The anonymous portrait had been donated to Mahlangu's family after his death. The stamp was sold as a souvenir sheet that bore the inscription "The Legend of Freedom!" It also cited the words *my blood will nourish the tree that will bare* [sic] *the*

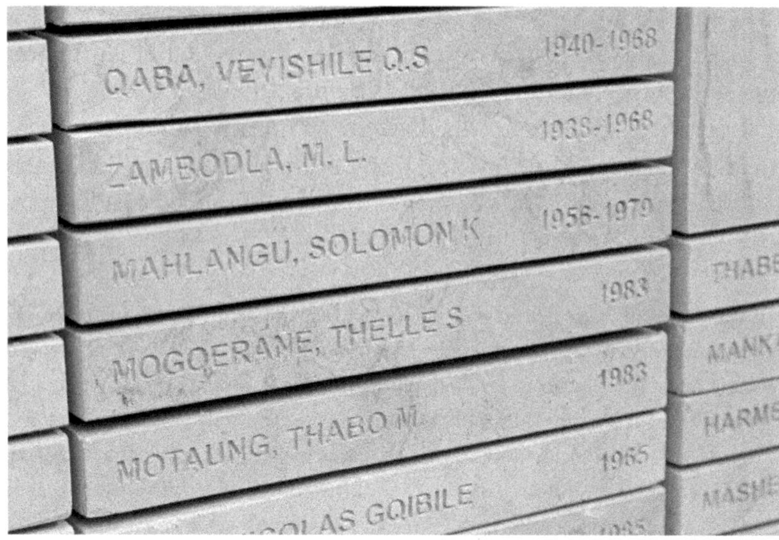

Fig. 6.3 Freedom Park. Detail of Wall of Names with Solomon Mahlangu included among those who were victims of "Executions/Hangings." *Photograph by Paul Mills.*

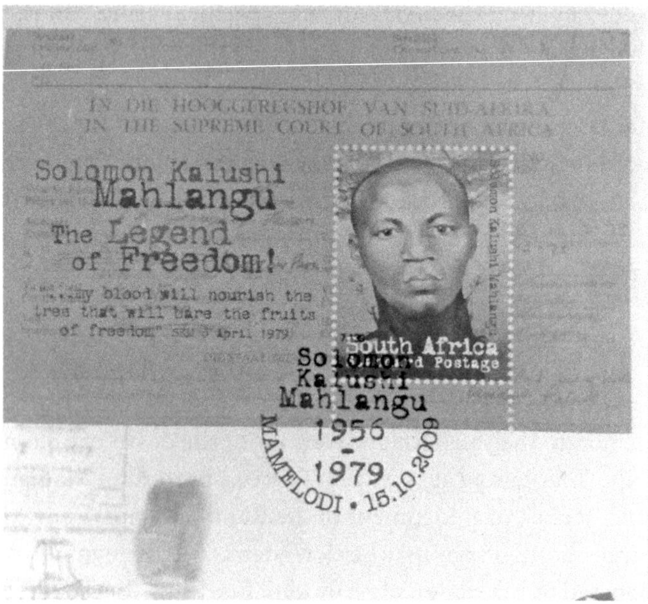

Fig. 6.4 Stamp produced by the South African Post Office to commemorate the thirtieth anniversary of the death of Solomon Kalushi Mahlangu (2009).

fruits of freedom, reputedly the last Mahlangu uttered before being hanged. These, as we already know, are not original and have been attributed to the nineteenth-century Italian nationalist leader Giuseppe Mazzini and if actually uttered by Mahlangu, were presumably memorized.

As I have already suggested, postage stamps are far from ideologically innocent or politically neutral. Stamp issuance policies serve as vehicles for identity creation and propagation and as mechanisms for regime legitimation (Deans and Dobson 2005, 6). As a government agent, the South African Post Office's philatelic services seek to project a certain image of the country. Representation of heroes fits into this commemorative ideological practice (Jones 2001). Its issue of the souvenir sheet underscores Mahlangu's immortalization as a martyr who was executed by the apartheid regime and thus sacrificed his life for the (national) liberation struggle. As far as I am aware, he is the first cadre to be honored in this manner. If a postage stamp is a visual signifier of official national culture, then Mahlangu is an icon.

How and why has Mahlangu been elevated to the status of a struggle icon? Who was he?

We have only snippets of information about Mahlangu's short life. But from what we are able to piece together, his story is typical of the so-called class of '76, those black youths who came of age politically in the harsh discriminatory and oppressive climate of apartheid South Africa in the 1970s.

Mahlangu grew up in the Pretoria township of Mamelodi where his mother supported the family on the meager wages of a domestic servant. He was unable to complete his schooling because he was caught up in the student uprising of 1976 that erupted following the imposition of Afrikaans as a medium of instruction in black schools. The demonstrations started in Soweto where students were fired upon by trigger-happy security police. Following these killings, the uprising spread to other townships such as Mamelodi where Mahlangu attended high school. He joined his peers in expressing his discontent and so became one of the many youths who faced the prospect of detention by the feared security police.

At the age of nineteen, Mahlangu fled South Africa and joined the ranks of MK. While in exile in Angola and Mozambique, he received military training and ideological instruction or indoctrination. He slipped back into the country via Swaziland in June 1977 as part of the Young Lions Detachment that sought to establish underground cells and conduct sabotage and other operations. Members of the detachment carried arms, explosives, and

ANC pamphlets in dead letter boxes. They successfully escaped detection until the security police cornered them while en route to a remembrance service for the victims of the 1976 uprising. Mahlangu and two other MK cadres who sought refuge in a warehouse in Goch Street, Johannesburg, were ambushed. In the ensuing exchange of fire, two white civilians were killed. Mahlangu and Monty Motloung were captured, but George "Lucky" Mahlangu evaded arrest.

Only Solomon Mahlangu stood trial as Motloung was severely assaulted by police and sustained brain damage that rendered him incapable of making a court appearance. Mahlangu faced two counts of murder and several charges under the Terrorism Act. He pleaded not guilty to the charges. Following the trial proceedings, the presiding judge accepted that he had not fired a shot and was not responsible for the deaths of the civilians. However, he was convicted on the grounds of common purpose and sentenced to death.

Mahlangu's sentence was widely regarded as testament to the legalized brutality of the apartheid regime. It was deemed a travesty of justice and sparked an outcry both domestically and internationally. Desmond Tutu, then secretary-general of the South African Council of Churches, appealed for clemency. The appeal was endorsed by the UN Secretary-General Kurt Waldheim, US President Jimmy Carter, the Organisation of African Unity, certain European governments, and the Anti-Apartheid Movement. For two years, solidarity organizations campaigned against Mahlangu's execution and called on the apartheid state to recognize all captured freedom fighters as prisoners of war rather than terrorists or common criminals (Reddy 1979). The campaigners produced posters, stickers, buttons, and a range of other paraphernalia to promote public awareness and create solidarity against the apartheid regime. However, the international community did not convince Premier B. J. Vorster to grant a pardon and thereby spare Mahlangu's life. He was refused leave to appeal his sentence by the Rand Supreme Court and subsequently by the Bloemfontein Appeal Court. He was duly executed at Pretoria Central Prison on April 6, 1979.

Video footage exists of Mahlangu on death row. It was apparently given to ANC members by prison wardens and policemen as a gesture of goodwill during the 1990s but has come to light only recently. The footage shows that Mahlangu carried himself with dignity to the end. But it does nothing to confirm that he went to the gallows shouting ANC slogans such as

"Amandla!" (Power!). The footage was screened by the SABC as part of a program that commemorated the thirtieth anniversary of Mahlangu's execution. Despite its ostensible documentary format, the program verged on advocacy journalism. It makes the case for Mahlangu as a hero-martyr of the liberation struggle, which is exactly how he has been depicted in the ANC's political narrative.

Mahlangu paid the ultimate price for his commitment to the armed struggle. If his execution was intended to scare potential MK recruits, it proved counterproductive. Thousands of youths left the country and swelled the ranks of the liberation armies. This, in turn, galvanized the ANC to pursue the liberation struggle with renewed vigor. The so-called Mahlangu Campaign included strategies such as applying pressure on governments to enforce sanctions in order to isolate the apartheid state. The campaign also included efforts to raise awareness via visual and other media. The aforementioned poster produced by Medu, depicting an armed ANC cadre in silhouette with words attributed to Mahlangu superimposed thereon, was disseminated via international solidarity organizations.

Mahlangu was further honored in 1979 when a college established for MK cadres in Tanzania was named after him. The Solomon Mahlangu Freedom College (SOMAFCO) became an institution where a generation of political exiles was educated. Following the political transition, SOMAFCO was relocated to Mahlangu's birthplace, Mamelodi, where it provides a service to the local community. Here, Mahlangu is remembered as one of the class of '76 who sacrificed education for the sake of liberation—a strategy only retrospectively recognized as having produced the so-called lost generation.

In 1991, an improvised and rather crude statue that pays tribute to MK's "fallen heroes" was erected in the renamed Solomon Mahlangu Freedom Square in Mamelodi. It was commissioned by the Mamelodi Civic Association and funded by the local community. A welder constructed a stylized figure made from square tubing holding aloft a wheel, shield, and spear—symbols derived from the ANC logo. The statue was unveiled by Chris Hani, then MK's chief of staff, who himself became a martyr-hero after his assassination by white extremists. The statue was targeted by reactionaries who attempted to destroy but only succeeded in partially damaging it. The statue was placed in safe custody until it could be re-erected in 1995. By this time, Mahlangu's remains had been exhumed from an Atteridgeville grave and reinterred in the square. Marschall (2010, 42) reckons that the makeshift MK statue had "immense historical importance" as the very first public memorial erected in honor of the liberation movement in post-apartheid South Africa. This may be so. But what commenced as a community project was subsequently co-opted by the ruling party and the state.

In 2005, the well-known South African sculptor Angus Taylor was commissioned by the Tshwane Metropolitan Municipality to produce a statue of Mahlangu for the site bearing his name (Masombuka 2005). Taylor recounts that he consulted with Mahlangu's mother and members of the Mamelodi community in order to gather information about his subject. He managed to source a photograph and an extremely poor quality video of Mahlangu exiting the courthouse during his trial. From these, he modeled a likeness in clay and then cast a bronze mold of a 3.7 meters high (twice life-size) statue of Mahlangu dressed in camouflage combat fatigues (http://www.angustaylor.co.za/). The unarmed figure was more of a generic combatant than a faithful representation of Mahlangu. It cradles a globe that possibly suggests a quest for learning rather than confrontation with the forces of oppression. The statue was unveiled in Freedom Square on September 17, 2005 (fig. 6.5).

In wishing to further divest the figure of its militancy, Taylor resolved to give material expression to the words *My blood will nourish the tree that will bear the fruits of freedom* attributed to Mahlangu. The statue's pedestal was designed to represent the roots of a tree and plaques signifying the "fruits of freedom" were affixed thereto. Taylor involved two Mamelodi primary schools in the project. Children were asked to visualize and draw what they considered to be these "fruits." The best drawings were chosen and the children were taught how to model these drawings into clay that Taylor's studio provided. A number of these clay reliefs were selected by Elizabeth Mahlangu on behalf of the Metro Council, cast into bronze plaques and attached to the plinth. Unfortunately, these plaques have been stolen for scrap, which might suggest that certain members of the local community have little invested in the project (Artefacts 2012). Even aesthetically acclaimed public art is unlikely to escape vandalism or enjoy pride of place in a community that has pressing material needs.

The substitution of the Mahlangu statue for that of an abstract MK soldier meant that he effectively came to embody or personify the armed struggle. Both members of the community and visitors to the site can literally look up to Mahlangu for he has become larger in death than in life. The

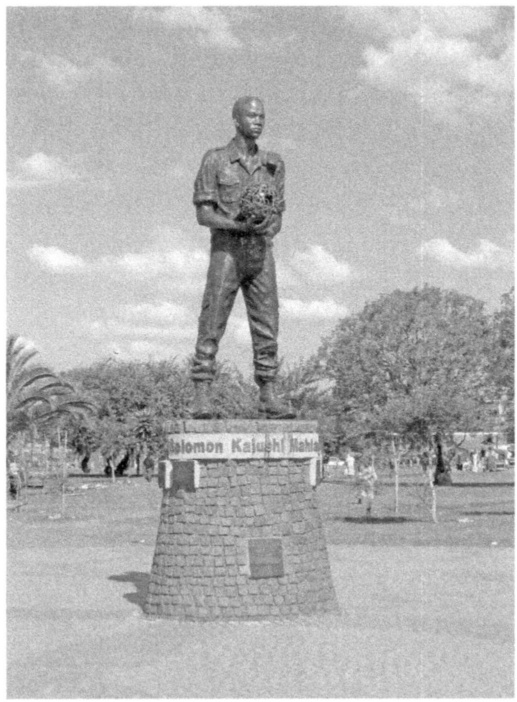

Fig. 6.5 Angus Taylor, *Solomon Mahlangu* (2005), bronze, Mamelodi, Tshwane. *Photograph courtesy of Sabine Marschall.*

very monumentality of this imposing statue legitimates the establishment of the new sociopolitical order by the ruling party (Marschall 2008). Thus, the precinct was not merely "upgraded" but inscribed with new meaning, with the ANC reclaiming a public space on behalf of the community that serves as a microcosm of the nation.

Following Mahlangu's canonization as a "Struggle" stalwart, the ruling party has sought to keep him in the public eye. Aside from the issue of the commemorative stamp and the erection of the statue, regular tributes have been paid to Mahlangu by ANC leaders and government spokespersons. In a lecture on the life of Mahlangu to the ANC Youth League Congress in 2008, Deputy President Kgalema Motlanthe proclaimed that Mahlangu's "courage and dedication to the people's cause . . . symbolised the spirit of the youth of 1976 and the fighting traditions of our people. He was a shining example of a revolutionary patriot to all future generations of South Africans" (Motlanthe 2008). In his 2009 state of the nation speech, Acting President

Motlanthe made a connection between Mahlangu and the warrior traditions of the indigenous African people who fought colonialism: "Solomon Mahlangu was continuing a tradition of the warriors of yesteryear, among whom we count those under King Cetshwayo who in 1879 defeated the British army in Isandlwana, in defence of the freedom of the indigenous people of our country and the sovereignty of their lands" (Motlanthe 2009). The speech invoked traditions of resistance against colonialism and suggested continuities with the anti-apartheid struggle. Mahlangu was placed on a par with warriors who died fighting for their independence.

In an address on the thirtieth anniversary of Mahlangu's death, President Zuma called the living "the custodians of the collective memory of fallen comrades." He would have been more accurate to assign this responsibility to the political elites. Zuma (2009) also reiterated that Mahlangu said that "my blood will nourish the tree that bears the fruits of freedom." The ANC has continued to invoke the spirit of Solomon Mahlangu on each anniversary of his death (Mthembu 2010). Statements issued on these occasions have taken on the character of ritualized incantations. They serve to reinforce the myth of the armed struggle that underscores the state-sanctioned narrative of liberation in post-apartheid South Africa.

CONCLUSION

The political elites and custodians of memory in the "new" South Africa have designated popular resistance to white domination as the national narrative. This triumphalist master narrative of the liberation struggle serves as the foundation myth of post-apartheid South Africa. Thus, Solomon Mahlangu has been elevated to the status of a hero-martyr whose cause was vindicated by the victory of the ANC over the apartheid regime. Accordingly, he has become an iconic figure in "The Struggle." The commissioning of a commemorative stamp and monument honoring Mahlangu bears testimony to this. However, the limited efficacy of the armed struggle has meant that MK's legacy is somewhat ambiguous. And the debunking of the myth of the armed struggle has only confirmed as much.

South Africa's memorial landscape is now dotted with "Struggle" sites (Harrison 2004; Marschall 2010). As befitting its flagship status as a heritage site, Freedom Park is spectacular and grandiose in style. However, it was not modeled on war monuments such as Heroes Acre that pay tribute to a revolutionary fighting spirit (and militarized masculinity) nor does it valorize the armed struggle. If anything, the curators of Freedom Park have ignored or deliberately disregarded the role of MK in the liberation struggle. For as much as the elites seek to construct a coherent narrative that serves the nation-building project, their story necessarily serves a particular political purpose: to justify the ANC's actions in the past and confer legitimacy on it as the ruling party. Indeed, the institutionalization of memory inscribed in public art can serve to reinforce this project.

According to Levinson (1998, 39), "art placed within [public] spaces is almost always the product of some instrumental purpose outside the domain of pure aesthetics." Yet, a particular reading of public art cannot be prescribed, nor can the inculcation of "appropriate" attitudes toward the public order be guaranteed. This is the case with respect to the commemoration of Mahlangu. Whereas the MK cadre's sacrifice once symbolized the movement's commitment to a selfless act for an oppressed people, it now represents an idealism betrayed by a cohort of greedy and corrupt politicians. The ANC's loss of moral authority has devalued the armed struggle and the principles for which it fought in liberating the country. Rather than affirming the ANC's liberation credentials and buttressing its legitimacy, Mahlangu's representation in various forms of public art has yielded little dividend for the ruling party. For the ANC's conduct in office has actually devalued his iconic status. "Struggle" martyr-heroes such as Mahlangu have become casualties once again.

Gary Baines is Professor and Head of the History Department at Rhodes University in Grahamstown, South Africa. He is the author of *South Africa's 'Border War': Contested Narratives and Conflicting Memories* and coeditor of *Beyond the Border War: New Perspectives on Southern Africa's Late Cold War Conflicts.*

Notes

1. Medu is a sePedi word meaning "roots."
2. Myth signifies the body of stories through which a certain group of people—in this instance the nation—relate its history. See Sabin (2013).
3. The eclipse of letter writing and its replacement by e-mail has meant that the issue of postage stamps are primarily for commemorative rather than utilitarian purposes. Nowadays, stamps are issued for the sake of collectors rather than to consumers wishing to pay the costs of postage. Alongside the decline of the numbers of

government-sanctioned postal stamps, privately produced artistamps or parastamps have proliferated during the last four decades. This constitutes a form of public art. See Anonymous (2007), the catalog of the Exhibition from the Artistamp Collection of Artpool Art Research Center.

4. The dispute over the definition of a "veteran" was politically charged. It encompassed debates regarding the status of former SADF members (and conscripts), as well as that of the Self-Defence Units (SDUs).

5. PMP, Commemoration of the 20th Anniversary of the Battle of Cuito Cuanavale, Official Short-Term Programme of Events 2008. This included a public forum at Rhodes University on May 28, 2008, that featured Ronnie Kasrils, then minister of intelligence services, and General Roland de Vries (ret.), commander of the SADF's 61 Mechanised Battalion during the battle of Cuito Cuanavale. For the text of Kasril's talk, see Kasrils (2008).

6. The Truth and Reconciliation Commission Archives was digitized, but it has not been always accessible to the public as the host site is unreliable.

References

Addison, G. 2008. "Fighting over the Memory of a Battle Nobody Won." *Business Day*, February 25, 2008.

African National Congress (ANC). 2008. "ANC Commemorates the Battle of Cuito Cuanavale." Accessed February 17, 2015. http://www.anc.org.za/ancdocs/pr/2008/pr0319a.html.

African National Congress National Executive Committee (ANC NEC). 2008. "Statement of the Second Ordinary Meeting of the Year, Ekurhuleni, 17 March 2008." Accessed February 17, 2015. http://www.anc.org.za/ancdocs/pr2008/pr0317.html.

Anderson, B. 1983. *Imagined Communities: Reflections on the Origins and Spread of Nationalism*. London: Verso.

Anderson, B. 1983. *Imagined Communities: Reflections on the Origins and Spread of Nationalism*, 2nd ed. London: Verso.

Anonymous. 2007. *Parastamp: Four decades of Artstamps, from Fluxus to the Internet*. Budapest: Szepmuveszeti.

Anonymous. 2008. "Fallen MK Soldiers Honoured." Accessed February 12, 2015. www.news24/SouthAfrica/Politics/Fallen-MK-soldiers-honoured-20080324.

Artefacts. 2012. "Statue of Solomon Mahlangu, Pretoria, Gauteng." Accessed February 12, 2015. http://www.artefacts.co.za/main/Buildings/bldgframes.php?bldgid=10357.

Baines, G. 1998. "The Rainbow Nation? Identity and Nation Building in Post-Apartheid South Africa." *Mots Pluriels* 7. Accessed March 6, 2015. http://motspluriels.arts.uwa.edu.au/MP798gb.html.

Baines, G., and S. Gear. 2013. "Military Veterans as Victims." In *Victimology in South Africa*, edited by R. Peacock, 263–73. Pretoria: Van Schaik.

Barnard, T. N.d. "Cuito Cuanavale (1987–88): A Dialogue on Commemoration." Unpublished paper. Accessed February 17, 2015. http://www.academia.edu/715057/CUITO_CUANAVALE_1987-1988_A_DIALOGUE_ON_COMMEMORATION.

Billig, M. 1995. *Banal Nationalism*. London: Sage.

Cherry, J. 2011. *Umkhonto weSizwe: A Jacana Pocket History*. Auckland Park, South Africa: Jacana Media.

Corrigall, M. 2012. "Mimicking the Master." *Sunday Independent*, June 10, LifeArt Section, p. 5.

Davis, S. R. 2010. "Cosmopolitans in Close Quarters: Everyday Life in the Ranks of Umkhonto we Sizwe (1961–Present)." Unpublished PhD diss., University of Florida.

Deans, P., and H. Dobson. 2005. "Introduction: East Asian Postage Stamps as Socio-Political Artefacts." *East Asia* 22: 3–11.

Ellis, S. 2012. *External Mission: The ANC in Exile*. Johannesburg and Cape Town: Jonathan Ball.

Harrison, P. 2004. *South Africa's Top Sites: Struggle*. Cape Town: Kenilworth New Africa Books.

Jones, R. A. 2001. "Heroes of the Nation? The Celebration of Scientists on the Postage Stamps of Great Britain, France and West Germany." *Journal of Contemporary History* 36, no. 3: 403–22.

Kasrils, R. 2008. "'Historic Turning Point at Cuito Cuanavale,' Address to Public Forum on the 20th Anniversary of Cuito Cuanavale." Rhodes University, May 28. Accessed February 17, 2015. http://www.pmpsa.gov.za/FILES/pdfs/Kasrils.pdf.

Leclerc, J. 1973. "Iconologie politique du timbre poste Indonésien (1950–1970)." *Archipel* 6: 145–83. [Translation: Scott, N., trans. 1993. "The Political Iconology of the Indonesian Postage Stamp (1950–1970)." *Indonesia* 57: 15–48.]

Levinson, S. 1998. *Written in Stone: Public Monuments in Changing Societies*. Durham, NC: Duke University Press.

Marschall, S. 2006. "Commemorating 'Struggle Heroes': Constructing a Genealogy for the New South Africa." *International Journal of Heritage Studies* 2: 176–93.

———. 2008. "Pointing to the Dead: Victims, Martyrs and Public Memory." *South African Historical Journal* 60: 103–24.

———. 2010. *Landscape of Memory: Commemorative Monuments, Memorials and Public Statuary in Post-Apartheid South Africa*. Leiden, the Netherlands: Brill.

Mashike, L. 2007. "'Some of Us Know Nothing Except Military Skills': South Africa's Former Guerrilla Combatants." In *State of the Nation: South Africa 2007*, edited by S. Buhluncu, J. Daniel, and R. Southall, 351–78. Pretoria: HSRC Press.

Masombuka, S. 2005. "Tshwane to Honour Hero Solomon Mahlangu." *Daily Sun*, May 9, 2005. Accessed February 12, 2015. http://152.111.1.87/argief/berigte/dailysun/2005/05/09/DS/04/02.html.

McEachern, C. 2002. *Narratives of Nation Media, Memory and Representation in the Making of the New South Africa*. New York: Nova Science.

Meskell, L., and C. Scheermeyer. 2008. "Heritage as Therapy: Set Pieces from the New South Africa." *Journal of Material Culture* 13, no. 2: 153–73.

Motlanthe, K. 2008. "A Lecture on the Life of Solomon Kalushi Mahlangu Delivered at the 23rd National Conference of the ANC Youth League Conference." Accessed February 17, 2015. http://www.anc.org.za/show.php?id=4075.

Motlanthe, K. 2009. "State of the Nation Address of the President of South Africa, Kgalema Motlanthe, to the Joint Sitting of Parliament, Cape Town, 6

February 2009." Accessed February 17, 2015. http://www.info.gov.za/speeches/2009/09020611061001.htm.

Mthembu, J. 2010. "Statement by Jackson Mthembu, ANC National Spokesperson, 'The ANC Salutes Solomon Mahlangu—Hero of Our Struggle.'" April 6. Accessed February 17, 2015. http://www.anc.org.za/show.php?id=2386.

Murray, M. J. 2013. *Commemorating and Forgetting: Challenges for the New South Africa.* Minneapolis: University of Minnesota Press.

Popescu, M. 2013. "War Room Stories and the Rainbow Nation: Competing Narratives in Contemporary South African Literature." In *National Myths: Constructed Pasts, Contested Presents,* edited by Gerard Bouchard, 190–205. Abingdon, UK: Routledge.

Reddy, E. S. 1979. "Speech at a Meeting of the Presidential Committee of the World Peace Council in Memory of Solomon Mahlangu by ES Reddy, Prague, 11 April 1979." Accessed February 17, 2015. http://www.anc.org.za/show.php?id=4266.

Parliament of the Republic of South Africa. 2008. "In Session, Cuito Cuanavale Commemoration, July 2008, 4." Accessed February 12, 2015. http://www.parliament.gov.za/content/insession%2015.08.081~1~1.pdf.

Sabin, E. 2013. *Revolution, Rebellion, Resistance: The Power of Story.* London: Zed Books.

Simbao, R. K. 2008. "The 30th Anniversary of the Soweto Uprisings: Reading the Shadow in Sam Nzima's Iconic Photograph of Hector Pieterson." In *Footprints of the "Class of 76": Commemoration, Memory, Mapping and Heritage,* edited by A. Hlongwane, 131–76. Johannesburg: Hector Pieterson Memorial & Museum.

South African Broadcasting Corporation News (SABC). 2008. "All Set for Angolan Battle Commemoration." March 21. Accessed February 12, 2015. http://www.sabcnews.com/portal/site/.

———. 2009. "SA Honours Struggle Hero, Solomon Mahlangu." April 6. Accessed February 12, 2015. http://www.sabcnews.com/portal/site/.

Suttner, R. 2008. *The ANC Underground in South Africa to 1976.* Auckland Park, South Africa: Jacana Media.

Taylor, A. "Angus Taylor." [Website] http://www.angustaylor.co.za/index.html.

Van den Muijzenberg, O. 2000. "Faces of the Nation in Postage Stamps." In *Old Ties and New Solidarities: Studies on Philippine Communities,* edited by C. J.-H. Macdonald and G. M. Pesignan, 269–99. Quezon City, Philippines: Ateneo de Manila University Press.

Zuma, J. 2009. "Address by ANC President Jacob Zuma on the Occasion of the Thirtieth Anniversary of the Execution of MK Hero Solomon Kalushi Mahalangu at Pretoria City Hall, 4 April 2009." Accessed February 17, 2015. http://www.anc.org.za/show.php?id=3761.

PART 3

ERASURES AND RUINS

CHAPTER 7

The Pain of Memory and the Violence of Erasure: Real and Figural Displays of Female Authority in the Public Sphere

KIM MILLER

If social change is, necessarily, about encountering resistance, negotiating power relations, and altering boundaries, it must engage in the politics of visibility in public space.
Adrienne Burk

DURING THE NIGHT OF January 26, 2011, two young white men visited a memorial site where a life-sized bronze statue depicting Nokuthula Simelane, a former female struggle activist, stood. Alone with the statue, the two men took a long rope out of their truck and tightly wrapped it around the figure. Once the body was sufficiently bound, the men fastened one end of the rope to the back of their truck, started the engine, and began to drive away. The bronze statue bent forward until the metal could no longer withstand the force of the tugging rope, at which point it toppled over, completely severing from its base. The men drove off, dragging the bronze body behind them through the streets of Bethel, a small town in South Africa's province of Mpumalanga. Police located the men the following day, engaged in the process of dismembering the statue while it lay in the back of their truck.[1] Police arrested the assailants and confiscated all of the statue's remains. All, that is, except for a single body part—a left foot. For unbeknown to the men, as they dragged Simelane's body away, the one foot remained secured to the base. The foot that remains acts as both witness to, and evidence of, the defacement that took place that night. It is a reminder of the violence that was enacted on the symbolic body of a militant black woman—at the time the only female liberation hero to be honored with a figurative statue in South Africa's post-apartheid era.[2]

Details of the theft are unnervingly similar to the traumas that Simelane's human body endured while she was alive. Nokuthula Aurella Simelane was abducted and then subsequently tortured and killed at the hands of apartheid secret police. An anti-apartheid activist, she was a member of Umkhonto we Sizwe, also known as MK, the military wing of the African National Congress (ANC) strategy of resistance, and helped the ANC to emerge "as the leading force in the liberation movement" (Kimble and Unterhalter 1982, 218). Within MK, Simelane served primarily as a link between ANC members working inside of South Africa and their exiled activists in Swaziland, transporting weapons, information, and banned literature between the two countries. Working under cover, she was known to comrades only by her covert MK name, Sbongile (TRC on the Disappearance of Nokuthula Simelane 1999). Shortly before her death, the twenty-three-year old woman had recently completed her degree at the University of Swaziland. On September 11, 1983, Simelane was sent to Johannesburg to carry out an MK mission. While there, she also planned to visit friends and family. She made arrangements to collect a special dress to be worn at her graduation ceremony from her parents' home, and she went to the Carlton Centre mall in downtown Johannesburg to purchase shoes for that occasion. However, while at the mall, Simelane was lured into a trap in the underground parking garage and then abducted by the apartheid government's security police. She endured several weeks of interrogation and torture. And then she disappeared. Nokuthula Simelane was never seen by friends or family again.

Following her disappearance, Simelane's family members searched tirelessly for any information on her whereabouts. Her parents had suspected her political involvement and thus understood that their daughter might have been abducted and killed by government forces. Thoughts of her suffering tormented them. Facing the possibility of her death, they also searched for clues to help locate their daughter's remains. According to her mother, they "searched heaven and earth for her after she disappeared without a trace," traveling as far as Swaziland and other countries. After two years of fruitless searching, in 1985 they appealed to the media for help. *The Sowetan*, a progressive newspaper, published Nokuthula's story and photograph, describing her as "MK's Mata Hari" (Mashego 2006, 28). In response, local authorities reopened her case, then ceased, claiming to have "investigate[d] [it] exhaustively." All attempts to find the missing woman were fruitless, and the long-lasting, crippling political silence that is all too familiar to families of the "disappeared" ensued.[3]

Elizabeth Jelin, an Argentinean scholar who writes about how societies come to terms with historical injustice, suggests that commemorative spaces can be effective tools to help individuals cope with the silences and absences that accompany traumatic pasts. Speaking, for example, about painful memories experienced by families of "the disappeared" in Argentina, she explains: "since the absence of bodies and the uncertainty of death make mourning almost impossible . . . *to have a material marker or a place* seems to help in that process of difficult mourning" (Jelin 2003, 140fn17, italics mine). At the unveiling of Nokuthula's commemorative statue, twenty-eight long years after disappearance, family members and former comrades responded to the memorial in ways that enacted Jelin's claim.

The statue's unveiling was highly ceremonial and celebratory: it began with a procession led by drummers and singers and included family members, local government officials, former allies from the struggle, and local residents. Arts and Culture Department spokesperson Sechaba Mphahlele spoke about the memorial's important role in documenting local history. He commented that the statue would establish Simelane's role "in the attainment of freedom in South Africa" and that it stood for "just recognition and honour of a true heroine whose patriotism gave birth to what South Africa is today." What was unexpected was the way in which the occasion was marked by a continued longing to find the remains of Nokuthula's real body. Gathering around Nokuthula's bronze likeness, her family engaged with the statue as if it were "real," touching it lovingly, they smiled and stood with it as if posing for family photographs. "For the Simelane family, the statue of Nokuthula represented their continuing connection with their daughter and sister . . . there is no grave site for the family. There are no known human remains. The statue of Nokuthula is the closest thing her family and those who loved her have to her body and personhood. It represents everything about her including her physical body."[4]

Nokuthula's sister, Thembisile Nkadimeng, further indicated the memorial's potential for healing when she described how the statue's presence helped ease her bereavement. She said the memorial represented "unfinished business, in terms of establishing the whereabouts of Nokuthula's remains."[5] Sammy Mpatlanyane, a spokesperson for local government, declared the memorial's intent to "immortalize [a] liberation struggle hero" and also give people a chance to "hear stories about how people went missing without a trace during apartheid" (Mogakane 2009, 10).

Just as the creation of the statue provided an opportunity for resolution and healing, its theft and destruction reversed that process and rekindled traumatic remembrance. For Nokuthula's mother, Ernestina, the statue's theft collapsed the distinction between actual violence and symbolic violence, reviving the anguish and grief she felt at the time of her daughter's abduction. When asked for her reaction to the theft, Ernestina responded not as if she were talking about the destruction of a statue but as if she was speaking about her daughter's actual suffering: "I am very sad and angry. I cannot find peace and closure. I appeal to those responsible for her disappearance to give me her remains."[6] In a statement given before parliament, ANC Member of Parliament Patrick Sibande reinforced this: "The Simelane family have come to regard her statue as the grave of this heroine of our people." Thembisile's response was similar. Distressed, she described the statue's theft as a form of assault against her sister: "We never buried Nokuthula. For us the statue was a symbol of her grave. What she went through while alive, she has gone through again in death" (Magagula).

The responses poignantly demonstrate the pain of memory, the importance of representation, and the violence of erasure. The particular way in which Simelane's representation was seized and dismembered shifts the meaning of the statue from a symbol of "just recognition and honour" to a painful reminder of the brutality she endured prior to her disappearance and ignites the unresolved aspects of that crime. It is also possible to understand the destruction as symptomatic of men's cultural anxieties about women's increasing advancements in the public sphere. Indeed, immediately after the statue's destruction, local black residents, media, and feminist nongovernmental organizations commented that the crime could be understood as an aggressive backlash by individuals who understand figural and real displays of female authority as a challenge to male power. Local activists described the vandalism as a "politically motivated crime" that was "tantamount to violating the late Nokuthula Simelane after death, as in the same breath she was violated when she was murdered by the police hit squad" (Mtshali 2011).[7] This particular episode is instructive for thinking through the relationship between violence and representation in the public sphere, what W. J. T. Mitchell (1990, 891) calls "the economy of violence encoded in public images."

How might this story—a story about a heroic woman, her demise, her commemoration, and its subsequent destruction—demonstrate the political function of visual culture and shed light on the gender politics underpinning commemoration in South Africa's public sphere? What can it tell us about the possibilities, and the limits, of public displays of female power and authority? As I will demonstrate, the destruction of Simelane's statue is symbolic of a larger failure to adequately memorialize South Africa's heroic women, and as we shall see, this failure is mirrored in a range of other commemorative efforts.

In the pages to come, I discuss how the desecration of this particular memorial speaks to the difficulties of achieving transformative political change, particularly for women, as it intersects with two pervasive post-apartheid narratives: the broader critique of the post-apartheid state (the ANC) and its failure to live up to its own democratic, gender progressive ideals, and the unresolved gender-based violence committed by the former apartheid state.[8] The latter will be considered in the context of South Africa's internationally acclaimed and most visible public memory practice, the Truth and Reconciliation Commission (TRC), and the TRC's inability to bring justice to women. Despite the important and very public role that the TRC played in South Africa's transformation, many scholars and activists have leveled strong critiques about the commission's failure to effectively deal with women's experience with violence, especially torture and sexual violence.[9] I have argued elsewhere that the resulting "gender blindness," as described by Beth Goldblatt and Sheila Meintjes, is paralleled in public arts and the processes of memorialization.[10]

THE STORY

As a memorial, Nokuthula Simelane's commemorative representation was, as Marita Struken (1991, 120) says, "situated within a particular code of remembrance . . . [m]emorials embody grief, loss, and tribute or obligation; in so doing, they serve to frame particular historical narratives." In this case, the historical narrative marked by silence and disappearance became both more complete and more complicated when details of Simelane's story finally emerged in the context of South Africa's TRC.

Sixteen years after Nokuthula Simelane was abducted, eight security branch officers who were responsible for the crime—all of them men—provided detailed testimony about their actions in the context of the TRC. The applicants—William Coetzee, John Williams, Jacobus Ross, Anton Pretorius, Minrod Veyi, Frederick Mong, M. L. Mkhonza, and M. L. Selamolela—were all members of the (then) South African Police, working as part of the Intelligence Unit.[11] The TRC (1999) ruled that "all of the Applicants were to a greater or lesser extent involved in the incident." In a separate, and concurrent, appeal, Simelane's family also filed her case with the TRC in a final attempt to decisively resolve the circumstances surrounding their daughter's disappearance and demise.[12]

At the end of the five-day amnesty hearing, the TRC determined with reasonable certainty that the following events occurred: the apartheid security police learned of Simelane's Johannesburg mission through an agent who had infiltrated the ANC in Swaziland. The agent then arranged to meet Simelane at a restaurant at the Carlton Centre, posing as an MK operative himself but with the purpose of abducting her. At the time, the agent did not know that his target was a woman. "It was only at that stage that it transpired that the MK member was a lady, Ms. Simelane." He went on to describe her as "young, attractive, soft-spoken and [with] a slender figure" (TRC Amnesty Committee 2001). To avoid a public spectacle, he lured Simelane to a more private space—the parking garage—where several men then "tackled and grabbed her." Simelane fought back. Her resistance was futile as she was "completely outnumbered by the members of the Security Police who were all male and physically superior to her" (TRC Amnesty Committee 2001). The men overpowered her, threw her to the ground, and forced her into the trunk of their car.

Simelane was then taken to a location in Norwood, a short distance away. She remained there for four to five days and was repeatedly tortured by as many as four men at a time. Coetzee—the lead officer throughout her interrogation and assaults—described how "we bagged [suffocated] her, we hit her with a fist, and we slapped her. . . . If I recall, everybody participated" (TRC Amnesty Committee 2001). A detached Coetzee pragmatically described this as his personal "handling methodology . . . the manner in which I worked" (TRC on the Disappearance of Nokuthula Simelane 1999).

In between periods of active torture and interrogation, Simelane was bound to a bed with hand and foot cuffs. She "appeared to be nervous." She was denied sleep and medical care.

Simelane was then moved to a secret farm where she endured a lengthy detention during which she was tortured continuously and with increasing severity.[13] In addition to beatings and suffocation, she was subjected to electric shock treatment. At least once, she was taken from the farmhouse and thrown into a dam full of freezing-cold water. She nearly drowned (Nkadimeng 2013, n.p.). One of her assailants recalled how, while being "bagged," the torture was so severe it caused the young woman to wet and soil herself (TRC on the Disappearance of Nokuthula Simelane 1999). As a result of the assaults, Simelane's physical condition had deteriorated to the point where her face and body were unrecognizable: "the way she was assaulted, she didn't look the same, her appearance changed. Her physical condition had changed completely" (TRC on the Disappearance of Nokuthula Simelane 1999). A second assailant testified how "she had great difficulty in walking and her physical condition had generally deteriorated quite badly" (TRC on the Disappearance of Nokuthula Simelane 1999). After five weeks, Simelane disappeared from the farm and was never seen again.

Just as the amnesty hearing filled in some gaps of Simelane's fate, it also revealed the complexities and challenges involved in reconstructing the past through the vehicle of testimony in the absence of the victim herself. At the amnesty hearing, Simelane's assailants split into "two conflicting camps": the white assailants (Coetzee, Pretorius and Mong) provided a story that fundamentally opposed that of the black assailants (Veyi and Selamolela). Coetzee and his two white colleagues alleged that soon after her abduction, Simelane agreed to work as an informant for the apartheid police and that her torture ceased as she revealed information about MK structures and operations. According to Coetzee, he drove Simelane back to Swaziland, after which she simply "disappeared." Veyi and Selamolela maintained that the severity of Simelane's torture increased *because* of her refusal to cooperate with the police: "She persisted with this stance right up to the end of her stay on the farm and there was never any question of her being recruited as an agent of the Security Police" (TRC Amnesty Committee 2001). Veyi testified that he last saw Simelane lying unconscious in the trunk of Coetzee's vehicle and alleged that Coetzee and Pretorius killed Simelane and disposed of her body (TRC Amnesty Committee 2001). Although the TRC ruled that the applicants failed to meet the criteria of full disclosure, they deemed the latter version of the story to be "basically truthful" (TRC Amnesty Committee 2001).[14]

The conflicting versions of the "truth" and the commission's inability to reach a definitive resolution to this story resulted in the denial of amnesty, for all men, on the charges of torture and murder. Tragically, it also meant that key elements of Simelane's experience would forever remain unknown.

In her work on women and the TRC, Fiona Ross highlights the limitations of the TRC in terms of its treatment of women: too few women came forward to speak about their own experiences with violence, instead testifying to the suffering of loved ones and causing the TRC to consider them only as "secondary victims"; feelings of shame and embarrassment led countless women to hold back from speaking about their experiences with torture and sexual violence; and the TRC undervalued and underestimated the complexity of women's experiences. As a result, in the TRC's final, authoritative report, women's experiences under apartheid are misrepresented and, in Ross's (2003, 3) words, "slip easily from the record."[15] In the case of Nokuthula Simelane, we see how women's experiences under apartheid slip away from both the historical record and public visual culture. In both instances, women are denied their rightful place in the telling of South Africa's struggle history.

From the perspective of Simelane's family, the knowledge they craved the most was what was denied to them. The testimony failed to reveal information that would lead them to the whereabouts of their daughter's remains.[16] And to their dismay, the TRC (2001) reached the devastating conclusion that "it is not necessary for the purpose of this matter to make a definitive finding on the eventual fate of Ms. Simelane." Speaking from the perspective of a witness, and in the context of the TRC Human Rights Violation Hearings, Mathew Simelane, Nokuthula's father, pleaded with the TRC: "I would like to know even more. What happened to my daughter and after the torture what was done to her. I want to know that. . . . All we want now are her remains so we can bury Nokuthula in a decent way. In our culture we bury people decently and we would like to do that" (TRC Human Rights Violations Hearings 1997).

David Bunn has observed that "for many, including . . . the relatives of those who died at the hands of the security police, there is a complete disjunction between personal suffering and public memory. Apartheid's worst torturers relied absolutely on the fact that it was possible to kill, maim, and massacre without any record of their actions passing into the public domain, let alone into the monumental tradition" (Bunn 1998, 116). Bunn's observation points us beyond the TRC and into the realm of visual culture and the restorative role that public arts can play in telling a political history. Indeed, the explanatory plaque on the base of Simelane's memorial is inscribed with the words *Nokuthula Simelane. Finally, she has come home.* The sculpture—its physical and public presence, restores the disappeared woman's visuality and allows her to reappear in sculptural form. In the case of Simelane's experience, her commemorative statue was the final effort to address the erasure of her story and to make one woman's history visible once again.

THE COMMEMORATION

In 2009, the Mpumalanga provincial government sponsored the creation of the memorial statue depicting Nokuthula Simelane to recognize her courageous contribution to the struggle and place her story in the public domain by way of "the monumental tradition." The provincial government awarded the commission to Ruhan Janse van Vuuren, an artist born and raised in Mpumalanga and now based in Pretoria. Janse van Vuuren was likely chosen for his connection to the region and for his expertise working on other public commemorative projects.

In Pretoria, while employed at Dionysus Sculpture Works, Janse van Vuuren worked on a representation of Chief Tshwane and the sculpture of anti-apartheid activist Solomon Mahlangu that Gary Baines discusses in chapter 6 (fig. 6.5). He also assisted artist Angus Taylor on the commemoration of singer Brenda Fassie as part of the *Sunday Times* Heritage Project. Most recently and notably, he collaborated with André Prinsloo on the larger-than-life bronze statue of Nelson Mandela that was unveiled at the Union Buildings in Pretoria shortly after Mandela passed away in December 2013 and is discussed in the introduction to this volume (fig. 0.4).

These projects help to establish Janse van Vuuren as an artist whose work largely conforms to a traditionalist style in his depictions of public figures. That is, his works tend to follow conventional European modes of commemoration: the style is realistic and presents a recognizable image of its subject, the works are life-sized or larger and elevated on a pedestal, and bronze is the chosen medium. The subjects, nearly always male, are typically presented heroically. A number of scholars have written about how such statues like this have historically been used by the state "in an attempt to impose its authority" (De Alwis and Hedman 2009, 12). For this chapter, it is important to also recognize that this traditionalist commemorative tradition typically excludes women and instead glorifies male achievement and the political power of men.[17]

In keeping with that style, Janse van Vuuren commemorates Nokuthula Simelane in a manner that conforms to some of these conventions: with a realistically rendered, life-sized, bronze statue, elevated on top of a platform that identifies the subject via a plaque that bears her name (figs. 7.1 and 7.2). While Janse van Vuuren's statue of Simelane may initially strike one as traditionalist in the sense that it is a realistic depiction and is crafted in bronze, it does in fact subvert that convention in some important ways. Set on a slightly elevated base, the statue is approachable and encourages public engagement. It depicts the subject in an informal moment, as conveyed through clothing and body language. Furthermore, in a context where Simelane's family experienced the disappearance of their daughter and were denied even the right to bury her, the rendition of her person representationally assumes increased importance here.

Dressed stylishly, as if on her way to a formal occasion, Simelane is depicted wearing a long-sleeved dress that fits loosely on her slender body. The dress has a collar, is cinched at the waist, and ends just below her knees. Because it is a replica of the cream-colored dress that Nokuthula planned to wear at her graduation ceremony, in this context the dress becomes an object that helps to reassert the presence of the disappeared. Janse van Vuuren reports that when he consulted with Simelane's family members about his approach to the subject matter, they "wanted to see her in her academic gown."[18] The actual dress, which was never worn, still hangs in a closet at the Simelane home (Mashego 2006, 28). A thin, loose cardigan sweater is layered over the dress; it is open at the front, and at the top, it has gently fallen down below her shoulders. Standing straight and erect, she is depicted by the artist as strong and solid, in spite of her slim figure. Her posture and stance convey self-assurance and vitality. Her posture is both relaxed and intense. Although she is not in motion, her left foot steps slightly forward, suggesting that she is alert, ready, and prepared to move. Two long, beaded necklaces, fancy earrings, and bracelets on both wrists add a layer of formality to her attire—a sense that is partly offset by the fact that she is barefoot. Simelane casually holds a pair of pointed dress shoes in her right

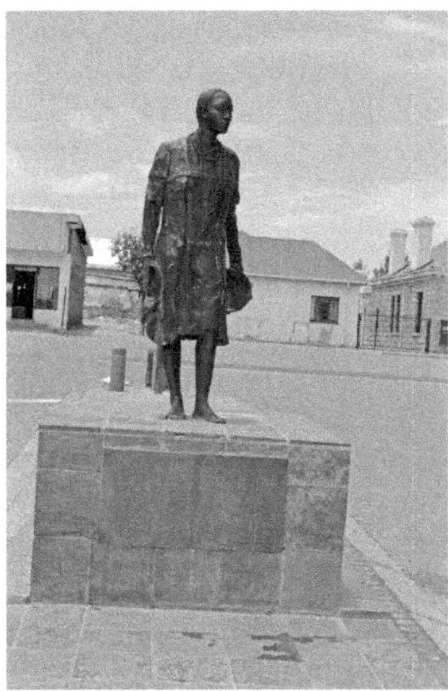

Fig. 7.1 Ruhan Janse van Vuuren, *Memorial for Nokuthula Simelane* (2009), bronze, Bethel, Mpumalanga. *Photograph courtesy of Ruhan Janse van Vuuren.*

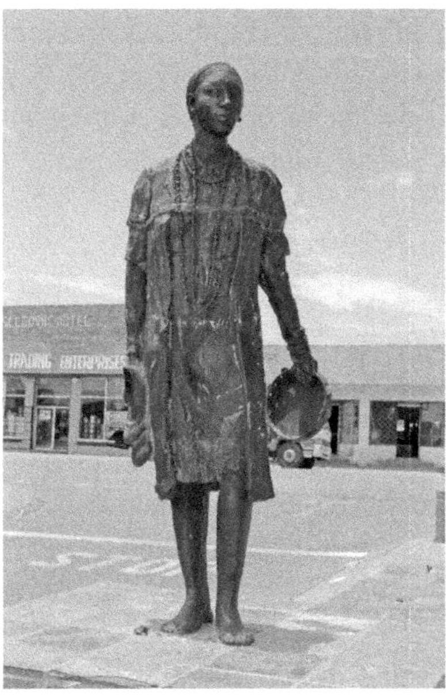

Fig. 7.2 Ruhan Janse van Vuuren, *Memorial for Nokuthula Simelane* (2009), bronze, Bethel, Mpumalanga. *Photograph courtesy of Ruhan Janse van Vuuren.*

hand. Given what we now know about her story, we can assume that we see her as she would have looked at the graduation ceremony she planned to attend. The dangling shoes are a reminder of the circumstances of her capture and of her final moments of freedom.

In this commemoration, there is no visible indication of her political associations or her political work. There is a kind of counterintuitiveness here—she does not appear as what we expect to see when we imagine a vision of military power. Instead, Janse van Vuuren depicts her as most people knew and perceived her: as a young, vibrant woman who fought in her country's freedom struggle, engaging in important, clandestine work, and whose political activity was a secret to family and friends. The success of MK relied on an individual's ability to maintain anonymity. Indeed, to the people around her, this is precisely what an MK operative looked like. Her appearance also reminds us that the liberation movement relied on, and was largely successful because of, the hard and perilous work of everyday people, many whose experiences remain unrecognized.

In his careful rendering of Simelane, Janse van Vuuren presents her in a manner that makes her recognizable and identifiable to us.[19] The young woman's hair is tightly braided and pulled back behind her ears and up from her face accentuating her high forehead. This also makes it easier for us to see, and remember, the details of her face. Her cheekbones are high and angular. She wears a serious expression that is suitable for the kind of clandestine political work we can imagine her doing: her mouth is closed, and her lips are full and slightly downturned. Behind her eyebrows, the muscles on her forehead constrict, and a furrowed brow conveys a sense of tension, worry, or concern. Although Simelane's body is positioned so that it faces the front of the pedestal, her face turns away, and she does not engage, or make eye contact with, the viewer. Instead, her attention is elsewhere. Her head is tilted back a bit, her chin raised ever so slightly into the air, and her gaze is steadily focused on something in the distance.

In his speech at the statue's unveiling, Mphalele commented that Simelane's commemoration was meant to be one part of a wider effort to "document history for the benefit of future generations," and thus stories of other struggle heroes who hailed from the town of Bethel were included in the public arts project. Simelane was placed in close proximity to a second commemorative sculpture of local activist Gert Sibande. Sibande is portrayed wearing a work shirt with rolled-up sleeves, overalls, and sturdy leather boots, attire that speaks to his life's work fighting on behalf of farmworkers to expose and transform the inhumane working conditions on Bethel farms.[20] An ANC activist and trade union leader, Sibande organized farm workers in the eastern Transvaal, founded a farmworkers association in the 1930s, and rose through the ranks in the ANC to become its provincial president.

An astute political activist, part of Sibande's success was in connecting the trade union movement to the broader political movement and in drawing media attention to the problem. Prominent progressive journalists and photographers documented and covered his cause. In 1947, with the help of Ruth First, *New Age* (the newspaper of the South African Communist Party) gave wide exposure to the near-slavery conditions on farms in an exposé which then led to a multipage story, illustrated with shocking images, in *Drum Magazine* (1952). He was subsequently banned by the government and deported to another region of the country, where he continued to organize farmworkers. Sibande eventually went in exile to Swaziland, died, and was buried there at the age of eighty-seven.

The two statues are situated near a third commemoration, the Nomoya Masilela Museum, and together, the three sites comprise Bethel's cultural precinct aimed to commemorate the region's struggle heritage and "immortalise liberation heroes" (Mogakane 2009, 10).[21] On the night of January 26, only Simelane's statue was desecrated, while the figure of Sibande was left untouched (though years earlier, both statues were vandalized when their surfaces were spray-painted white).

Two things are remarkable here. First, the positioning of Simelane—a female struggle hero—next to Sibande, a man, demonstrates that gender balance is a priority in Bethel's conception and display of its struggle history. She is positioned as a social and political equal to a man. Further, the similarities in how the two statues are depicted and positioned—both are bronze, life-sized likenesses of the individuals they commemorate—suggest that Simelane is valued and appreciated on equal par with Sibande. The two figures are positioned on separate pedestals, intended to be recognized visually and historically as individuals. This conveys the message that Simelane, like Sibande, is worthy of recognition as a political actor in her own right; in other words, she is not deserving of our recognition because of her relationship to family (as mother) or to men (as wife). I comment below on why this is important in the context of South African public arts.

Second, in giving us such a remarkably realistic rendering of Simelane's face, Janse van Vuuren creates an identifiable depiction of a female struggle hero. This is unusual: in spite of women's deep and widespread engagement in the liberation struggle, very few individual women have been commemorated in public arts. When they are, they tend to be depicted either in nonrepresentational terms, or else they are shown in relation to men. A memorial that honors Lilian Ngoyi, one of the most accomplished and prominent female anti-apartheid activists, in symbolic terms, is an example of the former.

Part of the *Sunday Times* Heritage Project public art initiative, the commemoration for Ngoyi offers little information about her extensive political career and instead conveys conservative messages about gender. Artist Steven Maqashela located his memorial at the site of Ngoyi's former house in Soweto. Maqashela represents Ngoyi's tremendous political career via a sewing machine (fig. 7.3), and it is impossible to ignore the powerful and pervasive gender politics underpinning the subject matter of this work.[22] This memorial, dedicated to one of the most prominent female icons of the liberation struggle, oddly uses an object that is associated with women's domesticity, not their liberation. Because of the memorial's singular focus on sewing, its subject matter and meaning rely on limiting patriarchal notions of women's sacrifice within the home, rather than transformative possibilities of their heroic work in the public sphere. Ultimately, this is a representation that reinscribes conservative ideas about gender and denies women their heroic status and contributes to the assumption that the normative political subject is male.[23]

Marina Walsh's 2009 memorial for Walter and Albertina Sisulu is an example of a figurative sculpture that recognizes a historic female figure but considers her only in relation to men (fig. 7.4). Located in the Diagonal Street Square in central Johannesburg, Walsh's memorial presents us with a slightly more complicated vision of political womanhood. The sculpture is a double political portrait, commemorating Albertina and Walter Sisulu together. As a pair, the Sisulus were one of South Africa's most famous political couples, and individually, they dedicated their lives to liberating South Africa.[24] The two are shown sitting down, facing each other and holding hands. The lower parts of their bodies merge together so that they become one. While it can be argued that the work might convey a vision of gender equality—the two figures are of equal height—depicting one of the most prominent female struggle heroes within the context of marriage

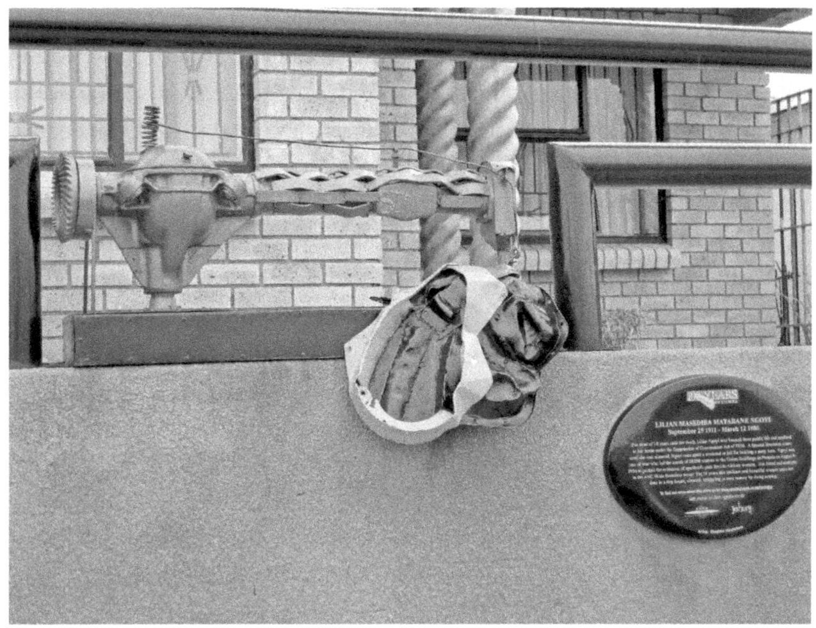

Fig. 7.3 Stephen Maqashela, *Lilian Ngoyi Memorial* (2006), metal, Soweto, Johannesburg. *Photograph by Kim Miller.*

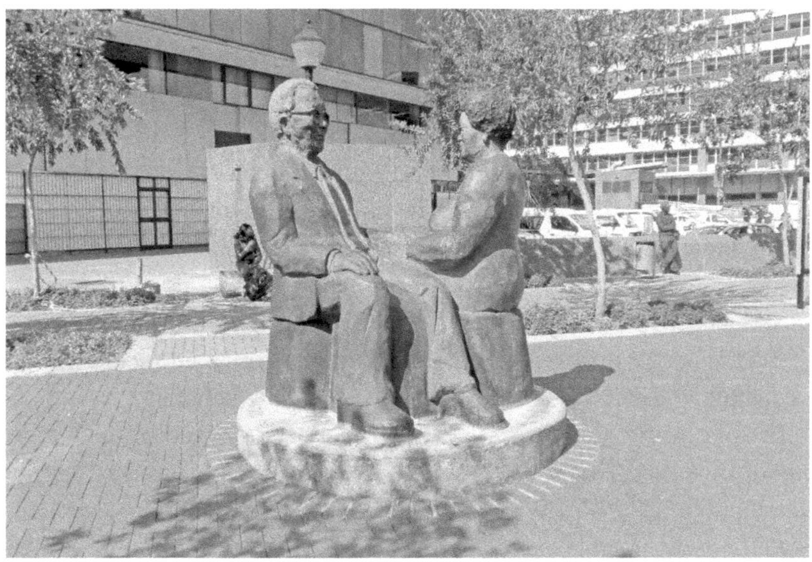

Fig. 7.4 Marina Walsh, *Memorial for Walter and Albertina Sisulu* (2009), concrete, Johannesburg. *Photograph by Kim Miller.*

dilutes her political authority and power.[25] Ultimately, the work recognizes Albertina Sisulu's power within a very circumscribed gender role—through marriage—and thus imposes a conventional narrative back onto a woman who was by no means conventional. It is a nonthreatening and comfortable way to publicly depict female political work.

Janse van Vuuren's political portrait works against these representational trends. He makes Simelane identifiable to a new audience and recognizable to those who knew her. Here, the artist effectively extends a small but significant visual iconography of women's political portraiture that has been critical in making particular women known *and recognizable* as political actors in their own right. Sue Williamson and Sandra Kriel, two apartheid-era artists who each produced a series of work featuring female activists, are most notable in this regard. Williamson's *A Few South Africans* (1983–87) and Kriel's *For Our Fallen Comrades* (1991–92) both depict political women through portraiture, combined with an iconography that tells the viewer something about the subject's life achievements.[26] Like Kriel and Williamson, Janse van Vuuren offers a realistically rendered work that gives us insight into Simelane's story and shows us her face. This adds to public knowledge of women as effective and powerful political subjects.[27]

Whereas the memorials for Ngoyi and Sisulu fail to disrupt, trouble, or challenge gender roles, the memorial for Simelane legitimizes women as viable, and heroic, political subjects in a commemorative landscape that is overwhelmingly male. Furthermore, this work significantly enriches the core narrative of anti-apartheid heroism and expands the canon of representations of women's experiences by offering us the depiction of a female political hero who was also an MK operative. Nokuthula Simelane was a militant woman. Here, we see a woman who was courageous and assertive enough to seek out acceptance in MK, who was strong enough to endure military training, and whose formidable power carried her through the ultimate physical and mental test of torture. Here is a woman who remained steadfast, loyal, and defiant while facing a group of men who would end her life.

In spite of the demonstrated role that women played in MK, depictions of them are almost entirely absent in post-apartheid visual culture, and in public arts nearly all depictions of MK members are gendered male. The most notable exception to this is at the Johannesburg Women's Jail, a former political prison that has been remade into a museum space.[28] The jail consists of a number of different exhibition areas narrating the varied experiences of women detainees, including a hallway of six isolation cells where former political prisoners were previously held in solitary confinement. Each cell tells the story of an individual woman via an object and a video: the object relates to the subject's political life, and the video allows her to narrate her experience. Outside of each cell hangs an explanatory panel with archival images and text that speak to the apartheid law corresponding to the reason for imprisonment.

One cell is dedicated to Lilian Keagile, a former activist whose story shares a number of similarities with Simelane's. Keagile received military training at an MK camp and worked as an underground MK operative. At the age of twenty-four, she was arrested, severely tortured, then convicted of terrorism under the 1967 Terrorism Act. She was sentenced to ten years in prison. Keagile is represented here primarily through a head wrap featuring text and imagery that relate to MK and its military power. The long narrow strip of cloth is crafted in the ANC colors of black, gold, and green. The words *Amandla Power Maatla* are written and repeated across the top, with a clenched fist bursting out of the *W* in the word *Power*. Beneath the text are female figures, all of them MK operatives who are depicted as warriors. One woman wears fatigues and is armed with an AK-47 on her back. The other stands facing the viewer in an empowered pose, her arms raised into the air, hands gripping, and breaking apart, a chain that runs along the top length of the cloth.[29] Janse van Vuuren's commemoration of Simelane, then, is only the second instance where a public representation of an MK struggle hero has a woman's face.

CONCLUSION

If we recall the words of philosopher Charles Griswold, who considered memorials "a species of pedagogy [that] seeks to instruct posterity about the past and, in so doing, necessarily reaches a decision about what is worth recovering" (Struken 1991, 120), then this chapter's focus investigates the extent to which women's contributions to the liberation struggle are considered as "worth recovering" based on what is assailable, and what is forgotten, in the commemorative landscape. If part of this work's success is in the depiction of a physically empowered female political subject, then what might its destruction tell us about the public response and tolerance for displays of female authority in the public sphere? How can we make sense of the circumstances surrounding its violent destruction, and what does it have to do with gender?

As cultural theorist Andreas Huyssen (2003, 4) comments, "inevitably, every act of memory carries with it a dimension of betrayal, forgetting, and absence." This chapter has illuminated those things that are forgotten, and those that are betrayed, in the creation and subsequent destruction of the commemorative sculpture of Nokuthula Simelane. Huyssen's claim also prompts us to think about one of the fundamental questions of this chapter in terms of those things that are forgotten, betrayed, and absent: what is at stake in how women are remembered? Janse van Vuuren's memorial is about more than the life of one woman—it is more broadly about how one remembers. It is both singular and indicative of a larger issue, which is this: women's agency is increasingly invisible in South Africa's public sphere, even as the telling of South Africa's struggle history is in the process of unfolding. This has long-lasting and dire consequences for our understandings of women as viable political subjects in a context where, as Nombiniso Gasa (2007, xxiii) states, women "have not been accorded the recognition, acknowledgement, and attention they deserve." And then, ultimately, in the words of Elizabeth Jelin (2003, 77), "gender [is] rendered invisible once again."

Kim Miller is Associate Professor of Women's and Gender Studies and Art History at Wheaton College in Norton, Massachusetts, and a research associate in the University of Johannesburg's Visual Identities in Art and Design (VIAD) research center. Miller's scholarship examines the relationship between visual culture, gender, and power in African arts.

Notes

1. See http://www.sowetanlive.co.za/news/2011/01/26/2-bust-for-theft-of-statue-of-heroine, accessed April 10, 2015.
2. I am deeply indebted to artist Judy Seidman for initially telling me about both the creation of Simelane's statue and its desecration.
3. Indeed, this effort is ongoing: Thembi Nkadimeng, Simelane's sister, continues to lead the cause to establish the whereabouts of her sister's remains. She most recently sought help from the Constitutional Litigation Unit of the Legal Resources Centre.
4. The quote comes from the website for Khulumani Support Group (www.khulumami.net), an advocacy group that aims to support and heal people who were harmed during apartheid. http://www.khulumani.net/truth-memory/item/463-simelane-statue-court-case-appearance-today.html, accessed April 15, 2015.
5. See houseofmemory.co.za, accessed April 9, 2015.

6. See http://www.khulumani.net/truth-memory/item/463-simelane-statue-court-case-appearance-today.html, accessed April 9, 2015.

7. In "The Backlash against African Women," recently published in the *New York Times*, Sisonke Msimang (2015) describes a widespread, and extremely hostile, backlash, or "cultural war against [African] women's advancements." She details advancements made by women in a number of African countries in the realms of the arts, film, literature, education, business, and politics: "nowhere has progress been more remarkable than in Africa's legislatures. Africans have significantly outpaced their female peers in America and Europe." In South Africa more than 40 percent of representatives in the National Assembly are women. Msimang then proceeds to describe the orchestrated, and very violent, backlash against these advancements. The backlash comes from individuals and institutions and can be seen in a number of locations, including churches, political parties, families, from traditional leaders, and rural officials. The backlash is forceful and violent: "outrage at bold women is both spontaneous and organized."

8. A number of scholars, activists, journalists, politicians, and others have commented on these two connected issues. As Troy Martens, former national spokesperson for the ANC Women's League, commented on August 3, 2012, "everyday women still suffer under a patriarchal system where men dominate and believe they are better than women."

9. See, for example, Goldblatt and Meintjes (1996, 1999), Graybill (2001), Krog (2000), and Ross (2001, 2003). Goldblatt and Meintjes (1999, 4) maintain that the commission failed South African women due to "the failure to utilize a gendered analytical framework," which, they rightly claim, had "serious implications for the telling of [South African history]."

10. I discuss this idea in relation to the Monument to the Women of South Africa at the Union Buildings in Miller (2011).

11. The hearing for Simelane's case began on Monday, May 17, 1999, at the Central Methodist Church in Johannesburg and lasted for five days.

12. Together, Matthew and Ernestina Simelane appeared before the TRC at the Human Rights Violation hearing in 1997. They were accompanied by other family members who were present for support. Speaking as witnesses to trauma and violence, they told the story of their missing daughter from their perspective and experience.

13. The once-secret farm that is described in the above testimony, where Simelane was tortured, is now known to all South Africans as Vlakplaas. Located on the outskirts of Pretoria, Vlakplaas covertly served as the headquarters for the South African Police counterinsurgency unit during the 1980s and 1990s. Vlakplaas operatives effectively functioned as the government secret police, capturing political activists like Simelane, then taking them to the farm where they were brutally tortured and then, usually, executed.

The existence of Vlakplaas and chilling descriptions of the horrific acts that occurred there were revealed to the majority of South Africans primarily in the context of the TRC hearings. The two former commanding officers, Dirk Coetzee and Eugene de Kock, revealed part of the secret history of the apartheid state as they described how the site was the location of many executions). De Kock—an assassin whom the press nicknamed "Prime Evil" in response to his TRC testimony about Vlakplaas operations—gave detailed accounts about ruthless murders of activists in front of stunned surviving family members who were present at the hearings

As each revelation about Vlakplaas emerged in the context of the TRC, as painful as it was, this knowledge filled in many of the absences and uncertainties from the apartheid past, and what happened at Vlakplaas became part of the public record. It is now a space that is seared into the country's collective memory and that is important to the historical memory of the struggle. South African citizens continue to try to come to terms with the knowledge of what happened there. Vlakplaas's history, like Simelane's story, is one that, in Butcher's (2001) words, has "yet to have its full history revealed." The single foot remaining at the site where Simelane's bronze likeness once stood now serves as a metaphor for the fragmented TRC testimonies that fail to offer full disclosure about what happened to her and other Vlakplaas victims and the searing/painful silences that persist.

14. In regard to Veyi and Selamolela, the Amnesty Committee ruled that "they have both made a very favourable impression upon us and their testimony has struck us as honest as well as a genuine attempt to convey all of the facts and circumstances concerning the incident to the best of their ability" (TRC Amnesty Committee 2001). Alternatively, they found "no merit" in the submission by Coetzee et al., whose testimony they described as "evasive" and was full of "long winded technical explanations" rather than direct answers (TRC Amnesty Committee 2001). Doubting the veracity of Coetzee et al., the commissioners further stated, "we have no doubt, that they have made common cause and orchestrated their testimony in an attempt to minimize their roles in the torture of Ms Simelane" (TRC Amnesty Committee 2001).

15. Amnesty was granted to all men for Simelane's abduction, kidnapping, and assault.

16. Simelane's family was not present at the hearing, thus sparing themselves the emotional shock of listening to her daughter's torturers detail her suffering, and instead they were represented by a Mr. van den Berg. Through him, they opposed the applications of Coetzee, Pretorius, and Mong but supported amnesty for the others, whose testimony they believed to be truthful.

17. It is also the case that throughout the world, in terms of public sculpture, realistic representations of females are often for the purposes of suggesting them as representative of abstract ideals, such as motherhood or the nation, rather than showing individual women directly.

18. Interview with Ruhan Janse van Vuuren, conducted via e-mail, March 17, 2015.

19. In my interview with the artist, Janse van Vuuren described how many photographs depicting Nokuthula, and belonging to the Simelane family, were destroyed or given to journalists and never returned. While working on this commission, he crafted his subject's likeness primarily through one photograph of Nokuthula wearing sunglasses, and with lots of assistance from the sister Tembi.

20. As the son of a tenant farmer and former farm laborer himself, Sibande witnessed and experienced the inhumane conditions that his people endured.

21. Nomoya Masilela was a high school student who was shot and killed during student protests in the township of Bethel in the 1980s.

22. As a commemoration, this strikes me as a highly unusual, if not offensive, choice. It is unlikely that a similar kind of object would be used on a memorial to honor and commemorate a heroic male figure.

23. Alternatively, a second example from the *Sunday Times* Heritage Project that honors the life of a female political activist provides an important example of how an untraditional monument can employ abstraction successfully, insofar that it enables

the female subject to be understood as empowered and as an individual. Ruth Sacks's commemoration of Cissie Gool, located on a busy pedestrian mall in Cape Town, is entirely abstract. It consists of a series of round, granite pedestals, each one inscribed with text that speaks to Gool's political work. While Gool is not represented directly, many of her accomplishments are represented very directly through detailed text. Furthermore, her agency is asserted visually through the repetition of her name, which is inscribed on each of the sixteen separate pedestals.

24. During her political career, Albertina Sisulu was instrumental in the 1955 launch of the Freedom Charter and helped organize the 1956 Women's March. She was elected national co-president of the United Democratic Front when it started in 1983, then elected deputy president of the ANC Women's League. In 1989, she led an overseas delegation to help persuade foreign governments to implement sanctions against the apartheid government, and in that capacity met with George H. W. Bush, Jimmy Carter, and Jacqueline Kennedy Onassis. She endured imprisonment, including solitary confinement, exile, and banning as a result of her political activity. In 1994, she became a Member of Parliament in South Africa's new democratic government.

25. Albertina Sisulu is also depicted in the context of the Johannesburg Women's Jail—one of the solitary cells is dedicated to showing her story. Even there, her political identity is framed in relation to family as she is figured primarily as maternal.

26. Williamson's series includes portraits of the following activists: Annie Silinga, Elizabeth Paul, Maggie Magaba, Winnie Mandela, Albertina Sisulu, Nokukanya Lutuli, Helen Joseph, Lilian Ngoyi, Amina Cachalia, Caroline Motsoaledi, Charlotte Maxeke, Virginia Mngoma, Mamphela Ramphele, Jenny Curtis Schoon, and Mariam Makeba.

Kriel's series includes portraits of Dulcie September and Ruth First. I have previously written about Kriel's series and its significance in the wider spectrum of anti-apartheid artistic production in my article, "Inter-Weaving Art and Activism: Sandra Kriel's Heroic Women" (Miller 2013).

27. Also, as two-dimensional, gallery-based works, Kriel's and Williamson's series have a very different audience and are received differently as compared to works like van Vuuren's that are positioned in the public sphere.

28. Located in the heart of Johannesburg, the former jail is now a museum and forms part of the heritage site known as Constitution Hill. Many people consider it to be the long-awaited women's equivalent to Robben Island (Coombes 2003, 105).

29. Popular depictions of MK from the apartheid era convey an iconography that is similarly militarized. When inclusive of women, such images are also heavily feminized through motherhood: MK women are typically shown carrying weaponry and also children. I investigate the meanings behind these images in my article, "Moms with Guns: Women's Political Agency in Anti-Apartheid Visual Culture" (Miller 2009).

References

Bearak, Barry. 2011. "Albertina Sisulu, Who Helped Lead Apartheid Fight, Dies at 92." *New York Times*, June 5.

Bunn, David. 1998. "Whited Sepulchres: On the Reluctance of Monuments." In *Blank: Architecture, Apartheid and After*, edited by Hilton Judin and Ivan Vladislavic, 93–115. Rotterdam: Architectural Institute.

Correspondent. 2011. "Metal Theft: Freedom Heroine Laid Low by Crime." In *Witness*. Accessed January 29, 2011. http://www.witness.co.za/index.php?showcontent&global[_id]=54688.

De Alwis, Malathi, and Eva-Lotta Hedman. 2009. "A Double Wounding: Aid and Activism in Post-Tsunami Sri Lanka." In *Tsunami in a Time of War: Aid, Activism and Reconstruction*, 121–138. Colombo: International Center for Ethnic Studies.

Gasa, Nomboniso. 2007. "Introduction." In *Women in South African History: They Remove Boulders and Cross Rivers*, xiii–xxxvii. Cape Town: HSRC Press.

Goldblatt, Beth, and Sheila Meintjes. 1996. *Gender and the Truth Commission: A Submission to the Truth and Reconciliation Commission*. Cape Town: Juta Publishing.

———. 1999. "Women: One Chapter in the History of South Africa? A Critique of the Truth and Reconciliation Commission Report." Paper presented at the conference *The Truth and Reconciliation Commission: Commissioning the Past*. Johannesburg: University of Witwatersrand.

Graybill, Lynn. 2001. "The Contribution of the Truth and Reconciliation Commission toward the Promotion of Women's Rights in South Africa." *Women's Studies International Forum* 24, no. 1: 1–10.

Jackson, Paul. 2015. "Prime Evil: Why South Africa Has Released Eugene De Kock." Accessed January 30, 2015. http://theconversation.com/prime-evil-why-south-africa-is-releasing-eugene-de-kock-37007.

Jelin, Elizabeth. 2003. *State Repression and the Labors of Memory*. Minneapolis: University of Minnesota Press.

Khulumani Support Group. 2011. "Simelane Statue Court Case Appearance." May 27. Accessed January 16, 2012. khulumani.net.

Kimble, Judy, and Elaine Unterhalter. 1982. "'We Opened the Road for You, You Must Go Forward': ANC Women's Struggles, 1912–1982." *Feminist Review* 12, no. 1: 11–35.

Krog, Antjie. 2000. *Country of My Skull: Guilt, Sorrow, and the Limits of Forgiveness in the New South Africa*. New York: Broadway Books.

Magagula, Thokozani. 2011. "Metal Theft: Freedom Heroine Laid Low by Crime." *The Witness*, January 29.

Mahlangu, Isaac, and Sashni Pather. 2012. "De Kock Must Rot in Jail." *Times Live*, January 29. Accessed January 14, 2015. http://www.timeslive.co.za/local/2012/01/29/de-kock-must-rot-in-jail.

Mashego, Goodenough. 2006. "All I Want Are My Daughter's Remains." *City Press*, April 16.

Mclea, Harriet, and Dominic Mahlangu. 2011. "Struggle Icon Albertina Sisulu Dies." *Times Live*, June 3, 2011.Accessed June 3, 2011. http://www.timeslive.co.za/local/2011/06/03/struggle-icon-albertina-sisulu-dies.

Miller, Kim. 2009. "Moms with Guns: Women's Political Agency in Anti-Apartheid Visual Culture." *African Arts* 42: 68–75.

———. 2011. "Selective Silence and the Shaping of Memory in Post-Apartheid Visual Culture: The Case of the Monument to the Women of South Africa." *South African Historical Journal* 63, no. 2: 295–317.

———. 2013. "Inter-Weaving Art and Activism: Sandra Kriel's Heroic Women." In *Bodies of Knowledge: Interviews, African Art, and Scholarly Narratives*, edited by Joanna Grabski and Carol Magee, 98–113. Bloomington: Indiana University Press.

Miller, Nancy K. 2003. "'Portraits of Grief': Telling Details and the Testimony of Trauma." In *differences: A Journal of Feminist Cultural Studies* 4, no. 3: 112–35.
Mitchell, W. J. T. 1990. "The Violence of Public Art: Do the Right Thing." *Critical Inquiry* 16, no. 4: 880–99.
Mogakane, Tshwarelo Eseng. 2009. "Statue to Honour Missing Freedom Fighter." *City Press*, p. 10.
Mokoena, Norman. 2008. "Gerd [sic] Sibande Remembered: Address at the Unveiling of the Statue." Accessed January 9, 2015. http://www.cosatu.org.za/show.php?ID=1712.
Moselakgomo, Alfred. 2012. "Struggle Icon's Statue Desecrated Again." *The Sowetan*, March 2.
Msimang, Sisonke. 2015. "The Backlash against African Women." *New York Times*, January 10.
Mtshali, Thokozani. 2011. "Family Want Statue Court Case Moved to Evander." *The New Age*, March 15. Accessed August 24, 2014.
Nkadimeng, Thembi. 2013. "My Sister's Heart." *City Press*, December 26.
Nyaka, France. 2012. "Struggle Icon's Statue Stolen Again." *The New Age*, March 5.
Ross, Fiona. 2001. "Speech and Silence: Women's Testimony in the First Five Weeks of Public Hearings of the South African Truth and Reconciliation Commission." In *Remaking a World: Violence, Social Suffering and Recovery*, edited by Veena Das, Arthur Kleinman, Margaret Lock, Mamphele Ramphele, and Patricia Reynolds, 250–79. Berkeley: University of California Press.
———. 2003. *Bearing Witness: Women and the Truth and Reconciliation Commission in South Africa*. London: Pluto.
Sibande, Patrick. 2011. "Motion without Notice by Honourable Patrick Sibande on the Vandalism of the Statue of uMkhonto we Sizwe Member, Nokuthula Simelane." March 1. ANC Parliamentary Caucus Document.
Struken, Marita. 1991. "The Wall, the Screen, and the Image: The Vietnam Veterans Memorial." *Representations* 35: 118–42.
Suttner, Raymond. 2011. "MaSisulu: A Life Sermon Written through Hard, Painstaking Work." *Daily Dispatch*, June 9.
The Unveiling of the Nokuthula Simelane Statue. Accessed January 28, 2015. http://houseofmemory.co.za/Nokuthula%20Simelane.pdf.
Thomas, Cornelius. 2007. "A Scrupulously Selfless Couple." *Safundi: The Journal of South African and American Studies* 5: 1–2, 1–3.
Truth and Reconciliation (TRC) Amnesty Committee. 2001. "Application in Terms of Section 18 of the Promotion of National Unity and Reconciliation Act, No. 34 of 1995." May 23.
Truth and Reconciliation Commission (TRC) Human Rights Violations Hearings. 1997. "Testimony by Mathew Simelane." June 3.
Truth and Reconciliation Commission (TRC) on the Disappearance of Nokuthula Simelane. 1999. "Statement Issued by the Truth and Reconciliation Commission." May 14.

CHAPTER 8

Transgressive Touch: Ruination, Public Feeling, and the *Sunday Times* Heritage Project

DUANE JETHRO

Erected between 2006 and 2008, the *Sunday Times* Heritage Project (STHP) comprised a series of thirty-six individually designed, site-specific narrative memorials located in four of South Africa's major provinces. Designed to be inconspicuous but also engaging and interactive, the memorials were also intentionally styled as evocative pieces of public art. Many were, however, badly vandalized or even destroyed soon after being unveiled. In this chapter, I would like to address this ruination and its implications. To ruin, Laura Anne Stoler (2013, 9, 11) cites, is an "active process," a "vibrantly violent verb," the "reappropriations, neglect, and strategic and active positioning of [ruins] within the politics of the present". It relates to the spoiling of material culture through a range of means and the place of ruined material in the world. Taking up the constructive vibrancy and violence of this term, I use the word *ruination* to refer to a state of decay induced either through purposeful destruction or neglect. I want to mobilize it to try and think about what it says about the memorials, the STHP in general and urban space and publicness in post-apartheid South Africa. My chapter builds on extant scholarly writing about the STHP, which addresses questions of public history and heritage (Kros 2008), gender and memorialization (Marschall 2010), as well as heritage and practices of mediation (Marschall 2011). In contrast, here, I focus on ruination and the afterlife of the memorials. Specifically, I will argue that ruination allows us to understand the relationship between the *Sunday Times* and the publics it attempted to address because it frames a conceptual and sensory interface, through the sense of touch, between human beings and valued material cultural forms that may provide an insight into public feeling about public history.

Feeling is important. Erika Doss (2010, 13) argues that memorials are "archives of public affect . . . repositories of feelings and emotions" that are "embodied in their material form and narrative content." For her, memorials are "bodies of feeling, cultural entities whose social, cultural, and political meanings are determined by the emotional states and needs of their audiences" (Doss 2010, 36). Derek Hook (2005, 701) has similarly proposed, "Monuments are the 'machines of ideology' which require a human component to power their affects." Affect has been growing topic of scholarly inquiry regarding memorials and commemorative culture (Allen and Brown 2011; Clark and Franzman 2006; Stevens 2009). Feeling is a deeply sensuous affective capacity particularly related to touch (Classens 2012). Anthony Synnott (1993) has shown that touch is physical, relating to the skin and contact, but also metaphorical, resonating in a host of metaphors that refer to states of feeling. Emotions are powerfully freighted through the language of touch. Indexing notions of connection and feeling, orientation and understanding, touch provides a useful metaphorical language for grasping at the complex acts of ruination perpetrated against the STHP memorials. Focusing on public feeling and the destruction of material culture, I hope to add to debate about the material turn in the humanities by showing how the creative power of ruination marks the articulation of public feeling as part of the process of staging claims to and about post-apartheid public spheres. Put another way, in this chapter, I explore the public reception of the STHP memorials through the relationships struck between ruination, the sense of touch and public feeling.

PUBLICS AND PUBLICITY

The *Sunday Times* stressed the public grassroots acceptance of its memorials. For example, the editor characterized the consultation process with stakeholders, the publics that would ultimately take ownership of the memorials, as defining the project's character: "This is what our Heritage Project is about: the lived experience of South Africans."[1] Further reinforcing the everyday character of the project, design criteria stipulated the STHP memorials not only be situated in public locations with high pedestrian traffic but also that they incorporate some interactive component. They were meant to break with the omnipotent, monumental authority evoked by colonial and apartheid memorials, categorized as "Big Men on Bronze Horses," in the words of one of the coordinators, Charlotte Bauer (2007).

The STHP memorials were designed to be small scale and site specific, with some purposefully inviting active physical, tactile interaction on the part of their publics.[2] For example, the *Mannenberg* memorial allowed passers-by to play a few notes from a jazz track by running sticks along a few carefully cut metal pipes. The *Mohandas Gandhi* memorial was similarly interactive. Erected to commemorate the 1908 pass-burning riot led by Mohandas Gandhi outside the Hamidia Mosque in central Johannesburg, it took the form of a cooking pot similar to that used during the protest and featured a zoetrope device that, when rotated, depicted the burning of a pass book. Inviting a range of physical interactions such as touching and feeling, pulling and pushing, tapping and sounding, sitting, rotating, and seeing, the interactive materiality of the memorials evoked a range of sensory experiences. As public art works situated at or near locations of direct significance to the narratives they commemorated and the publics that it was assumed remembered them, the STHP memorials also engaged with particular, complex notions of site specificity (Kwon 1997; 2004). By emphasizing everydayness, innovative aesthetics, and site specificity, many of the *Sunday Times'* memorials were not only meant to enjoy a kind of inconspicuous publicness but were also meant to stake public histories in very particular ways.

Concerted effort to gain acceptance for the memorials by their intended publics did not, however, equate to their actual protection. By 2008, at least five of the *Sunday Times* memorials had been ruined, with the majority eventually being defaced, damaged, or simply left in a bad state of disrepair due to a lack of maintenance.[3] Clearly, addressing the "lived experience of South Africans" did not necessarily make the memorials compelling. It also posed a serious challenge. For that reason a crucial difficulty project designers faced was "the need to look after sensitive artworks in places where . . . neglect seemed to reign."[4] A major design condition was that the memorials had to be resistant to the forces of both the natural and social environment. They had to be durable and enduring, "time-proof, people-proof, and weather-proof."[5] Erected for the public, the STHP memorials therefore had to also be protected from the public.

The notion of the public is clearly central to understanding who the *Sunday Times* tried to address and engage with these memorials. Jürgen Habermas (1991, 1) expressed the messiness of publicness in *The Structural Transformation of the Public Sphere,* saying that "the words 'public' and 'public sphere' betrays a multiplicity of concurrent meanings" that linger in both common and academic language despite their complexity. Michael Warner (2002; 2005) affirms this confusion when he says that often no distinction is made between ideas of *a* public or *the* public. Accordingly, two specific configurations of what is meant are often interchangeably implied, namely a public as "a social totality" and "as a concrete audience" (Warner 2002, 413). This overlap often works to elide the conditions under which such publics are framed. For him, publics emerge through "texts and their circulation" as discourses: "a public is a space of discourse organized by nothing else than discourse itself" (Warner 2002, 414). Locating publics in the reflexive operations of the production and circulation of texts, for Michael Warner and others (Fraser 1990; Hauser 1999), publics are entities bound and forged through practices of dialogue and the production of discourse. I employ these ideas cautiously, noting their lack of emphasis on the materiality of the means and modes of mobilizing and inscribing texts.[6] Through discussing specific cases of ruined *Sunday Times* memorials, I will engage directly with the relationships between the production of forms of language, materiality, and the constitution of post-apartheid publics.

RUINATION AND TOUCH

Concerns about the security of the *Sunday Times* memorials were well founded because the vandalism of material heritage forms was prevalent in South Africa. Suspending David Freedberg's (1985) propositions about the mystery of "iconoclasts and their motives," I would like to suggest that, perhaps, intuitively, in the South African context we can infer two sets of motivation for such acts of ruination. On one hand, some material heritage forms were vandalized for the purpose of making clear political statements. For example, in 1998, in East London in the Eastern Cape Province, a statue erected in honor of the Black Consciousness icon Steve Biko was vandalized by unknown members of the public who sprayed the signature of the Afrikaner Weerstand Beweging (Afrikaner Resistance Movement), a right-wing paramilitary organization, at its feet.[7] On the other hand, material heritage forms were also vandalized for purely material reasons. In Cape Town in

2008, for example, the life-sized bronze sculptures of Coline Williams and Robbie Waterwitch, installed to commemorate their tragic death while planting an explosive device at a municipal voting station during apartheid, was toppled and spirited away in the early hours of the morning. In a tragic irony, the assailants were exposed when they tried to sell broken chunks of the effigies for their value in metal.[8]

What conceptual language can we use to interpret this destruction of public property? The art historian Dario Gamboni (1997) provides a useful outline of the complexity that surrounds the use of terms and concepts to describe such phenomena. He shows that the term *vandalism* emerges out of the volatility of the French Revolution. Coined by Abbé Grégoire, who designated it to mean "barbarous, ignorant, or inartistic treatment devoid of meaning," he intended it to carry to the implication of "excluding the vandal from the community of civilized mankind . . . neighbourhood, city, nation, etc." (Gamboni 1997, 18). In its classical sense, vandalism was imbued with condescending connotations regarding the character of destroyers of material property (Merrills 2009). Iconoclasm, traditionally referring to the destruction of religious images, alternately implies "intention, sometimes doctrine" but more precisely, that "the actions or attitudes thus designated have meaning" (Gamboni 1997, 19). The assumed ascription of motive, and classes of those perpetrating destruction, therefore distinguishes vandalism from iconoclasm as engagements inspired either by meaningful intention or mindless malice. Yet iconoclasm introduces its own set of problems. It refers to the destruction of religious images specifically and, relatedly, that the spoiling of these material representations is secondary to the spoiling of what they signified (Gamboni 1997, 17–22). Despite this reductive interpretation of religious meaning and material forms, overall, we can see the conceptual language framing the destruction of material cultural forms as loaded with historical meaning that have clear religious resonances. This is further evident when we make another conceptual distinction through the notion of defacement. Describing the actual act of spoiling, this term conveys the notion of willful intent to damage. In Michael Taussig's (1999, 1) consideration, however, defacement is construed as a particular form of desecration where the power of the material representation is not undermined but, rather, amplified: "a strange surplus of negative energy is likely to be aroused from within the defaced thing itself." In this "state of desecration," artifacts and images of the cultural value "can come across as being more sacred than sacred." For Taussig (1999, 2), defacement is a powerful form of truth telling that is "not a matter of exposure which destroys the secret" but, rather, "a revelation which does justice to it." Whether in reference to secrets, religious images, or material cultural forms, this conceptual lexicon outlines the complexity of different modes of classification of the destruction of culturally significant material.[9]

The apparently neat relations between violence, publics, and material cultural forms are not always that clear, as W. J. T Mitchell (1990, 886–87) prompts: "Is public art inherently violent, or is it a provocation to violence? Is violence built into the monument in its very conception? Or is violence simply an accident that befalls some monuments?" For him, monuments as public art are violent because the concept itself is encoded with political forces that exclude certain publics and facilitate the erasure of histories since they inherently assert the authority of the narratives permeating their design. And how do we address instances of material violence where the motive is not entirely clear? In South Africa, vandalism as a form of ruination, was, however, also sometimes inspired by obscure, indeterminate motives that Bruno Latour (2002, 17, 21) would term iconoclash, where "one does not know, one hesitates, one is troubled by an action for which there is no way to know . . . whether it is destructive or constructive" and where "there is uncertainty about the exact role of the hand at work in the production of a mediator." The vagaries around motives and the classes of perpetrators reveal the insufficiency of a universal language of classifying material violence. In the following three sections, I will engage in a case-by-case interpretation of such incidents, highlighting the kinds of modalities of ruination, touch, and public sentiment they appeared to index.

BANKIE GEDAGTES

Between 1950 and 1990, the apartheid state forced South Africans to be classified into an ever-finer series of racial categories that would govern their experience of everyday life. The Race Classification Board (RCB), which during the 1960s sat at the High Court Annex, was charged with policing these categories. It was this legacy of racist discrimination and its effects on the psyche of South Africans that the *Sunday Times* wanted to reflect on when they commissioned Roderick (Rod) Sauls to design and install a commemorative artwork (fig. 8.1). The narrative was selected, researched, and composed by journalist Sue Valentine. It stated:

> In the 1960s, a room in what is now the High Court Annex was the scene of formal hearings of the most bizarre and humiliating kind as ordinary people came before an appeal panel to argue about what "race" they should be labelled. The classification was subjective, and families were split apart when paler or darker skinned children or parents—or those with curlier hair, or different features—were placed in separate categories.[10]

Sauls's professional credentials marked him out as well suited for such a project. His life and career as an artist and educator seemed to be tied up in urban commemorative projects. Born and raised in District Six, a site of race-based forced removals, Sauls was engaged in pursuing a PhD in art and education at the University of the Western Cape at the time of the commission. He also worked at the District Six Museum, an important institution commemorating the histories of forced removals in Cape Town (Rassool and Prosalendis 2001). He clearly had a close connection to this particular narrative, which was one criterion used for the selection of artists commissioned for the project.[11]

Sauls developed a concept for the RCB narrative that engaged with the elaborate textual culture of the apartheid legislative apparatus and its real material affects and effects. The Population Registration Act of 1950 mandated that all South Africans be racially classified at birth as white, black, or colored. The RCB, located in a room in the High Court Annex on Queen Victoria Street in central Cape Town, would adjudicate appeals for reclassification. Board members would use a range of arbitrary, humiliating criteria such as anatomical measurements to assess the merit of such appeals. Highlighting the life-altering significance of these capricious classifications, Sauls developed a concept comprised of a pair of wooden and concrete public benches that were respectively designated "Whites Only" and "Non-Whites Only," in reference to the Separate Amenities Act of 1953. The Act demarcated public amenities on the basis of race. Sauls's artwork engaged with the legal power of apartheid authority because their wooden slats were inscribed with clauses from the Population Registration Act, and quotes from the *Government Gazette* about incidents of reclassification.[12]

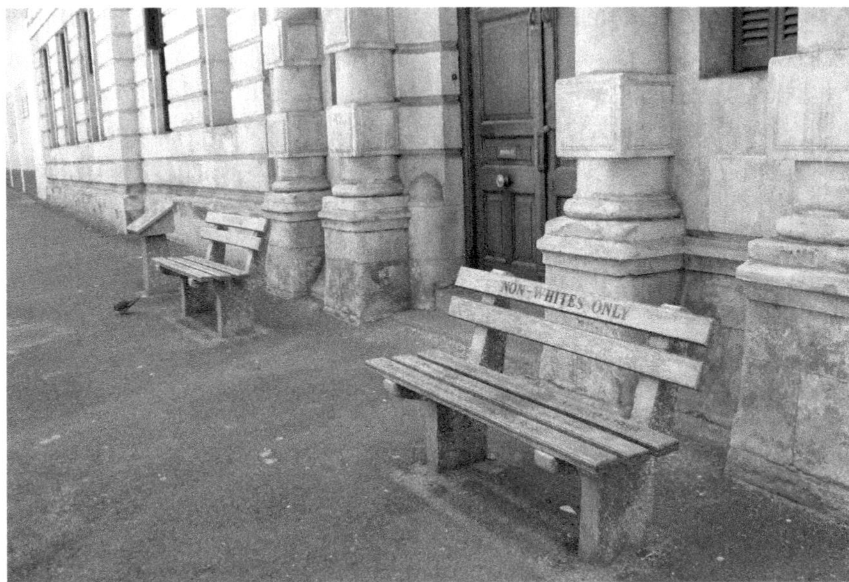

Fig. 8.1 Roderick (Rod) Sauls, *Race Classification Board*, Queen Victoria Street, Cape Town. *Photograph by Duane Jethro.*

Officially titled the *Race Classification Board,* Sauls's first working title was *Bankie Gedagte* which, translated literally from Afrikaans, meant "bench thoughts," an idiomatic reference to closed-mindedness in Cape colored patois.[13] The pejorative ascription was not meant to cast aspersion on the publics who may have internalized the apartheid-era racial demarcation of urban space. Instead, it was intended to call attention to the feelings of fear that such designations were meant to engender. As he explained, "In the old days, because of how people were divided between non-whites and whites, people would walk past a bench [designated white] and never sit there. There was nobody around but still they would not sit there; people were just scared."[14] The title of the benches captured its symbolic meanings because Sauls's original proposal claimed that the benches were meant to signify the notions of "body and soul," with "the three dimensional construction of the bench" representing the physical body, and the text inscribed thereon, standing as "a symbol of the soul."[15] By developing a concept that drew attention to the subtle yet painful petty denigrations the apartheid legal apparatus evoked around racial inscription on the bodies and in the souls of South Africans, *Bankie Gedagte* highlighted the affective power of institutionalized racism as inscribed in material space. The memorial therefore reflected on the legacy of a denigrating legal apparatus and its effect on the heart and soul of black South Africans' experience of urban space.

The memorial was a provocative, popular attraction among passers-by. Over some twenty hours of fieldwork observation in 2010, it became clear to me that pedestrians who noticed the benches typically perceived them as absurd, as if it was ludicrous that such distasteful public markers of apartheid segregation could still remain in place. Whatever their perceived visibility or authenticity in representing a palpable yet almost-forgotten aspect of social history, the benches could also evoke heavy emotions and memories. This was made evident in an encounter I had with a middle-aged, colored gentleman while sitting on the benches. When I asked him whether it would have been good to retain some of these signs as a reminder to young people, my interlocutor whom I will name Matthew, said the memorials evoked strong feelings about apartheid that were best forgotten.[16] "No, it's derogatory to us [people of color]." Reason being, "if you see some of the signs it brings back that bad memories of the time we had . . . you see we all trying to forget it . . . because of the bad experiences that most of us had." Sometimes, commemoration of the bad past for better futures could simply arouse bad feelings that some would prefer to never feel again. As he explained: "The thing is this, it's a thing that we are trying to forget and don't want to remind our children what we went through and we want our children to grow up to be equal." The past, and the burden of bad feelings about being made to feel inferior, about the petty humiliation, was not something that needed to be remembered but, rather, forgotten. He also provided some insight into how the race classification system worked, saying:

> Time of apartheid . . . if a woman gives birth and she wants to go and register that child . . . you had to physically take your child to that counter, there's a small window . . . an old white woman, a white lady that hasn't got any education works behind that counter . . . she looks at the child, she looks at the type of weave of the child's hair, then she will decide "colored," "black," "Other colored." That's how they classified us.

While prompting unhappy memories, the memorial was not so much vandalized as ruined through exposure, what is sometimes referred to as wear and tear. Over time, the inscriptions on the wooden slats faded into obscurity as the glossy, varnished finish became weathered and worn. One of the slats was broken, and by the time Mathew shared his story with me, the memorial was in a state of serious disrepair.[17] Sauls, was not, however, concerned with the state of his piece but, instead, viewed its deterioration as part of the natural life of a public artwork.[18] This natural deterioration could be interpreted as a metaphor for the ephemerality of the feelings and memories the benches evoked in this interlocutor. It served as a material reminder of how, over time, the bad memories related to the difficult feelings of discriminatory racial classification were indeed slowly being forgotten. The material frailty of the RCB Benches therefore indexed how touch and physical interaction through constant use and weathering interfaced with notions of memory and the painful feelings about race and apartheid. Tapping into the feelings of ordinary passers-by who suffered injustice and humiliation, the benches also touched on the emotions skirted over by the Truth and Reconciliation Commission process and pointed to a national body politic that was still quietly grappling with the bad memories, the hurt, and the pain of the apartheid past.[19]

PIPES OF PROTEST

Early on the morning of May 31, 1981, a slight of stature, blond student named Bruce Fordyce joined thousands of runners in Durban to compete in that year's Comrades Marathon. Established by Vic Chapman in 1921 as a tribute for World War I soldiers, this ultramarathon was meant to celebrate "camaraderie and mankind's ability to triumph over adversity." Staged annually on Commonwealth Day, May 24, the inaugural marathon covered 89 kilometers (55 miles) of hilly terrain between Durban and Pietermaritzburg. The 1981 race did not, however, mark the celebration of these English, commonwealth traditions but was instead scheduled to coincide with the twentieth anniversary of Republic Day, a public holiday that commemorated the apartheid state's break from the commonwealth family of nations. Bowing to political pressure, organizers of the marathon incorporated the race into nationwide state-sanctioned festivals (Cameron-Dow 2011). Fordyce and a number of other runners protested the celebration of Republic Day by wearing black armbands. Walking up to the starting line, he was booed, sprayed with water, and bombarded with tomatoes. Despite this animosity, he won the race in record time, and, subsequently, a further eight times in a row, showing his mettle and unrivaled athletic prowess. To quote from the official STHP narrative text, "Fordyce, who is acknowledged to be one of the world's greatest long distance runners, has said that 'wearing the black armband to protest apartheid that day was, and is, one of the proudest moments in my life.'"[20]

Journalist Shelly Said researched this virtually forgotten moment of courageous sports political protest, and Doung Jahangeer was commissioned to design and install a public artwork honoring Fordyce (fig. 8.2). It was to be sited opposite the Royal Hotel in Durban City Centre, very near where Fordyce was first ridiculed. Using 4 centimeter (1½ inch) polished steel rods, Jahangeer developed a concept that reflected the narrative's predominant themes of running and resistance. Two-meter (6½ feet) lengths of steel were shaped and fused into an abstract, shimmering fascicle representing a runner. When some of the pipes were pulled, the sculpture would vibrate as if mimicking the rhythmical cadence of a runner in motion. Dubbed "Pipes of Protest" by one local newspaper, the memorial vividly reflected the themes of movement and opposition that flowed through the occasion of the black armband protest.[21]

Within a month of its installation, one of the steel rods was crudely broken off. Over time, the plaque was stolen, and gradually, more of the rods were broken off until the memorial was entirely destroyed.[22] Despite its interactive element rendering the piece vulnerable to the stress of excessive force, its polished steel was in fact of little monetary value, and as an abstract representation with no clear political import, it was reasonable to assume that the vandalism was motivated by undefined malice. Initially, Jahangeer was upset and hurt by the news. But gradually, he interpolated the destruction as representing an elaboration of a set of concepts, such as in-betweenness, the constitution of apartheid in urban space and the place of public art in the third world, that he had been thinking about in the years leading up to the commission.

Jahangeer construed in-betweenness in both personal and political terms. On one hand, it registered in his identity as a South African–based "Mauritian-born, Creole, Muslim-raised male of Indian descent."[23] And on the other, in-betweenness registered in his experience of Durban's urban landscape. As he explained, "When I started walking, I noticed this constant stream of people walking along the freeway, hanging around desolate parking lots and underneath freeways. These places are generally known as lost, neutral or non-spaces."[24] Neither here nor there, these lost spaces inspired

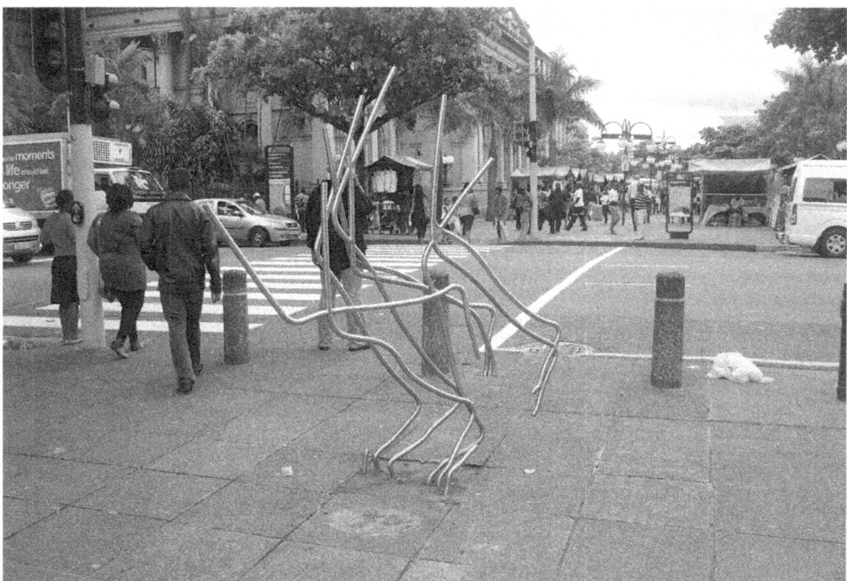

Fig. 8.2 Doung Jahangeer, *Memorial for Bruce Fordyce* (2008), opposite the Royal Hotel, Anton Lembede Street (formerly Smith Street), Durban. *Photograph by Duane Jethro.*

him to launch a project called CityWalks, guided walking tours that focused on "investigating spaces of in-between, in a city urban area."[25] Walking the side streets of Durban, observing the flow of people between places, Jahangeer imagined himself actively engaging with Michel de Certeau's (1984) notions of tactics and strategies while navigating the modern apartheid-designed cityscape. Relatedly, he was also concerned with the racial constitution of urban space and how and in what ways it related to notions of freedom and citizenship in the post-apartheid context. In his observation, after apartheid "non-white South Africans continued to use public spaces merely as a means to an end," like moving from one part of the city to the other or for setting up shops to sell goods. This instrumentalist utilization of public space perpetuated the imposed notion that "public spaces were places where they were not allowed to be free" (Jahangeer 2012, 9). He considered public art the best instrument for interpreting the complexities of post-apartheid public space and a critical tool that could potentially interrupt their legacies of containment, control, and constraint. Through the production of new public art, Jahangeer believed he could constitute new public spaces that would facilitate the richer participation of those marginalized in public life.

One of his first experiments in this regard was his contribution to the collaborative art project *Memories of Modernity* in 2006, for which he came up with a concept titled *Urbanamnesia*. Comprised of a knot of coiled steel wires, the art intervention was mounted underneath a Durban highway underpass. Over time, it was gradually broken and eventually destroyed by unknown members of the public. "The express purpose of the piece was to document its demise as it slowly became re-appropriated by steel recyclers until it disappeared entirely. The process took no more than a couple of weeks" (Jahangeer 2012, 10). In its decay, deterioration, and eventual destruction, *Urbanamnesia* did not register notions of erasure and forgetting as much as it marked the recovery of the meaning of public art in "lost" urban space.

Against this background, Jahangeer realized that the creeping destruction of the STHP memorial was not a further instance of wanton vandalism on the part of a silent, invisible mob but was instead a creative act of deconstruction that communicated sophisticated relationships between notions of public art and urban space in the post-apartheid cityscape. "Public art in the context of the third world, needs to be reassessed in terms of what function it is actually serving. If it is about the 'upliftment' of the city dwellers, then it cannot really exist in the form that public art traditionally has," he observed (Jahangeer 2012, 12). Here, Jahangeer appeared to invoke W. J. T. Mitchell's notion of public art as engendering violence. Following Mitchell's reasoning, Jahangeer seemed to suggest that third world public art was violent because it perpetuated value systems misaligned with the reality of its audience. Put another way, public art seemingly violently imposed the idea of art as an inherent aesthetic good, as uplifting and beneficial, on its audience. Post-apartheid urban space called for a new way of understanding the constitution of public art and how and in what ways it was meant to figure notions of place and publics. By abandoning the notion of public art as an inherent public good, Jahangeer was able to appreciate the subversive, critical power of the destruction of work as a creative act that progressively revealed the true nature of ordinary life in the post-apartheid city. Erecting public art then became an "effective and qualitative détournement of a practice of 'civilized' art into the participatory public where art became as much a process of investigation as it is a final intervention" (Jahangeer 2012, 10). Rerouting the flows of meaning forms of public art were meant to initiate, Jahangeer attempted to open up debate about public art practice itself.

Against the background of Jahangeer's ongoing exploration of the nature and locus of public art, the everyday and the legacies of racial urban planning, the vandalism perpetrated against the Bruce Fordyce memorial could be reinterpreted as an elaborate critique of the post-apartheid urban spatial order perpetrated by a virtually invisible, yet highly conspicuous public who harbored feelings of being left out. This was a nonwhite, poor, and urban-dwelling counterpublic, "a subset of the public . . . constituted through a conflictual relation to the dominant public" (Warner 2002, 423). Physically handling, forcing, and eventually breaking the steel frame of the Bruce Fordyce memorial, this counterpublic could be seen to be dramatically exerting force over material in an urban landscape from which they felt removed. Figuring motion and resistance, powerlessness and invisibility, the *Bruce Fordyce* memorial, could be construed as indexing this public's threshold of tolerance for forces constraining post-apartheid urban space and their sense of not being seen and heard, of belonging.

A BOOK

The June 16 youth uprisings, when students gathered to organize a march to protest against the Bantu Education Department's institution of Afrikaans as a medium of instruction, command a central place in the post-apartheid nation's cultural memory. It spawned a number of commemorative projects across Soweto, many of which were concentrated on a vacant plot the site opposite Morris Isaacson High school (see Oei and Staal 2011). Many were dedicated to those who were injured or died in the events that unfolded on that day, as was the case with Hector Pieterson. The *Sunday Times* also chose to participate in this commemorative culture, choosing, per its general narrative mandate of newsworthiness, to place emphasis on the origins and agents that initiated the event. This is made clear in the narrative description of the memorial, which read:

> At 8am on June 16, 1976, Tsietsi Mashinini interrupted the school assembly to lead the first group of students out of the gates and on the march that started the Soweto uprising. They were protesting the use of Afrikaans in schools. A reward was posted for his capture . . . [Mashinini] escaped detection by dressing up as a girl. After the march he never slept at home again and fled the country two months later.

This narrative was researched and written by Gillian Anstey, the journalist responsible for the Johannesburg area. This memorial did not focus so much on the student mass action as on Tsietsi Mashinini's role in leading the student masses in the march against the oppressive policies of the apartheid regime. Tsietsi Mashinini was a charismatic, intelligent, and handsome youth who became politically conscientized as a learner at Morris Isaacson High School. Three days before the protest, on June 13, Tsietsi Mashinini was elected the chairperson of the Action Committee established to coordinate activities. In the days leading up to June 16, he coordinated a plan for students from schools throughout Soweto to join a march that would culminate in a mass rally at the Orlando stadium. Anticipating an encounter with the police, Mashinini insisted that the march be peaceful. On the morning of June 16, he rallied students at Morris Isaacson High School to march, initiating the protest that would rock the country.

Having experienced the June 1976 riots firsthand as a boy, Johannes Phokela, the artist commissioned for this narrative, was inspired to design an art piece in the form of a mural, but one that was sculptural in form. In so doing, he wanted to emphasize "hope more than anything else."[26] Situated on the plot opposite Morris Isaacson High School, his memorial sculpture was shaped in the form of an open textbook placed on a raised plinth and directed to face the entrance of Morris Isaacson High. As he explained, "After much experimentation, I decided to do a wall that looked like a textbook. It is covered in tiles and on a podium which could be used for other projects, such as poetry sessions."[27] The tableau facing the school featured a collage of images and text in the shape of a map showing the route the march took through Soweto. It featured a prominent image of Mashinini in the center and was peppered with iconic images of other unnamed students and the slogans and exclamations of defiance they passionately exclaimed on the day. The plaque was placed on the rear, and the book was titled, "June 16, 1976, Wait This Is Our Day!" Through placing emphasis on Mashinini, the memorial therefore served as a powerful commemoration of the values and ideology of the unknown 1976 youth he inspired, doing so through a keen reflection on the social significance of the school as a locus of political action.

How have the memorial's intended audience—present-day learners—received the commemorative piece?[28] How has this memorial touched its intended audience? When I visited the site in August 2010, the memorial

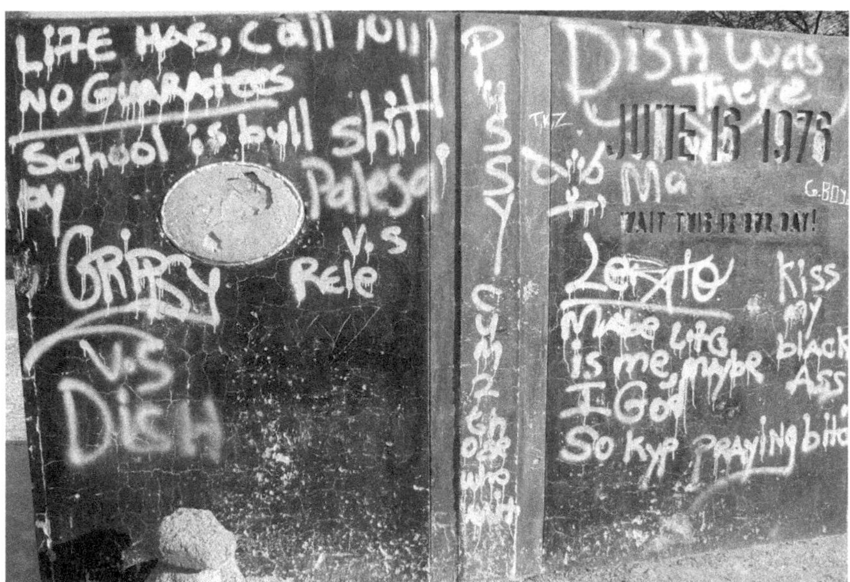

Fig. 8.3 Photograph taken in August 2010 that shows the defacing of Johannes Phokela's *Memorial for Tsietsi Mashinini* (2006), opposite Morris Isaacson High School, Soweto, Johannesburg. *Photograph by Duane Jethro.*

had been seriously defaced (fig. 8.3). The tiles of the collage were broken or cracked, and the images had faded due to exposure. Walking around the back, I discovered that the plaque had been removed. More strikingly, the dark rear surface was covered in neon-yellow graffiti. Other *Sunday Times* memorials erected in the Johannesburg area suffered similar vandalism.[29] While the other cases of vandalism in the Johannesburg area left few clear indicators of reception and motivation, the defacement of the Mashinini memorial was a more accessible archive of public sentiment. The luminous-yellow writing adorning its rear presented as a complex text expressing a range of perceptions about school going and township youth life. It marked the constitution of a public insofar as "a public space is the social space created by the reflexive circulation of discourse" (Warner 2002, 420). Discounting the other, smaller inscriptions that appear on the memorial, this main body of text can be read as a reflection of the perceptions of one of the memorial's intended publics. Using a series of phrases and terms that appear on the sculpture, peeling through the layers of discourse it relates to, it is possible to interpret how and in what ways the memorial may have affected this public and the kinds of feelings it evoked.

First, the wild, profanity-strewn graffiti sprayed across the back of the memorial directly addressed the issue of the school as an institution of discipline and control. This was reflected in the plain but powerful phrase "school is bullshit!" Ironically signaling solidarity with the values of their 1976 predecessors, despite the vast difference in sociopolitical context, the redactor also confirmed the memorial's success in tapping into public feeling about a relevant and enduring social issue.[30] Second, the graffiti brought attention to the feelings and experience of being a township youth living in post-apartheid South Africa. This was evidenced by the phrase "Life has no Guarantees, call 1011"—a reference to the official emergency rescue number, which appeared to index the anxieties of living in an unpredictable world where only distant agents of the state provided a sense of security. Third, the graffiti focused on the social significance of touch by reflecting on the power dynamics that underwrote forms of intimate bodily contact. For example, the phrase "Kiss my black ass!" spoke to a fascination with tactility and the skin through its implicit contemplation of intimate oral contact with a racialized body. While the phrase "Pussy cum to those who wait," sprayed down the spine of the book, highlighted the urgent yet frustrated corporeal desires of contemporary male youths and the objectification of women's bodies. Indeed, Michael Warner (2002, 417) notes, "public speech can have great urgency and intimate import." These nuggets of public speech touched on notions of masculinity, femininity, and the unequal, even violent gender dynamics among township youths. As Anthony Synnott (1993, 164–70) has shown, the sense of touch was often gendered and used to maintain particular gender distinctions and hierarchies of association and power.[31]

Taking the Tsietsi Mashinini memorial's form literally, it is apparent that it emphasized the political significance of the school as an institution of civil education and disobedience and the political significance of the textbook as an educational tool. The memorial could therefore be seen as figuring the past as a contested discursive space, where students protested against the use of a particular language as a medium of instruction. The vivid, expressive graffiti defacing the memorial therefore manifests as an evocative public commentary that ironically affirmed the memorial's discursive figuration of the past. Touching the memorial, breaking its tiles, handling the spray can to mark bold messages across its vast black canvas, the perpetrators also sought to outline their feelings of defiant rebellion against institutional authority, assert particular versions of masculinity, and cast opinions about the angst-ridden world of township life in post-apartheid Johannesburg.

BLAME

For the journalists, arts administrators, and artists involved in the project, the dilapidated condition of many of the memorials was painful. It felt like a failure. As Charlotte Bauer declared, it was "a damn shame."[32] Participants tried to make sense of the phenomenon by attributing blame. The failure of the sensitive creativity expressed in the material heritage forms to capture the hearts of the South African publics they addressed only made sense through ascribing blame on the *Sunday Times* for a lack of real long-term financial commitment or the South African public's lacking a culture of civic value. The *Sunday Times* was blamed for failing to make adequate financial provision for the long-term maintenance of the memorials. As Sabine Marschall (2010, 51) notes, the *Sunday Times* "assured municipalities from the outset that maintenance costs would be borne by the newspaper," yet "no funds were actually set aside for this purpose." Because no financial provision was made for the maintenance of the memorials, their "donation" could be construed as a form of abandonment, a form of neglect that could also be seen as staging the conditions for the memorials' ruination.

What is elided in these ascriptions is whether the *Sunday Times'* aesthetic choices and initial financial investment doomed the project from the beginning. Were the artists provided with sufficient material resources to design artworks that would stand a better test of time? By stipulating that the memorials incorporate an element of public interaction, did the *Sunday Times* not leave the memorials vulnerable to such destruction? What kinds of resources and alternate aesthetic choices could have been employed in designing interactive memorials of such variety that would be more impervious to acts of defacement?

Participants also remarked that the ruination represented an overly ambitious miscalculation of the South African public's appreciation of public art: the public just could not handle it. As former *Sunday Times* editor Mondli Makhanya explained, the newspaper anticipated this, forging ahead despite feelings of trepidation about the consequences of putting the works of fine art out in the public domain. "It was a risk that we knew from the onset . . . people in the industry, artists municipalities and so on were telling us that there were certain areas where they had to fence off public art works because they were just vandalised." Despite looming fear about the possible public life of the memorials, and skepticism about the South African public's perceived tolerance for such a project, Mondli Makhanya insisted that the *Sunday Times* had to grasp the nettle and go ahead. As he explained, "But the question is do you sit back and wait, do you sit back and wait another fifty years for the public to be ready? . . . Some people said, 'Are you crazy wanting to put something like that here?' . . . But you know what? You actually have to hope that people will get to appreciate their heritage and get to appreciate art."[33] The process of erecting artistic memorials in places where neglect seemed to reign required a suspension of judgment, fortitude, and blind faith. Commenting on the ruined memorials, Michael Barry, one of the arts administrators explained, in all sympathy, "What is it with these people, hey? You have to have nerves of steel when you put these things out there."[34] Other stakeholders could also be drawn into sharing the burden of responsibility for the state of the memorials. Sabine Marschall (2011) argues that municipalities and communities of immediate interest should also take some responsibility because in many cases, they failed to take advantage of the memorials for tourism or public history projects. While parties contest the ruins of the material component of the STHP, some of the memorials endure in public spaces all across South Africa, whether in a defaced, dilapidated state, or rarely in a pristine condition, especially in places where they were appropriated by, or perceived to be under the care of, an immediate community of interest.

CONCLUSION

Pitched between arguments about immature civic culture and a lack of financial commitment, the question of whether the vandalism of some of the memorials indeed marked the failure of the STHP enabled such exercises in blame. These attempts to work out who was responsible for the destruction of the *Sunday Times* memorials concerned deliberations about who bore the burden of responsibility for arbitrating over notions of public history and high culture as a force of influence over civic values that pervaded post-apartheid society. Framed in this way, these contests alluded to another central stake in this debate, which Sabine Marschall (2010, 54) defines as the question of how and in what ways we can gauge the efficacy of the memorials: "do they foster a democratic exchange about the meaning of the past, which is connected to public debate and participation in civil society?"

I have tried to engage with this question by arguing for ruination and its usefulness for understanding the relationship between the *Sunday Times* and the publics it attempted to address. I have tried to show the constructive meaningfulness of ruination as a practice that concerned the working out of publicness in post-apartheid South Africa by looking at three ruined STHP memorials. Exploring relationships among notions of ruination, touch, and public feeling in post-apartheid South Africa, I have engaged with how and in what ways these incidents marked instances of exchange about the meaning of the past as occasions of debate about public space, belonging, and citizenship in post-apartheid South Africa. By engaging with materiality, publicness, and public feeling, I have hoped to argue that such an approach contributes to the study of heritage and the senses by showing how practices engaging with material cultural forms staged representative sets of public feeling. Clearly, strong feelings were on display in some of the cases discussed.

ACKNOWLEDGMENTS

The research toward this chapter was developed within the Netherlands Organisation for Scientific Research (NWO) project, Heritage Dynamics: Politics of Authentication and Aesthetics of Persuasion in Brazil, Ghana, South Africa and the Netherlands, led by Professor Birgit Meyer and Professor Mattijs van de Port. I hereby acknowledge the funding provided by the NWO for conducting this research.

Duane Jethro is a 2017 Alexander von Humboldt Post-Doctoral Fellow based at the Centre for Anthropological Research for Museums and Heritage, CARMaH, at the Humboldt University, Berlin. His post-doctoral project, *Aesthetics and Difference,* looks at the work of commemorations under changing social and temporal conditions in Berlin.

Notes

1. "Heritage Virgins Come of Age." See http://heritage.thetimes.co.za/article.aspx?id=570377, accessed December 20, 2013.
2. I understand interactiveness as relating to a range of intentional relations of tactile, physical engagement staged by the artworks that include occasions of engagement

that were not overt, active and direct. They could relate to the act of sitting on the bollards of the Cissie Gool memorial in Cape Town, for example, or on one of the three bench-style memorials erected in Cape Town, Johannesburg, and the Eastern Cape, or the handling and touching of the metal crosses of the Olive Schreiner memorial in Cape Town, or feeling the dimpled, tiled surface of the colorful Bessie Head memorial in Durban.

3. "Fifth *Sunday Times* Commissioned Sculpture Vandalised," *South African Art Times*, July 2008, accessed December 20, 2013, http://issuu.com/arttimes/docs/saatjuly08/4.

4. "Public Art Meets History's Heart," accessed December 20, 2013, http://issuu.com/arttimes/docs/saatjuly08/4. I don't see this article featured in the link provided.

5. "Public Art Meets History's Heart."

6. I am convinced that discourses do not so much "create the objects of which they speak," to paraphrase Foucault, but, rather, they are a fundamental reality of the material stuff that renders them sensible.

7. "Dispatches: Blacks Chip Away at Monuments to Afrikaner Power," accessed December 20, 2013, http://www.independent.co.uk/news/despatches-blacks-chip-away-at-monuments-to-afrikaner-power-1240902.html.

8. "The Abandoned Robert Waterwitch/Colleen Williams Memorial," accessed December 20, 2013, http://152.111.1.87/argief/berigte/dieburger/2008/03/04/PQ/3/srstatue-811.html.

9. In this chapter, I refer to ruination, drawing on Laura Anne Stoler's ideas of ruination as a process of despoiling, to avoid the pejorative associations that may attach to this conventional lexicon, and in recognition of the active-passive conceptual slippage between notions of neglect versus vandalism.

10. "Race Classification Board," accessed December 20, 2013, http://sthp.saha.org.za/memorial/race_classification_board.htm. This is a truncated version as are the other quoted narratives for brevity. To my knowledge, these narratives were provided as informative vignettes. I do not know whether they have been contested or debated.

11. The selection criteria were described in a document discussing the Commissioned Artists (n.d.). Selection was done on "a closed-commission basis," rather than open competition. Commissions were awarded on the basis of "recognition for [artists'] work and appropriateness to the project." Furthermore, "Only South African contemporary artists" living and working in South Africa were chosen. In many cases, this meant artists were selected from the province in which a series of memorials were being erected. Artists had to show a portfolio that demonstrated "successful experience in producing corporate and/or public commissions or similar projects," as well as "a special focus on public space and an interest in South African heritage, history and local narratives." Sometimes, artists were commissioned because of their "existing knowledge, involvement or proven interest in one of the specific stories or sites" such as Rod Sauls. Moreover, "a diversity of artists, in terms of style, interest, concept and media across the spectrum of race, gender and age were contacted and employed."

12. See http://heritage.thetimes.co.za/memorials/WC/RaceClassificationBoard/, accessed December 20, 2013.

13. Official Census data records racial demographics using five categories, African, White, Coloured, Indian/Asian, and Other that respondents are invited to self-identify

with. Following this scheme of classification, here coloured and coloureds as those who are considered to be, but necessarily of, mixed racial descent. Taking this position, I fully acknowledge that racial categories are fraught, loaded and socially constructed.

14. "The Lightbulb Moment," accessed December 20, 2013, http://sthp.saha.org.za/memorial/articles/the_light_bulb_moment_the_artists_concept_9.htm.

15. Rod Sauls, "Artist Proposal," August 2006, 1.

16. I do not have demographic data to show how representative Matthew was as a visitor to the site, but his comments and ideas were some of the most frank and generous.

17. This was the case with a number of other memorials in the STHP that were erected in Cape Town. For example, Barbara Wildenboer's memorial dedicated to Olive Schreiner was badly weathered, with paint flaking and the metal crosses pinned into its central pond either having been bent or simply removed. The entire memorial was removed in 2016. The series of bollards that made up the memorial to the activist politician Cissie Gool was also in a bad state of disrepair with chunks of concrete plaster flaking off and the plaque having been removed and never recovered. The area around the memorial was also often unkempt and litter strewn. Later, in 2016 the memorial was updated and cleaned up.

18. As of 2014, the benches have been repaired but not to their original condition, which included the full legislative inscriptions on the slats. The plaque is also missing.

19. The Truth and Reconciliation Commission was a legislative institution established in 1996 to investigate incidents of gross human rights violations between 1960 and 1994, assist with the rehabilitation and restoration of the dignity of victims, and investigate and assess perpetrators appeals for amnesty on the basis of their full disclosure to the commission. Various groups and individuals came forward to make submissions to the commission, and a series of public hearings were staged around the country between 1996 and 1998.

20. Undated narrative brief.

21. "Pipes of Protest," *Natal Witness*, March 7, 2008, p. 3.

22. I am not sure if the series of memorials erected in the Durban area were subject to similar acts of ruination. There was very little public information about them, and the ones I did manage to find were generally in a good state of repair in early 2011.

23. "Take a Walk: Interview with Doung Jahangeer, Part 1," accessed December 20, 2013, http://www.cascoland.com/2007/dag/13feb.html.

24. Ibid.

25. Ibid.

26. "The Lightbulb Moment."

27. Ibid.

28. "Learners" is the official term for school goers in contemporary South Africa, while they are referred to as pupils or students in historical sources.

29. For example, Usha Seejarim's *Mohandas Gandhi* memorial, was vandalized soon after its unveiling. Trash had been placed inside the pot and set alight, damaging the zoetrope images. And in Newtown, not far away, the Brenda Fassie memorial also suffered repeated incidents of vandalism, with the microphone head, the central interactive component of the piece, having broken off and repaired on a number of occasions. See, for example, "Brenda Fassie Intact Again," accessed February 23, 2015, http://

www.joburg.org.za/index.php?option=com_content&view=article&id=7940:brenda-fassie-intact-again&catid=122:heritage&Itemid=203.

30. One cannot equate this disaffection with that of students of 1976, and their conviction that the education of black township youths in the democratic dispensation was seen as an important means of transforming their material circumstances.

31. Synnott's observations are crafted in relation to the sociology and anthropology of the senses, where he broadly relates the sense of touch to different perspectives on the place and use of touch in human development, depth of human relations, and gendered notions of tactility, physical intimacy, sex, and power.

32. Telephone interview with Charlotte Bauer, January 18, 2010.

33. Personal interview with Mondli Makhanya, January 26, 2011.

34. Personal interview with Michael Barry, February 7, 2010.

References

Allen, Matthew J., and Steven D. Brown. 2011. "Embodiment and Living Memorials: The Affective Labour of Remembering the 2005 London Bombings." *Memory Studies* 4, no. 3: 312–27.

Bauer, Charlotte. 2007. "Goodbye to Big Men on Bronze Horses: When the *Sunday Times* Turned 100 Last Year, It Decided Not Only to Celebrate, but to 'Give Back' by Getting into the Heritage Business." *Rhodes Journalism Review* 27 (September): 36–41.

Cameron-Dow, John. 2011. *Comrades Marathon—The Ultimate Human Race*. Johannesburg: Penguin.

Clark, Jennifer, and Majella Franzmann. 2006. "Authority from Grief, Presence and Place in the Making of Roadside Memorials." *Death Studies* 30, no. 6: 579–99.

Classens, Constance. 2012. *The Deepest Sense: A Cultural History of Touch*. Urbana: University of Illinois Press.

de Certeau, Michel. 1984. *Distinction: A Social Critique of the Judgement of Taste*. New York: Routledge and Kegan.

Doss, Erika. 2010. *Memorial Mania: Public Feeling in America*. Chicago: University of Chicago Press.

Fraser, Nancy. 1990. "Rethinking the Public Sphere: A Contribution to the Critique of Actually Existing Democracy." *Social Text* 25/26: 56–80.

Freedberg, David. 1985. *Iconoclasts and Their Motives*. Maarssen, the Netherlands: Schwartz.

Gamboni, Dario. 1997. *The Destruction of Art: Iconoclasm and Vandalism since the French Revolution*. London: Reaktion Books.

Habermas, Jürgen. 1991. *The Structural Transformation of the Public Sphere: An Inquiry into a Category of Bourgeoisie Society*. Translated by Thomas Burger with assistance by Frederick Lawrence. Cambridge, MA: MIT Press.

Hauser, Gerard. 1999. *Vernacular Voices: The Rhetoric of Publics and Public Spheres*. Columbia: University of South Carolina Press.

Hook, Derek. 2005. "Monumental Space and the Uncanny." *Geoforum* 36, no. 6: 688–704.

Jahangeer, Doung. 2012. ". . . Just Passing Through . . ." In *Shoe Shop*, edited by Marie-Helene Gutberlet and Cara Snyman, 7–12. Auckland Park, South Africa: Fanele.

Kros, Cynthia. 2008. "Prompting Reflections: An Account of the *Sunday Times* Heritage Project from the Perspective of an Insider Historian." *Kronos* 34, no. 1: 181–214.

Kwon, Miwon. 1997. "One Place after Another: Notes on Site-Specificity." *October* 80 (Spring): 85–110.

———. 2004. *One Place after Another: Site-Specific Art and Locational Identity*. Cambridge, MA: MIT Press.

Latour, Bruno. 2002. "What Is Iconoclash?" In *Iconoclash: Beyond the Image Wars in Science, Religion, and Art*, edited by Bruno Latour and Peter Weibel, 16–40. Cambridge, MA: MIT Press.

Marschall, Sabine. 2010. "Private Sector Involvement in Public History Production in South Africa: The *Sunday Times* Heritage Project." *African Studies Review* 53, no. 3: 35–59.

———. 2011. "The *Sunday Times* Heritage Project: Heritage the Media and the Formation of National Consciousness." *Social Dynamics: Journal of African Studies* 37, no. 3: 409–423.

Merrills, A. H. 2009. "The Origins of 'Vandalism.'" *International Journal of the Classical Tradition* 16, no. 2: 155–75.

Mitchell, W. J. T. 1990. "The Violence of Public Art: Do the Right Thing." *Critical Inquiry* 16, no. 4: 880–899.

Oei, Vincent G., and Jonas Staal. 2011. "The Missing Link/Monument for the Distribution of Wealth." *Continent* 1, no. 4: 242–52.

Rassool, Ciraj, and Sandra Prosalendis. 2001. *Recalling Community in Cape Town: Creating and Curating the District Six Museum*. Cape Town: District Six Museum.

Stevens, Quentin. 2009. "Nothing More Than Feelings: Abstract Memorials." *Architectural Theory Review* 14, no. 2: 156–72.

Stoler, Laura Anne, ed. 2013. *Imperial Debris: On Ruins and Ruination*. Durham, NC: Duke University Press.

Synnott, Anthony. 1993. *The Body Social: Symbolism, Self and Society*. London: Routledge.

Taussig, Michael. 1999. *Defacement: Public Secrecy and the Labor of the Negative*. Stanford, CA: Stanford University Press.

Warner, Michael. 2002. "Publics and Counterpublics (abbreviated version)." *Quarterly Journal of Speech* 88, no. 4: 413–25.

———. 2005. *Publics and Counter Publics*. New York: Zone Books.

PART 4

EPHEMERAL PROJECTS

CHAPTER 9

Public Art, Troubling Tropes: An Unsettling Intervention in Cape Town

SHANNEN HILL

The kind of aesthetic understanding that should ensue from a reading of public art, literature and expressive culture is a very different thing to that demanded by a nation building project. It is important to acknowledge that the role of art is to forge a sense of the independent, enquiring, skeptical mind.
Valmont Layne, 2001

IF THE MID- TO late 1990s was a period of developing a highly visual, publicly commemorated version of the "story of liberation struggle" in South Africa, then the early years of the new millennium may be remembered as a time that such singular narratives were challenged and modes of telling were re-calibrated. Heritage, a noun, was viewed post-apartheid as a code for culture that could be easily filed in a multicultural manner, neatly placed side by side to realize a "Rainbow Nation" for global consumption. Although this tidy rhetoric was challenged even while it was taking shape, it took nearly a decade and numerous debates before some sectors began to conceptualize heritage as a verb: what historian Ciraj Rassool (2000, 5) called "an assemblage of arenas and activities of history-making" that required individuated articulation to be made meaningful. Approaching heritage in this way dislodges it from authoritative claims such as the "nation building project" Layne describes in the epigraph (what Sabine Marschall [2010, 177] calls South Africa's "foundation myth"), and it enables us to fully appreciate voices and visions that do not trouble themselves with academic hierarchy and grammar's dictates.[1] In challenging what falls within and outside history's lens, Rassool (2000, 4–5) suggests that we need "a sociology of historical production in the academy as well as the public domain and an enquiry into the categories, codes and conventions of history-making in each location and in all its variability." I support this bid and offer an account of a public art intervention by a collective once deeply involved with troubling the dictates of both multiracialism and nonracialism (different vantages that are too commonly swathed in the same light) witnessed in heritage building post-apartheid. The BLACK ARTS COLLECTIVE (1998–2003), or BLAC, mounted an outdoor, freely available public exhibition called *Returning the Gaze* in 2000 in response to Cape Town's "One City" rhetoric, a trope that embraced the harmonious glow of rainbowism attractive to tourists. As will become clear, I believe that future public arts commissions would do well to embrace BLAC's methodology as it is more meaningful to South Africa's population, purveyors of heritage on the move.

Founded in Cape Town by Zayd Minty, BLAC was first and foremost a "quiet space" for building discourse around race, identity (or heritage), and power that enabled individuals to air their disenchantment with the rainbow rhetoric and develop a means of redress. Through regular meetings, a seminar series, an exhibitions program, and an online forum that encouraged public response to debates, BLAC sought to trouble the limiting frames of blackness that had settled into South Africa's arts institutions and its mainstream commercial market, both of which fed global perceptions of the rainbow's harmonious glow. Importantly, BLAC relied on an interpretation of blackness as originally promoted by Black Consciousness (BC) activists in the 1970s: one that united all people commonly oppressed by nationalists regardless of skin color, itself a radical break from much anti-apartheid activism at that time. Unlike those political parties that signed the Freedom Charter (a multiracial document of 1955), BC united people consigned to Indian, Coloured, and Bantu, and it thus rejected self-definitions that mirrored the Population Registration Act of 1950.[2] The BC minded enabled the regional realization of a transnational, tricontinental vision (today constituted by the Global South) that had fueled anticolonial activism for decades. Minty and his colleagues made use of this tradition to vocalize and visualize a more inclusive definition of blackness than that promoted by gallerists and museum personnel in the 1990s.

A word on historicizing South African racial politics is imperative here because liberation narratives, both popular and scholarly, frequently cast multiracial and nonracial methods as one and the same, but they are distinctly different. So, too, do they cast BC as fundamentally racial. Multiracialism is conservative in that it interprets race as biological difference. Nonracialism, as Michael MacDonald (2006, 92) put it, "means a number of things" today, but consistent among them is a rejection of racialist ideas (and, problematically, their consequences) in all forms.[3] The term's origins are in the Cape Colony of the mid-to-late nineteenth century where they were couched in cultural terms.[4] Whereas multiracialism can be described as a gathering together of difference with an aim to acknowledge and potentially appreciate it, nonracialism is best understood as a dismissal of racial notions in favor of a common and diverse humanity. BC is seen as racially determined mainly by those who continue to put too much emphasis on the color that consciousness names. It was (and is) entirely antiethnic and does not concern itself with whiteness. Power is its focal point and enabling self-determination among those commonly oppressed by colonial histories is its aim. Still, scholars of visual culture who consider BC (Peffer 2009; Wylie 2008) tend to elide the distinctions between multiracial and nonracial approaches, and they tend to cast BC as ineffectual in realizing apartheid's end.[5]

By using media not commonly understood as public art and explicitly looking back at those who set its parameters, BLAC's *Returning the Gaze* project intervened on the norm. For instance, in fig. 9.1 we see a work within Berni Searle's well-known *Colour Me* series (1998–2000) reproduced on T-shirts worn by University of Cape Town students who walked the city passing out artists' postcards. This body of work launched Searle's international career and has been written about extensively in interesting ways (Bester 2003; Coombes 2003; Gqola 2005; Schmahmann 2009; Van der Watt 2004); she created it during the same period in which she took part in BLAC seminars (Hill 2015). So, too, has her *Not Quite White*, another work in which Searle covered her body with a substance used to prepare meals (Bester 2003; Schmahmann 2004). But too few scholars record the context of *Not Quite White*—it was a billboard displayed beside the busy N1 highway as part of *Returning the Gaze*—to secure the place of BLAC's intervention in its history (Hill 2015; Minty 2001b). Searle was a regular and reliable member of this group since its first year, both contributing to and benefiting from its mission. So committed was she that she sat on BLAC's board of directors (Annual Report 2001). BLAC's influence is present in these works and must be historicized.

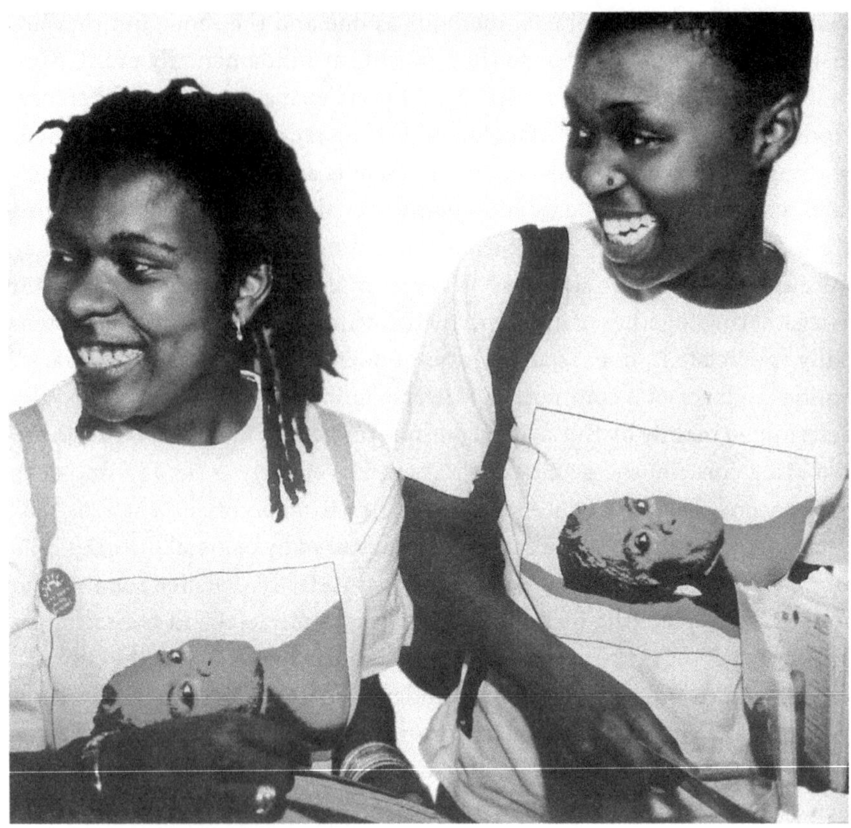

Fig. 9.1 University of Cape Town students distributing postcards at the One City Festival, 2000. The woman at left holds Brett Murray's *Mantra* and Alexander Smith's *Untitled*. The woman at right displays Cameron Platter's *Care-Race*. A work from Berni Searle's *Colour Me* series is reproduced on their shirts. *Photograph by Nicholas Aldridge.*

Scholarly omission and confusion over terms are important to address because they deny counterparts to South Africa's foundation myth, itself overbearing and inaccurate. It miscasts BC as an outdated approach, and groups that adopt it, like BLAC, as threatening to the nation's welfare. For instance, Cape Town's arts professionals, including some involved in Public Eye, the best-known organization devoted to creating public art in the area, took issue with BLAC's approach. As BLAC member Thembinkosi Goniwe put it, "Once you say BC people panic," and indeed response to his BC infused approach register it.[6] For example, Henri Vergon of Afronova Gallery described the artist's "badly digested BC background" as cause for his own reluctance to engage with him. Once the artist proved himself "humble and measured," the gallerist was willing to work with him. Revealing his own limited understanding of BC as an ideology centered on skin rather than mind/power, Vergon said of Goniwe, "I think he did have those racial prejudices, but he has moved on. He's more relaxed" (de Vries 2010, 48). In interviews, Minty, Paul Hendricks, Donovan Ward, and Emile Maurice (the last two also of BLAC) all concurred that local nonracialists either brushed off BC-derived projects or effectively silenced their efforts by showing no interest.[7] In short, BC was seen as racial instead of hybrid, oppositional instead of embracing varied tones.

It's important, too, because BLAC's methods and objectives model how public art commissions might best be realized. BC offers space for open discussion with careful attention to voices and visions outside the mainstream; listening instead of heady talking can realize art that more people find meaningful. BLAC participant Ice7 (aka Tony Coetzee) told me that such ventures enable him to sense "a deeper, more universal connection through an informed, personal identity."[8] In adopting BC at its founding, BLAC secured a stage to contest Cape Town's powerful art base, discomforting it in the process. Finally, it placed public art on the move by adopting T-shirts and postcards, media important to heritage studies in South Africa.[9] Periodic, well-placed interventions in the public arena of the kind discussed here cause us to pause and reconsider the efficacy of both dominant mediums and messages. If public art aims to record histories inherited through time (for this is what the noun *heritage* reflects), then those who commission it would do well to encourage alternative narratives, no matter how uncomfortable, because these may resonate more meaningfully.

BLAC: ITS GOALS, ACHIEVEMENTS, AND WHY IT CHOSE BLACK CONSCIOUSNESS

In 1990, a rapid rise in international attention accompanied the end of the United Nations–sanctioned cultural boycott of South Africa, and throughout that decade, select South African artists and other arts professionals found themselves at the epicenter of a global contemporary market.[10] As the decade progressed, the nation grappled with countless changes; in the cultural sphere these included how to meaningfully incorporate diverse historical perspectives once understood to be separate. Both Annie Coombes (2003) and Sabine Marschall (2010) historicize the debates that took place and critique the limited frames that arose with adopting a narrative of national unity over, as Coombes (2003, 206) put it, "the contradictions and tensions of a more dynamic model of history and society." Issues of heritage—the whos, whys, and how to best represent it—were debated amid an ambition, in the first part of the decade, to realize a Rainbow Nation of equally proportioned bands and, in the decade's later years, to realize South Africa's role in leading an African Renaissance that heralded the continent's global import to the new millennium. In short, the rhetorical swings of multiracialism and nonracialism (or color blindness) gave way to that of black entrepreneurship (or self-determination). Although talk of a renaissance eventually sputtered out along with its progenitor, President Thabo Mbeki, innovative projects continued to be realized.[11]

When the BLAC formed in 1998, it did so within a cultural climate that had a narrow vision of what constitutes black art in both political and aesthetic terms. In the African National Congress's (ANC's) rainbow-infused rhetoric, "African" referred to skin color, and art by men and women so designated either reflected black life in content or it "looked" African in form. Such was the template desired by most visiting curators who organized international exhibitions of South African art, and largely, though not entirely, by museum and gallery management that promoted it at home. BLAC challenged this vision, and it chose several modes of action to do so. First, members chose to define black not by skin color but by common access to power. In this way, they mirrored blackness as first articulated by BC adherents who, beginning in 1968, limited their target audience to "people who have, as a result of Apartheid, been marginalized on the basis of race"—that is, Black, Coloured, and Indian societal sectors (Minty 2001a). Second, like its better-known counterpart, the MEDU ART ENSEMBLE (1977–85, Gaborone, Botswana), which was also founded by the BC-minded, BLAC eventually welcomed white members who were willing to cede the platform to otherwise marginalized voices, if not fully accepting BC as a meaningful ideology in their lives. Third, BLAC adopted the same aesthetic values promoted by artists-activists in the United Kingdom who also championed, beginning in 1981, BC in the realm of culture: Rashid Araeen, Eddie Chambers, Mona Hatoum, and Gavin Jantjes among them. In this vantage, "black art is contemporary art that has nothing to do with AfroAsian traditions" (Araeen 1988, 5). In other words, the inherent political positioning of black art as promoted by BLAC and its predecessors refused cultural domination and essentialist reductions. In these ways, BLAC optimized the self-determination of BC-inspired initiatives and challenged the global preference for the nonracial rainbow, itself promoted uncritically through Cape Town's first One City Festival in 1999, among other nodes in cultural capital.

Founded and largely shepherded by Zayd Minty, BLAC was conceived of as a "discourse building project" around intersections of "race, identity, and power," each of considerable interest to heritage and other cultural brokers, tourist professionals, and academics. It "embraced contestation," aimed to provoke fresh insights, and promoted adherence to "principles of positivity, proactivity, nurturance and respect." BLAC achieved many things over its five years of existence. Funded by several entities, BLAC ran seminars (with a record of nine in 2000) on topics of heritage, art, and identity and included "predominantly black cultural workers" around Cape Town who made music, art, fashion, film, poems, graphics, and who danced and spun tunes. Its "creative pool" also included academics, journalists, writers, publishers, producers, technicians, and arts administrators (Minty 2001a). BLAC hosted a web-based forum (with a chat function that encouraged debate) for networking, editorializing, and promoting events. Most visibly, it organized two large-scale public offerings: *Returning the Gaze* (2000), discussed here, and a symposium called *Liberating Zones: Cultural Movements in the 80s in Cape Town* (2002).

Creating a space in which black arts professionals could communicate their ideas and perspectives made BLAC special. Minty said the aim was to "cross boundaries, so we made a very conscious effort with BLAC to have . . . cross-cutting forums and cross-cutting speakers" gather about every six weeks. He called these "talk shops" with about twenty to thirty people who shared their practice and what it meant, or "what they were about," professionally. He described discussions in the first year, when white arts practitioners were not allowed: "A lot of it was about the pain of being black, about being marginalized, or deeper issues of ethnic difference and how it has impacted our new society, marginalizing them even further. . . . How difficult it is [as an artist] to break through in the current environment and find opportunities." This "quiet space" of restricted membership was upturned a bit in 1999 when BLAC opened membership to whites. While it continued to profile only black speakers, Minty found that the "quality of the discussion did change." BLAC "wasn't the place" for nonracial liberalism, and Minty believes some newer members "battled to come to grips with . . . broader discussions" that might discomfort.[12] Thembinkosi Goniwe disagreed with Minty's decision to open BLAC to an audience other than that welcomed by BC. In our interview of 2011, he observed that the presence of white cultural interests "flattened debate" within seminars, as original members grew quieter. Ice7 concurred.[13]

Minty confirmed that particular tensions arose over BLAC's initial BC-derived approach with some founders of Public Eye, a Section 27 company founded in 1999 to promote public art within Cape Town. While Minty described their response as a "severe attack," Donovan Ward noted a "sense of hostility" toward BC from those who would establish Public Eye when he and others mounted an exhibition devoted to it at the District Six Museum in September 1997.[14] Called *The Legacy of Steve Biko Twenty Years Later,* the exhibition coincided with the better publicized and funded *The District Six Public Sculpture Project*; they neighbored each other in District Six and opened within the same two weeks.[15] Eventually, tensions between BLAC and Public Eye subsided and both bodies came to praise the work done by the other. And in one case, the two were reconciled: Brett Murray, a Public Eye cofounder, created a work called *Mantra* that BLAC included in its *Returning the Gaze* exhibition of 2000.[16] This exhibition forms the bulk of what follows, but first, let us consider the venue in which it was staged: Cape Town's One City Festival, a setting wherein public art interventions take place. BLAC's impact here registers best by comparing it with its first incarnation, staged in 1999.

1999: THE ONE CITY FESTIVAL WITHIN A RAINBOW NATION

Ryland Fisher, then editor of the *Cape Times,* conceived of the One City Festival to promote intercultural tolerance after a terrorist-planted bomb exploded during dinnertime at Cape Town's Planet Hollywood on August 25, 1998 (Fisher 1999, 3).[17] Subtitled *One City, Many Cultures,* the full-week festival stretched over Heritage Day, September 24, a national holiday established to celebrate diversity, the variety of which "has a profound power to build our new nation," said President Nelson Mandela in 1996 ("National Heritage Day").[18] In an article that Ciraj Rassool wrote (derived from a paper commissioned by BLAC for one of its public dialogue sessions), he rightly critiques the commodification of heritage, such as that touted by the One City Festival, as "a primordial one, in which culture is seamlessly constituted by a traceable purity or demonstrable authenticity." He evaluates the 1999 festival, among other things, and the "heady mix of advertising, corporate competition and [the] role call for democracy" that characterized the lead-up to it as the *Cape Times* ran a daily series over twelve weeks, across two broadsheet pages, aimed at understanding "how different religions and cultural groups relate to certain rites of passage and other important issues of life." The newspaper identified every Capetonian by religion since the violence that prompted the festival's creation was one of religious intolerance.[19] Readers wrote in their response, and aside from the occasional word about hybridity, debates were waged over rites and customs practiced. As the festival neared, locals were told "All roads lead to the One City Festival," and indeed the map itself appeared rainbow-inflected: Revelers were advised to "Take the green route for visual art or the yellow for cultural tourism. [Music can be had if you] follow the blue marked posters to lead you to the right venues." Or one could enjoy the full spectrum of colors at one site—the Cape Metropolitan Council developed an "African Theme Park" at the city's fringe, replete with Ndebele, Xhosa, and Zulu villages, a museum, an auditorium, a restaurant, gift shop, and parking lot (Rassool 2000, 8–10).

The 1999 festival largely took place in the city's Central Business District (CBD) with free bus service running a circular route to participating locales along its edges.[20] Free off-site programming could be enjoyed in Noordhoek, Hout Bay, Kirstenbosch, Plumstead, Parkwood, and Mannenberg (all but one are affluent enclaves along the skirt of Table Mountain), but activities in Athlone, Gugulethu, and Crossroads (townships that dot the Cape Flats) charged fees. Further, while the festival offered "alternate tourism routes" by appointment, those within the CBD ran on a predetermined schedule. Rassool (2000, 9) credited Public Eye contributions—a Gugulethu street signs project; murals and billboards at the railway station, bus shelters, De Waal Drive and other main roads; and a CBD public sculpture "intervention"—for beginning to undermine "the static pre-ordained cultural framework through which heritage was constructed" within the neatly packaged spectacle of *One City, Many Cultures*. But he conceded that the *Cape Times* hardly noticed, and it seems that such valued interventions were rather obscure amid so much investment in making rainbow rhetoric real. For instance, Gugulethu sign makers were to direct tourists toward historically significant local sites, but they *began painting* on the festival's first day. One wonders how many of these sites actually received visitors. Thus the festival fell well short of its goal to "humanize" Cape Town by encouraging respectful engagement with the *Many Cultures* that comprise this *One City* because it upheld the notion that heritage is necessarily a noun, fixed in place, instead of a verb that roams.

An exception was the festival's Lecture Series, which Zayd Minty coordinated as a series of give-and-take dialogues like those BLAC practiced the previous year. At the Centre for the Book, festivalgoers could engage in panel discussions on freedom of expression, music history, ending violence against women, cultural tourism, and notions of an African renaissance; they could take part in debates on cultural appropriation or crime and a dialogue about business and art; and they could see an illustrated lecture about memorializing slavery. Most relevant for this book, a panel discussed "Revitalising and Democratising Public Spaces in Cape Town," and another addressed "Chasing the Rainbow: Racism in the Western Cape." These were BLAC concerns, and they were given a pronounced place in the One City Festival of 2000, which Minty was hired to coordinate. This in itself registers the positive local impact of his work.[21]

2000: ANOTHER SCENE/SEEN ALTOGETHER—*RETURNING THE GAZE*

Whereas the One City Festival of 1999 promoted the nation's "Rainbow People," its 2000 version was subtitled *Celebrating Difference,* which Minty cast as a rejection of rainbowism. The multicultural mantra was set aside for an approach that praised difference for the vitality it brings to personal experience. In other words, culture and heritage were not things to be observed, or gazed upon, as spectacle but felt or lived through and registered within. The festival's program of 2000 opens with the coordinator's column, and here Minty chose to quote hip-hop artist Pharoh Sanders in his epigraph: "We have been socialized into a way of looking at the world which associates difference with degradation, rather than understanding difference for difference." Minty expounded: "culture is dynamic and . . . positive change comes through both a pride in heritage and an acceptance of change itself." As festival coordinator, he promised that the art on view could "shake us and transport us" and urged the public to do more than engage at a distance; rather, they were prominently called forth. The festival, like BLAC before it, sought "a positively reconstructed view of our present and future realities," which Minty (2000a, 2000b) believed required "YOU, the audience, to add your ideas and voice to the debate!" In this way, the 2000 One City Festival adopted and adapted BLAC's approach to broadening public dialogue about race, identity, and power—troubling touchstones for those who felt more comfortable with a singular-tract liberation story: an arched rainbow of distinct colors that despite its nonracial glow, continued to register as largely white.

BLAC and its approach gained center stage; its primary visual arts component, an outdoor, city- and township-wide public arts project called *Returning the Gaze,* formed the center spread of the festival program (fig. 9.2). In the months leading up to the festival, BLAC issued a call for artworks across a wide swath of the city and its environs, and it aimed to infiltrate these locations with public artwork in both conventional and unconventional forms. In the end, a committee of three (Valmont Layne, Graham Falken, and Ciraj Rassool) selected for inclusion seven postcards that would be handed out by a team of theater students (see fig. 9.1), four billboards, three murals, a T-shirt design, one online work, and two poems to be performed at the festival. Although the project's title suggests a volley of sort—a reflexive response to a term, "the gaze," that visually fixes its subject into a classified object—Layne indicates that the panel favored submissions that "thought about the gaze in terms that went beyond narrow inversion or binaries in its interpretation of the gaze." Indeed, BLAC's approach, like that of BC before it, understood that the gaze, metaphor for a complex set of power relations manifest in visual spheres, has been effectively internalized by those subjugated to it; one can become complicit in one's own oppression. As Layne (2001, 8–9) saw it, "*Returning the Gaze* necessarily involves an admission of this complicity. It challenges us towards a sense of irony. It asks us to be open to exploring these honestly."[22] Fitting this bill were works like Murray's *Mantra,* a postcard with the anxious worry of one newly gazed upon in the period of Mbeki's African Renaissance—"I must learn to speak Xhosa"—repeated as chalk on a board, like a schoolboy's punishment (see the script that lightly fills the background of fig. 9.2) and Ward's *Leisure Time,* title for a billboard image of three women diversely occupied (see fig. 9.2, upper right): a white windsurfer; an elegantly dressed, long-necked women of light brown complexion; a black nanny holding a pale-skinned baby, the person who's comparatively "di$EMPOWERED." Thembinkosi Goniwe's *Untitled* billboard, discussed next, was also ironically staged. Like Searle's contributions to *Returning the Gaze,* this work has also received attention but more have historicized the context of its making (Goniwe 2001; Hill 2015; Minty 2001b, 2004; Proud 2007).[23]

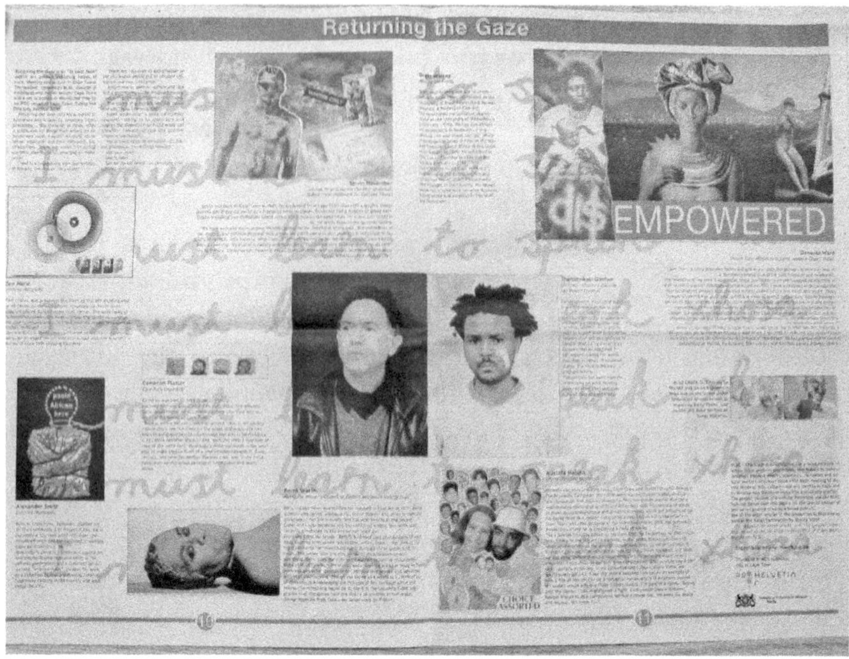
Returning the Gaze

EMPOWERED

Fig. 9.2 *Returning the Gaze*, exhibition preview as centerfold of the One City Festival Program, pages 10–11. *Cape Times*, September 2000.

Hung from a building opposite the Baxter Theatre on Main Road in Rondebosch, an affluent neighborhood that abuts the east side of the University of Cape Town's main campus, Goniwe's *Untitled* (fig. 9.3) confronted a mix of people who understood themselves as equal despite the vast inequalities (material and ontological) propagated within South Africa's recent past. The piece is brilliant because its rather simple form belies its deep conceptual content. Two men, both artists—Malcolm Payne at left and Goniwe at right—share the space and complement each other in several respects. Payne's black clothing balances the white that Goniwe wears, and both sport V-necks, thus they are commonly fashioned. The graying hair at Payne's temples is aligned with the bead near Goniwe's ear. Payne's pale skin color and dark hair cause his face and neck to jump out against a black background much as Goniwe's darker skin and hair cause his features, set against white, to do the same. Despite the stark complementary contrasts, each wears gray, a color that has recently indicated antireductive politics.[24] The combination here conveys what Layne (2001, 9) called a "yin and

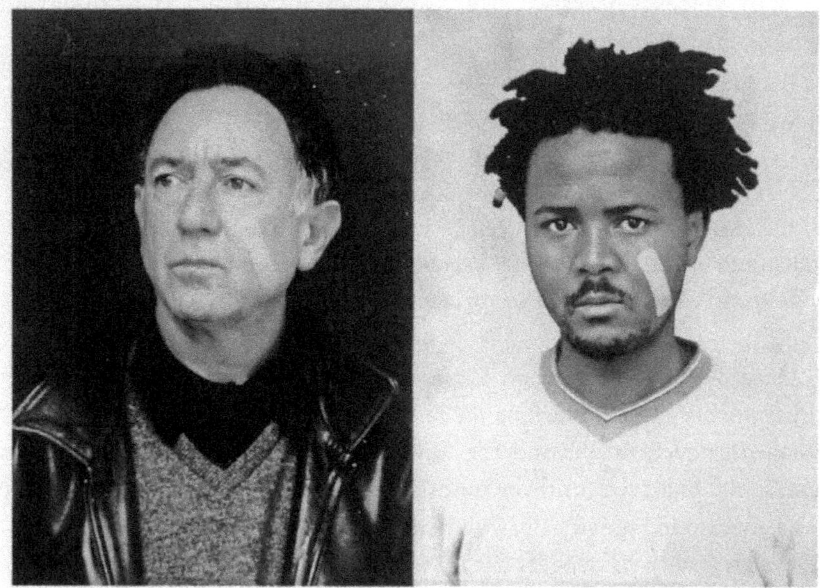

Fig. 9.3 Thembinkosi Goniwe, *Untitled*, 2000. Billboard in Rondebosch, Cape Town. *Photograph by Nicholas Aldridge.*

yang . . . interconnectedness" appealing to passersby. The challenge arises with racism's common wound, identically bandaged but dis-commonly felt. Payne, visibly less wounded, his attention diverted elsewhere, is the embodiment of a vantage that takes its own centeredness for granted. Goniwe, meanwhile, locks to us with a steady questioning eye that causes us to register the wound present and persistently in the now.[25]

Goniwe locates the origins of this work in two arenas: first, frustration with the varied "posts" of academic life—postcolonial, post-apartheid, the post-racism implied by rainbow rhetoric and, most absurdly, postblack as it was theorized in the United States—because each conveyed a decision to *not engage* with pressing realities experienced daily by billions worldwide.[26] He views these as "racist constructs" (Goniwe 2001) that he must actively challenge, and he cites the Pan Africanist Congress (PAC) as his ideological home. He enjoyed BLAC seminars that led up to this project and, akin to others I interviewed, noted that those excluded from it in the first year saw its adoption of BC's approach as "reverse racism." He questioned the importance of making others comfortable, and with this I agree. Discomforting dominant voices is necessary; it awakens their investment in listening and learning. He lamented:

> We spend too much time on white people, and not enough on us. We need to spend energy and time on us. Like Biko said, we need to take care of ourselves. We cannot love the other without loving the self. Apartheid denied us this time and energy. Our parents worked for whites and now we reproduce that in debates about art. . . . For me, BC was able to shift that attitude of living for apartheid or the other. The shift was to take care of the self.[27]

Curators Zayd Minty and Carol-Ann Davids matched the site of particular works within *Returning the Gaze* with the audience quite well. The billboards stayed up beyond the One City Festival; Goniwe remembers them being displayed for three months. Others included Searle's *Not Quite White,* mentioned previously, which hung above the Community Arts Project, eye level with passengers in cars traveling along the N1, a busy highway connecting the CBD with nearly everything east of it.[28] Ward's *Leisure Time* was displayed in Langa, a township about 14 kilometers east from the CBD, near Guga S'Thebe, a newly established heritage site that exhibited *Langa Histories* during the One City Festival, a show that celebrated legendary musicians, athletes, and politicians who grew up in the neighborhood. Municipal red tape delayed the hanging of Selvin November's billboard *Naked Truth* (a version of which is seen in fig. 9.2, upper center) on the east side of the Customs House building, itself situated at the cross-section of the N1 and N2, Cape Town's major highways. Regrettably, the work—a colorful vertical piece that includes a bare-chested (and seemingly naked, save for dark sunglasses) male figure striding outward, an inset postcard of a stylized female African sculpture with splayed genitalia, and the words *Returning the Gaze*—was never hung at this location.[29] Chosen as the centerpiece of *Returning the Gaze,* it was suspended as a banner at The Granary, venue for the festival's largest visual art exhibition, *True Stories,* curated by Roger Van Wyk and Robert Weinek. Three murals were commissioned for *Returning the Gaze*: an untitled painting by Ricky Dyaloyi, Duke Norman, and Timothy Zantsi at the Langa Civic Hall reproduced a March 30, 1960 photograph of PAC youth leader Philip Kgosana and others marching from Langa to Cape Town to protest pass laws; *Township 2000* was made by Evaron Orange and Antonio (Tony) Coetzee on a wall along Klipfontein Road, a thoroughfare

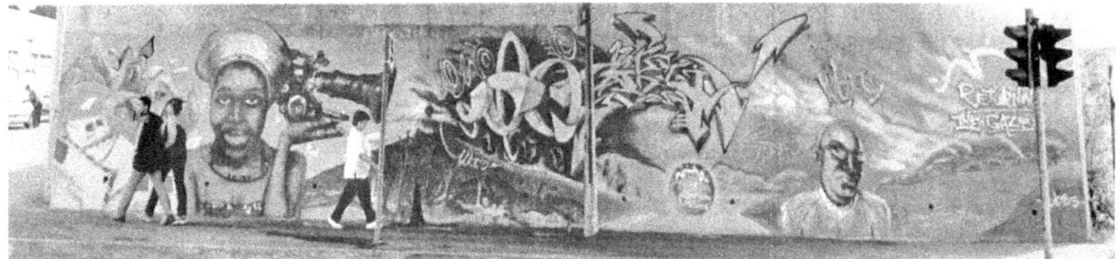

Fig. 9.4 Evaron Orange and Antonio Coetzee (aka Sky 189 and Ice7), *Return to Sender*, 2000. Mural beneath an overpass on Buitenkant Street in the Central Business District, Cape Town. *Photograph by Nicholas Aldridge.*

that runs from Gugulethu to Athlone; and *Return to Sender* (fig. 9.4), a mural by the same duo, was painted on Buitenkant Street in the CBD.[30]

Orange and Coetzee are best known by their tag names, respectively Sky 189 and Ice7.[31] (They are shown at work along the right side of fig. 9.2.) Their names are recorded here in the "wild-style" graffiti at the mural's center, legible only to fellow aerosol artists. Such secrecy is both practical because it evades unwanted attention and exclusive because it promotes, within a desired sphere, one's sly ability to tag public space unlawfully. The hand is Sky 189's chosen font, whereas Ice7's script is "original style," with a gothic flare (e.g., "Returning the Gaze" at right). At varied points throughout, one sees WOTS (Word on the Street), acronym of an award-winning aerosol art and advertising collective that the two founded in the late 1990s with Smirk, a female Swiss graffiti artist (Smith 2001, 29). Elsewhere—in the sky and water at right, for instance—are stylized graphics that connect varied forms, like the township at far right with the male figure in the foreground and, in turn, with the island to his right, at center.

The two principle figures here, the man just mentioned and the woman at left holding a camera, convey the viewpoints of BLAC's principle members: men and women who remain marginal to those who customarily regard, or gaze upon, townships as places of spectacle, entirely other to "the norm." The male, a figure Ice7 created specifically for the festival (he appears on the mural *Township 2000* as well), scowls at viewers from behind glasses with a certain skepticism. Sky 189 conceived of the female figure as "the world through the eyes of an African," and she shares her mind, on which the lens finder rests, through her stare directed straight at us. Unlike her male counterpart, she wears dress conventionally called "traditional" but altered for tourists: Her hat resembles forms (but not colors) worn by Zulu women on significant occasions. Her beaded tubular necklace is akin to (but smaller than) those worn by Ndebele women on similar events. Her dress is like that seen any day on any woman anywhere. In these ways, she is both a standard bearer for "Africa" and its conceptual opposite to those who fix her as such. Through the camera lens, her mind's eye is trained on an island, "possibly Robben Island" where she witnesses words "flying to the centre" (Smith 2001, 31). These loud cacophonic voices, which are the artists' own, emanate from the township at right situated just beyond the man's shoulder. They blast over and above a pale-skinned, small-scale trio at the shore, people who blithely sun themselves at a site of great historical weight. Their idle preoccupations are not those of the mural's makers. Rather, these men would "return to sender" the spectacle that is township life for such tourists.

Orange (aka Sky 189) hails from Athlone and Coetzee (aka Ice7) is from Mitchell's Plain.[32] Both studied graphic design at Peninsula Technikon and practiced as graffiti artists mainly in the many townships that constitute the Cape Flats. In 1996, they took part in a collective of local aerosol artists (including the now well-known Mustafa Maluka) called the Black Fist Art Movement, the name of which conjures an icon born of BC ideals like no other.[33] Ice7 created what he called "a live mural" of Steve Biko (meaning he made it during daylight, before an audience) as part of the *District Six Public Sculpture Project* mentioned previously.[34] Both Sky 189 and Ice7 have international careers that ultimately led them to leave South Africa, but they have returned on occasion; the latter most recently to complete a mural commissioned for the World Cup in 2010. In our interview, Ice7 described an "identity crisis within local 'mixed race' communities" that endeavors like the Black Fist Art Movement and BLAC counteract. Still, he came to BLAC through the *Returning the Gaze* project and said that despite BLAC's efforts, he noted less participation on the whole from the township residents, most of whom were well familiar with graffiti as an established, recognized "informative tool." He wished BLAC had explored still further means to involve marginalized people who, for instance, could not easily avail themselves of initiatives like its web-based project.

One such work was created for *Returning the Gaze*: Stacey Stent's *Nat-Gal* ran for the duration of the One City Festival (and a bit beyond it) on www.blaconline.org. Stent is known as South Africa's first female political cartoonist: she gained a following as author of *Who's Left* (1987–91), a strip cartoon created for the *Weekly Mail* that challenged liberal (i.e., nonracial) vantages. In the context of BLAC, which sought, in part, to bring attention to the acceptance of black perspectives—and black employment at the highest levels—within Cape Town's arts institutions, Stent found a ready target in Marilyn Martin, who directed the South African National Gallery from 1990 to 2001.[35] Cast as *NatGal,* Martin's animated likeness offered "A Dissertation on Art in 3 Languages." As she spoke, her jaw dropped and disconnected with her face, returning to a satisfied stare between greetings: "'kunjani' . . . . 'middag' . . . . 'hello' . . . ." (Long pause.) She looked to and read from a script that she then held on screen, her jaw intact as she smiled broadly: "'ndithanda IAfrican art.' 'thank you dankie enkosi,'" she murmured with closed eyes, evidently pleased with this vacuous synopsis. Surely Stent's animated work cut to the bone, thus it discomforted in the way one might, or must, in order to register the desired effects: a less limited understanding of what black means, and what blackness is, for those who so self-identify.[36]

Although postcards do not typify public art, they do frequently reproduce it. Postcards were the most abundant medium in *Returning the Gaze,* and these were passed out in venues throughout the festival. Others included Selvin November's *Scanning the Past,* an experiment with graphic style in shades of blue and orange that challenges any suggestion of a "clear-cut line" to understanding history. He layered graphic/technological arcs, an eye, a simplified version of Table Mountain in profile, and a Zulu-type shield to suggest history's many layers, always contingent on where one stands. In a surprisingly bland work, the otherwise-talented Mustafa Maluka contributed *Choice Assorted*: a postcard with twenty-six heads (including his own) surrounded by rainbow stripes and placed above cookies/biscuits from a box that promises variety (fig. 9.2, lower center). Also on hand was Cameron Platter's *Care-Race,* which reproduced photographs of four black men within squares that have layered blocks of gray and pale red printed over them (fig. 9.2, center left). They are united by their endless classification: A stream of letters repeats the word *race* horizontally in a computerized font across the full card, edge to edge. Handwritten in blue atop the portraits (which register as mug shots) is the word *care,* a simple reordering of the letters in *race.* Platter's vision underscores the need for "Care, respect, and new perspectives towards race" in Cape Town and the larger nation. Zen Marie's *Untitled* postcard (fig. 9.2, upper left) reproduced in quadruplicate a plaster cast figure from the South African Museum alongside spinning discs that suggest both recordings of black voices housed there and a modernist disinterest in the perspectives they captured. Finally, Alexander Smith's *Untitled* was also distributed as a postcard (fig. 9.2, lower left). A violent work that rails against local "imprisonment" to the ANC's "capitalist ethic," it records a body in a straightjacket with an American flag and Nike emblems upon it. The figure's head is merely dotted in outline and the words *paste African here* appear within. A chain encases the neck and is drawn taut to an unseen element stage left.

NEW BEGINNINGS, OLD FRIENDS

Zayd Minty returned to coordinate the One City Festival in 2001, an indication that its 2000 version was deemed successful. While there is no real way of accounting for the full number of people who saw *Returning the Gaze*, BLAC's most visible public art project, it was at least in the tens of thousands. After all, the *Celebrating Difference* program (see fig. 9.2) entered over 220,000 households.[37] By March 2001, diverse audiences became the subject of a panel at BLAC's seminar, where actor Marc Lottering, dancer Jaqui Jaob, and artist Berni Searle led a discussion on "the changing face of South African audiences" (Minty 2001a). And although some among that audience interpreted *Returning the Gaze* in rather simplistic ways (usually as a response to whiteness, e.g., Sobopha 2000), most would have at least grasped that a new sensibility was afoot in what Ciraj Rassool (2000, 1) once called South Africa's "culture wars." BLAC offered Capetonians and tourists multiple ways of understanding blackness, and this was its strongest contribution to a city and arts scene that in refusing BC's approach, continued to fix black too neatly rather than engage its hybrid character. It challenged this stream of thought as embedded in the One City Festival of 1999 and in so doing it called up the "'Black is Beautiful' in Black Consciousness thinking," as Zimitri Erasmus put it at a BLAC seminar in August 2000, as contributors to *Returning the Gaze* neared completion of their work. By this he meant beautiful realization of self.

The urgency of adopting a BC-inspired vision of blackness was particularly strong at this time because, as Erasmus (2000, 1–2) cautioned, "in this post-apartheid era, notions of diversity and difference [wherein black is a politically privileged shade] function to obscure continued white domination" in realms like culture. Although today one finds a somewhat more varied register of voices guiding such institutions and businesses within Cape Town, BLAC was altogether necessary for its time and place. No matter what detractors of the late 1990s assumed, BLAC was at the forefront of encouraging a deeper understanding of difference, a search for connections across racial boundaries, and the articulation of shared intimacies in art and writing about it. This quest has not yet ended, and public art commissions in South Africa can surely benefit from adopting BLAC's methodology of "quiet space" consultation. Many former BLAC members continued to work with Minty in other public arts projects he forged, like the Visual Arts Network of South Africa (VANSA), founded in 2003 (Minty 2005). Indeed, every BLAC participant with whom I have spoken says that Black Consciousness is still needed today for several reasons: to instill pride, to curb racism (of color, of ethnicity), to preserve languages, to harness capitalism, to restore integrity, to enhance ethics, to open ears, to celebrate life, to heal hearts, and to invigorate minds.

BLAC's *Returning the Gaze* intervention was needed in 2000 because those with the power to select and define public art in South Africa would not acknowledge that nonracialism's dominance left much unsaid and unseen. Although the efficacy of BC had by then been analyzed by scholars (Pityana et al. 1991) and understood by people on the ground for decades (Hill 2015), it still did not sit comfortably within the foundation myth actively being constructed at that time. BLAC unsettled those within Cape Town's art power base, which wields strong influence internationally. It discomforted, pressed for fresh vantages, and caused those who witnessed its work to rethink whether something was not quite right with such clean liberation narratives. Interventions of the kind BLAC advocated pose questions that those who realize public art—its agents and its audience—must address if we are to ever supplant the limiting frame of racial awareness for one that consciously addresses power.

ACKNOWLEDGMENTS

Thanks to Zayd Minty for sharing his archive and to the artists who were willing to speak to me about the Black Arts Collective. Its work and political position were controversial to some artists who subsequently chose not to engage.

SHANNEN HILL is Associate Curator for African Arts and Head of Department, Arts of Africa, the Americas, Asia and Pacific Islands at the Baltimore Museum of Art. She is the author of *Biko's Ghost: The Iconography of Black Consciousness.*

Notes

1. In repositioning heritage as a verb, one recalls strategies Henry Louis Gates Jr. employed to dislodge a noun that "signifies" into its activating vernacular form: "signifyin." See his classic, *The Signifying Monkey.*

2. This act was amended to include Indians in 1962. The Coloured Peoples' Congress, South African Indian Congress, African National Congress (ANC), and South African Congress of Democrats aligned to sign the Freedom Charter. In 1955, only the South African Communist Party was nonracial in membership. By "nationalists" I mean the National Party *and* the ANC because both actively suppressed BC since the mid-1970s. See Hill (2015).

3. In considering South African monument making in the 1990s, Marschall (2010, 176, 181) critiques the National Legacy Project's "token gesture [of] . . . consultation" with those invested in critical issues, its fear of "giving offense," and a vision whereby "struggle is portrayed as an historic process that ultimately benefited all people. Members of the white minority, it is intimated, can also celebrate the advent of freedom . . . as they have been liberated from the moral burden of benefitting from racial injustice."

4. Indicative of a British liberal ethos, nonracialism secured voting rights for Cape-based Africans and so-called Colored people who both owned property and, after 1892, passed an educational exam. See MacDonald (2006).

5. Scholars in other fields acknowledge BC's layered contribution to nonracialism in this decade include Gordimer (1983), Mzamane et al. (2006), and Pityana et al. (1991).

6. Author interview with Thembinkosi Goniwe, Braamfontein, Johannesburg, January 14, 2011.

7. Author correspondence with Paul Hendricks, August 25, 2011; Author interview with Emile Maurice, Woodstock, Cape Town, January 12, 2011.

8. Author correspondence with Tony Coetzee (aka Ice, Ice7), January 26, 2015.

9. Whereas postcards frequently record sites of historical weight, T-shirts that record political martyrs are well known in this nation. The shirt Dikobé Martins designed for Steve Biko's funeral on September 20, 1977, is likely the first.

10. Beginning in 1950, the United Nations passed several resolutions denouncing apartheid prior to its December 1980 decree to boycott South Africa's cultural and academic programs (United Nations 1980).

11. Mbeki's African Renaissance echoed the outmoded tenor of apartheid's racial categories because the ANC identified South Africans as Indian, coloured, white, or African (meaning black). This is not as the BC-minded would have it, and under President Jacob Zuma (Mbeki's successor), such racialized categories continue to foment societal tension.

12. Author interview with Zayd Minty, Greenpoint, Cape Town, January 5, 2011.

13. Correspondence with Coetzee, January 26, 2015.

14. Interview with Minty, January 5, 2011. Author interview with Donovan Ward, Woodstock, Cape Town, January 7, 2011.

15. Ward participated in both exhibitions and felt that "the mainstream art world," including those who met at the museum to advance the *District Six Public Sculpture Project*, registered "a silence, as if [the Biko exhibition] didn't happen." See Hill (2015)

for more about this exhibition. Public Eye was founded by Kevin Brand, Lisa Brice, Bruce Gordon, Lizza Littlewort, Brett Murray, Andrew Putter, Robert Weinek, and Sue Williamson. Minty sat on its board for a time but described some founders as "really angry . . . really upset" when he drew attention to the lack of diversity within the company proper (interview with Minty, January 5, 2011).

16. Illustrated in Hill (2015).

17. Spurred by ongoing wars over religious tolerance that stem from Israel and Palestine, a group called Muslims Against Global Oppression claimed responsibility for the bomb, detonated in response to the United States' attacks in Sudan and Afghanistan one week prior (Associated Press 1998).

18. The Inkatha Freedom Party first proclaimed September 24 "Shaka Day" in honor of the Zulu kingdom's founder, murdered this day in 1828. Mandela expanded this celebration to include all South African cultures.

19. Rassool (2000, 8) describes the "new imagining of nation . . . as one of firm boundaries. Everyone in the city was put into naturalized cultural categories that lay at the heart of the campaign: Christian, Muslim, Jew, Hindu, or Xhosa."

20. All data in this paragraph gleaned from the 1999 *One City Festival Program*.

21. By then, Minty was known as an arts professional having directed the Community Arts Project and arts programming for the Robben Island Museum, co-curated (with Tumelo Mosaka) *Isintu—Ceremony, Identity, and Community, a South–South Dialogue* (another project aligned with BC), established and promoted BLAC, and run the dialogue series in the 1999 One City Festival.

22. In 2000, Layne, a musician, worked for the District Six Museum; Falken directed the Community Arts Project; Rassool was Senior Lecturer in History and Museum and Heritage Studies at the University of the Western Cape.

23. Although others locate it within *Returning the Gaze* (de Vries 2010; Gule 2004) they do not engage with BLAC.

24. Although Breyten Breytenbach (1984) frequently refers to security officers as "Greys," recently the color carries connotations of antireductionist black/white historicizing (Atkinson and Breitz 1999; Peffer 2009, 1–40).

25. Goniwe earned his BFA and MFA at the Michaelis School of Fine Art, University of Cape Town. He found Payne to be among the few people there with whom he could discuss matters of race and politics (interview with Goniwe, January 14, 2011).

26. Ibid.

27. Ibid.

28. As in her *Colour Me* series, Searle was photographed without clothing. The billboard derived from another work, *Off-White: Back to Back* (1999). She lies on the ground beneath a blanket of white flour that covers her body and pools around its edges. The photograph has been spliced into four parts, each of which is slightly misaligned with its neighbor. A measuring bar appears above and below Searle's portrait. The words *Not Quite White* fill the lower register, equally proportionate to the artist's body; given in white script, the words stand out sharply against the black background. See Hill (2015) for analysis.

29. This piece shares central components with a postcard titled *Whites Only* made for the exhibition. See Hill (2015) for reproductions of works by Searle, Ward, and November.

30. *Township 2000* is reproduced in Hill (2015). In discussing their *Untitled* mural in Langa, those who made it incorrectly identify Mr. Kgosana as "Philip Rhosana" and do not provide historical context (Smith 2001, 33).

31. In 2000, the artist was known as Ice. The pseudonym stems from his love of B-boying (break dancing) and the fact that one freezes (holds postures) at the end of moves to taunt opponents. He later added the number because it is auspicious: it records the number of letters in Antonio, his birth name (Coetzee 2015). All information about this mural comes from this source unless otherwise cited.

32. Sandra Klopper (2000, 180) records Mitchell's Plain as "the Mecca of South African hip-hop" and graffiti as "the visual artistic expression of those embracing hip-hop and its ideologies."

33. Hill (2015) historicizes this gesture and secures its South African origins to BC.

34. Correspondence with Coetzee, January 26, 2015. Klopper interviewed another aerosol artist, Wealz130, founder of the group YMB (Your Millennium's Best) who accredited "all that BC stuff" to his growth as a young man mindful of how to combat what Klopper (2000, 185) called "the state's ongoing role in marginalizing already disempowered youth."

35. Although the National Gallery hired people like Emile Maurice (an active BLAC member) and Vuyile Voyiya in the mid-1990s, they worked as educators, thus were second string to the curatorial vision that drove exhibitions. Both ultimately left the South African National Gallery frustrated by such limitations (interviews with Emile Maurice, Gardens, Cape Town, January 12, 2011, and Vuyile Voyiya, Gardens, Cape Town, January 7, 2011).

36. This work and those following are reproduced in Smith (2001). Summaries are based on artists' statements within this same publication.

37. It is estimated that "well over 50,000 people" enjoyed the festival in 1999 (*One City Festival Program* 2000, 3).

References

Annual Report, 2001. BLACK ARTS COLLECTIVE. Archive of Zayd Minty.

Araeen, Rashid. 1998. *The Essential Black Art*. Exhibition catalog. London: Chisendale Gallery and Black Umbrella.

Associated Press. 1998. "1 Dead, 24 Hurt in Bombing at S. Africa Planet Hollywood." *Los Angeles Times*, August 26. Accessed March 21, 2015. www.articles.latimes.com.

Atkinson, Brenda, and Candice Breitz. 1999. *Grey Areas: Representation, Identity and Politics in Contemporary South African Art*. Johannesburg: Chalkham Hill.

Bester, Rory. 2003. *Float: Berni Searle, Standard Bank Young Artist 2003*. Cape Town: Bell-Roberts.

Breytenbach, Breyten. 1984. *The True Confessions of an Albino Terrorist*. Johannesburg: Taurus.

Coombes, Annie E. 2003. *History after Apartheid: Visual Culture and Public Memory in a Democratic South Africa*. Durham, NC: Duke University Press.

de Vries, Fred. 2010. "Pieces of a Man." *Art South Africa* 8, no. 4 (Winter): 48–51.

Erasmus, Zimitri. 2000. "Returning the Gaze." BLAC seminar paper offered August 1. Archive of Zayd Minty.
Fisher, Ryland. 1999. "We Deserve the Most Beautiful Festival." In *One City Festival Program*, 3. Cape Town: Cape Times.
Gates, Henry Louis Jr. 1988. *The Signifying Monkey: A Theory of African-American Literary Criticism*. New York: Oxford University Press.
Goniwe, Thembinkosi. 2001. "Questioning 'Post-Racism.'" *Network News*, July. Accessed March 21, 2015. www.getnet.org.za.
Gordimer, Nadine. 1983. "Art and the State in South Africa." *The Nation*, December 24, pp. 657–61. This article prints the paper "Relevance and Commitment," her keynote to *The State of the Art* conference, University of Cape Town, July 4–11, 1979.
Gqola, Pumla Dineo. 2005. "Memory, Diaspora and Spiced Bodies in Motion: Berni Searle's Art." *African Identities* 3, no. 2: 123–38.
Gule, Khwezi. 2004. "Thembinkosi Goniwe." In *10 Years 100 Artists: Art in a Democratic South Africa*, edited by Sophie Perryer, 130–31. Cape Town: Bell-Roberts.
Hill, Shannen. 2015. *Biko's Ghost: The Iconography of Black Consciousness*. Minneapolis: University of Minnesota Press.
Klopper, Sandra. 2000. "Hip Hop Graffiti Art." In *Senses of Culture*, edited by Sarah Nuttall and Cheryl-Ann Michael, 178–96. Oxford: Oxford University Press.
Layne, Valmont. 2001. "Returning the Gaze on the Occasion of the One City Festival." In *Returning the Gaze: Public Arts Project at the Cape Town One City Festival* (exhibition catalog), edited by Candice Smith, 7–11. Cape Town: BLAC.
MacDonald, Michael. 2006. *Why Race Matters in South Africa*. Cambridge, MA: Harvard University Press.
Marschall, Sabine. 2010. *Landscape of Memory: Commemorative Monuments, Memorials and Public Statuary in Post-Apartheid South Africa*. Leiden, the Netherlands: Brill.
Minty, Zayd. 2000a. "Message from the Festival Co-ordinator." *One City Festival Program*, 2.
———. 2000b. "Lecture Series." *One City Festival Program*, 6.
———. c. 2001a. *What Is BLAC*? Pamphlet produced by the BLACK ARTS COLLECTIVE. Archive of Zayd Minty.
———. 2001b. "Returning the Gaze." In *Returning the Gaze: Public Arts Project at the Cape Town One City Festival* (exhibition catalog), edited by Candice Smith, 7–11. Cape Town: BLAC.
———. 2004. "Finding the 'Post-Black' Position." In *A Decade of Democracy: South African Art 1994–2004 from the Permanent Collection of Iziko: South African National Gallery*, edited by Emma Bedford, 110–19. Cape Town: Double Storey Books.
———. 2005. "Transformation and the Visual Arts in South Africa: Building Diversity in the Public Sector." *Artthrob*, no. 99 (September). Accessed April 19, 2012. www.artthrob.co.za.
Minty, Zayd, and Graham Falken. 2003. "BLAC Bows Outa." *Artthrob*, no. 66. Accessed November 23, 2009. www.artthrob.co.za/03feb/reviews/blac.html.
Mzamane, Mbulelo Vizikhungo, Bavusile Maaba, and Nkosinathi Biko. 2006. "The Black Consciousness Movement." In *Road to Democracy in South Africa, 1970–1980*, vol. 2, edited by South African Education Democracy Trust, 99–160. Pretoria: University of South Africa.

"National Heritage Day." Accessed January 18, 2015. www.sahistory.org.za.
One City Festival Program. 2000. Cape Town: Cape Times.
Peffer, John. 2009. *Art and the End of Apartheid*. Minneapolis: University of Minnesota Press.
Pityana, N. Barney, Mamphela Ramphele, Malusi Mpumlwana, and Lindy Wilson, eds. 1991. *Bounds of Possibility: The Legacy of Steve Biko and Black Consciousness*. Cape Town: David Philip.
Proud, Hayden. 2007. *Scratches on the Face: Antiquity and Contemporaneity in South African Works of Art from Iziko Museums of Cape Town*. New Delhi: Iziko Museums of Cape Town.
Rassool, Ciraj. 2000. "The Rise of Heritage and the Reconstruction of History in South Africa." *Kronos: Journal of Cape History* 26: 1–21. Accessed January 17, 2015. www.reference.sabinet.co.za/webx/access/journal_archive/02590190/545.pdf.
Schmahmann, Brenda. 2004. *Through the Looking Glass*. Johannesburg: David Krut.
———. 2009. "Bodily Issues as Subject Matter: Abjection in the Works of Penny Siopis and Berni Searle." In *Expressions of the Body: Representations in African Text and Image*, edited by Charlotte Baker, 97–117. Oxford: Peter Lang.
Smith, Candice, ed. 2001. *Returning the Gaze: Public Arts Project at the Cape Town One City Festival* (exhibition catalog). Cape Town: BLAC.
Sobopha, Mgcineni. 2000. "'Returning the Gaze' at the Cape Town Festival." *Art Throb*, no. 38. www.artthrob.co.za.
United Nations General Assembly Resolution A/RES/35/206E, "Cultural, Academic and Other Boycotts of South Africa." 1980. 98th Plenary Meeting. December 16.
Van der Watt, Liese. 2004. "Tracing Berni Searle." *African Arts* 37, no. 4: 74–79, 96.
Wylie, Diana. 2008. *Art + Revolution: The Life and Death of Thami Mnyele, South African Artist*. Charlottesville: University of Virginia Press.

CHAPTER 10

Unsettling Ambivalences and Ambiguities in Mary Sibande's *Long Live the Dead Queen* Public Art Project

LEORA FARBER

THE JET-BLACK, HIGHLY POLISHED body of a monumentally scaled, mannequin-like figure towers over the gritty urban landscape of Johannesburg's inner city. From her indigo-colored dress, which incorporates the three components characteristic of the South African domestic worker's uniform—the front buttoned-down overall, white apron and collar edged with machine-made lace, and *doek*[1]—one might identify her as a domestic worker. Yet puzzlingly, her dress, with its puffy sleeves, fitted bodice, voluminous skirt, and excessive use of fabric, also recalls the lavishness of the upper-class Victorian woman's ball gown. Her closed eyes imply that she is in a trancelike state, swept up in a flight of fantasy. At once demure and serene, majestic and imperial, dominant and imposing, her figure, set against an empty off-white background, looms larger than life over its Afropolitan surrounds.

The above describes[2] one of the large-scale digital prints of a fictional South African black domestic worker named Queen Sophie that comprise the public art project titled *Joburg City, World Premier Exhibition, Long Live the Dead Queen* (hereafter "the project") by Johannesburg-based artist Mary Sibande (fig. 10.1). The images are printed onto vinyl and mounted like advertising billboards or building wraps that usually scaffold the outer facades of strategically located buildings. From June until September 2010, twenty-two images of Queen Sophie featured as billboards and building wraps on

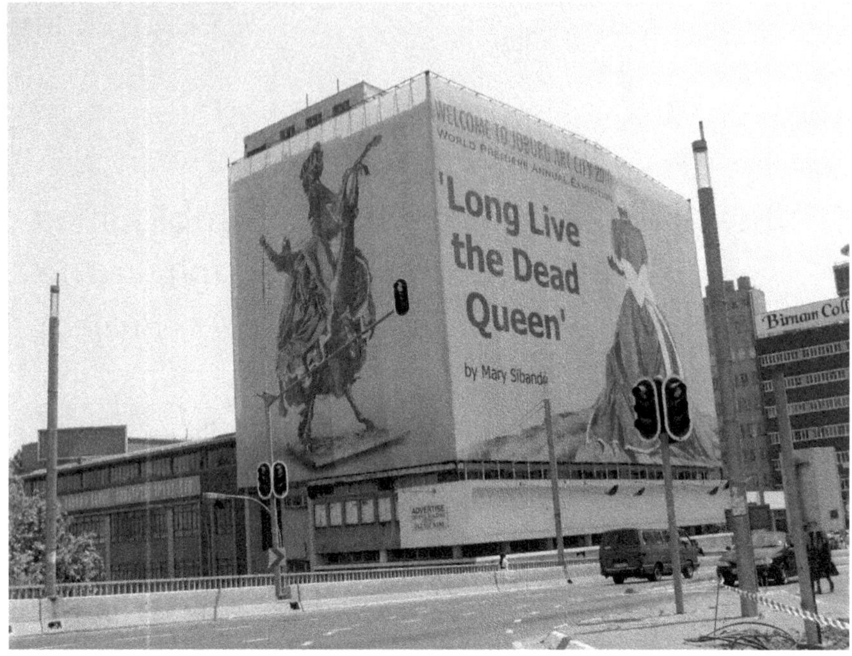

Fig. 10.1 Mary Sibande (2010), *Joburg City, World Premier Exhibition, Long Live the Dead Queen*. Installation view, Braamfontein, Johannesburg. *Photograph by Alexander Opper.*

nineteen buildings in Johannesburg's inner city, attracting a public audience, and effectively transforming this urban area into the largest outdoor art gallery in the city's history (Opper 2010, 46).[3]

Queen Sophie made her debut into the public realm as Sophie Ntombikayise, the domestic worker who was the protagonist of Sibande's first solo exhibition, titled *Long Live the Dead Queen*, held at the Gallery MOMO, Johannesburg, in 2009. In the exhibition, she takes the form of four life-sized sculptures made from fiberglass casts of Sibande's body. In each sculpture, Sophie wears a different version of the functional domestic worker's uniform that Sibande has refashioned to integrate the stylistic elements of an elaborate Victorian dress. The sculptures were exhibited together with a series of digital prints, ranging in scale from 35½ x 23½ to 43½ x 31½ inches, in which Sibande, wearing her fantastical dresses, performs Sophie's persona. The images featured in the project were therefore not made in relation to the specific public sites in which they were exhibited; the sculptures were photographed in a studio setting and thereafter, together with the digital prints shown at the exhibition, were enlarged to billboard scale and mounted across building facades in downtown Johannesburg.[4]

In the project, Sophie's persona conjoins female figures from a wide geographic and temporal terrain, spanning Victorian England, late nineteenth-century southern Africa, the apartheid era (1948–94), and post-apartheid South Africa. They include the upper-class Victorian lady, Queen Victoria, the contemporary black domestic worker and her historical counterpart under colonialism and apartheid, as well as Sibande herself.[5] These figures come into play through use of Sibande's body as a performative medium and in the form of body casts and images and through her fusing of the practical domestic worker's uniform with ornate Victorian gowns. The stylistic references to Victorian fashion in her garments are pronounced enough to allow the dress to operate as mnemonic device that prompts recollection of cultural associations with the broader Victorian era and, specifically, in a southern African context, the high point of colonialism. In connoting the servitude of the colonized black female worker and dominance of the white female colonizer as mistress, Sophie's refashioned dresses locate domestic service within modern colonial histories and the colonial relations of race.

In the dream world of her imagination, signified by her consistently closed eyes, Sophie assumes numerous identities (in the project, these include an African queen, adorned in traditional beadwork; a member of one of the South African Zionist Christian Churches [SAZCC];[6] and Queen Victoria). However, all of these identities are contingent on her domestic worker–cum–Victorian dresses that empower her to reclaim her own agency by imaginatively embodying the stereotypical positions of her colonial white mistress and contemporary (white) madam. Assuming the attire of both the highly politicized figure of the domestic worker and the colonial mistress/madam enables Sibande to problematize and parody the structures of a colonial past and to metaphorically redress white southern and South African women's historical upholding of supremacy and privilege in subversive terms.[7]

Unlike the domestic worker who was expected to be an invisible presence relegated to the background of domestic life, in the public space of the inner city, Queen Sophie's figure is arrestingly, almost overwhelmingly, materially present. This is partially due to the theatricality of her staging—manifest in the stark iconicity of her silhouettes and dramatic forms of display—and the magnitude of her supersized bodily proportions.

Her presence is rendered even more imposing by the scale of her dresses whose mammoth skirts, comprising vast swaths of fabric, spill outward into the empty space around her in epic proportions. The monumentality of her presence disallows Homi K. Bhabha's (1994) conception of the ambivalent colonial gaze in which the colonized subject is only partially seen: Queen Sophie cannot be overlooked; she commands center stage, asserting herself as hypermaterially present within the public domain.[8]

While the materiality of Sophie's presence is also asserted in the gallery space, primarily through the physicality of the sculptures, when shown in the inner city as images without their three-dimensional counterparts, her presentness becomes more nuanced. In the discussion to follow, I suggest that in the context of the project, Sophie's material presence takes on an unsettling ambiguity. Following Gabeba Baderoon's (2014, 180) contention that because "domestic work marks a crucial entry point for black women into the world made by the colonial encounter, household labor and its ambiguities continue to haunt black women's presence in public space in South Africa," I consider how, despite her strong visual and material presence in the inner city, Queen Sophie is also a disembodied, ghostlike figure that haunts the post-apartheid urban landscape with the spectral presence of absence. Like the ghost, which is neither present nor absent, neither living nor dead, Queen Sophie is infinitely suspended in an interstitial realm, oscillating between the stasis of visual materiality and fugitive ephemerality.

In their discussion around the relations between private lives and public cultures in contemporary South African society, Kerry Bystrom and Sarah Nuttall (2013, 307) identify Sibande's project as a visual realization of "spatial itinerancy," wherein "things that have historically been considered to be properly confined to the home or the domestic, surface in public spaces and become knitted into public discussions around these surfacings." They cite Sibande's representations of domestic servitude, and specifically those featured in the project, as examples of an emerging constellation of cultural production in South Africa that "focuses on the work of 'intimate exposure' in order to shape a public-private sphere, which in turn forges forms of citizenship unavailable, or submerged by, a history of segregation."[9] For Bystrom (2013, 333), Sibande's representations of "intimate exposures"—a term Bystrom and Nuttall (2013, 310) use to describe "a set of diverse acts that involve revealing inner aspects and places of the self and self-making"—are prime examples of how artworks that expose the intimate in a public realm have emerged in contemporary South African art as vibrant, fresh ways of "thinking in public and thinking the public."

Basing my discussion on Bystrom and Nuttall's conception of intimate exposures in relation to Sibande's public art project, I extend this premise, showing how, in the project, spatial itinerancies are realized through interplay between, and blurring of, the historically determined, gendered and hierarchical binaries of presence and absence. Drawing on Badaroon's (2014, 173) contention that in contemporary South Africa, the house is a place of "silences, ghosts and secrets" infused with the domestic worker's spectral presence, and what Shireen Ally (2015, 51–54) calls the "dialectic of distance and intimacy" in colonial and apartheid domestic relations, wherein "closeness, familiarity, and intimacy coexist with distancing, estrangement, and dehumanization," I explore the interstices between the binaries of presence and absence in relation to Sibande's inner-city project, how the work implicates and impacts upon the domains of the public and private, interior and exterior, and what is concealed and revealed within these domains.

PUBLIC POLITICS/PRIVATE PROXIMITIES

In a photograph documenting one of Sibande's building wraps located in downtown Johannesburg featuring the sculptural work titled *Sophie-Mercia* (fig. 10.2), Queen Sophie's image dominates its surrounds: her gigantic proportions fill the length and breadth of a building wall. The refinements of privilege, evident in the opulent, cascading folds of her indigo-colored dress, with its crisply starched white collar and sparklingly clean white apron, and the pristine off-white background color against which her image is set, contrast sharply with the dilapidated surface on which the wrap is mounted.

Some of the buildings used as installation sites for the project were built in the 1940s and reflect art deco architectural influences; others, built during the 1960s to 1980s, are examples of South African architects' emulation of, and aspirations toward, European modernism during these years. From the 1940 to 1980s, they were used as industrial spaces, factories, warehouses, and residential apartments located in the then-economic hub of the Central Business District (CBD). These inner-city spaces were abandoned during the 1990s with the flight of white capital to the northern Johannesburg suburb of Sandton. White flight from the CBD took place partially in response to informal traders setting up "illegal" vending stalls on the pavements, use of Bree Street (a main road in the CBD) as the central rank for minibus taxis

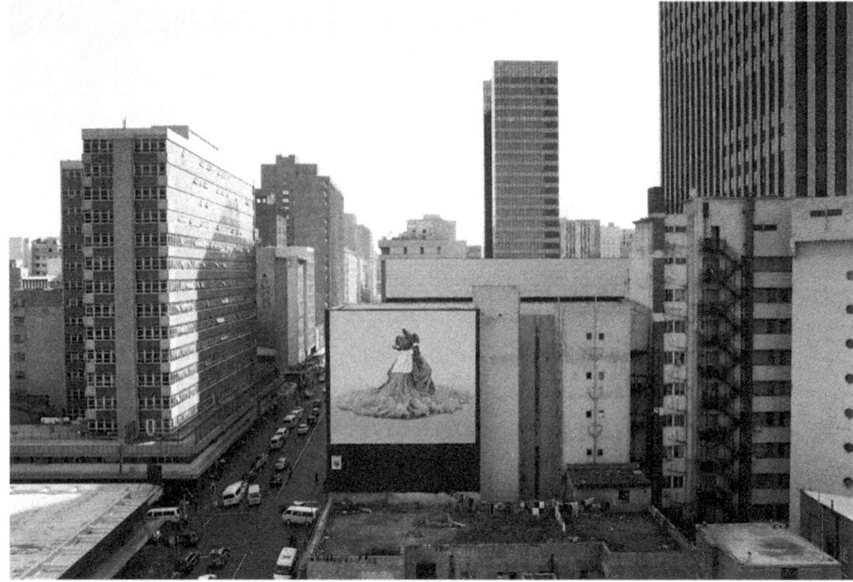

Fig. 10.2 Mary Sibande (2010), *Joburg City, World Premier Exhibition, Long Live the Dead Queen.* Installation view. Courtesy of Gallery MOMO. *Photographer ©Dean Hutton/2point8 Photography.*

servicing black commuters, the influx of South Africans and foreign nationals, and as a consequence of these factors, what was perceived as a sharp increase in crime rates and deterioration of the urban environment.

In 2000, the Johannesburg City Council embarked on an extensive Inner City Regeneration Program aimed to reestablish private investment in the inner city[10] (Reshaping Johannesburg's Inner City 2015). Despite the substantial resources the Johannesburg City Council invested in the Inner City Regeneration (or gentrification) Program, from documentary photographs of Sibande's project (see fig. 10.1), it is evident that in 2010, inner-city spaces were being used as housing for the urban poor, living in overcrowded, squalid, slum-like conditions.[11] Lacking maintenance, basic services, and modern amenities, these buildings speak of abject poverty and urban decay in the form of broken windows, littered rooftops, and stained walls. In this sense, Sibande's building wraps act as exterior facades that literally mask signs of deterioration on the structures they are scaffolded across.

Forming the second iteration of Joburg Art City 2010 Project that aimed to use public art as a means to revitalize the inner city, Sibande's project was closely connected to the Johannesburg City Council's Joburg 2030 vision of "transforming Johannesburg." The Joburg Art City 2010 Project was linked to the Johannesburg City Council's Regeneration Program in which an intention was to bridge class divides by taking visual art, usually exhibited in Johannesburg's private gallery spaces, into the public realm (Singer 2012, 44). The first iteration of the Joburg Art City Project took place in 2002. Sponsored by the mobile phone company Cell-C, it was intended to promote South African artists and showcase the council's urban renewal projects through a series of annual large-scale public art installations in the inner city. However, as the late Lesley Perkes—then-CEO of the company Artists at Work (AAW) that managed the installations—admitted, their initial conceptualizations of the project, and ways of realizing it, were misguided:

> We thought that we would transform Jo'burg. . . . We wanted to make . . . the impossible spaces between . . . the townships and . . . the inner city . . . beautiful. But we didn't understand the political nature of what we were doing, how contested these spaces were. . . . The works didn't speak to one another in terms of design . . . we hadn't really interacted with the walls of the buildings; [or] curated the city as a gallery. (Perkes cited in Brodie 2010)

Undeterred, after eight years of fund-raising, Perkes secured an amount of 814,551 rand from the National Lottery Distribution Trust Fund to realize *Long Live the Dead Queen* as the flagship urban art project of Joburg Art City 2010.[12] It was intended to be the first of what would become an annual outdoor solo exhibition in the inner city, featuring the work of a different artist each year.[13] Presumably, the decision to feature the work of a single artist was intended to achieve greater visual and conceptual coherency across the installations and to set up a sustained dialogue among the artworks, the sites in which they are installed, and the users of those spaces. It seems difficult to ascertain information as to who was responsible for the selection of Sibande's work, reasons for choosing her as the featured artist, and the identification of, and reasoning behind, choices of specific installation sites. Little or no mention of AAW having consulted with local residents and workers seems to be made. While some of the artworks appear to be placed in ways that draw formal visual correlations with specific sites (e.g., in fig. 10.4, the end point of Queen Sophie's scepter visually correlates with the triangulated point of the building on which the image is mounted), Sibande's images do not seem to be placed in ways that set up any discernable correlation between the specificities of the site and the content of the image.

IN THE INTERSTICES BETWEEN INTIMACY AND ESTRANGEMENT

In the context of Johannesburg's inner city, Sibande's images represent an ambivalent form of intimate exposure by opening up realms of the private for public perusal, while making public space more intimate and "homely" by imbuing it with personal narratives. As instances of spatial itinerancy, her intimate exposures could potentially enable members of the public to "enter into" the privacy of living spaces, or as Meg Samuelson (cited in Bystrom and Nuttall 2013, 316) puts it, imaginatively "[walk] through the door and [inhabit] the house." Ironically, the interior of the home, or objects and furniture that identify it as such, are not represented; it is through the figure of the black female domestic worker that the usually hidden, domestic interior—a space historically gendered as feminized[14]—is exteriorized and exposed. Sibande's personal narratives are manifest in her use of her body as a performative medium and in the form of the cast that visually describes her outer bodily contours—through the hollow casts infused with the artist's "ghostly presence" (Baderoon 2014, 173, 181, 186) but also form empty shells that metaphorically contain the spectral presences of her maternal great-grandmother (Sophie-Elsie), grandmother (Sophie-Merica), and mother (Sophie-Velucia), who were domestic workers during, and prior to, apartheid (Dodd 2010, 472). References to her matriarchal legacy are evident in the titles of three sculptures exhibited on Sibande's 2009 exhibition, each of which is named after one of her forbearers.[15] Sibande's public commemoration of their lived experiences of domestic servitude also extends to the title of the exhibition and project, *Long Live the Dead Queen,* in which her deceased grandmothers and mother are venerated as royalty and whose memories are upheld within the public consciousness of the present. The antonym of the project's title points to the figure of the specter, that if read in light of Jacques Derrida's (1994, xvii) conception of hauntology, is located between two apparently exclusive terms, such as life and death. Supplanting its near-homonym ontology, hauntology replaces the priority of being and presence with the figure of the ghost. The specters of Sibande's maternal forbearers could be said thus to represent a hauntology of South Africa's troubled legacy of domestic servitude under colonialism and apartheid. Located in an interstitial realm, they are neither present nor absent, neither living nor properly dead; they haunt life in the post-apartheid city with the prospect of death, while ultimately withholding the finality of that prospect.

Neelika Jayawardane (2013, 191) extends this idea, observing that "the Sophies of South Africa are a palpable—if unspoken of—trace. They are remainders and reminders of apartheid, and the structural, economic, and social inequalities that remain unresolved . . . in the neo-liberal present." While representing the intimacies of Sibande's maternal family history of domestic labor, her representations of Sophie also engage the broader public histories of women who endured domestic servitude under South Africa's legacy of racial and gender-based subjugation and exploitation under colonialism and apartheid.[16] Sophie therefore acts as a metonym for black women who were, and often remain, ghostly traces in the domestic sphere.

In representing a concentrated site where race, gender, and class differences came into direct contact, Anne McClintock (1995, 271) considers the colonial home to be a "contest zone of acute ambivalence." Although distinctions between the domains of public and domestic space were rigidly segregated under colonialism and apartheid, homes represented "places of juncture": "highly regulated but also fragile and overdetermined spaces," imbued with the psychic and affective anxieties of racialized intimacy (Ally 2015, 51–54). Employers attempted to manage the disquieting effects of such intimacies and the so-called contaminating effects of familiarity by establishing psychological and physical mechanisms for the construction, maintenance, and reinforcement of social and physical distance between themselves and their employees. These mechanisms included degradation and forms of marginalization, one being the "suppression of perception" (Dagut 2000, 561)—a practice of overlooking, or "not seeing" the servants despite their close proximity and the employer's awareness of their presence. Yet, despite her sidelined position within the home, through her labor, the black domestic worker was also "deeply implicated in . . . the close personal contact; the emotions, the experiences, and intimacy that is the fabric of family and households" (Ally 2015, 51). Domestic workers carried out the daily, intimate tasks of housecleaning and cooking, and, under apartheid, often played a key role in caring for and raising their white employer's children. Her ambiguous position, located in the interstices between intimacy and distance in the colonial and apartheid household and the fraught historical relationship between domesticity, privacy, and subjectivity that it fostered, leads Baderoon (2014, 178–80) to the poignant observation that in contemporary South Africa, "the house is a haunted place" whose memories, objects, and rooms remain "shadowed" by a history of servitude, sexual violence, and uncanny intimacies, and the "temporality, architecture, and subjectivities it has shaped."

As "remainders and reminders" of South Africa's troubled legacy of domestic labor, Sibande's intimate exposures of the domestic could potentially evoke a sense of identification with, or empathy for, the domestic worker, in the viewer. Bystrom (2013, 333) contends that the intimate exposures Sibande portrays, through what she terms the "'risky' but necessary work of sharing oneself with others in public," potentially give rise to "new forms of public intimacy." In support of this contention, Bystrom draws on the writings of Njabulo Ndebele (cited in Bystrom 2013, 339), who proposes that "'making public spaces intimate' by infusing into the public domain . . . genuine, reflective, if sometimes agonized, personal testimony . . . allows for the public sharing of vulnerabilities as the basis for the restoration of public trust . . . and makes possible a world of new, interpersonal solidarities." Extending Ndebele's thesis, Bystrom proposes that sharing intimate exposures in the public realm may be a way of breaking down distances between people in the imaginative realm. If considered against the backdrop of secrecy, repression, and censorship that underpinned apartheid society, such acts of (self-)exposure through artworks could potentially open up "new ways of thinking and feeling as well as moving, acting and relating to others" (Bystrom 2013, 334).

REDRESSING RELATIONS OF POWER/THE POWER OF DRESS

Sibande (cited in Ally 2015, 45) states that in her representations of Sophie, she does "not want to represent yet another image of a victimized maid" and that she hopes "to highlight the individuality [behind the maid's uniform] that years of stereotypes have hidden and even eroded" (Sibande cited in "Sophie Takes Over Inner City" 2010). She disrupts the overdetermined stereotype of the domestic worker as a disempowered, vulnerable, victimized, devalued, and exploited figure by purposefully not employing references that tend to evoke affective responses in the viewer (Corrigall 2009). Instead, Sibande subverts the way in which the black domestic worker has been cast in South African visual culture by locating Sophie's presence within the realm of the theatrical: through her performances in which she animates her fantastical garments by assuming dramatic poses and impassioned gestures, Sophie acts out her intimate fantasies and desires. Sophie's closed eyes suggest a dreamlike state, wherein she is able to imagine herself as being whomever or whatever she chooses to be. In entering this imaginative state, she occupies a kind of "private theater"—an interiorized and inviolate space. Despite her highly visible presence in the inner city, her closed eyes and dreamlike state discourage interaction with her viewers: positioned as spectators, the viewing public are made privy to this interiorized space but cannot access it. Her self-containment suggests that, like white Victorian women whose voice and agency was stifled under the authority of the Victorian paterfamilias, Sophie does not speak through verbal means. Linguistically silent, she engages in a bodily praxis that enables her to create and enact her narrative. As Baderoon (2014, 188) puts it, "The ecstatic silence in these installations is not the silence of erasure and stiflement but of unbounded invention."

For Sophie, the act of donning her garments seems to induce in her a psychological shift of attitude, self-perception, and behavior; wearing them gives her license to discard the attributes of victimization associated with a heritage of servitude, and, emancipated from the drudgery of domestic chores, to transcend her lowly socioeconomic status by assuming the white madam/colonial mistresses' privileged position of power. Furthermore, by drawing on her personal histories, Sibande honors her mother and grandmothers by "giving free reign to their imagined desires, liberating their spirits from the ordained strictures of remembrance" (Dodd 2010, 467).

It is through her manipulation of the domestic worker's uniform that Sibande disrupts and overturns the depersonalized, gendered stereotype. As a visual trope through which domestic workers are represented, the uniform carries dual associations: it acts as a signifier of female domestic labor and subservience and denotes that she has assumed the persona of a domestic worker by removing signs of her interiority and individuality (Baderoon 2014, 187). As Hlonipha Mokoena (2010) puts it, "for the maid to do her work she has to strip herself of all accessories and clothes that make her unique. She has to become nondescript, inconspicuous, non-threatening. For her to perform her duties, she has to be seen to be submitting to the discipline of sameness." Thus, as Baderoon (2014, 186) observes, by imbuing Sophie with the attributes of imagination, creativity, desire, agency, autonomy, and power, Sibande opens up "an expansive reimagining of the interior life of the women inside the uniform; a gesture that stands in overt opposition to silencing and erasure."

In early representations of Sophie, such as the digital prints titled *Caught in the Rapture* (2009) and *I Put a Spell on Me* (2009) (fig. 10.4), that are reproduced as images in the project, Sophie's dresses lean more toward the functionality of the domestic worker's uniform and the restrained gowns of the late Victorian era. With its swaths of pale blue tulle that emanate from under a ballooning indigo-colored skirt, the image derived from the sculpture titled *Sophie Mercia* (2009) (fig. 10.1) marks a transition from the simple fusion of the domestic worker's uniform-cum-Victorian dress to more flamboyant, exaggerated versions of Victorian gowns consistently combined with the white *doek* and apron. In their more extreme forms, Sophie's dresses portray the excessive style elements characteristic of upper-class Victorian women's clothing popular in the 1850s to 1870s: V-shaped waists; tight-fitting bodices featuring frilled necklines and ruffs; bell or leg o' mutton sleeves; widespread skirts that trailed on the floor as she walked; copious use of flounces, lace, and bows as well as abundant swaths of layered, draped, or ruched fabric. Sibande (cited in Corrigall 2010) acknowledges that this element of excess becomes more pronounced over time: as the folds of her dresses extend farther, and the material consumes greater ranges of space on the invisible floor plane, Queen Sophie seems to be growing into, and beyond, her mistress/madam's place as she occupies a continually increasing space of agency and personal power.

In the billboard-scale image featuring the sculpture titled *Sophie Ntombikayise* (2009), Queen Sophie's royal status is signified by the rich purple color of her dress and the way in which her exaggeratedly raised ruffled collar with its lacy edging encircles her head like a tiara. Sibande clearly associates the color purple with royalty: "The clergy and the royalty of England wear, or wore, purple if they were meeting an important person. Purple dye was expensive so only the rich were able to wear it." She continues that for her, the color purple denotes privilege: "I am attempting to use this privilege afforded to me by those who have fought for it" (Sibande cited in Krouse 2013).

In this image, the cotton fabric of her purple skirt is overlaid with shimmering, semitransparent blue organza that gathers in a frothy circle around her. No longer simply tied in a knot at the back of her dress, her apron culminates in a dramatically oversized white satin bow. Her imperial presence, already evident in the sculpture from which the image was derived, is amplified in the massive horizontal building wrap. Here, the image of her full figure is flanked by two close-up details of the front and back of her body from the waist up. Due to the superscaling of her bodily proportions in these details, in documentary photographs of the work, her gargantuan, almost monstrous, presence dwarfs everything and everyone around her.

In another image reproduced as a building wrap, depicting a sculpture titled *The Reign* (2010; fig. 10.1), Queen Sophie–as–Queen Victoria valiantly attempts to stay mounted on a monumentally large-scale bronze sculpture of a rearing horse. Here, Sibande uses parody as a means of conveying multiple possible readings of the work. One reading might be that her majesty, Queen Victoria, whose stance in photographs and paintings is conventionally upright and imperious, appears highly undignified as her billowing, royal blue skirt, with its columns of heavily ruched fabric, flounces up over the horse's hindquarters to reveal her purple petticoat. Seated at an anatomically impossible angle on the bucking horse, her highness literally and figuratively struggles to maintain her "rein," while her precarious position suggests that she is in danger of toppling off her equestrian pedestal. Such a fall from grace would ridicule her imperial status, metaphorically pointing to the end of Queen Victoria's reign and, by extension, the possibility of colonialism's demise. Alternatively, following Ruth Simbao's (2010) reading of the work, the angle that Queen Sophie leans back at indicates her imaginative ability to "magically def[y] gravity." Through this stunt, Queen Sophie parodies the celebrated status of "heroic" male soldiers and statesmen monumentalized in South Africa through a tradition of bronze equestrian statues. "Reveling in her new-found ability to do the humanly impossible," Queen Sophie "reigns supreme" (Simbao 2010) as she claims her position in South African history and triumphs in her victory over its legacies of masculine heroism and political power.

In the billboard-scale image of the digital print titled *I'm a Lady* (2009; fig. 10.3), the combination of Sophie's cobalt blue–colored tulle skirt, oversized concertinaed sleeves attached to the upper register of the domestic workers uniform, and dainty parasol embellished with white feathers, forms an overblown ensemble that parodies the hyperfeminized dress style of the Victorian lady. Inasmuch as the domestic worker's uniform was, and is, a marker of the wearer's socioeconomic position, so the opulent costumes worn by the upper-class Victorian woman signified her

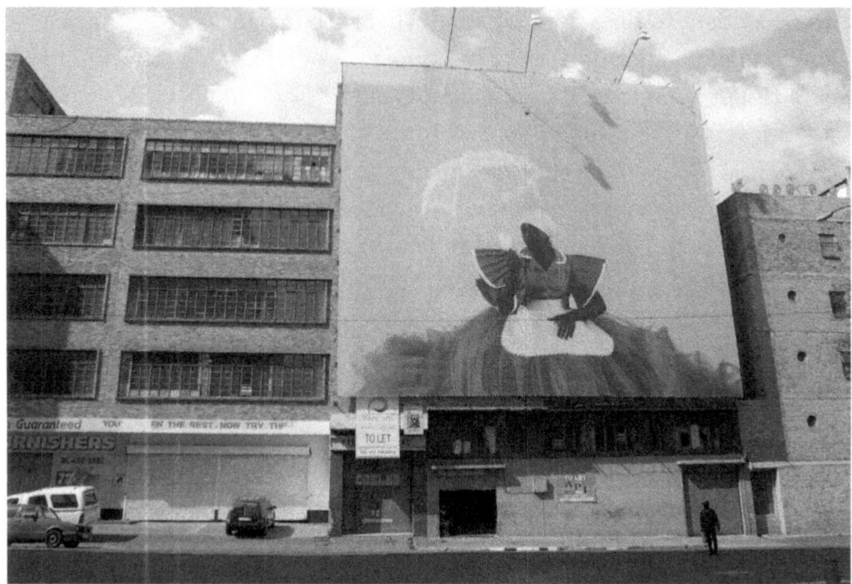

Fig. 10.3 Mary Sibande (2010), *Joburg City, World Premier Exhibition, Long Live the Dead Queen*. Installation view. Courtesy of Gallery MOMO. *Photographer ©Dean Hutton/2point8 Photography.*

husband's economic prosperity and class, declaring her status as a "lady of leisure."[17] Her ornamental place in Victorian society was buttressed by the volume of her dresses, created through a cumbersome layering of undergarments, petticoats, bustles, crinolines, and hoop skirt frames, the combination of which restricted her movement, while corseting forced her into a rigidly upright position and stifled her breath. With its exaggerated volume and extravagant pleating, gathers, and ruffles, Sophie's gown parodies the upper-class Victorian ladies' ornamentality: the dress renders her as physically incapable of performing simple household tasks, let alone menial labor. The inability to do domestic work and the inactivity and passivity it produces is a marker of Victorian femininity: her dress renders her a functionless, helpless, and disempowered creature needing to be waited upon.

According to Sibande (cited in Corrigall 2010), the opulence of Sophie's dresses and other references to affluence, consumption, and excess are intended to draw a parallel between Victorian upper-class women and those of South Africa's rising black middle class, who express their social status

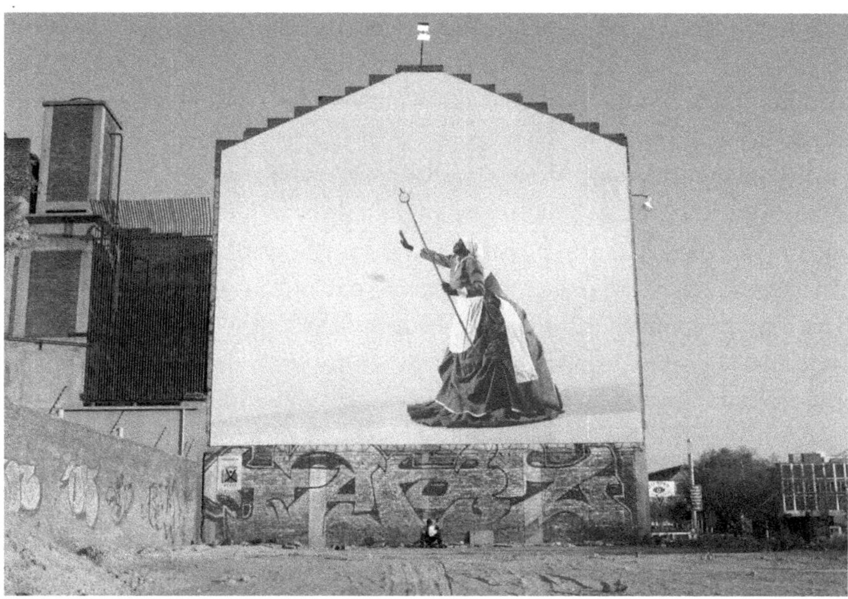

Fig. 10.4 Mary Sibande (2010), *Joburg City, World Premier Exhibition, Long Live the Dead Queen*. Installation view. Courtesy of Gallery MOMO. *Photographer ©Dean Hutton/2point8 Photography.*

and financial success through the avaricious pursuit of material goods, particularly designer clothing. In this regard, Sibande comments that "You see a lot of rich people in the township wearing a lot of bling. They have 10 rings on their fingers, wear the latest wigs [*sic*]. It's excessive. . . . [They] think the more [they] have the more [they] are getting there."

Sibande expresses the idea of consumption of material goods and visual displays of wealth as a means of showcasing one's material prosperity and economic success, through Sophie's costume, which parades and parodies the visual markers of servitude and wealth. Overt references to material prosperity are evident in the building wrap featuring the digital print shown on her 2009 exhibition, titled *I Put a Spell on Me* (2009; fig. 10.4), in which Sibande explores what she sees as connections between church garments, faith, and fashion, drawing parallels between the religious devotion of female SAZCC members, their religious apparel, the worship of fashion and conspicuous consumerism.

In this image, Sophie, clothed in a Victorian-inspired version of the emerald green–and–white robes worn by SAZCC members, carries a scepter adorned with replicas of Louis Vuitton logos (Dodd 2010, 469). Sibande (cited in Simbao 2010) explains that this work was influenced by the SAZCC members' processions that take place outside her studio on Sunday and likens the procession of worshipers—clad in crisply starched robes and uniforms—to a fashion show (Simbao 2010). With her closed eyes that turn upward as if looking for divine guidance from a higher spiritual power and one outstretched arm pointing toward the heavens, Sophie appears as if deeply immersed in prayer, or as having entered a trance-like state, perhaps even religious rapture. Earlier, I suggested that the act of donning her domestic worker's uniform–cum–Victorian-inspired dress enables her to transcend her lowly position of domestic worker and its stereotypical connotations. In this instance, it is not only her dress but also this particular dress, with its strong visual links to the robes and uniforms worn by SAZCC members that enables her to enter into a state of transcendence.

QUEEN SOPHIE IN THE PUBLIC EYE

For Sibande (cited in Brodie 2010), the project's importance lies in its attempt to convert the inner city into an outdoor exhibition space and the potential this offers for showcasing public art as a means of prompting public discourse. In this case, the public includes those who live, work, shop, drive, or walk in the inner city, as well as motorists driving through the city on the M1 highway. As Sibande states:

> People in the city don't go to galleries. Most of the galleries are in the northern suburbs. But if we take the gallery and put it in front of them . . . people might ask: What is this? Why is this in the city? Who is that woman, and why is she wearing blue? And part of the experience is that no one is going to answer those questions. In the city no one will talk to you.

In the project, the billboard and building wrap, both of which usually function as advertising space on the city skyline, are transformed to be platforms for public engagement and dialogue. Their conventional use is destabilized and visual languages appropriated so as to foreground the potential impact the large-scale display of art in public inner-city spaces might have. As Perkes (cited in Brodie 2010) states, "For the first time artworks took the place usually reserved for alcohol, cigarette, insurance and beauty advertising . . . allowing Sibande's . . . work to hold its own against the combined weight of Vodacom, Absa, Nike and Telkom et al. It's Sophie the domestic worker, taking on the corporate giants."

Alexander Opper (2010, 46) contends that the intersection of the artwork and the consumer-driven aesthetics of the billboard surfaces that surround representations of Queen Sophie—such as a woman in a similarly exuberant but more contemporary dress, holding an oversized credit card from a particular bank—represents a successful curatorial decision regarding the artwork's placement. For Opper, the juxtaposition of Sibande's work with images depicting public and private aspirations and desires could, potentially, be a means of prompting questions and setting up dialogues for, and among, passers-by.

However, in public understandings of the work, the juxtaposition of Sibande's artwork, which, as I have shown, deals with Sophie's aspirations toward, and fantasies of, material consumption, with surrounding on billboards and building wraps, might lead to the notion that Sibande's artworks are the same as, or similar to, these advertisements, particularly given the references to fantasy and desire that they both purport. This understanding is borne out in responses to a series of interviews conducted by Lise van Wyk, a journalist for the weekly newspaper *Mail & Guardian*, in which she asks passers-by to comment on Sibande's images. One responds by saying: "I . . . think they are advertising a label or something"; another says, "I think it's representing OMO" (Van Wyk 2010). Both interviewees conflate the artwork with an advertisement. The second respondent makes a visual correlation between Sophie and the stereotype of the domestic worker who, dressed in an indigo-colored uniform with white trims, is often depicted doing the laundry using OMO or Surf washing powder on billboards situated at the entrances to provincial South African towns. Other respondents indicate that they "like" the work but do not know how to read its content:

> It's beautiful but I don't understand it . . . ; I might not have an idea but it's just a nice thing to put on top [*sic*]. . . . It's a beautiful thing. . . . I liked it the minute I saw it. . . . I even shoot it on my photo [*sic*]; it's a good idea . . . because the art . . . goes together with the cultures and here in Johannesburg is lots of cultures [*sic*].

Some respondents consider the project to be a positive intervention because it showcases South African art to an international audience, particularly as Joburg Art City 2010 was timed to coincide with South Africa's hosting of the FIFA Soccer World Cup: "Here in Africa we always dream about art . . . people . . . like to see art . . . when they come to our place, they see that kind of art they are happy [*sic*] . . . ; most tourists . . . want to see . . . African art and culture." By responding, "It's . . . welcoming me. . . . I feel [like a] partaker in the city," one interviewee points to the potential impact and value of artwork that bring sites of invisibility into the public realm. His feeling "part of" or "at home" in the inner city suggests that Sibande's imbuing of the public space with personal narratives could contribute to making the potentially alienating inner city more intimate and homely. However, for others, the productive post-apartheid possibilities of artwork that foregrounds intimate exposures in the public realm and its potential to foster democratic public engagement seems to have been lost, or is greeted with skepticism:

> We ask ourselves many questions . . . what is this art for there [*sic*] because I can see it's me, but with an umbrella with this apron . . . the apron with the umbrella it's not on, no . . . ; That picture doesn't even have the message [*sic*] . . . I don't understand it. I always look at it when I go this way but the message and the layout the design and everything [*sic*] it's not that [impressive] . . .

While Sophie's figure visually consumes the public space of the inner city, she also enters the public realm discursively, through the critical commentary her works attract (Bystrom and Nuttall 2012, 315). As Bystrom and Nuttall (2012, 315) observe, such discursive commentary and public exposure open up platforms for discussing questions of domestic service—a topic that, as they note, like "dirty laundry," remains largely invisible in South African discourse. Since her 2009 exhibition, several manifestations of Sophie have been exhibited globally, in major cultural centers such as Paris, Venice, Helsinki, Rio de Janeiro, and Dakar. Her work has generated considerable interest and debate, expressed and disseminated through art critics' reviews, articles published in academic journals, and interviews with the artist. Sophie has also been popularized through the mass media, featuring in magazines and newspaper supplements, as well as publicity material distributed by Gallery MOMO.

CONCLUSION

Queen Sophie shifts from the invisibility of domestic work, to the public space of the art gallery, to a larger-than-life reclamation of the inner-city space and beyond, into the discursive public realm. These shifts from inner to outer, private to public, may be seen as foregrounding her liberation, as she is released from the confines of domesticity and the limitations of the white cube.

As ghostlike figures, Queen Sophie, and the maternal Dead Queens that precede her, remain suspended in an unsettling space of ambiguity: their presences speak of absences, while their absences are insistently present. Their present-absences haunt both the interiorized, private space of the South African household and the urban landscape of the post-apartheid city.

In its intimate exposures, Sibande's work recasts white women's supremacy and privilege under colonialism and apartheid in the postcolonial present. By grappling with the meaning of, and the possibilities opened by, making her private histories public and reworking the material and cultural baggage embedded in collective histories of domestic servitude, Sibande unravels the tightly bound colonial binaries of Self/Other that haunt understandings of difference in South Africa. In so doing, she undoes distinctions between the public and private, interior and exterior, opening up possibilities for ways in which cultural redress might take place on personal and collective terms.

LEORA FARBER is the Director of the Visual Identities in Art and Design (VIAD) Research Centre, Faculty of Art, Design and Architecture, University of Johannesburg, where she is Associate Professor.

Notes

1. Colloquial Afrikaans term for "headscarf."

2. In this chapter, I use "visual analysis" as a primary methodology, first providing a formal description of the work from which subjective, interpretative deductions are made. In so doing, I acknowledge that the particular interpretative deductions made through my visual analysis of Sibande's public art project may not necessarily be shared by readers of this text. Indeed, one of the challenges of Sibande's public art work is that it offers the potential for open-ended rather than narrowly didactic meanings and may be read in very different ways by different individuals and publics.

3. The buildings are located on 10,000 square meters of space on either side of the M1 South highway—the main motorway running through the inner city, linking Johannesburg's northern suburbs with Soweto and the southern suburbs.

4. Sites include Pritchard Street (a main road that horizontally connects the west and east ends of the inner city), Newtown (a semi-industrial area in which buildings are

used as warehouses, manufacturing spaces, residences, and venues for cultural events), and August House (a modernist structure situated at the corner of End and Moseley streets, Doornfontein). August House was built in the 1940s, when Doornfontein was Johannesburg's manufacturing hub. Artists, including Sibande, used the former warehouse as studio and residential space until it was taken over by property developers in 2014.

5. Sibande is of the post-1994, Generation Y of young black artists currently working in South Africa who are grappling with this country's troubled colonial legacy through performances of the self. Others working in similar ways include Nicholas Hlobo, Nandipha Nmtanbo, Nelisiswe Xaba, and Kudzanai Chiurai. Through their visual remaking of South African history, these artists disrupt entrenched colonial constructs of racial and sexual difference to give rise to forms of identity making that have relevance in a postcolonial context.

6. As a conglomerate body, the SAZCC comprises several denominations. Each practice a mixture of traditional African beliefs and a form of Christianity rooted in the tradition of the Catholic apostolic revival movement. While the style and color of the garments worn by female members the SAZCC vary according to their denomination, their starched white bonnets and collars and indigo, royal blue, or emerald green–and–white robes strongly resemble the design and colors of some of Sophie's dresses.

7. One reading is that Sophie "repeats" the stereotype of the colonial mistress/contemporary white madam but, drawing on Linda Hutcheon's (1985, 6) definition of parody, does so with a "critical distance, which marks difference rather than similarity."

8. Bhabha (1994) explains that in the construction of Self/Other underpinning colonial discourse, otherness is a relativized construct, based on visual markers such as blackness and whiteness. The Self is constructed in an ambivalent and visual relationship to the Other; as Bhabha states, "to exist is to be called into being in relation to an otherness, its look or locus." He describes the colonial gaze as the manner in which the colonized subject's identity is negated by the colonial's inability to "look at" or fully perceive their existence: "as even now you look/but never see me" (Bhabha 1994, 63, 67, 79).

9. Bystrom and Nuttall identify Penny Siopis, Usha Seejarim, Terry Kurgan, and Zanele Muholi as examples of other female South African contemporary artists who articulate personal narratives and private or interior spaces in which subjectivities are shaped in a public realm.

10. Some of the components listed on the Johannesburg City Council official website are "intensive urban management, including improvements to service quality, strict enforcement of by-laws, management of taxis and informal traders"; upgrading and maintenance of infrastructure; providing support for economic sectors that could potentially thrive in the inner city; discouraging properties that are abandoned, overcrowded or poorly maintained; and encouraging investments that uplift the area ("Reshaping Johannesburg's Inner City" 2015).

11. As of April 2015, the inner city has 217,000 residents in 37,000 dwelling units. Approximately 800,000 commuters enter and leave the city daily, and between 300,000 and 400,000 migrant shoppers from various African countries as well as rural areas of South Africa visit the inner city annually ("Reshaping Johannesburg's Inner City" 2015).

12. At an exchange rate of 12.13 rand to US$1.00, this amount translates to US$479,352.93.

13. There have been no further iterations of the Joburg Art City Project since 2010.

14. The historical divide between the domains of the public and private may be traced back to the Victorian paradigm of gender hierarchies, wherein women were economically, socially, sexually, and creatively placed in the lesser position (Malan 1996, 12). Women were associated with domesticity and the home, while men inhabited the public sphere of business, politics, and finance (Lemmer 2007, 48).

15. The fourth sculpture, titled *Sophie Ntombikayise,* portrays Sophie as Sibande herself.

16. Historically, domestic labor has been the most sustained avenue for black women's participation in the South African economy. In contemporary South Africa, due to high unemployment rates and difficulties immigrant black women face in finding employment through formal channels, domestic service remains a sought-after form of employment. According to Sithiabile Ntombela, approximately one million women work as domestic workers in South Africa, making up 8 percent of the country's workforce. Although institution of the Domestic Worker's Act of 2002 has, to some extent, regulated the industry by setting a minimum wage and determining improved working conditions, domestic work remains a low-status, low-paying employment sector. Women working in this sector often come from economically impoverished backgrounds, lack skills and training, and are disadvantaged by poor education and are therefore open to exploitation and abuse (Ntombela 2012, 132).

17. Sophie's parasol is one indicator of her aspirations toward social and economic status, as only wealthy Victorian women used these as a daily accoutrement. Its purpose, aside from being frivolously decorative, and thus a signifier of femininity, was to protect their fair complexion from the sun. A pale, porcelain-like white skin was considered a mark of gentility, as it indicated that unlike "common women," an upper-class lady did not have to work, and certainly not outdoors.

References

Ally, Shireen. 2015. "Domesti-City: Colonial Anxieties and Postcolonial Fantasies in the Figure of the Maid." In *Colonialisation and Domestic Service: Historical and Contemporary Perspectives*, edited by Victoria Haskins and Claire Lowrie, 45–62. New York: Routledge.

Baderoon, Gabeba. 2014. "The Ghost in the House: Women, Race, and Domesticity in South Africa." *Cambridge Journal of Postcolonial Literary Inquiry* 1: 173–88.

Bhabha, Homi K. 1994. *The Location of Culture*. London: Routledge.

Brodie, Nechama. 2010. "Look Up, Up, Up." *Mail & Guardian*, July 9. Accessed March 15, 2012. http://mg.co.za/article/2010–07–09-look-up.

Bystrom, Kerry. 2013. "Johannesburg Interiors." *Cultural Studies* 27, no. 3: 333–356.

Bystrom, Kerry, and Sarah Nuttall. 2013. "Introduction: Private Lives and Public Cultures in South Africa." *Cultural Studies* 27, no. 3: 307–32.

Corrigall, Mary. 2009. "Mary Sibande: Domestic Fantasy." *Incorrigible Corrigall*, August 5. Accessed September 20, 2014. http://corrigall.blogspot.com/2009/08/mary-sibande-domestic-fantasy.html.

———. 2010. "Interview with Mary Sibande." *Incorrigible Corrigall*, July 25. Accessed July 3, 2014. http://corrigall.blogspot.com/2010/07/interview-with-mary-sibande.html.

Dagut, Simon. 2000. "Gender, Colonial 'Women's History' and the Construction of Social Distance: Middle-Class British Women in Later Nineteenth-Century South Africa." *Journal of Southern African Studies* 26, no. 3 (September): 554–72.

Derrida, Jacques. 1994. *Specters of Marx*. Translated by Peggy Kamuf. New York: Routledge.

Dodd, Alexandra. 2010. "Dressed to Thrill: The Victorian Postmodern and Counter-Archival Imaginings in the Work of Mary Sibande." *Critical Arts* 24, no. 3: 467–74.

Hutcheon, Linda. 1985. *A Theory of Parody: The Teachings of Twentieth-Century Art Forms*. New York: Methuen.

Jayawardane, Neelika. 2013. "Of Bastards, Creoles, and Incommensurable Remainders in the Transnation: Postcolonial Studies and Contemporary South African Literature." *Journal of Commonwealth and Postcolonial Studies* 1, no. 1: 192–207. Accessed November 14, 2014. http://www.oswego.edu/Documents/english/Jayawardane1.pdf.

"Joburg Art City with Mary Sibande and the Dead Queen." 2011. *Art at Work*. Accessed April 11, 2012. http://www.artatwork.co.za/web/experience/special-projects/item/128-joburg-art-city-with-mary-sibande-and-the-dead-queen.

Krouse, Matthew. 2013. "Mary Sibande: The Purple Shall Reign at Grahamstown's Arts Fest." *Mail & Guardian* Art and Culture, June 21. Accessed April 11, 2015. http://mg.co.za/article/2013-06-21-mary-sibande-the-purple-shall-reign-at-the-fest.

Lemmer, Catherine. 2007. "Victorian Respectability: The Gendering of Domestic Space." Unpublished master's diss., University of Pretoria.

Malan, André. 1996. "The Use of Historical Photographs as Source for Cultural History: The Sammy Marks Photograph Collection." Unpublished master's diss., University of Pretoria.

McClintock, Anne. 1995. *Imperial Leather: Race, Gender and Sexuality in the Colonial Contest*. New York: Routledge.

Mokoena, Hlonipha. 2010. "Anybody Can Be a Maid." *Africa Is a Country* (Blog), December 6. Accessed September 16, 2014. http://africasacountry.com/anybody-can-be-a-maid/.

Moletsane, Rebebohile, Claudia Mitchell, and Ann Smith, eds. 2012. *Was It Something I Wore?: Dress, Materiality, Identity*. Cape Town: HSRC Press.

Ntombela, Sithiabile. 2012. "Do Clothes Make a Woman?: Exploring the Role of Dress in Shaping South African Domestic Workers' Identities." In *Was It Something I Wore?: Dress, Materiality, Identity*, edited by Rebebohile Moletsane, Claire Mitchell, and Ann Smith, 132–47. Cape Town: HSRC Press.

Opper, Alexander. 2010. "The Art of Being Public." *Art South Africa* 9: 44–49.

"Reshaping Johannesburg's Inner City." 2015. *The Official Website of Johannesburg's Inner City*. April 7, 2015. Accessed April 7, 2015. http://www.joburg.org.za/index.php?option=com_content&id=126&Itemid=9.

Sibande, Mary. 2009. "Artist's Statement." *Artthrob*. Contemporary Art in South Africa. Current reviews. Accessed January 30, 2015. http://www.artthrob.co.za/Artists/Mary-Sibande.aspx.

Simbao, Ruth. 2010. "Mary Sibande: *Long Live the Dead Queen*." *Gallery MOMO*. Accessed April 12, 2015. http://www.gallerymomo.com/wp-content/uploads/2011/09/Mary-Sibande-English1.pdf.

Singer, Elizabeth. 2012. "'Sophie' Reigns over Dominant Display Practices: Negotiating Power in Mary Sibande's Installations." Unpublished master's diss., University of Texas, Austin. Accessed October 4, 2014. http://repositories.lib.utexas.edu/handle/2152/ETD-UT-2012–05–5685.

"Sophie Takes Over Inner City." 2010. *Joburg, My City, Our Future: Growth and Development Strategy 2040*, July 22. Accessed January 3, 2015. http://www.joburg.org.za/index.php?option=com_content&task=view&id=5478&Itemid=193.

Van Wyk, Lise. 2010. "Sophie in the Joburg Skyline." *Mail and Guardian* Entertainment, October 14. Accessed February 2, 2015. http://mg.co.za/multimedia/2010–10–14-sophie-in-the-joburg-skyline.

CHAPTER 11

Unsanctioned: The Inner City Interventions of Julie Lovelace

KAREN VON VEH

JULIE LOVELACE IS A ceramic artist who makes small, whimsical ceramic sculptures. A public art project she embarked on in 2011 as part of her master's degree[1] is, however, a marked departure from the generally sheltered and rarified milieu of the fine art galleries in which her work had hitherto been exhibited.[2] *Unsanctioned,* as the title suggests, consists of a number of unsolicited, noncommissioned art interventions placed into the forgotten corners and liminal spaces of downtown Johannesburg. Lovelace likens her interventions to the impromptu public events ("interjections") staged by South African performance artist Steven Cohen or the unheralded appearance of images by the British graffiti artist Banksy. Such examples indicate the gap between commissioned art that has been selected and legitimately placed in a public space by representatives of a city's governing bodies and works that, while not subject (initially) to censorship or any form of authority, might nevertheless be labeled "illicit" or even "illegal."

Julie Lovelace was born in England on October 7, 1963. She moved to South Africa in 1998 on a five-year contract, deciding subsequently to remain in the country.[3] Lovelace (2014a, 1) explains that her project for *Unsanctioned* grew from her immigrant status in South Africa and her resultant feeling of being "betwixt and between" (Turner 1967, 93) as if straddling two identities and not quite belonging to either. This feeling of liminality encouraged her to explore how the liminal is manifest in other migrant experiences and in the spaces they inhabit. The city of Johannesburg has been identified in newspaper reports and on websites as the fastest growing city in Africa with migrants and emigrants pouring in daily from elsewhere on the continent as well as from rural areas in South Africa.[4] The lack of population controls with the end of apartheid, and the resulting influx of African migrants looking for a better life, has created a city where the existing infrastructure is not adequate to support the growing population. Living space is severely limited, there are not enough jobs for the numbers of inhabitants, and people often exist in substandard housing, slums, or shacks that are set up underneath bridges and alongside highways.[5] The liminal inhabitants of Johannesburg are the primary audience for Lovelace's *Unsanctioned* project, which consists of small ceramic sculptures inserted into unused corners, broken bridges, on walls underneath motorway overpasses, or in storm-water drains. Combining made and found objects overlaid with writing and graphic images, they also include toys and mementoes from Lovelace's own childhood. They attest to her personal history by evoking a sense of nostalgia for her past, and as I indicate in this chapter, they assert her present liminal (immigrant) identity in the spaces often inhabited by other immigrants or seen by passers-by.

The interventions are discreet insertions that appear almost overnight in an apparently spontaneous manner and are intentionally ephemeral. Many of these interventions appear and disappear in a manner similar to the miniature cityscapes inserted by Charles Simonds into the broken bricks of New York City's buildings.[6] In a few cases, however, they have surprisingly been embraced by some neighborhoods as part of their local cultural manifestations and taken on a more permanent existence. Whether transient or permanent, they present an element of playful surprise that challenges the normal relationship experienced between artist and audience when encountering sanctioned public displays. Lovelace (2014a, 3) believes that by choosing to work independently in public spaces, she allows for the possibility of transformation and new mediation to happen spontaneously between her work and those who might encounter it. For this particular response, the artworks need to occur outside of the normal social structures such as galleries, museums, or monuments where visitors to such delineated sites arrive expecting a particular kind of experience. When inserting the artworks she has had to engage with the people who inhabit or pass through the spaces in which she works (Lovelace 2014a, 66), so the process of installing her small interventions allow for personal interactions with people who might never enter an art gallery, speak to an artist, or take much note of monumental public art. In these cases, the spectator may become a cooperating participant, sharing the responsibility of the work's realization and its very existence, as works are sometimes stolen ("repurposed") or vandalized in some cases, or become a valued part of the environment in others. Her interventions thus encourage explorations into the dynamics of the public space they inhabit.

In this chapter, I consider three of Lovelace's interventions in detail, analyzing both the inspiration for their existence and their life-span in situ. The works are discussed in terms of the way they engage with the multifaceted nature of liminality: in terms of their identification as "liminal art works," in terms of their placement in "liminal spaces," and as a reflection of the liminality of their creator and the people who encounter them. Liminality is identified by Victor Turner (1967, 94) as space and time where transformations can take place, a transitional situation fueled with ambiguities and contradictions. Homi Bhabha (1997, 5) further writes that liminality is related to the concept of cultural hybridity, and the placement of these works demonstrates Bhabha's (1997, 54) notion of the hybrid "third space" where social identities are questioned and negotiated giving rise to something new and independent. Using this theoretical framework, I argue that Lovelace's unsanctioned public art interventions maintain a fluidity that grows from their ability to "repurpose" a space, and in doing so, they reflect the nature of Johannesburg in its present incarnation as a melting pot for local inhabitants, immigrants, and refugees. Furthermore, Johannesburg is itself in a state of "becoming," with constant interventions to upgrade and reimagine some areas, while others fall into disrepair and are taken over by slumlords. I suggest that Lovelace's works provide an appropriate counterpoint to commissioned public sculpture as they respond to the very instability that characterizes Johannesburg. Some of her works are transient, some are more permanent but are reembellished, and/or repaired or altered when necessary. Her work thus taps into the prevailing ethos and engages with local inhabitants in an attempt to create a "third space" that breaks binaries and shatters imposed cultural homogeneity (Bhabha 1997, 37), and where imaginative individual expressions of identity and renewal can be experienced.

INTERVENTIONS 1 AND 2

The first of Lovelace's unauthorized interventions, *If You Go Down to the Woods Today* (fig. 11.1) is an understated and relatively discreet collection of ceramic plates of various sizes, grouped together almost haphazardly and affixed halfway up an upright support for the overhead highway (a bridge bent) on the corner of Berea Street and Fox Street in Johannesburg. The plates appear surprising in this rather industrial and somewhat grimy urban setting, as unexpected as a tea party in a railway station. The installation was created in December 2011 in response to an open call for submissions by the Immigrant Movement International. This was part of an ongoing project initiated by Cuban artist Tania Bruguera (2011) and supported by Creative Time and the Queens Museum of Art in New York for actions to take place around the world at 2:00 p.m. (local time) on December 18, 2011. The date had been designated International Migrant's Day by the United Nations, and the call was for artists, immigrants, or any interested member of the public to stage an action that would in some way respond to the recognition of migrants as a "global class" who were united by their common human experience of migration with its resulting social and political conditions. Bruguera (Creative Time 2011) explains: "As migration becomes a more central element of contemporary existence, the status and identity of those who live outside their place of origin starts to become defined not by sharing a common language, class, culture, or race, but instead by their condition as immigrants." Participants were invited to visit the immigrant-movement.us website and submit their idea for an action. The website enabled users to track these events as they happened in real time across the globe, by presenting an interactive map of the world with a description of each action.

The plight of migrants in South Africa, however, is more complex than mere displacement and alienation, and the experience of liminality due to migrant status in South Africa is largely dependent on a person's country of origin. Immigrants from elsewhere in Africa, many of them refugees from conflicts in their home countries, or legal migrants working in South Africa, have been subject to sporadic upsurges of violent xenophobic attacks since May 2008. The first wave of attacks, beginning in Johannesburg, was marked by an unprecedented scale of violence and displacement in which all African foreigners were stereotyped as "illegal refugees" (SAHRC 20010, 8). The *Mail & Guardian* newspaper (May 31, 2008) reported that between May 19–31, 2008, 62 people were killed, 670 were wounded, and literally thousands were driven from their homes and businesses and left destitute. The South African Human Rights Commission responded to the initial 2008 attacks in a report on xenophobic violence published in 2010.

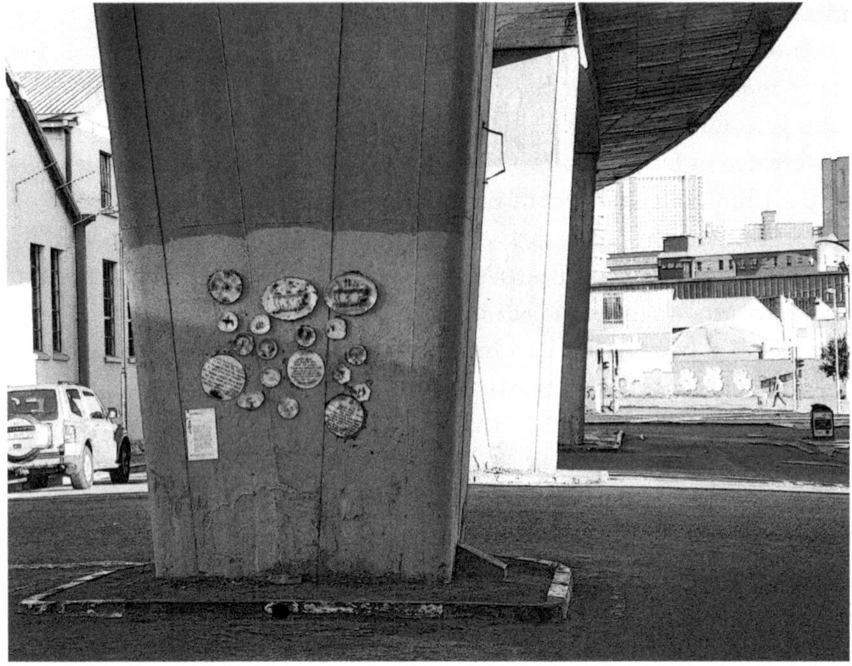

Fig. 11.1 Julie Lovelace, Intervention 1: *If You Go Down to the Woods Today* (December 2011). Installation. *Photograph taken by the artist in February 2012.*

The introduction to the report (SAHRC 20010, 8) puts the plight of migrants into perspective:

> The 2008 mobilisation against non-nationals can only properly be understood within the country's broader history of xenophobia and South Africa's "culture of violence" (Harris 2001, 6). Despite our formal transition to equality and democracy, violence is often still viewed as a legitimate means of resolving issues (Harris 2001, 6). Non-nationals resident in South Africa are all the more likely to fall prey to violence, as South Africans often blame them for crime and unemployment, and view them as responsible for depriving "more-deserving" citizens of jobs, housing, and other economic goods. Outsiders are, therefore, often subject to intense discrimination and hostility from local communities. (Harris 2001, 10)

Despite studies and reports such as this and official social interventions to assist in the integration of African immigrants and refugees, there is an ongoing simmering tension between local inhabitants and other African dwellers, particularly in Johannesburg where many of the immigrants choose to come and look for work. Further attacks were reported in a Johannesburg township in 2010, prompting officials to erect refugee shelters at the main border between South Africa and Zimbabwe for people fleeing the country (Mail & Guardian 2010). In 2011, a spate of attacks, primarily aimed at Asian, Somali, and Ethiopian traders, occurred in Gauteng (Misago and Wilhelm-Solomon 2011). Threats of xenophobic attacks created fear and anxiety among the foreigners living in Mayfair, a working-class neighborhood of Johannesburg, during 2012 (Parker 2012). Newspaper reports state that during that year at least 120 foreigners were killed and 250 were injured across South Africa, indicating that xenophobia is spreading across the country (Landau 2013). There are many more examples culminating in the latest wave of mass violence that made headline news in Johannesburg during January 2015 (Sosibo 2015). Philip de Wet (2015) suggests that xenophobic violence has escalated in the last few years, and foreign nationals are the most vulnerable residents in South Africa. Their situation is exacerbated due to the perceived lack of interest from local authorities who fail to offer support or protection when necessary and, in addition, the possible political instability arising from local government elections coming up in 2016 (De Wet, 2015).

It is clear that African migrants are marginalized due to ongoing attacks and distrust, which further contributes to their liminal status. It is also true that Lovelace, as a white European immigrant, is not subject to xenophobia and therefore possesses the security and privilege to raise the fraught issues of migrant experience in Johannesburg without the fear of violent xenophobic reprisals or censure. Lovelace's position of security allows her to create works that bring to light complexities of displacement and relocation that would seem to have resonance to those immigrants who do not share her position of privilege.

Lovelace (2014a, 43) explains that she responded to Bruguera's call and the plight of local migrants by carefully selecting a site that would express liminality and therefore resonate with the experiences of migrants in Johannesburg. She identifies the particular bridge bent chosen for this intervention as a transitional or liminal space because it could be defined, in Marc Augé's terms (O'Beirne 2006, 38–50), as a nonplace: "If a space can be defined as relational, historical and concerned with identity, then a space which cannot be defined as relational, or historical, or concerned with identity, will be a non-place." As Emer O'Beirne (2006, 38–50) explains, Augé coined the term *non-lieux* [nonplaces] to describe architectural and technological spaces that are designed to be passed through rather than appropriated. They would include bridges, doorways, stairways, pavements, or public spaces such as bus stops or airports—places that retain little or no trace of our engagement with them.

Lovelace's choice of an indeterminate space is deliberate because she identifies nonplaces as filled with playful possibilities, precisely because they are not defined and therefore not limited in any way (Lovelace 2014a, 14). The title of her first intervention, *If You Go Down to the Woods Today,* refers to the playful nature of her work and its links with childhood as the words come from a well-known children's song, written originally in the 1930s and perennially popular with children in both England and South Africa, "The Teddy Bear's Picnic."[7] The "big surprise" referred to in the song is also evoked by the unexpected nature of finding an art intervention in such a "nonplace." Lovelace identifies her chosen liminal spaces as "thresholds" because they exist between two different existential planes, and she notes "actions on thresholds are often publicly tolerated as they are not perceived by others as lasting and dangerous" (Lovelace 2014a, 13). Her thinking was influenced by studies in the liminal aspects of ritual and performance undertaken by the anthropologist Arnold van Gennep in 1909 and further developed by Victor Turner in the mid-twentieth century. While buildings often provide a sense of order or a defining framework for specific activities, a threshold frames an escape from social convention and adds to the exploration of new possibilities due to encounters outside cultural frames of reference or defined relationships. Turner (1969, 128–29) suggests that an in-between space allows for an active exchange of ideologies and concepts. Liminal space might therefore be defined as a metaphorical realm where artistic, political, cultural, and social beliefs are in constant states of contestation and negotiation, flux and change.

This particular position under the highway is a relatively busy thoroughfare where many people converge on a daily basis while en route to other destinations in the city. It allows for relatively uncontrolled encounters with strangers, and as Erving Goffman (1982, 117) notes, in such settings, chance and risk are always present. The area covered by the highway is generous in scale and is a suitable setting for informal use as it affords some protection from the weather for traders, passers-by, and Lovelace's public interventions. This area of Johannesburg, named the Maboneng precinct, is part of a "regeneration project,"[8] where formerly unused or derelict industrial structures are in the process of being reimagined as cultural venues. The particular bridge bent, on which Lovelace's first intervention is situated, faces a busy arts and culture center called Arts on Main. Because the area is in the process of transformation and is frequented by so many diverse people, there are security staff and surveillance cameras to monitor the area and ensure the safety of citizens and visitors.

Lovelace (2014a, 44) explains that the diversity of this area and the fact that it is difficult to categorize in social and economic terms is at the root of her choice of this space for an intervention based on exploring and exploiting liminality in the city. She further notes that a particularly complex collection of energies abound in a place that has been lost or degraded over time and is subsequently reappropriated and reimagined. There is a need to negotiate between the new economically privileged participants and the preexisting inhabitants—the street-level economies made up of urban dwellers who trade there or pass through the area on a daily basis. These conditions particularly appear to foster transience and liminality, making this position an ideal setting for her intervention as it fulfills the requirements of Homi Bhabha's "third space," which provides the potential for transformation and for constructing a new experiential engagement with the city. Bhabha (1997, 217), in *The Location of Culture,* has defined the "third space" as a place of hybridity, liminality, and ambivalence, where boundaries are dissolved, where singularity is fragmented and which enables other positions to emerge "*in-between* the claims of the past and the needs of the present" (Bhabha 1997, 219, emphasis mine). The result is a space that allows for future developments, that is opened to new possibilities with new structures of authority and new initiatives, creating an expectant space of exploration. It forms a counterpoint to institutionalized political arenas or "legitimized" formal spaces.

Lovelace's interventions placed directly into the street, therefore, respond to their locale in a way that sanctioned and commissioned art works in predetermined loci or within the controlled confines of the art museum cannot. Lovelace (2014a, 44) explains that her art is a form of resistance against the museum establishment or sanctioned public sculpture, as her works are uncommissioned, unsigned, and are aimed at subverting and repurposing her chosen spaces. The objects constituting her first "unsanctioned intervention" are a collection of found and slip-cast ceramic plates of various sizes, attached to the bridge bent. The objects were carefully selected, according to Lovelace (2014a, 44, 45) because of the historic context of ceramic crockery that relates to domestic and utilitarian use. They are thus invested with their own narratives that are subsequently altered by Lovelace through her manipulation of the surface decoration. Many of the plates are mass-produced consumer objects purchased from charity shops or antique shops (Lovelace 2014b, 14). They are already embellished with nostalgic floral patterns that echo the "old English" aesthetic of the crockery owned by Lovelace's grandmother and parents. Some have thin, worn glazing, creating a rough surface. Some are cracked or chipped and some have worn gold luster on the edges. The perceived flaws in the objects are valued by Lovelace (2014a, 45) as evidence of the history they carry. In her manipulation of the surfaces, she deliberately draws attention to cracks and chips by working the added glazes around the imperfections so that they will be enhanced and reveal the past life of the object. She then adds various kitsch images denoting "stereotypical notions of idealized childhood" and line renditions of antique rococo furniture to evoke a sense of nostalgia (Lovelace 2014a, 45).

The children and other figures or objects superimposed on these floral backgrounds are created from black decal silhouettes, also referring to historic prototypes as they are similar to those used on postcards, by travelers and immigrants, before the camera was invented. Lovelace (2014b, 15) suggests that she was drawn to these silhouettes because of their ability to present the essence of a subject in a minimal way. "Shadow people" could also denote a liminal state of being, particularly as they look anomalous in these traditional floral ceramic settings (fig. 11.2). The figures are children playing, dancing, going fishing and the exotic or magical creatures and people they might encounter in fairy stories or when going "down to the woods" as the title of the work implies. There are gypsies, musicians, animals, and some animal human combinations connoting childhood adventures and happy endings. In between these shadow figures, Lovelace has also placed commercially bought decals of large colored flowers that appear to deepen the sense of make-believe or unreality. The apparently innocuous and frivolous imagery is subverted, however, by guns placed into the hands of some children or silhouettes of tanks and weapons of war inserted into the painted idyllic scenery on several plates.

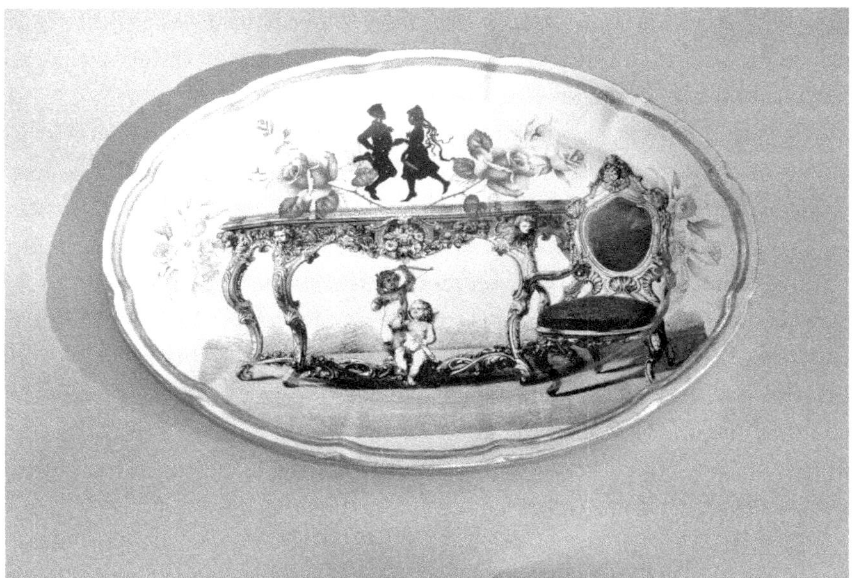

Fig. 11.2 Julie Lovelace, Intervention 1: *If You Go Down to the Woods Today* (December 2011). Detail of oval plate. *Photograph taken by the artist in February 2012.*

Lovelace has also overlaid the words of a hip-hop/rap song, "Little Weapons" (2007), written and performed by Lupe Fiasco.[9] The song presents three crime scenarios perpetrated by young children with guns, reflecting the detrimental effect of gun use, violence, and intolerance on children around the world. Fiasco's theme is particularly pertinent to the city of Johannesburg, which has gained a reputation for violent crime. Fear of crime has resulted in an extremely high percentage of private gun ownership (Hirsch 2013), and statistics report that more than 40 percent of the murders recorded in South Africa are committed with guns.[10] The allusion to children and guns also perhaps raises the specter of child soldiers and the gun violence that could have been experienced by immigrants and refugees who come to South Africa to escape from other African countries embroiled in conflict. The imagery in Lovelace's installation thus creates a duality where some iconography explores nostalgic scenes of childhood innocence and others evoke the harsh reality of present existence. This dichotomy refers to Lovelace's (2014a, 39) own feeling of existing "betwixt and between" two cultures and illustrates the ambivalence of her feelings about the city in which she now lives. Her experience of Johannesburg is placed on display through these eclectic objects that are exhibited in a position that is also categorized as liminal: halfway between the ground and the flyover, in a nonspace under the highway, and positioned to capture the attention of the many migrants and city dwellers who pass through this area daily. According to Lovelace (2014b, 12), "Words and images are made solid for an ephemeral moment, turning a 'non-place' into a 'place,' by creating an engagement between the intervention, the street and the viewer, to illuminate a marginal space and introduce an element of surprise to those who notice." Lovelace photographically documented her intervention and put her images onto the Immigrant Movement International website as part of Tania Bruguera's worldwide initiative. To emphasize the purpose of her work, she also printed a copy of the Migrant Manifesto, taken from the website, and pasted it onto the bridge support just below her plates.[11]

Lovelace's first installation has achieved some recognition at home, completely independent from its original purpose, due to a local photographic initiative in the Maboneng precinct titled (rather ironically in this instance) the I Was Shot Foundation. This project, which began in 2009, provides photographic training for the homeless street children from Hillbrow and the areas around Maboneng. The children are given disposable cameras, taught how to use them, and encouraged to take photographs of their neighborhood and the people they encounter. The first exhibition of their photographs was held at Arts on Main in December 2009 and was called *Joburg on Monday Afternoons: Through the Eyes of 15 Street Kids.* It was such a success that a stand was opened at the Market on Main, in the Maboneng precinct, to sell products made with the images (printed napkins, key rings, fridge magnets etc.) and to generate an income for the street children (iwasshot in Joburg). An image of *If You Go Down to the Woods Today* (December 2011) is one that can be purchased from the market or from their internet site, iwasshot.com.

If You Go Down to the Woods Today (2011) was further developed by Lovelace in 2012 in response to a second call for submissions by the Immigrant Movement International. She revisited the site and found, to her surprise, that it was relatively undamaged with only a few of the original pieces missing, possibly thanks to the surveillance systems and twenty-four-hour security in the area (Lovelace 2014a, 47). She decided to repair the remaining pieces and add new works to them, choosing to rename the

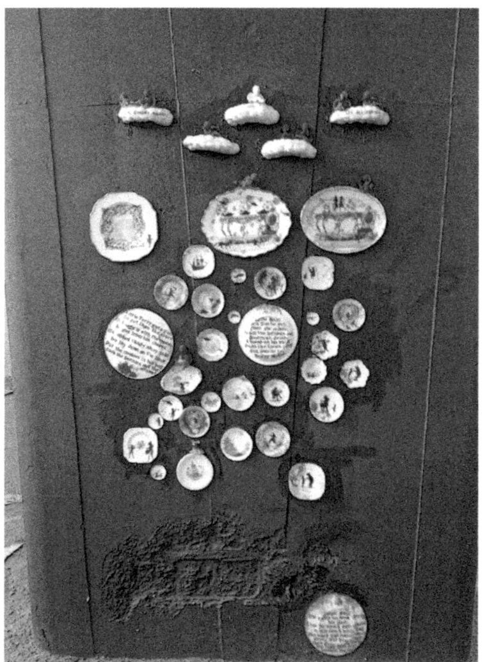

Fig. 11.3 Julie Lovelace, Intervention 2: *We Are All Migrants* (December 2012). *Photograph by the artist.*

expanded intervention *We Are All Migrants* as a response to International Migrant's Day (fig.11.3). The bridge bents had all been repainted a dark gray since the original installation, and each had one of the letters of Maboneng painted in large capitals on the upper part of the support.[12] The painters had worked carefully around Lovelace's plates, perhaps tacitly accepting their existence as a fixture of the neighborhood.[13]

The date of the second action was December 18, 2012, and Lovelace (2014b, 21) recounts that as she arrived at the underpass to begin her installation, she was surprised to find the area populated by city council employees, dressed in red overalls and armed with crowbars. These "Red Ants," as they are known, demolish informal settlements and evict illegal squatters at the order of the sheriff of the court. On this particular morning, they were there to evict the squatters from a derelict building situated about fifty meters from her intervention. The evicted inhabitant's belongings were all placed on the side of the road in heaps, and Lovelace (2014b, 21) felt traumatized at witnessing this event unfolding around her and the ensuing "pandemonium" while she was working. She decided to photograph the Red Ants at work and post these images on the Immigrant Movement International website instead of continuing working on her intervention that day, and like the documentation of her previous intervention, these photographs went out globally in "real time," illustrating the need for recognition of the plight of many contemporary immigrants (Lovelace 2014b, 21). This event was also a harsh reminder of the particular fate suffered by both migrants and other indigent dwellers in Johannesburg.

When she returned later to continue her work, many of the evicted inhabitants had moved their belongings near to her installation as they were able to find shelter under the highway and live on the street in relative safety due to the security systems in the area. Her nonplace had become a place of refuge through this inhabitation. Lovelace (2014a, 48) explains that some families inhabited the area for several weeks while they looked for alternative accommodation. Her work was concluded while she was surrounded by families, some with children returning from school daily and doing their homework under the highway.[14] It is ironic that these people, many of them immigrants, illegal aliens, or migrants from rural areas, found themselves homeless and temporarily marginalized in the direct vicinity of an art installation dedicated to affirming the rights of migrants on International Migrant's Day. Their treatment at the hands of the Red Ants and their resulting liminal status is doubly ironic in the light of Ban Ki-moon's address to the UN General Assembly in October 2013. He spoke about the importance of making migration work because "migration is an expression of the human aspiration for dignity, safety and a better future. It is part of the social fabric, part of our very make up as a human family" (Ban 2013).

In response to such sentiments Lovelace (2014b, 18, 20) installed five white, slip-cast ceramic clouds above her plates. One carries the inscription "We are all migrants" and another, "We are immigrants" in black letters. Clouds are representative of the visible movement of nature through time and space, yet they are also liminal in their lack of substance and permanent form. In this installation, they metaphorically refer to the nature of migrants who move from place to place and have to transform or adapt to their new environments (Lovelace 2014b, 20). On top of each cloud and arbitrarily situated above some plates, she placed a range of "cute kitsch" black cherubs/angels. Some blow kisses, some are praying, and some cover their eyes, mouths, or ears in the typical manner of "hear no evil, speak no evil, see no evil" figurines. The angels, like the clouds, are ambiguous and liminal creatures who move between heaven and earth and can "migrate" anywhere and everywhere. Lovelace has placed tiny guns finished with a silver luster alongside some of the angels, possibly referring to the guns held by children in the silhouette imagery and alluding to the dangers of migration—particularly in South Africa.

The plates that remained from the initial intervention were also supplemented by more plates and saucers, with fairy-story silhouettes superimposed over floral decoration or painted hearts. While she was finishing the installation, Lovelace (2014b, 21) recounts that she was approached by a young man called Bheki who conducted walking tours of the area for visitors. His tours included the local "street art," and he explained that his clients always asked to stop at this particular intervention. They were drawn to the words written on the plates and often asked him about the artist and the meaning of the images. He had also been approached by journalists writing about the area who would like to know about the artist and the work. He asked if Lovelace would e-mail an explanation of the work so he could be better informed for his clients. Lovelace (2014b, 21) explains that she has subsequently seen her intervention and discussions about it on multiple blog sites, and she notes that "Bheki seems to have become the neighborhood's accidental steward of local street art."

What is interesting about the initiatives discussed thus far is that despite the unsanctioned nature of the work, they have in a sense become sanctioned by local inhabitants and thus part of the local culture. Lovelace has, indeed, repurposed these nonplaces and created a "third space" of transformation that seemingly adds value to one's experience of the city. Other installations did not fare so well, however. For example, Lovelace's seventh intervention created in August 2013 and also named *If You Go Down to the Woods Today* had the shortest life-span of her unsanctioned works perhaps because the choice of site was "edgier" and the area was less controlled than that of her earlier installations.

INTERVENTION 7

In August 2013, Lovelace chose to "rebuild" the crumbling brickwork of a bridge over a polluted storm-water drain on Anderson Street (near the Berea Street crossing) in the manner of Charles Simonds's interventions.

She (Lovelace 2014a, 60) explains that she was initially drawn to this site because it reminded her of a bridge that she used to play near as a child. The surrounding area in this location, however, is the antithesis of rural England. The bridge is situated near the Mai Mai Market, which is huddled beneath yet another portion of Johannesburg highway. According to the official website of Johannesburg (Majola n.d.), it is the oldest market in Johannesburg, with tiny overcrowded shops selling medicinal ingredients (muti) to traditional healers and sangomas. The shops are often dark, crammed with animal parts and herbs hanging from ceilings, and shelves lined with jars containing unidentifiable substances. The area is known for the preservation of indigenous knowledge practices and is also home to a close-knit community of about 600 people, mostly family and relatives of the traders. According to Desmond Sweke, who conducted a survey of the inhabitants for the municipality in the 1990s, to profile and register hawkers, "The trajectory of the Mai Mai is closely linked to the influx of first-generation migrants to Joburg who remained insulated from local communities since the 1950s" (Majola n.d.). The Mai Mai Market is described online as not properly maintained, with blocked storm-water drains and crumbling infrastructure making it "in but not of the city" (Majola n.d.). The market is thus identified as a liminal space, idiosyncratic, populated by migrants, and overlooked by the organizational structures of local government.

Adjacent to the market and the chosen bridge, there is also a small park, situated between the Joe Slovo Street on and off ramps from the highway. The park has been repurposed by the inhabitants and is now used regularly for open-air church services. There is also a busy taxi rank situated next to the market and the park, bringing people into and out of the space constantly and surrounded by the informal hawkers who are drawn to the trading opportunities of such sites. Across the road, a large recycling center is situated alongside a shebeen,[15] so the area is vibrant and constantly full of a diverse mix of urban dwellers on the move. For Lovelace (2014b, 50), it was the perfect situation for an intervention as the street holds many relatively unregulated thresholds, where diverse experiences flow over onto the street and possibilities for surprise encounters and cultural exchange are magnified. The chosen site thus fulfills Turner's (1969, 129) identification of an in-between space that fosters dialogue. It allows for a space where nationalities and identities can be performed and negotiated in a contingent and open

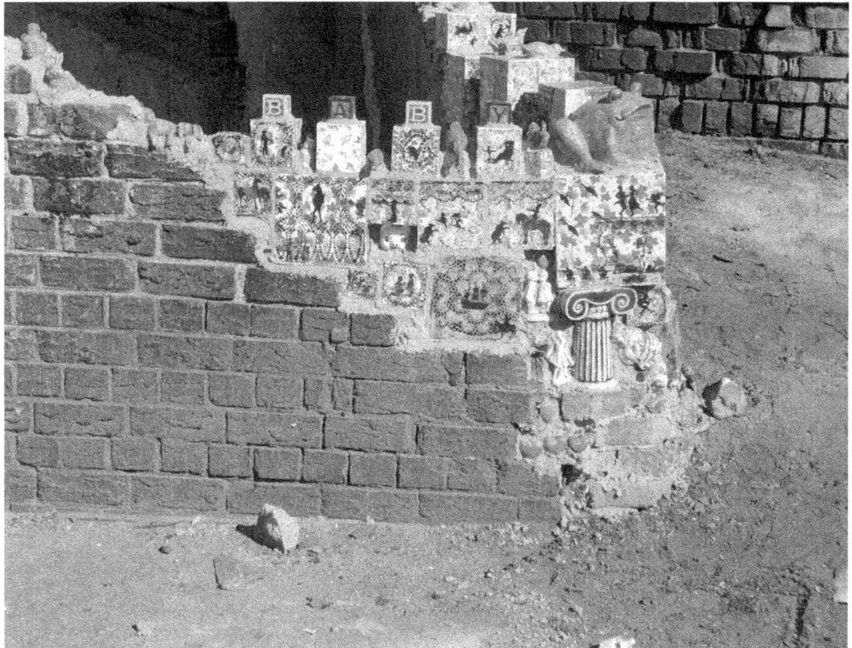

Fig. 11.4 Julie Lovelace, Intervention 7: *If You Go Down to the Woods Today* (August 2013). *Photograph by the artist.*

way, where, as Bhabha (1997, 219, emphasis mine) explains, "difference is neither One nor the Other but *something else in-between*."

Lovelace's intervention in this instance also resides in the in-between space of being an art work and/or a structural repair to a broken bridge. Her repairs to the crumbling brickwork were achieved with ceramic blocks of various sizes covered in colorful patterns and sealed with glazes to withstand the elements (fig. 11.4). Lovelace (2014b, 50) notes that blocks are modular and easy to use as substitutes for bricks; they also form the substructure for varied decorative finishes applied with floral decals (reminiscent of her grandmother's tea service), lace (inspired by the lace curtains from her childhood home), silhouette images of figures and animals, and some of the floral patterning that was seen on the plates in her first intervention. There is a strong sense of childhood memories and childish kitsch in both the coloring and overlaid imagery on the blocks. The smallest blocks at the top of the wall are babies' alphabet blocks, and interspersed throughout the wall, one can see found and slip-cast toys and ornaments with a large turquoise toad surmounting the corner.

The complexity of this intervention meant that Lovelace was working in the area for two full days to erect the bridge "repairs." This afforded her an opportunity to engage with the inhabitants in the area who were passing by on the street. One Sunday, Lovelace was there for an entire day and most of the local community was not at work. She recalls, "Some kindly invited me to church, some staggered into me on the way back from the shebeen, and a couple of street children, who earn a living by recycling, stopped to try and sell me objects which they thought I could incorporate into my installation" (Lovelace 2014b, 50). All the responses were positive. Mothers expressed relief that their young children would no longer be in danger of falling into the polluted drain because of the broken brickwork. Many people described the colorful insertions as beautiful, and several expressed their surprise that Lovelace was repairing the bridge at her own expense and without any recompense from the municipality (Lovelace 2014b, 50). The responses are articulated from each viewer's cultural background or their personal assignation of importance to the intervention. This "act of spectatorship and interpretation" (Ramos 2000, 5) is the liminal moment whereby the artwork transcends the sum of its parts and becomes meaningful to the local inhabitants in ways that the artist may not have foreseen.

Sadly, when she returned the day after completing the intervention, some of the more vulnerable pieces had been stolen. By the following week, the installation had been badly vandalized with many of the ceramic blocks smashed or missing (Lovelace 2014b, 50). Part of the substructure was still intact, however, and while Lovelace was documenting the damage with her camera, one of the young women who worked at the shebeen came to talk to her. She expressed her sadness at the destruction as so many people in the area had been delighted that the bridge was now safe and beautiful.[16] She also said the vandalism had been carried out by the street children who sleep in the area (Lovelace 2014b, 50). These children "are most especially harmed on the streets by the harsh physical conditions, by violence and harassment, [and] by labour exploitation" (Richter 1991, 8). They often sniff glue or use other substances to alleviate hunger and to cope with the realities of their existence; their behavior is therefore erratic and often aggressive and is a direct result of their marginal existence. The life-span of Lovelace's liminal artwork was in this instance delineated by the social effects of liminality, reflected in the marginality of the spaces the street children occupy and the lives they lead. Malcolm Miles (1997, 76) suggests, "Sub cultural space as such does not guarantee freedom from constraint, but for some does provide a site of reflection and negotiation." Lovelace's intervention highlights the need for reflection specifically on the plight of homeless children in the city, who are further marginalized by the "new" South Africa's capitalist economy. Their aggressive response to the blocks may be "a response to the alienation from society they experience every day" (McKay 2000, 1). Lovelace (2014a, 62) notes that by positioning a fragile and decorative ceramic intervention in the midst of such poverty, she is also highlighting the contradictions of the "new" South Africa where differences between privileged and underprivileged communities appear to be widening daily.

The interest and enthusiasm of this poverty-stricken community reflects an issue raised by Turner (1969, 95) related to the liminality of what he terms threshold people who "elude or slip through the network of classifications that normally locate states and positions in cultural space." Marginalized social groups in a liminal state of existence, like immigrants or the extreme poor, allow for an unstructured arrangement of personal and social interrelations developing from a shared existence. Turner (1969, 96) has termed their resulting social arrangement "communitas," which he explains is the antithesis of the Western societal "norm" identified as "a structured, differentiated, and often hierarchical system of politico-legal-economic positions with many types of evaluation, separating men in terms of 'more' or 'less.'" Communitas emerges from a liminal position and can arise spontaneously in response to an event that requires cooperation for survival. The plight of the migrants who were evicted by Red Ants and took up residence near Lovelace's first artwork might illustrate spontaneous communitas. The boundaries between hierarchies and social positions is dissolved by their communal problem and a sense of equality and solidarity is engendered by their need to work together to survive. Lovelace (2014b, 50) states that she also experienced communitas while working near the Mai Mai market in 2013 because the local community had taken time to converse with her and engage with her work, expressing pleasure in the intervention and empathy with her when it was vandalized. Their liminal existence in the city and her engagement with them led to a sense of commonality that exposed her to the role of communitas as it is manifest in marginalized communities.

CONCLUSION

There is a difference in the way unsanctioned public art and commissioned public art negotiate and transform public spaces. Unsanctioned cultural expression, not validated by a gallery or museum space or by a formal commission, can be dismissed as nonart and in some cases has the possibility to cause conflict: graffiti, for example, can be identified as vandalism and is likely to engender a hostile response from city officials or property owners. Lovelace's unsanctioned interventions, however, allow her to express her liminal, hybrid identity in an open and inclusive way that not only repurposes certain areas or structures but also functions as a third space providing the potential for transformation and an alternative engagement with the city. In some instances, her work has become "sanctioned" in a way, through its acceptance by the local communities, but this is a sanction that emerges as a positive outcome from the third space she creates rather than from governmental impositions.

An unexpected outcome of her interventions arose from her experience of communitas among the liminal inhabitants of Johannesburg. Relationships were fostered with both the people and the places in which she worked, and this has contributed to a tangible sense of her connection with the city (Lovelace 2014a, 66). As noted in the discussion above, Lovelace's art interventions also appear to have had an effect on many of the people who encountered them. Whether her works are permanent or transient, they provide a means to playfully celebrate alternatives and to reflect on the integration of people who might come from a different background, race, gender, or class. The liminal nature of the interventions also achieves what sanctioned public art, perhaps, cannot in terms of imaginatively encouraging participation and a fostering a sense of belonging. Remarks Achille Mbembe made in an interview with Vivian Paulissen (2009), while about the recognition of contemporary art and creativity in general rather than specifically about temporary interventions such as those of Lovelace, are nevertheless pertinent in this regard: "[South Africa] needs to distance itself from an understanding of culture as pastness, a simple matter of customs and traditions, monuments and museums. We have to realize that culture is not yet another form of 'service delivery.' It is the way human beings imagine and engage their own futures."

ACKNOWLEDGMENTS

I wish to sincerely thank Julie Lovelace who set aside time to discuss with me factors surrounding her interventions in the city and the responses from the people she encountered while engaged in her project. She has also kindly allowed me to use some of the photographs that she took of individual works and those in situ to illustrate my discussion. Research for this chapter was undertaken with the assistance of the South African National Research Foundation (NRF) who have granted me research funding. Please note, however, that any opinions, findings, or conclusions expressed in this chapter are mine, and the NRF does not bear any liability with regard to them.

KAREN VON VEH is Associate Professor of Art History and Head of the Visual Art Department at the University of Johannesburg. She is coauthor of *Taxi-013: Diane Victor* and author of *Diane Victor: Burning the Candle at Both Ends.*

NOTES

1. I was the supervisor for Lovelace's master's degree in visual art at the University of Johannesburg, and this chapter draws on theoretical underpinnings for her work that were discussed and developed in close consultation with me and that formed the basis for her master's thesis. While I have drawn on the ideas developed with Lovelace during our collaboration, it was not appropriate for us to coauthor the article. First, I have introduced some discussion that was not in her thesis and have developed a context to underpin my argument. Second, Lovelace prefers the role of maker rather than writer (unless the writing is about the practical aspects of her ceramic works), and she therefore particularly requested that I write about this project for publication.

2. Lovelace's work has been included in the following group exhibitions:

   2014: *Twenty: An exhibition of Contemporary Art from South Africa at the Appalachian State University,* USA. Curated by Gordon Froud.

   2014: *"Cathedra": a group exhibition of chairs.* Curated by Gordon Froud.

   2014: *Turbine Art Fair.* University of Johannesburg master's students' exhibition. Johannesburg, South Africa.

   2014: *Bayliss Gallery.* Johannesburg, South Africa.

   2014: *"Deconstructing Dogma: an exhibition of transgressive Christian iconography in South African art.* Curated by Professor Karen von Veh. University of Johannesburg.

   2013: *Re-envisioning the Anglo Boer War (South African) War,* Johannes Stegmann Art Gallery, Sasol Library, University of the Free State. Curated by Janine Allen and Angela de Jesus.

2013: *Tom Waite's for No Man*. Traveling exhibition at the ABSA BankGallery, the Klein KarooNasionaleKunstefees (art festival) in Oudtshoorn. University of Johannesburg Art Gallery, Johannesburg. Le Grand Provence Gallery, Cape Town. Curated by Gordon Froud.
2013: *101 Place Setting*. Castle of Good Hope, Cape Town, South Africa.
2012: *Thami Mayele Fine Art Awards Exhibition*.
2012: *101 Place Setting*. Castle of Good Hope, Cape Town, South Africa.
2010: *Roof Top Exhibition*, University of Johannesburg Art Gallery.
2010: *Ceramics South Africa*, National Exhibition.
2010: Le Grand Provence Gallery, Cape Town, South Africa.
2009: Solo exhibition. GordArt Gallery.
2008: *Faculty of Art Design and Architecture Exhibition*, University of Johannesburg.
2008: *Ceramics South Africa*, Regional Exhibition.
2007: *Faculty of Art Design and Architecture Exhibition*, University of Johannesburg.

3. Telephone discussion between Julie Lovelace and Karen von Veh on November 4 and 20, 2014.

4. According to the Department of Human Settlement's Urban Strategy Review (2012/13 and 2013/14), Johannesburg has at present more than 4.4 million inhabitants, and the city is growing faster than the entire Gauteng region. The *Local Government Handbook* indicates the rate of growth of the Johannesburg Metropole at 3.18 percent and the unemployment rate, according to 2013/14 statistics, stands at 25 percent, although this is thought to have grown to 30 percent in 2015.

5. The city of Johannesburg's official website states the following statistics regarding the status of overcrowding and lack of services, as of February 4, 2015: "Some 20% of Johannesburg residents live in abject poverty, in informal settlements that lack proper roads or electricity or any kind of direct municipal services. Another 40% live in inadequate housing, with insufficient municipal services. The poor are largely black (72%), earning less than R25,000 per annum. Johannesburg is also a magnet for illegal immigrants from other African countries, in sufficient numbers to put a major strain on city and provincial services, which are allocated on the basis of legal populations. 16% of households lack municipal sanitation, 15% do not receive municipal electricity, 3.6% do not have water supplies. Unemployment is at 30%, up from 27% three years ago. Some 116,827 families live in informal settlements. Some 108,000 families live in illegal backyard dwellings. There are some 4,500 homeless 'street people.' The present conditions are also, to an extent, a continuation of the poor housing and overcrowding suffered by 'township dwellers' under the old apartheid system of racially segregated areas designated for housing."

6. In the 1970s, Charles Simonds created a mythology of the "little people," and over the next two decades, he built tiny dwellings for them in corners of buildings in gaps where there was broken brickwork, or on windowsills in downtown Manhattan (Princenthal 2012). He chose any position where he could construct buildings out of minute mud bricks. They would appear unheralded and their existence was dependent on the weather or the response of the public who encountered them. He deliberately did not try to protect them and stated, "Their effect is enhanced by their destruction and disappearance" (Simonds and Molderings 1978, 19).

7. The first verse of "The Teddy Bear's Picnic" song referred to by Lovelace is as follows:

> If you go down to the woods today you're sure of a big surprise,
> If you go down to the woods today you'd better go in disguise,
> For every bear that ever there was is gathered there for certain because
> Today's the day the Teddy Bears have their picnic.

8. The Gauteng Tourism website states, "regeneration in Johannesburg has seen the transformation of areas that, for years, were declared no-go zones as a result of urban decay and crime. The Maboneng precinct east of the city is one of them."

9. Little Terry got a gun, he got from the store,
He bought it with the money he got from his chores,
He robbed candy shop told her lay down on the floor,
Put the cookies in his bag took the pennies out the drawer.
Little Kalil got a gun he got from the rebels,
To kill the infidels and American devils,
A bomb on his waist, a mask on his face,
Prays five times a day, and listens to Heavy Metal.
Little Alex got a gun he took from his dad,
That he snuck into school in his black book bag,
His black nail polish, black boots and black hair,
He's gonna blow away the bully that just pushed his ass
—Lupe Fiasco, "Little Weapon," 2007

10. The shooting of Reeva Steenkamp by Oscar Pistorius brought the matter of gun violence in South Africa into worldwide prominence. In an article on this event, Murray Williams (2013) reports that 15,910 were murdered in South Africa (according to the police reports of 2012/13), and of that number, 42 percent were killed by a firearm. In the latest official statistics, that number has gone up to 17,068 murders for 2013/14 (Institute for Security Studies and Africa Check 2014).

11. Telephone discussion between Lovelace and Von Veh, November 4 and 20, 2014.

12. The general upgrading and repainting was commissioned by the property development company responsible for the Maboneng precinct, which had a vested interest in improving and regenerating the area (Lovelace 2014b, 20).

13. When she went to prime the wall before adding to the installation, however, she was approached by security and taken to speak to the precinct manager who was wary of further interventions. Lovelace pointed out that he did not own the public area, and he responded that her intervention had only been preserved thus far due to the protection of his security systems and the maintenance they afforded for the area (Lovelace 2014b, 20). After ensuring that the work she undertook would not damage or mess the newly cleaned and painted wall and agreeing to regrout and mend the damaged pieces, Lovelace was given permission to proceed.

14. The displaced families were given permission by the management of Maboneng to use the precinct's washing and toilet facilities while they were waiting for new accommodation (Lovelace 2014b, 21).

15. A shebeen is the local name for an illegal establishment selling alcohol.

16. Lovelace told the young woman that she would repair the bridge and is now in the process of creating stronger pieces that could withstand further vandalism with which to rebuild her installation. She has not yet returned to effect the repairs to the bridge

but has started re-creating the blocks in her studio to replace the broken pieces. She will return to the site as soon as she has made enough to complete the repair (personal telephone correspondence between Lovelace and Von Veh, November 4 and 20, 2014).

References

Ban, Ki-moon. 2013. "Message for International Migrant's Day." *United Nations*. Accessed November 13, 2014. http://www.un.org/en/events/migrantsday/.

Bhabha, Homi. 1997. *The Location of Culture*. New York: Routledge.

Bruguera, Tania. 2011. *Immigrant Movement International*. Accessed November 7, 2011. http://www.taniabruguera.com/cms/486–0-Immigrant+Movement+International.htm.

City of Johannesburg. N.d. "Fighting Poverty: Apartheid and the Root of Johannesburg's Problems." Accessed February 3, 2015. http://www.joburg.org.za/index.php?option=com_content&task=view&id=709&Itemid=9

Creative Time. 2011. Accessed December 13, 2011. http://creativetime.org/about/.

Department of Human Settlements. N.d. "2012/13 and 2013/14 USDG Review." Accessed November 4, 2014. http:/pmg-assets.s3-website-eu-west-1.amazonaws.com/doc/2013/130619joburg.pdf.

De Wet, Philip. 2015. "Xenophobia: Danger Brewing for 2016 Elections." *Mail & Guardian*, January 26. Accessed February 9, 2015. http://mg.co.za/article/2015–01–25-xenophobia-the-danger-of-2016-elections.

Goffman, Erving, ed. 1982. *Where the Action Is*. New York: Pantheon.

Hirsch, Afua. 2013. "Fear and Self-Arming in South Africa." *The Guardian*, February 14. Accessed November 13, 2014. http://www.theguardian.com/world/2013/feb/14/fear-arming-south-africa-guns.

Institute for Security Studies and Africa Check. 2014. "Factsheet: South Africa's Official Crime Statistics for 2013/14." *Africa Check: Sorting Fact from Fiction*. AFP Foundation. Accessed November 12, 2014. http://africacheck.org/factsheets/factsheet-south-africas-official-crime-statistics-for-201314/.

i was shot in joburg :). Accessed October 24, 2013. www.iwasshot.com.

Landau, Loren. 2013. "Xenophobic demons linger in S.A." *Mail & Guardian*, May 17, 2013. Accessed February 12, 2015. http://mg.co.za/article/2013-05-17-00-xenophobic-demons-linger-in-sa.

Lovelace, Julie. 2014a. "Expressions of Liminality in Selected Examples of Unsanctioned Public Art in Johannesburg." Unpublished M-Tech diss., University of Johannesburg.

Lovelace. Julie. 2014b. *Unsanctioned*. Unpublished catalog/documentation of *The Unsanctioned Interventions of Julie Lovelace*.

"Maboneng Precinct." *Gauteng Tourism*. Accessed January 13, 2012. http://www.gauteng.net/attractions/entry/maboneng_precinct/.

Mail & Guardian. 2008. "Toll from Xenophobic attacks Rises." *Mail & Guardian*, May 31. Accessed February 9, 2015. http://mg.co.za/article/2008–05–31-toll-from-xenophobic-attacks-rises.

Mail & Guardian. 2010. "Migrants Attacked in Johannesburg, Five Hurt." *Mail & Guardian*, July 20. Accessed February 9, 2015. http://mg.co.za/article/2010-07-20-migrants-attacked-in-johannesburg-five-hurt.

Mail & Guardian Staff Reporters and Sapa Sapa AFP. 2008. "Gauteng Reels under XenophobicAttacks." *Mail & Guardian*, May19. Accessed February9, 2015. http://mg.co.za/article/2008-05-19-gauteng-reels-under-xenophobic-attacks.

Majola, Bongani. "Mai Mai Market." *Official Website of the City of Johannesburg.* Accessed November 17, 2014. http://www.joburg.org.za/index.php?option=com_content&view=article&id=308:mai-mai-market&catid=53&Itemid=188.

McKay, Anne. 2000. "Finding Depression behind Aggression." *CYC-Online* 18. Accessed September 22, 2013. http://www.cyc-net.org/cyc-online/cycol-0700-mckay.html.

Miles, Malcolm. 1997. *Art, Space and the City: Public Art and Urban Futures.* London: Routledge.

Misago, Jean-Pierre, and Matthew Wilhelm-Solomon. 2011. "Foreign Traders Are Fair Game." *Mail & Guardian*, May 20. Accessed February 10, 2015. http://mg.co.za/article/2011-05-20-foreign-traders-are-fair-game.

O'Beirne, Emer. 2006. "Mapping the Non-Lieu in Marc Augé's Writings. *Forum for Modern Language Studies.* 42 (1).

Parker, Faranaaz. 2012. "Xenophobia Rears Its Head as 'War' Declared in Mayfair." *Mail & Guardian*, September 3. Accessed February 10, 2015. http://mg.co.za/article/2012-09-03-xenophobia-rears-its-head-in-mayfair.

Paulissen, Vivian. 2009. "African Contemporary Art: Negotiation the Terms of Recognition." (Interview with Achille Mbembe), September 9. Johannesburg Workshop in Theory and Criticism blog. Accessed June 13, 2015. http://jhbwtc.blogspot.com/2009/09/african-contemporary-art-negotiating.html.

Princenthal, Nancy. 2012. "Review: Charles Simonds, New York, at Knoedler." *Art in America*, February 15. Accessed November 10, 2014. http://www.artinamerica magazine.com/reviews/charles-simonds/.

Ramos, Rufel F. 2000. "Homi Bhabha: The Process of Creating Culture from the Interstitial, Hybrid Perspective." *Essays*, November 20. Accessed July 14, 2013. http://rowenasworld.org/essays/newphil/bhabha.htm.

Richter, Linda. 1991. "Street Children in South Africa." *The Street Care Worker* 9, no. 8: 7–9.

SAHRC. 2010. "Report on Xenophobic Violence." South African Human Rights Commission. Accessed February 12, 2015. http://www.sahrc.org.za/home/21/files/Reports/Non%20Nationals%20Attacks%20Report_1-50_2008.pdf.

Simonds, Charles, and H. Molderings. 1978. *Schwebende Stadte und andere Architekturen/Floating Cities and Other Architectures.* Münster: Westfalischer Kunstverein, Munster.

Sosibo, Kwanele. 2015. "Thousands of foreigners seek refuge in Mayfair." *Mail & Guardian*, January 28, 2015. Accessed February 12, 2015. http://mg.co.za/article/2015-01-27-thousands-of-foreigners-seek-refuge-in-mayfair.

Yes Media. 2014. "City of Johannesburg Metropolitan Municipality (JHB)." *The Local Government Handbook: A Complete Guide to Municipalities in South Africa.*

Accessed November 4, 2014. http://www.localgovernment.co.za/metropolitans/view/2/city-of-johannesburg-metropolitan-municipality.

Turner, Victor. 1967. *The Forest of Symbols: Aspects of Ndembu Ritual.* Ithaca, NY: Cornell University Press.

———. 1969. *The Ritual Process: Structure and Anti-Structure.* Piscataway, NJ: Transaction.

———. 1974. *Drama, Fields, and Metaphors: Symbolic Action in Human Societies.* Ithaca, NY: Cornell University Press.

———. 1982. *From Ritual to Theater: The Human Seriousness of Play.* New York: P. A. J. Publications.

Van Gennep, Arnold. 1960. *The Rites of Passage.* Translated by Monika Vizedom and Gabriella Coffee. London: Routledge.

Williams, Murray. 2013. "SA's Gun Death Toll Shooting Up." *IOL News,* March 15. Accessed November 12, 2014. http://www.iol.co.za/news/crime-courts/sa-s-gun-death-toll-shooting-up-1.1486924#.VX05i-edrwM.

CHAPTER 12

Rage against the State: Political Funerals and Queer Visual Activism in Post-Apartheid South Africa

KYLIE THOMAS

Producing and populating a humanized public space is, in part, our challenge.
Colin Richards, "Retouching Apartheid: Intimacy, Interiority and Photography."

THE STRUGGLE FOR QUEER rights in South Africa has emerged as a key issue that makes visible many of the paradoxes and challenges that define the post-apartheid condition. Queer activists are also producing what are some of the most interesting, vibrant, and critical forms of cultural engagement in South Africa today, across a range of media. At the same time, people who defy heteronormative patriarchy are frequently subject to hate speech and violent assault, and queer cultural producers, particularly those who are black and economically disadvantaged, operate under the threat of death (see Bennett et al. 2010). In this chapter, I focus on queer visual activism in contemporary South Africa and engage with the political funerals of queer black South Africans who have been raped and murdered and with visual works made in response to these deaths. I consider these, on one level, as a manifestation of "public art" but also, on another, as visual expressions that highlight the difficulties associated with publicness for queer people in South Africa. I focus in particular on the work of photographers and visual activists Collen Mfazwe, Zanele Muholi, and Jabu Chen Pereira to explore queer strategies for mourning and commemoration and for the expression of rage and grief.[1]

Visual activism can be understood as the use of visual forms to make visible what those in power prefer to keep invisible. It describes work produced by artists to raise awareness about particular social issues and forms of injustice and to describe the work of activists who employ visual forms in order to protest and subvert the dominant order. The term *visual activism* in South Africa emerges from the context of the struggle against apartheid to refer to documentary photographers and visual artists who produced art in response to and against the regime. While many documentary photographers, such as some of the members of the anti-apartheid photography collective, Afrapix, understood themselves to be activists first and photographers second, the term *visual activism* came into circulation after the end of apartheid and has been applied retrospectively.[2] I first noted the term being used by South African documentary photographer Gideon Mendel to describe his work that focused on the struggle for access to treatment for people living with HIV/AIDS in 2001.[3] The relation between art making and the struggle to bring about social justice in South Africa is not uncomplicated, and there have been powerful arguments about the need to delink art from the imperative to represent political struggle, perhaps most famously articulated by Albie Sachs (1991). There have also been less nuanced arguments made about documentary photography under apartheid, and as Jon Soske (2011) has observed, for several years it was derided as "the paradigmatic form of 'struggle art'" that allegedly "codified a one-dimensional and thus dehumanising image of black life." The limits of such critique, as Soske points out, and as recent works on the history of photography in South Africa make clear, lie in overlooking both the range of images produced and the multiple ways in which they can be read. The ability of visual activism to bring about social change is not without limits, and one obvious point of critique is how such works can and have been commodified and their radical potential somewhat neutralized in the process.

In this chapter, I consider how the visual repertoires used by queer visual activists in South Africa both draw on and transform established modes of resistance. I engage with three instances of public art made in response to the death of twenty-eight-year-old Thembelihle Sokhela, who was murdered on September 14, 2014, in Daveyton, a township in Gauteng province, not far from the city of Johannesburg. Sokhela was a lesbian person who was killed by Thabo Molefe, who had only recently been released from prison for another rape and murder.[4] Sokhela's body was found two days after her death behind Molefe's bed. She was found wrapped in a blanket with blood pouring through her nostrils, ears, and mouth (Dumse 2014). It should be noted here that Sokhela is one of many black South African lesbians who have been murdered, and the visual activists who have responded to her murder have also produced images and texts and created performances and protests in response to the deaths of others.[5] Collen Mfazwe describes the politicized and contested terrain of queer visual activism that centers on the ongoing violation of the rights of queer South Africans and explains that "each and every LGBTI [lesbian, gay, bisexual, transgender, and intersex] funeral is documented, she was part of us, so we have the right."[6] In this formulation, claiming the right to grieve is also a claim to belonging and instantiates community in the face of the violent unmaking of hatred, rape, and murder.

Queer activism in the present draws on the visual repertoires of AIDS activism both inside and outside of South Africa and extends back to the struggle against apartheid and political funerals in particular.[7] Queer political funerals are an assertion that queer lives matter in the face of a society that turns away from the ongoing persecution of gender nonconforming people, a society that largely affirms what Keguro Macharia (2014) has termed the "disposability" of black queer bodies. The works discussed below signal a refusal to allow Sokhela's death to go unmourned and unmarked. Through the work of public mourning, queer visual activists lay claim to the right to occupy the spaces from which queer people are violently excluded and contest the normative limits that define both private and public space.

PERFORMING QUEER LOSS

In her account of the funeral of Thembelihle Sokhela, Lerato Dumse relates how, like that of many other black South African lesbians who have been raped and killed because of their sexual orientation, Sokhela's funeral became a site not only for grief but for activism: "In the dying minutes of the service, some LGBTI members who had gathered outside the tent (having arrived when all seats were taken), started singing political songs, drowning out the pastor's voice, while he tried to close the first part of the funeral service with prayer" (Dumse 2014).

In spite of their solemn purpose, funerals are not devoid of conflict, as families, church leaders, and queer activists sometimes compete for space to mobilize and mourn. Nor are political funerals private spaces, and the desires of the family are often overwhelmed by the agendas of political parties and activist groups. For instance, the African National Congress (ANC) Women's League was out in full force at the funeral of Duduzile Zozo, a lesbian woman who was murdered in 2014. The gruesome way in which Zozo was killed and the way in which her body was mutilated (she was found with a toilet brush inserted in her vagina) partly accounts for the wide circulation of reports of her death and for why political parties responded to the murder. Zozo's death also coincided with a period of intense electioneering and the presence of members of the conservative ANC Women's League at the funeral was regarded with contempt by activists who considered the "solidarity" of the Women's League to be purely opportunistic.

Writing of political funerals during apartheid, Mamphela Ramphele (1996, 106) argues that "the enlargement of the circle of mourners to incorporate the body politic to which the deceased also belonged brings added support and tension." She goes on to write that "political formations naturally want to make as much political capital as possible out of the death of a comrade. The funeral becomes a form of political theater that has to be managed to achieve the desired outcomes for the political formation involved. Inevitably, problems arise in balancing the wishes of the family and the desires of the politicians" (Ramphele 1996, 106).

Queer political funerals in the present are complicated even further by the position queer people occupy in relation to the nation-state, which technically, constitutionally, offers an equal place for all in the body politic, but actually, materially, in word and deed, violently excludes those who do not conform to heteronormative forms of gendered being. Queer forms of kinship also present a fundamental challenge to heteronormative conceptions of the family and queer forms of embodiment destabilize singular notions of the body politic.

Funerals are also sites for the expression of queer subjectivity and solidarity and in this sense queer activism at funerals can be understood as a form of public performance. Such "performances" are spontaneous, in that there is no rehearsal for what unfolds, but in a certain sense, they can also be understood as choreographed, as a purposeful, coherent claim to queer collectivity. Such performances entail dressing in a certain way that marks a person as queer or in wearing clothing emblazoned with slogans that refer to hate crimes and sexual and gender identity and discrimination.

A photograph included on inkanyiso.org website portrays mourners at Sokhela's funeral and was taken by Zanele Muholi, who attended the funeral both as a member of the grieving queer community and as a visual activist and photographer.[8] Muholi's photograph shows a large group of people, all of whom are singing or chanting, and moving, clapping their hands, raising their arms skyward and pointing, their faces full of emotion. It is an image that conveys the loud energy of the scene in a multitude of colors, the clothing of those depicted providing a visual echo of the large banner emblazoned with letters painted in rainbow stripes, asserting queer identity. Almost all the people in the image appear to be women, some of them masculine-presenting lesbians. There are two men in the image, and their presence is striking as they are both wearing brightly colored T-shirts, one red, the other pink, both of which bear the words *HIV Positive*. These shirts identify them as members of the Treatment Action Campaign (TAC), and for those familiar with the history of AIDS activism in South Africa, their presence immediately links Sokhela's funeral to the political funerals of those who have died as a result of AIDS-related diseases. The composition of the image as well as its subject evokes Gideon Mendel's iconic image of TAC activists holding hands and toyi-toying at the International AIDS Conference in Durban in 2000.[9]

Three people occupy the foreground of Muholi's photograph of Sokhela's funeral and provide the focus for the image. These three mourners are shown at a remove from the group assembled behind them and are dancing in an open space and are completely immersed in their movements. Two of the mourners are crouched down low to the ground and appear to be about to lift themselves back onto their feet. On the far left of the image is a person whose whole body and spirit is given over to the movements that flow from the fusion of grief and rage that is carried in the bodies of those who participate in protests against injustice in South Africa.

Queer activists also claim and/or disrupt funeral spaces by dancing and singing political songs, as in the case of Sokhela's funeral at which their voices succeeded in "drowning out the pastor's voice." In their refusal to participate in the rites of mourning in the manner determined by the church or by long-standing community practices, queer people assert their right to exist in public space on their own terms. Collen Mfazwe describes the funerals of those who have been raped and murdered as a "battleground" and argues that "all LGBTI funerals are the same, there is chaos, we as lesbians, we take over. There are divided groups but as lesbians we are together."[10] Mfazwe also describes how family members are often marginalized by activists at funerals and "lesbians stop the pastor" and correct their version of accounts of people's lives. Mfazwe describes the emotions of activists at funerals as "super-angry, and at the same time, it's sad."[11] Queer mourners claim their right to grieve those they identify as part of their own community, whether they knew the person who was killed or not, and in this way mourning comes to play a constitutive part in forming and maintaining queer solidarity.

As a result of the tireless activist work of Zanele Muholi, the funerals of people who have been killed as a result of hate crimes are also now extensively documented in words and images. Muholi has been responding to violence against black lesbians by photographing hate crimes and queer funerals since the first cases were recorded in South Africa in 2004.[12] Another photograph taken at Sokhela's funeral includes Muholi herself at the graveside, her camera in hand, capturing the burial and the mourners gathered at the open grave.[13] Muholi now increasingly also works together with other members of the Inkanyiso collective who also take photographs at funerals, film the events, and write about hate crimes in South Africa. Muholi's video works of funerals have appeared alongside her photographs at her exhibitions, but they also appear online and in this way circulate in public space.[14] This circulation is limited, however, as in order to see these works, a viewer has to seek them out, and for this reason, they only play a small part in overturning and transforming prejudice. However, the existence of these documents of queer loss affirms the resilience of queer communities. The making of these photographs and films insists on the significance of queer lives and deaths.

"NO SENSITIVE VIEWERS"

"No Sensitive Viewers" is the trigger warning that appears at the beginning of Collen Mfazwe's video piece documenting a performance that took place on September 27, 2014, when three women interrupted the Soweto Pride March to give visual expression to the grief and fury they felt in response to Sokhela's murder. Their performance piece draws on the tradition of protest theater and of the street as a space for the public expression of outrage.[15] At the same time, it is an exceptional work that is without precedent.[16] Mfazwe, who conceptualized the performance with Nontsikelelo Mbaso, Elizabeth Sebesho, and Katlego Mogola, members of a theater group based in

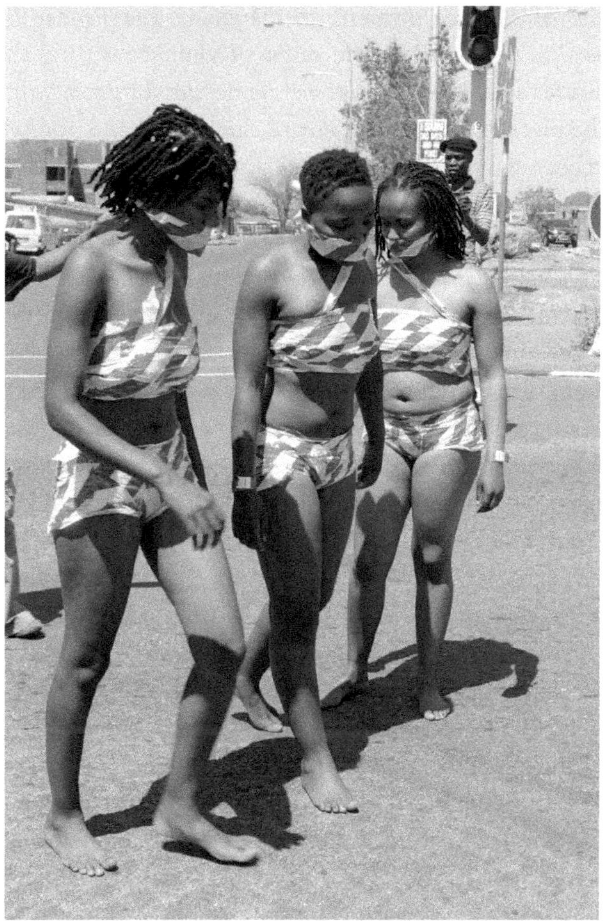

Fig. 12.1 Performance conceptualized by Collen Mfazwe and including performers Nontsikelelo Mbaso, Elizabeth Sebesho, and Katlego Mogola, at the tenth anniversary of Soweto Pride in September 2014.

Daveyton, a township just outside of the city of Johannesburg, describes the piece as "fighting violence through arts." The choreographed work is born of rage, and it powerfully conveys the emotions of the performers.

Mfazwe's video of the performance shows the startled audience gathered in a large circle around the performers who begin a physical theater performance that contains elements of dance and that disturbingly portrays the rape and murder of one of the performers (Mbaso) by another who enacts the part of the male perpetrator (Mogola). The piece is called "State of Emergency" and references the reign of violence during the states of emergency under apartheid when the state declared martial law. At the beginning of the piece, all three women are clad only in red-and-white plastic tape that has been wrapped around their bodies to form a kind of makeshift underwear. The performance begins when the performers tear the tape from their mouths, and one of the group begins a call, a long mournful dirge, that continues for several minutes. The other two performers begin to move in unison, not facing each other, slowly at first and then, colliding with each other, their pace quickens. Their movements convey desire but also danger, their movements are no longer in time with each other, and their dance becomes increasingly disturbing. Mogola, who enacts the part of the rapist, tears off the tape that covers her chest and bares her breasts. Mabaso enacts being raped, her movements indicate terror, and she cries out. Mogola then picks up a pair of soccer boots, the laces of which are tied together to form a long cord and strangles Mabaso, dragging her across the gravel street. Mabaso lies on the ground, calling out, and Mogola pours a bucket of water over her body. Mogola, the bare-breasted perpetrator, slaps her own thighs loudly and performs a taunting dance. She then climbs on the back of Sebesho, who until this point has been singing, and forces her to the ground and enacts assaulting her on her head and strangling her.

The tape wrapped around the bodies of the performers is what is used to cordon off an area, such as a construction site, and evokes the site of a crime that has been partitioned off by the police. The tape signifies the desire of the performers to be protected, off-limits, to have the sanctity of their bodies respected, and at the same time, it signifies that they have been violated. During this performance, the audience tried to protect the performers from the police: "Police were trying to stop the performance. That was the fucked-up part. Other people were fighting the police in the background."[17]

Mfazwe describes how the audience reacted to the collective's intervention and states that "people did not understand this performance thing." For the most part, people who were witness to the performance were disoriented and disturbed by the fact that the performers seemed to be in genuine pain, both emotional and physical. In addition to trying to stop the police from interfering, members of the audience also shouted at the performers and called for Mogola to stop attacking Mbaso. Toward the end of the performance, Mbaso picks up the soccer boots and puts on a soccer kit to convey that she is a "butch" lesbian and to evoke a number of cases of soccer players who have been murdered, such as that of Sihle Sikoji.[18] At the very end of the piece, the performers begin to speak in phrases that are enunciations of pain: "In my silence, I became nonrecognized and acknowledged"; "My soul is in pain"; "I have seen silences of my brothers and sisters turned into political rallies"; "I was found in a pool of water"; "And I was found in a bed of shame"; "For they have mouths to feed and empires to build"; "They never invest in my safety"; "My name is Thembelihle Sokhela, and I was found wrapped under this bed of shame"; and finally, "In my silence, be my voice, in my silence, be my voice." Before the audience dispersed, the performers gave out small printed notes that contained information about hate crimes, and a woman wearing a T-shirt printed with the words *My blood speaks of the horror you've done to me* cries out, "Long live the spirit of Thembelihle, long live; Long live the spirit of Gift Disebo Makau, long live; Long live of the spirit of Eudy Simelane long live," and the audience responds, "Long live," after each name.[19]

The performance can be compared with a protest held in Rosebank, a formerly white neighborhood of Johannesburg, in 2012 when activists staged a "die-in" and blockaded the road during the Joburg Gay Pride Parade. The activists were part of the One in Nine campaign, which had been formed in 2006 in solidarity with Fezeka Kuzwayo, the woman who accused Jacob Zuma of rape, and which offers support to women who have been raped. (The campaign draws its name from a study conducted by the Medical Research Council of South Africa in 2005 that found that only one in nine women who are raped report the crime.) They briefly brought the march to a halt, holding banners that read "Dying for Justice" and "No Cause for Celebration" and calling for one minute of silence. The video footage of the protest is chilling to watch—the predominantly white marchers in the parade pick their way over the prostrate bodies of the protestors lying in the street. The footage captures activists being told they had no right to be at the parade and people at the parade, including members of the pride board, shouting, "This is my route" and "Drive over them."[20] The protestors were also threatened by police officers, who eventually forced them off the street. Pride marches signify the production of and claim to public space as inclusive of queer lives. The interruption of the march, and in particular the dominant response to the One in Nine campaign activists, makes visible the lie that queer people have access to public space and indeed underlined why rapes are reported so infrequently. This incident makes clear that public space in South Africa not only remains deeply divided but that the legacy of apartheid produces new and painful forms of racist hatred.

The performance staged by Mfazwe's collective was more effective in engaging participants and spectators than the One in Nine protest, and this may have been, at least in part, because of the absence of the racist white South Africans who caused the violent and ugly scene at the Joburg march two years earlier.[21] The performance at the Soweto Pride March in 2014 provides a striking instance of the power of public art to profoundly challenge what feminist literary scholar Helene Strauss (2009, 79 as cited in Baderoon 2014, 328) describes as "silences and complicities" that "facilitate the normalization of gender-based violence." The collective intends to conceptualize and perform similar works in response to hate crimes in the future. Mfazwe notes, however, that "resources are holding us back, but we are trying so hard to get resources so that we can continue."[22] S/he also said that the next piece would take place in a shopping mall or in a busy road outside of the context of the Pride March, which offers a form of protection to the performers as it is intended to be a queer-friendly space. In response to my query about whether the performers would be afraid to perform the piece in a different location, Mfazwe replied, "It sounds quite scary, but we need to take that risk and see how people react."[23] Gender nonconforming writer and visual activist Neo Musangi has spoken of feeling safer during and after their performance piece in central Nairobi than when they are moving through public space in the course of ordinary life.[24] Musangi (2014, 54) describes the experience of walking in the streets of Nairobi as a queer person in the following way: "To be so often harassed in these streets is to signal the danger of your being: It is to take a risk with yourself. To continue walking these streets is to understand that your body presents itself as available for insults, advances, rape, for jokes. The body, presenting itself in privileging but vulnerable ways. It is to come to terms with what Keguro Macharia calls "disposability" and the ever increasing *killability*."

Charting the connections and disconnections between public space and political life in post-apartheid South Africa is highly charged, not least because spatial segregation was a lynchpin of the apartheid state. Raising the question of who has the right to enter, move through, and occupy public spaces in the most unequal society in the world makes visible how, as cultural theorist Sarah Nuttall (2004, 741) argued more than a decade ago, "the new South African city is still a space where nightmarish divisions may be witnessed and where the fear of crime delimits dreams of truly public space."

At the same time, in her work, Nuttall (2004, 731) is concerned with charting contemporary social forms in the aftermath of apartheid and calls for "theories and ways of reading culture which take into account the extent of the transformations that have taken place." The works discussed in this chapter cast light on the massive shifts that have occurred in social and political life post-1994, as well as on the emergence of terrifying forms of violent policing of ways of being that challenge retrogressive and heteronormative conceptions of the nation-state. Achieving the "dream" of public space would be to move beyond the looming shadows of apartheid-era Christian-Nationalist notions of "*Eendracht Maak Magt*/Unity Is Strength," and to embrace difference and dissent, even within collectives.[25] Bringing "truly public space" into existence requires refusing to prematurely celebrate the advent of democracy but to continually insist upon remembering, registering, and refusing the limits of post-apartheid belonging.

RADICAL MOURNING

Iranti-org is a queer visual media activist collective based in Johannesburg founded by queer activists Jabu Chen Pereira and Neo Musangi. Along with Inkanyiso, the queer visual activist collective founded by Muholi, Iranti-org is playing a critical part in drawing attention to the crisis of violence against queer people in South Africa. On January 15, 2015, Iranti-org released a press statement regarding the case of Thembelihle Sokhela, criticizing the police for failing to collect evidence at the scene and for neglecting to recognize Sokhela's murder as a hate crime: "Until now, the police failed to get a statement saying Thembelihle was a lesbian and sexual orientation was a motive in this heinous crime. The police have also been slack in the gathering of vital evidence, leaving behind the victim's clothes, her underwear and the blanket that wrapped her body at the scene of the crime.[26]

The collective also staged a powerful advocacy piece in response to the murder that incorporated an installation of images on a wall on the outside of a building in Johannesburg. The images included a copy of a page of Sokhela's identity book and photographs of evidence relating to the murder taken by members of the collective immediately after Sokhela was killed. Beneath these images was a person who lay prostrate on the ground below the images, completely wrapped in a blanket that appeared to be blood-stained and that represents the way that Sokhela's body was found.[27]

Like the One in Nine campaign activists who staged a "die-in" at the Pride March, and like Zanele Muholi's appearance in a glass coffin at her 2014 exhibition opening in South Africa, this piece by the Iranti collective brings the "corpse" into public view.[28] In this way, the collective makes visible and resists the erasure of queer lives.

The advocacy piece created by Iranti-org claims a place in public space for queer lives at the same time as it marks this as an impossibility—the collective insists on the possibility of shared mourning even as it documents the devastating effects of Sokhela's murder. Like Duduzile Zozo, whose dead body was discovered with a toilet brush inserted into her vagina in July 2013; like Gift Makau who was strangled to death in August 2014 and found half-naked and with a piece of wire around her neck and a hosepipe stuck in her throat; like Noxolo Nogwaza who was raped and stabbed to death in 2011, the manner of Sokhela's death is one to which it is difficult, if not impossible, to come to terms. The small but significant acts of radical mourning practiced by queer visual activists are slowly but surely being recognized and are increasingly seen by wider audiences that extend beyond the bounds of South Africa. The question of how to open and transform local public spaces from zones of exclusion and violence, and very occasionally of queer protest and resistance, to sites of belonging remains.

In response to the crisis of violence against queer people in Africa, Jabu Chen Pereira and Zethu Matebeni coordinated "Critically Queer," a multimedia exhibition that included works by queer artists from across the continent and that formed part of a four-day series of events and discussions.[29] The event also included two public performances, one by Selogadi Mampane and the other by Neo Musangi, both of which took place on the University of Cape Town campus. These groundbreaking works, and the discussions and exhibition that accompanied them, were largely attended by queer visual artists, theorists, and activists. In South Africa, simply being queer in public space is to expose oneself to violence, and as the incident at the Pride Parade in 2014 makes clear, this is all the more so for black people. For this reason, it is misguided to call on queer black artists to challenge racist heteronormative society and to criticize them for failing to "claim" their right to public space. Before this can take place, dominant ways of thinking require radical transformation. A participatory public art project focused on how people think about and perform their sexual identities and how they understand gendered being, along the lines of Terry Kurgan's Hotel Yeoville Project, is sorely needed. Hotel Yeoville engages with the experiences of people who have moved to South Africa from other places to Yeoville, an inner-city neighborhood of Johannesburg, and makes use of innovative methods involving participatory photography, storytelling, and digital exchange.[30] Without these kinds of interventions, funerals will continue to be at the center of queer visual activism in South Africa.

PUBLIC QUEER PRESENCE

In a fascinating essay on the significance of urban public space for social and political life, social geographer Ash Amin argues that the connection between the central spaces of the city and civic culture and democratic politics has long gone unquestioned. He points to the differences between classical Rome and Renaissance Florence in which public life was shaped in public spaces, and contemporary political and social life, in which "urban public space has become one component, arguably of secondary importance, in a variegated field of civic and political formation" (Amin 2006, n.p.). Amin notes the significance of, among others, the media (and in the wake of the Arab Spring, one would include online activism in particular), of books, and of transnational organizations in shaping public culture in the present. He observes not only that "civic practices—and public culture in general—are shaped in circuits of flow and association that are not reducible to the urban" but also that "following those who stress the plural sources of civic and political culture in contemporary life, that sociality in urban public space is not a sufficient condition for civic and political citizenship" (Amin 2006, n.p.).

Amin's insight that the material public spaces of a city are only one site where community, belonging, and public culture can be forged is interesting to consider in relation to how all three visual activists (and collectives) discussed in this chapter make use of online spaces for the production and circulation of queer visual activism. Digital space can be understood as an important, and relatively safe, public space for activist work and for queer public art. However, virtual spaces cannot substitute for material spaces. In her essay, "Bodies in Alliance and the Politics of the Street," Judith Butler (2011) notes the crucial interrelation between physical and digital spaces: "Although some may wager that the exercise of rights now takes place quite at the expense of bodies on the street that twitter and other virtual technologies have led to a disembodiment of the public sphere, I disagree. The media requires those bodies on the street to have an event, even as the street requires the media to exist in a global arena."

Drawing on Hannah Arendt's thinking about public space and political life, Butler (2011) argues that "to be precluded from the space of appearance, to be precluded from being part of the plurality that brings the space of appearance into being, is to be deprived of the right to have rights." The works discussed here make the reasons for the mostly digital and largely transitory nature of queer interventions in public space in South Africa painfully clear: public space is overdetermined by the threat of violence and the experience of violation. The absence of permanent installations of queer public art in South African cannot be remedied simply by placing artworks in city streets but requires challenging those who argue that the national body holds no place for queer lives. At this point, the struggle for the right to live and love freely as lesbian/gay/trans/queer/asexual/non-gender-conforming/intersexed people is being waged by a very small number of people, most of whom are themselves at risk of experiencing both psychic and physical violence.

There are those who argue that it is precisely the visibility of black lesbians in South Africa, and in particular masculine-presenting black lesbians, that renders them vulnerable to being raped and killed. If this is indeed so, it is up to those who are not themselves at risk to stand in solidarity with those who are most vulnerable and to make queer presence not only possible but desired. This is to refuse the genocidal logic of the course laid out for us by the apartheid state and to speak out against homophobia, xenophobia, and racist hatred. It is to learn about how and why violence reaches particular bodies and how it passes over others.[31] It is to recognize that we cannot name the spaces we occupy "public" when they exclude the majority of those who dwell in the "dehumanisation zones" that encircle our cities.[32] And it is to understand how no one can, no one should, walk in peace if that right cannot belong to all. The work of the visual activists discussed here tirelessly reminds us of the names of those who have been killed and whose deaths teach us that what Richards (2013) termed a "humanized public space" is not yet in reach.

ACKNOWLEDGMENTS

I am grateful to the artists and activists discussed here for their powerful work and to Collen Mfazwe for allowing me to include the photograph of the 2014 performance in this chapter.

Kylie Thomas is a research associate at the Institute for Reconciliation and Social Justice, University of the Free State, South Africa. She is the author of *Impossible Mourning: HIV/AIDS and Visuality after Apartheid*.

Notes

1. Zanele Muholi is a critically acclaimed South African photographer and visual activist. Her most recent book, *Faces and Phases 2006–14*, was published by Steidl in 2014 and is a testament to the powerful work she has created over time. The book has been shortlisted for the Deutsche Börse Photography Prize. Collen Mfazwe is a photographer and member of the queer visual activist collective Inkanyiso. Muholi founded Inkanyiso in 2009 in order to create a space for queer visual activism and to support emerging activists, writers, and photographers in South Africa. The inkanyiso.org site contains an already-extensive and growing online archive of documents and images that chronicle queer experiences post-apartheid. Jabu Chen Pereira is a photographer and visual activist and the founder, together with Neo Musangi, of the Johannesburg-based queer visual media platform Iranti.org.

2. On the Afrapix collective and the relation between photography and activism during apartheid, see Hayes (2011), Jacobs (2012), Soske (2011), and Thomas (2012).

3. See my chapter on Mendel's work, "Traumatic Witnessing: Photography and Disappearance" in Thomas (2014).

4. See Lerato Dumse's report: http://inkanyiso.org/2014/09/26/2014-sept-26-man-appears-in-court-for-lesbian-murder/.

5. Muholi's work is emblematic in this regard and provides a comprehensive visual history of hate crimes in South Africa. Her work has opened the way for young visual activists to produce their own works, and Collen Mfazwe, for instance, is currently collaborating with performance artist and activist Selogadi Mampane to produce a video work that commemorates the murder of Duduzile Zozo (interview with Collen Mfazwe, March 18, 2015).

6. Interview with Collen Mfazwe, March 18, 2015.

7. On AIDS activism in the United States before antiretroviral treatment was widely available, see Weiner (2012).

8. Performance at the funeral of Thembelihle Sokhela, Daveyton, September 28, 2014, by Zanele Muholi. See https://inkanyiso.org/2014/09/30/2014-sept-28-an-emotional-farewell-for-the-recent-victim-of-hate-crime/, accessed December 6, 2016.

9. This image appears at the end of Gideon Mendel's (2001) book, *A Broken Landscape*.

10. Interview with Collen Mfazwe, March 18, 2015.

11. Interview with Collen Mfazwe, March 18, 2015.

12. Mpho Setshedi, a lesbian soccer player, was murdered in Johannesburg in 2004, and in 2006, Zoliswa Nkonyana was stoned and beaten to death in Khayelitsha, Cape Town. The number of hate crimes against queer people in South Africa has steadily increased since then. See the time line in Muholi's (2014) *Faces and Phases*, which includes brief notes on hate crimes committed in South Africa between 2004 and 2014.

13. The photograph described here accompanied Dumse's account of the funeral and can be viewed at inkanyiso.org.

14. See, for instance, Muholi's video piece about the murder and funeral of Duduzile Zozo (https://www.youtube.com/watch?v=5IW_WomkExc) and about the murder of Sihle Sikoji (https://www.youtube.com/watch?v=k8Mmz95YSA4).

15. The street was the primary place of protest in South Africa during apartheid and remains so in the present.

16. In my interview with Mfazwe, I asked whether the collective had been witness to other performances that are similar to the work they created, but according to Mfazwe, they had not.

17. Interview with Collen Mfazwe, January 2015. It is a horrible irony that the police were attempting to prevent the performers from protesting about gender-based violence. One hundred and forty cases of rape involving members of the South African Police Service were reported to the Independent Police Investigative Directorate (2014, 42) between April 1, 2013 and March 31, 2014.

18. In Muholi's video piece documenting the funeral of Sikoji, a football can be seen among the flowers placed on the coffin.

19. Apart from Bianca Bothma's article, "Born This Way: Gay Pageant Helps LGBTI Community Feel Safe" (http://www.enca.com/south-africa/born-way-gay-pageant-helps-lgbti-community-feel-safe) in which an image of the performance appeared, there were no newspaper reports or reviews about the performance. The video piece was screened at "Thinking against Violence: Queer Perspectives" at the Centre for African Studies Gallery at the University of Cape Town in November 2014 and in Berlin, Germany, in July 2015 at the Second Gender, Violence, Visual Activism Workshop, a project I am coordinating with activists, artists, and writers from South Africa and Germany.

20. See LGBT activists disrupt Joburg Gay Parade: https://www.youtube.com/watch?v=Hnxip-T_Hnw&sns=em. For reports and critical commentary on the protest, see Rebecca Davis, "'This Is My Route!': Race, Entitlement and Gay Pride in South Africa," accessed January 27, 2015, http://africasacountry.com/this-is-my-route-race-entitlement-and-gay-pride-in-south-africa/ and Gillian Schutte, "No Cause to Celebrate a Racist Pride," *Mail & Guardian*, October 12, 2012, accessed January 27, 2015, http://mg.co.za/article/2012–10–12–00-no-cause-to-celebrate-a-racist-pride.

21. See McLean (2014) for a detailed discussion of the aftermath of the protest in 2012.

22. Interview with Collen Mfazwe, January 2015.

23. Ibid.

24. Musangi raised this point during the Gender, Violence, Visual Activism Workshop held in Cape Town in November 2014.

25. *Eendracht maak Magt* was the slogan on the South African coat of arms before the end of apartheid.

26. The court hearing of Sokhela's case has been postponed five times.

27. Images of the visual activist work produced by Iranti-org in response to Sokhela's murder can be viewed at http://www.iranti-org.co.za/content/Press_Releases/2015-Thembelihle-Sokhela/Thembelihle-Sokhela_2015_gallery/index.html.

28. At the opening of "Of Love and Loss," which appeared at the Stevenson Gallery in Johannesburg from February 14–April 4, 2014, Muholi lay naked in a glass coffin for

the duration of the event. Muholi was also showing a related body of work titled "Mo(u) rning" at the Wits Art Museum at the same time. This work formed part of the Queer and Trans Art-iculations exhibition that also included the groundbreaking series of portraits and films "Proudly African and Transgender" and "Proudly Trans in Turkey" by Gabrielle Le Roux. See Humbane (2014), Lloyd (2014), and Smith (2014) for reviews of the exhibition.

29. The Critically Queer exhibition, curated by Jabu Chen Pereira, was first held at the University of Johannesburg, September 10–17, 2013. In 2014, it was displayed at the Centre for African Studies Gallery at the University of Cape Town (UCT) in association with a series of discussions and events, "Queer in Africa: Confronting the Crisis," coordinated by Zethu Matebeni and held May 29–June 2, 2014, at the Institute for Humanities in Africa, also at UCT. The exhibition was accompanied by a book edited by Matebeni, *Reclaiming Afrikan: Queer Perspectives on Sexual and Gender Identities.*

30. For an insightful reading, see Alex Dodd's (2013) essay, included in the publication that resulted from the project, *Hotel Yeoville* (Kurgan 2013).

31. See Anderson (2000), Andrews (1999), Britton (2002), Bennett (2010), Goldblatt and Meintjies (1998), Gqola (2010), Jewkes and Abrahams (2002), and Wood (2005) for a range of perspectives on gender-based violence in South Africa both during and after apartheid.

32. The Tokolos Stencils collective inscribed the phrase *dehumanisation zone* in large letters on the concrete walls of open-air toilets used by township residents and visible from a large national highway, the N2. The city of Cape Town painted over the words within a few weeks. To view this and other works, see http://tokolosstencils.tumblr.com.

References

Amin, Ash. 2006. "Collective Culture and Urban Public Space." Accessed March 22, 2017. http://www.publicspace.org/en/text-library/eng/b003-collective-culture-and-urban-public-space.

Anderson, Michelle J. 2000. "Rape in South Africa." *The Georgetown Journal of Gender and the Law* 1: 789–821.

Andrews, Penelope E. 1999. "Violence against Women in South Africa: The Role of Culture and the Limitations of the Law." *Temple Political and Civil Rights Law Review* 8: 425–57.

Bennett, Jane. 2010. "Editorial: Rethinking Gender and Violence." *Feminist Africa* 14: 1–6.

Bennett Jane, Nonhlanhla Mkhize, Relebohile Moletsane, and Vasu Reddy. 2010. *The Country We Want to Live In: Hate Crimes and Homophobia in the Lives of Black Lesbian South Africans.* Cape Town: HSRC Press.

Britton, Hannah. 2002. "The Incomplete Revolution: South African Women's Struggle for Parliamentary Transformation." *International Feminist Journal of Politics* 4: 43–71.

Butler, Judith. 2011. "Bodies in Alliance and the Politics of the Street." Accessed February 4, 2015. http://www.eipcp.net/transversal/1011/butler/en.

De Lange, D. 2012. "Call to Suspend ANC MP for Opening Fire on Gay Rights." *Cape Times*, May 8, p. 4.

Dodd, Alex. 2013. "A Public Variation on the Theme of Love." In *Hotel Yeoville,* edited by Terry Kurgan, 1–16, Johannesburg: FourthWall Books.

Dumse, Lerato. 2014. "An Emotional Farewell for the Recent Victim of Hate Crime." *Inkanyiso.org,* September 28. Accessed January 28, 2015. http://inkanyiso.org/2014/09/30/2014-sept-28-an-emotional-farewell-for-the-recent-

Goldblatt, Beth, and S. Meintjies. 1998. "A Gender Perspective on Violence during the Struggle against Apartheid." In *Violence in South Africa: A Variety of Perspectives,* edited by E. Bornman, R. van Eeden, and M. Wentzel, 227–50. Pretoria: HSRC Press.

Gqola, Pumla. 2010. *What Is Slavery to Me? Postcolonial Slave Memory in Post-Apartheid South Africa.* Johannesburg: Wits University Press.

Humbane, Aluta. 2014. "Black South African Visual Artist Lesbian, Zanele Muholi, in Transparent Coffin of Love and Loss." *Inkanyiso.org,* February 24. Accessed March 31, 2014. https://inkanyiso.org/2014/02/24/2014-feb-14-black-south-african-visual-activist-lesbian-zanele-muholi-in-a-transparent-coffin-of-love-and-loss/.

Independent Police Investigative Directorate. 2014. "Annual Report, 2013–2014." Accessed March 22, 2017. http://www.gov.za/documents/independent-police-investigative-directorate-annual-report-20132014-29-sep-2015-0000.

Jewkes, Rachel, and Naeema Abrahams. 2002. "The Epidemiology of Rape and Sexual Coercion in South Africa: An Overview." *Social Science and Medicine* 55: 1231–44.

Lloyd, Ang. 2014. "Zanele Muholi's New Work Mourns and Celebrates South African Queer Lives." *Africa Is a Country* (Blog). Accessed February 3, 2015. http://africasacountry.com/zanele-muholis-new-work-mourns-and-celebrates-south-african-queer-lives/.

Macharia, K. "Imagine Freedom." *Gukira: With(out) Predicates* (Blog). Accessed February 4, 2015. https://gukira.wordpress.com/page/3/.

Matebeni, Zethu. 2013. "Intimacy, Queerness, Race." *Cultural Studies* 27: 404–17.

———. 2014. *Reclaiming Afrikan: Queer Perspectives on Sexual and Gender Identities.* Cape Town: Modjaji Books.

McLean, Nyx. 2014. "Digital as an Enabler: A Case Study of the Joburg Pride 2012 Clash." *Feminist Africa* 18: 25–42.

Mendel, Gideon. 2001. *A Broken Landscape: HIV & AIDS in Africa.* London: Network Photographers.

Muholi, Zanele. 2014. *Faces and Phases 2006–14.* Göttingen, Germany: Steidl.

Musangi, Neo. 2014. "In Time and Space." In *Reclaiming Afrikan: Queer Perspectives on Sexual and Gender Identities,* edited by Zethu Matebeni, 53–58. Cape Town: Modjaji Books.

Nuttall, Sarah. 2004. "City Forms and Writing the Now in South Africa." *Journal of Southern African Studies* 30, no. 4: 731–48.

Ramphele, Mamphela. 1996. "Political Widowhood in South Africa: The Embodiment of Ambiguity." *Daedalus* 125, no. 1 (Winter): 99–117.

Richards, Colin. 2013. "Retouching Apartheid: Intimacy, Interiority and Photography." In *Rise and Fall of Apartheid: Photography and the Bureaucracy of Everyday Life,* edited by Okwui Enwezor and Rory Bester, 234–47. New York: International Center of Photography and Prestel.

Robins, Steven, and Bettina von Lieres. 2004. "Remaking Citizenship, Unmaking Marginalisation: The Treatment Action Campaign in Post-Apartheid South Africa." *Canadian Journal of African Studies* 38, no. 3: 575–86.
Smith, Michael. 2014. "The Constitution of Love and Loss." *Artthrob*. Accessed February 3, 2015. http://www.artthrob.co.za/Reviews/Michael_Smith_reviews_The_Constitution_of_Love__Loss_by_Zanele_Muholi_at_STEVENSON_in_Johannesburg.aspx.
Thomas, Kylie. 2010. "Zanele Muholi's Intimate Archive: Photography and Post-Apartheid Lesbian Lives." *Safundi* 11: 421–36.
———. 2012. "Wounding Apertures: Violence, Affect and Photography during and after Apartheid." *Kronos: Southern African Histories* November: 204–18.
———. 2013a. "Digital Visual Activism: A Profile of Inkanyiso." *Feminist Africa* 18: 79–81.
———. 2013b. "Homophobia, Injustice and 'Corrective Rape' in Post-Apartheid South Africa." Cape Town: Centre for the Study of Violence and Reconciliation and Centre for Humanities Research, University of the Western Cape.
———. 2014. *Impossible Mourning: HIV/AIDS and Visuality after Apartheid.* Johannesburg: Wits University Press.
Weiner, Andrew. 2012. "Disposable Media, Expendable Populations—ACT UP New York: Activism, Art and the AIDS Crisis, 1987–1993." *Journal of Visual Culture* 11: 103–9.
Wood, Kate. 2005. "Contextualising Group Rape in Post-Apartheid South Africa." *Culture, Health and Sexuality* 7, no. 4: 303–17.

CHAPTER 13

Telltale Signs: Unsanctioned Graffiti Interventions in Post-Apartheid Johannesburg

MATTHEW RYAN SMITH

Natives—men, women and children—should only be permitted within municipal areas in so far and for as long as their presence is demanded by the wants of the white population.
Stallard Commission 1922

As early as 1897, geographic maps of Johannesburg indicate that municipal authorities made an attempt to segregate groups of individuals according to their ethnicity. At the same time, they created laws to limit the physical and visual contact between African, colored, Indian, and white residents. Their initial efforts were unsuccessful (Apartheid Museum 2006, 22); however, they helped to establish a racial hierarchy in Johannesburg. In these spaces of the city, where the marginalized were once unwelcome through systemic racial discrimination, class bias, and forced separation, now appear unsanctioned graffiti. The physical presence of these bodies while producing unsanctioned graffiti markings in post-apartheid spaces should not be ignored, namely because it represents a radical act of transhistorical dissidence. Unsanctioned graffiti is a complex form of autobiographical representation that facilitates the physical presence of the body and the politic of the inscription. These artists and writers challenge the historical legacy of apartheid by using graffiti as a strategy of resistance. Graffiti interventions have aided in the reclamation of former sites and spaces of exclusion. In this sense, it is through graffiti that they generate "a moment of identity performance in place" that marks and remarks critical subjectivities in real space and time (Heddon 2002), while enacting defiance against status quo ethnic and class discrimination. Within this matrix of political resistance and body politics, these radical subjectivities raise questions about how unsanctioned graffiti performs criticisms of place.

Unsanctioned graffiti artists and writers in Johannesburg demonstrate a growing frustration with structural and systemic inequality that continues to hamper economic growth and social amity in urban environments and surrounding suburbs. Here, they take aim at the proceedings of local government, social welfare policies, corporate exploitation of labor, the (post)colonial project, violent crime, lack of employment, gender inequality, sexual assault, and other pressing social conditions. The visibility of unsanctioned graffiti projects in and around Johannesburg point to an experiential viewing dynamic that frames a kind of oppositional politics. While graffiti–as–social commentary is not a new phenomenon in Johannesburg, the artists and writers who engage in this complex form of visual communication employ historical references and events related to the city, and South Africa more generally, in order to load their texts and images with personal and collective meaning. In this sense, unsanctioned graffiti in Johannesburg frequently takes on a dimension of activism in that it employs non-neutral forms of visual communication in an attempt to destabilize discrimination, prejudice, and xenophobia. Nevertheless, there exists an altogether-distinct category of unsanctioned graffiti in Johannesburg that is more concerned with the global popularity of hip-hop graffiti style and consequently remains apathetic to the political potential of graffiti marking. This is precisely the reason why several controversial graffiti projects by nonresident writers and artists such as Faith47 and ABOVE have been crucial in presenting an outsider's perspective and a distinct political conviction. Ultimately, however, Johannesburg's graffiti culture is unique precisely because it negotiates between historical trauma and the promise of renewal.

In this chapter, I explore unsanctioned graffiti practices in post-apartheid Johannesburg by proposing that inscriptions made by graffiti artists and writers deconstruct post-apartheid geographies. To better understand these apparatuses of social expression, I analyze the ways that graffiti artists mark the walls of Johannesburg to critique the colonial and apartheid project for which poverty, frustration, and inequity function as visible reminders of its legacy. The first section of this chapter draws on interviews conducted with writers and graffiti artists to locate and analyze the evolution of urban street culture in Johannesburg since the fall of apartheid. I then move to debates around the city's nuanced laws surrounding the criminalization of graffiti and how this pertains to the city's 2006 public art policy. Drawing on cultural theorists such as Jürgen Habermas and Michael Warner, I use the notion of the modern public sphere in order to explore the tensions between public art and graffiti, while demonstrating how unsanctioned forms of visual expression can function democratically. The second section in this chapter conceptualizes how the physical body is utilized in unsanctioned graffiti interventions to shift relations of power, pose an oppositional politics, and enact resistance. This includes, among other things, how the graffiti tagging of personal signatures in South African indigenous languages such as isiXhosa perform a politics of place through embodiment. I conclude this section with a discussion of the paradoxical relationship between unsanctioned political graffiti and hip-hop graffiti to understand how urban street culture in Johannesburg exists within a complex set of global trends and cultural significations. The third and final section of this chapter responds to the first and second by demonstrating how some of the most politically consequential works created in Johannesburg are the product of nonresident graffiti artists and writers. These projects, and others similar to them, present what filmmaker and activist Oliver Ressler calls embedded art, or projects that contain elements of participation and performance (quoted in Cronin and Robertson 2011, 10). I outline how Johannesburg's architecture operates as a blank slate to criticize the city's socioeconomic conditions and historical traumas. In my conclusion, I use the work of urban theorists to discuss how Johannesburg has effectively redrawn boundaries of segregation since the fall of apartheid through various urban development projects, and how the destruction of graffiti now forms an indicator of separation on a grand scale.

CITY DRAWING

With a population of nearly 4,400,000, Johannesburg is the largest city in South Africa and one of the most ethnically diverse in the world. As the provincial capital of Gauteng, it remains the commercial hub of South Africa—namely, for hosting the corporate headquarters of European, American, and Asian mining interests. From 1993 to 2007, Johannesburg ranked 171st out of the largest three hundred metropolitan economies in the world, later improving its ranking to 85th from 2011 to 2012. The numbers are significant because they point to a recovery from major economic recession, and while marginally improving on employment rates, the city still lags on gross domestic product per capita (Brookings Institution 2014). Yet Johannesburg exists in a strange paradox, forever negotiating nominal economic growth with the most extreme poverty.[1] It is a place where severe class and racial disparity has become another cliché, which many of the city's intelligentsia chose to overlook, ignore, or deny (Enwezor 2004, 25).

Within this climate of social discord, coupled with the city's problematic colonial and post-apartheid history, graffiti has proven a highly productive area of critical discourse (see Bremner 2002; Klopper 2000; Landau and Kaspin 2002; Peffer 2009; Waddacor 2014). From 1999 to 2014, the development of unsanctioned graffiti in Johannesburg encountered numerous transformations corresponding to periods of social unrest, the availability of materials, state-sponsored sporting events, enthusiastic younger generations, and the introduction of new hip-hop graffiti styles. For writer and graffiti artist Cale Waddacor, the graffiti and street art scene in Johannesburg has gradually shifted to encompass a more inclusive cultural discourse. During the early to mid-1990s, there existed "unwritten rules" pertaining to graffiti writers' aesthetic expression and antiestablishment ideals, which essentially restricted its social and cultural development. Questions such as "Why didn't you do a second outline?" or "Why are your letters not the same size as each other?" appeared to matter more than the benefits of stylistic innovation, pedagogy, and community engagement. Bullying and verbal threats put pressure on other artists and writers to conform to these conventions; thus, the graffiti produced during the early to mid-1990s in Johannesburg is somewhat adverse to the congenial atmosphere of the global hip-hop graffiti art movement that exploded in the early 2000s. With the continued global acceptance of graffiti art and other forms of urban street culture—triggered by artists such as Banksy, Shepard Fairey, Invader, and David Choe, among numerous others—including mural painting, rap music, and break dancing, freedom of individual expression gained impetus. The rules that previously dictated style and subject matter in Johannesburg subsided to the point where new writers were accepted and mentored into prospering cultural communities such as Newtown and Fordsburg.[2] Works of unsanctioned graffiti , then, are not only joined to the architecture of the city but also to a cacophony of social, political, and economic dynamics that help forge a greater sense of community (Heartney 1994, 162).

As much as the graffiti community in Johannesburg has grown since the fall of apartheid, graffiti artists and writers hold the rather unique position of cultivating a distinct cultural movement with little to no historical precedence to borrow from. This is in part due to the strict banishment of, and fierce prosecution for, any type of graffiti marking during the apartheid era. In this regard, Johannesburg's graffiti culture is surprisingly little more than two decades old, which is barely enough time for two generations of artists and writers to learn and share their knowledge. The formal development of graffiti in Johannesburg and its neighboring districts is dependent on the hand of time itself. Often overlooked, the introduction of specific painting and writing tools, including stronger stencil materials, more durable markers, and premium spray paints, such as those manufactured by Montana and Molotow, have also contributed, in their own way, to this core development.[3] The resulting shift has seen graffiti writers and urban artists who honed their skills by generating unsanctioned work on the streets, such as Gogga, Mak1one, Falko, Curio, and Rasty, garnering major commissions for corporate- and state-sponsored graffiti projects, acquiring representation in commercial art galleries, and being selected to participate in major curated exhibitions. As is often the case with forms of visual expression that attempt to make political statements, it becomes co-opted and assimilated by the cultural elite, and thus loses its political authority (Searle in Cronin and Robertson 2011, 5).

In cities around the world, police crackdowns on graffiti and other forms of urban street culture threaten the very energy of contemporary city life (Klein 2002, 311). Johannesburg has had an ambiguous relationship with graffiti art and writing since the end of apartheid. The city of Johannesburg establishes vague terminology surrounding the lawfulness of unsanctioned graffiti murals, while simultaneously condemning tagging and other kinds of "unsightly" markings. Even the city's official proclamation that it is "now considered the capital of graffiti art in South Africa" encompasses contradictory signifiers of illegality (graffiti) and socially accepted norms of visual expression (visual art) (City of Johannesburg 2014). Still, the production of unsanctioned graffiti remains a criminal offense in Johannesburg, and carries with it the possibility of a jail sentence. The city's most recent Public Art Policy, dating back to 2006, demonstrates a clear commitment to enhance the urban environment and the enjoyment of public space. The policy claims that public art is intended to confer "shared symbols" for constructing "social cohesion," "civic pride," and the forging of a "positive identity" for the city. "Through this art," the policy reads, "the City projects its collective identity and vision, while individuals and community groups in neighborhoods are also empowered to also express their unique identities." Point sixteen on the policy breakdown addresses "The Removal of Unwanted Graffiti":

> Special attention should be given to keeping major landmarks and declared heritage sites clear of unwanted graffiti. Working under the direction of the Manager: Public Art, an Anti-Graffiti Rapid Response Unit will be responsible for the timeous removal of objectionable and unwanted graffiti from key points. Further, the City should be pro-active in protecting prominent sites from unsightly graffiti by, where appropriate, applying treatments to discourage and/or repel graffiti. (City of Johannesburg 2006, 9)

In effect, the references to unsanctioned graffiti and the policy's vague rhetoric toward "objectionable," "unsightly," and "unwanted" graffiti illustrate the fallibility of homogenizing graffiti's most basic idioms—pieces, murals, bombings, tags, stickers, stencils, or wall art—within a comprehensive judicial and visual category. Moreover, there exists little to no transparency for who is responsible for adjudicating what graffiti is permissible and what gets destroyed or removed, assumedly placing the onus of responsibility on individual city workers, which, by mediating graffiti's locations and messages, positions them as arbiters for taste, beautification, and censorship.

More recently, questions surrounding unsanctioned graffiti, street art, murals, wall art, tagging, bombing, and other forms of mark making as acts of vandalism have been the subject of passionate discourse by various media sources, citizens, and journalists. Published reports on the state of unsanctioned graffiti in Johannesburg center on its visibility in public spaces, its inherent social dimensions, and the indeterminacy of its illegal dynamics. According to one article, "If Johannesburg is to maintain a positive image and work against the escalation of crime, then 'petty' crimes like vandalism must be addressed before the environment of degradation and impunity worsens"; adding, "keep in mind that the prevention of petty crimes is a significant step towards the prevention of major crimes (Witherden 2010)." What is often overlooked is the idea that Johannesburg's policy toward unsanctioned graffiti carries with it strong ethnic and class bias. The spaces in the city with some of the highest concentrations of poverty, violent crime, and nonwhite residents, such as the "inner-city suburbs" like Hillbrow and "northern" townships like Diepsloot, are where the city of Johannesburg states the most frequent instances of graffiti marking occur (City of Johannesburg 2014). Thus, the strong correlation between municipal policy, ethnicity, and graffiti indicates a systemic prejudice toward whom and what is being targeted in the prevention, removal, and potential prosecution of graffiti in Johannesburg.

As the most transgressive form of public art, a categorical definition of unsanctioned graffiti rests in the idea that the creative environment of the street is a *medium* and *resource* open to boundless exploration, exploitation, and intervention.[4] But the issue of the criminalization of graffiti is less about a hierarchy of artistic practices and more about the fact that it is being executed in public spaces, on the privately owned sites of corporations, homeowners, and small businesses. According to an unnamed expert referred by the legal compliance department of the city of Johannesburg's local government, the act of graffiti "may" not be illegal, though the place where it is inscribed qualifies its illegality; specifically, when the wall, signboard, or bridge is the property of an individual, local government, or state (see Witherden 2010).

Part of the official crackdown on graffiti in Johannesburg is premised on the idea that these forms of social communication and visual aesthetics occupy the very bottom of the hierarchy of the arts. Yet "despite what they say," remarks Banksy (2007, 8), "graffiti is not the lowest form of art"; rather, it punctures geographies of the city "with moments of fracture, spaces of disruption, and subjective uses of territory" so as to manifest a vibrant urban culture and public communication forum (see Deitch et al. 2011, 19–24).[5] Often, these marks of defiance represent strategies of resistance against the intrusion and proliferation of corporate advertising imagery overwhelming the public spaces of Johannesburg. Specific locations such as government property, operational infrastructure, and Euro-American commercial advertising billboards mired in object fetishism have become a proverbial target for culture jammers and *détournement*. Graffiti artists and writers often hijack advertising space to corrupt corporate images through defacement, thereby transforming their original meaning into something new and antithetical. For Kim Dovey, Simon Wollan, and Ian Woodcock (2012, 22–23), graffiti addresses a "captive audience" that it shares with architecture and advertising, yet differs in its informality, illegality, and transgression of codes. In effect, the rampant criminalization of graffiti is "not merely a war on vandalism and social chaos fought along strict legal boundaries as its agents often claim, but part of a war against all messages legal or otherwise that distract from the dominant presentation" (Weinberg quoted in Ouzman 2008, 244). Unsanctioned graffiti interventions are part of a larger strategy of reclamation intended to recapture sites and spaces of the city that have been sold to corporate advertising interests (Schiller and Schiller 2010, 11). In cities such as Johannesburg, the rules that apply to private property take precedence over the rights of freedom to self-expression (see Seno 2010, 23).

Those who comprise a public may not necessarily relate to visual categories of inclusion but instead to ontologies of address. For Habermas, the modern public sphere is both a conceptual and physical environment where criticisms of society at large are based on the basic principles of democracy. Within this environment, groups of individuals engage in free discussion (see Holub 1991). This, according to Pauline Johnston (2006, 12), is "a mode of interaction in which participants conduct themselves without regard for social status, believing that the authority of the better argument should be allowed to prevail . . . this newly emerging 'public' insist[s] on a principle of openness and inclusion." For Warner (2004, 10), "To address a public or to think of oneself as belonging to a public is to be a certain kind of person, to inhabit a certain kind of social world, to have at one's disposal certain media and genres, to be motivated by a certain normative horizon, and to speak within a certain language ideology." Under apartheid, notions of "public" were divided across racial lines—the public was predominantly a white public, and therefore the potential for democratic discourse, following Habermas's logic, was an impossible dream. Paradoxically, after the end of apartheid, every graffiti tag, mark, or inscription created on previously segregated walls by the nonwhite victims of forced separation may have in fact helped to forge a healthy modern public sphere. These works incorporated once silenced voices into an open dialogue of democratic communication (albeit through illegal modes of address). Consequently, then, the challenge to Johannesburg is finding a productive way to reconcile inclusive social practices with prohibited modes of visual communication.

TELLTALE SIGNS

As a postmodern city, Johannesburg functions as a conceptual, geographic, and critical space that lends itself to history making through the inscription and circulation of graffiti, whose visibility can be usurped to move the powerless to the powerful (see Sassen 2011, 574). Graffiti tagging, in particular, may operate as a complex marker of social unrest, disenfranchisement, or economic inequity, but it may also operate more strategically, as a physical and conceptual reclamation of space. More specifically, "tagging" references a different kind of vernacular self-representation, one that was forbidden as an act of vandalism, trespassing, and as a form of political radicalism under apartheid. In effect, tagging is the blanketing of the city's surface with pseudosignatures that stand in for absent physical bodies. "Described as pollution, dirt, deviance, criminal defacement, or, more benignly, folk art," Timothy Cresswell explains, it "has also been variously theorized as a marking of territory; or an expression of, or an insistence on, identity" (Heddon 2002). Tagging, among other things, is a form of autobiographical marking that remains resistant not only to the category of visual art but also to the limits of respectable aesthetic expression (Whitlock and Poletti 2008, xiii). It remains a mode of autobiographical intervention that confronts the everyday person as an egotistical pollution of the urban environment. As a distinct category of graffiti, it operates discursively and spatially, forming a kind of autotopographical mode of resistance because it simultaneously occupies and defines space (Heddon in Whitlock and Poletti 2008, xiii–xiv). Tagging in Johannesburg may be closely related to the idea of reoccupying both tribal homelands and desegregated geographies, representing, quite literally, the reinsertion of oneself in colonially-occupied space for the purposes of visibility, self-insistence, and embodiment. The autobiographical act of tagging is a postcolonial interventionist strategy of resistance to the ethnic and geographic separation that Johannesburg is founded upon.

Tagging and other forms of text-based graffiti in Johannesburg are also subject to linguistic taxonomies rooted in indigenous African language, colonialism, and hybrid speech. One such example is the increase of the inscription "AMANDLA TATA"—meaning "Power Father"—written in isiXhosa, one of the eleven official languages of South Africa—near Mandela's one-time residence in Soweto during the period immediately following his death. The presence of text-based graffiti on Johannesburg's walls written in languages such as English and Afrikaans is a particularly strong example of colonialism's sustained presence on the physical topography and social identity of the city. Moreover, the intrusion of nonnative language structures among colonized peoples of the Global South typifies yet another layer of European imperialism that enforces cultural hegemony through language. A second strong example refers to graffiti stating "WE WON'T MOVE" in the area of Sofiatown (once Triomf), a place known for its forcible removal of the black populace in 1955 under apartheid. While Sophiatown remains one of Johannesburg's most ethnically diverse districts, graffiti reading "WE WON'T MOVE" appears frequently as a visible reminder of the township's unsettled relationship with the past. The veritable frequency of this type of unsanctioned graffiti is directly related to the idea of transhistorical resistance; more specifically, that the appearance of graffiti marking related to this event may function to prevent forgetting and encourage the production of collective memory. The intensity of anger, pain, and victimization experienced by the collective consciousness long after the forcible removal represents the presence of intergenerational trauma, defined as the diffusion of trauma and trauma's aftereffects following a critical historical event.

Similarly, Sabine Marschall (2002) argues that urban murals and rural wall decoration illustrate an understated and deep resistance to colonial and apartheid legacies by having the physical body enter previous geographies of exclusion. While essentially a transgressive act of opposition to political hegemony—many of which still exist today—these mural and wall-based works represent possibilities for inclusivity and social change: "Murals appropriate spaces and buildings, and through these sites they celebrate cultural difference; they recover history and aspects of traditional heritage; they offer unpretentious, candid glimpses into the activities and environment of daily life. Murals essentially acknowledge and assert the presence of people who were not permitted to occupy these spaces in the past or whose identity and cultural heritage were and often still are ignored or discredited" (Marschall 2002, 51). The contemporaneous inscription of unsanctioned graffiti onto spaces clearly demarcated across racial or ethnic lines decades before, confronts history with a strategy of recovery. Graffiti can operate as a proclamation of physical presence and the embodiment of inclusion, where interventions into post-apartheid topographies—be they physical, conceptual, aesthetic, or otherwise—fundamentally criticize earlier social policies and dominant ideologies. In this sense, unsanctioned graffiti is a different method of "delegitimation" that, as Stuart Hall (in Gerin 2013, 155) explains, occurs when cultural or ideological manifestations can be made vulnerable,exposed, and essentially stripped of their legitimacy.[6]

In recent years, Johannesburg and its districts have been inundated with subversive graffiti that responds directly to Hall's notion of delegitimation,such as the graffiti images featuring Hector Pieterson in the arms of Mbuyisa Makhubo in Soweto (fig. 13.1). This example engages with the concept of delegitimation through its reference to the 1976 student protests in Soweto over the application of Afrikaans Medium Decree, a domestic policy reform that sought to force black students to use Afrikaans and English languages during classes, which essentially devalued (and delegitimized) the students' indigenous dialects. On June 16, 1976, tens of thousands of black students left school to peacefully protest the measures at Orlando Stadium until a riot broke out and left many students, including Hector Pieterson, shot to death by the police. The presence of images of the lifeless Pieterson hanging from the arms of fellow student Mbuyisa Makhubo are marked, and continue to be marked, by artists and writers on the architecture of Soweto and elsewhere in South Africa. Not only does this work, and works similar to it, attempt to delegitimate the incursion of colonial and apartheid forces on indigenous African cultures, but it also strikes out against the systemic protraction of racism and the devaluing of ethnic traditions by erecting unofficial graffiti monuments dedicated to the event and its victims.

Urban art discourse in Johannesburg—for which graffiti and street art is a part of—does not exist in a vacuum but derives from the global urban art movement, most especially from New York City and Europe. The global popularity of hip-hop graffiti art and culture is directly related to the lack of political graffiti in Johannesburg, though the same may be said for other cities around the world. For Waddacor, "Graffiti is connected with hip-hop and that is how it was brought to this country. Young teens found a bond with the culture and sub-culture and began to replicate what they saw."[7] Although hip-hop graffiti may remain altogether local and regional in its execution, urban street culture's aestheticism circulates under the rubric of its cultural limitations. Klopper suggests that hip-hop's influence on graffiti grew out of the New York City scene of the 1960s; however, once it traveled

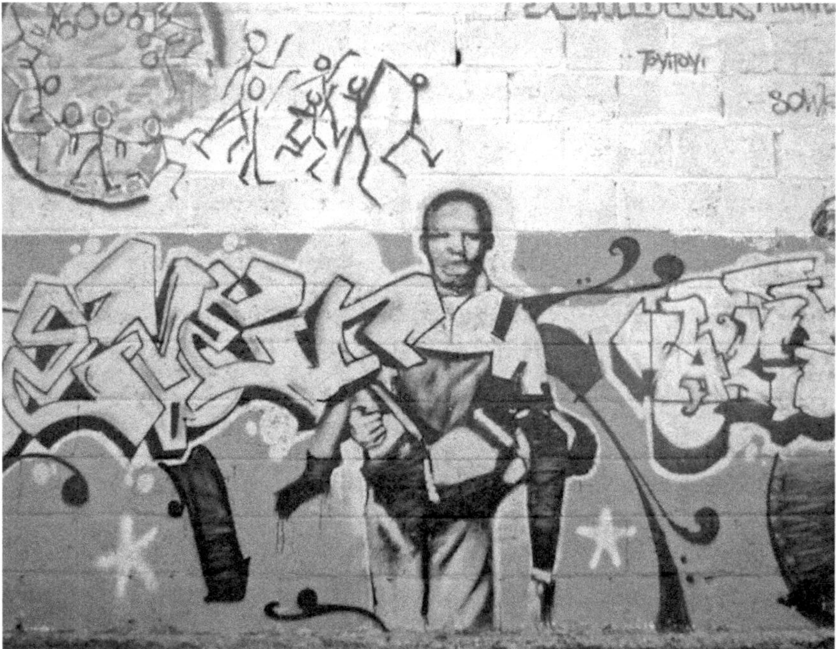

Fig. 13.1 Anonymous. Hector Pieterson in the arms of Mbuyisa Makhubo (date unknown), Soweto, near Vilakazi Street, Johannesburg. *Photograph courtesy of Charlotte Hayes.*

to South Africa, it was employed by marginalized youths from poor urban neighborhoods to speak as a form of autobiographical expression about their experiences. "Even so," she writes, "when it first emerged in South Africa, hip hop probably had more in common with earlier cultural movements that had sought to express opposition to the apartheid government by turning to America for inspiration than with the Mass Democratic Movement of the 1980" (Klopper 2002, 181). In recent years, the younger generation of graffiti artists, with little to no knowledge or memory of apartheid, has taken to the streets with spray cans. Tumelo Mosaka (2004, 31), curator of the exhibition "A Decade of Democracy: Witnessing South Africa," produces a similar observation suggesting that since a decade after the fall of apartheid, a younger generation of visual artists, though socialized under apartheid, is unburdened by its tragedies—their work does not engage or respond to local politics or political vernaculars. During apartheid, graffiti and other forms of urban street art discourse were treated as antagonistic acts of defiance to the state, and people were jailed for graffiti because it was viewed as an uprising.

The lack of political graffiti in Johannesburg may be directly related to the idea that the city has fallen far behind others in terms of responding to the global urban street art movement, so artists and writers are attempting to strategically place themselves within it rather than draw their attention to a graffiti that encourages oppositional politics. In the period following 1999, while many resident graffiti artist and writers engage with the global urban street art movement, unsanctioned graffiti projects executed by outsider, nonresident artists and writers, including Faith47, ABOVE have embraced an oppositional politics, using it to expose and critique Johannesburg's inimitable relationship with global capital, apartheid, and resistance.

OUTSIDE LOOKING IN

In 2012, California-based graffiti artist ABOVE visited Johannesburg to produce a controversial work that soon received the critical attention of global media (fig. 13.2). ABOVE persuaded a community arts and cultural development organization to commission an enormous street-level wall text located on the east security wall in a district of Johannesburg known as Jewel City. Jewel City is the corporate base of operations for nearly three hundred mineral companies and reportedly the largest diamond exporter in the Southern Hemisphere, whose worth is estimated at more than seven billion rand (approximately US$7,000,000) (Smith 2012). ABOVE originally proposed to inscribe the words *Diamonds are a women's best friend* in stylized black-and-white letters, an appropriation of the phrase *diamonds are a girl's best friend* made popular by the actress Marilyn Monroe. Unbeknown to the commissioners of the project, he supplemented the phrase with the quip "And a man's worst enemy" at the time of the work's creation. "What the owners didn't know," says ABOVE, "is that I lied to them and was hijacking their wall. . . . I assume the owners were so busy trading diamonds inside the mega centre that they never took the time to come out and see that I was painting a controversial wordplay about the diamond trade and how it's fuelled so much bloodshed in wars, making it one of man's worst enemies" (Smith 2012). For ABOVE, deception is a necessary, though Machiavellian evil: "I have justified my lying as I feel it created an epic social and political piece" (Kanani 2012). *DIAMONDS ARE A WOMAN'S BEST FRIEND AND A MAN'S WORST ENEMY* blurs the categorical distinctions between sanctioned and unsanctioned graffiti by employing bureaucratic means of

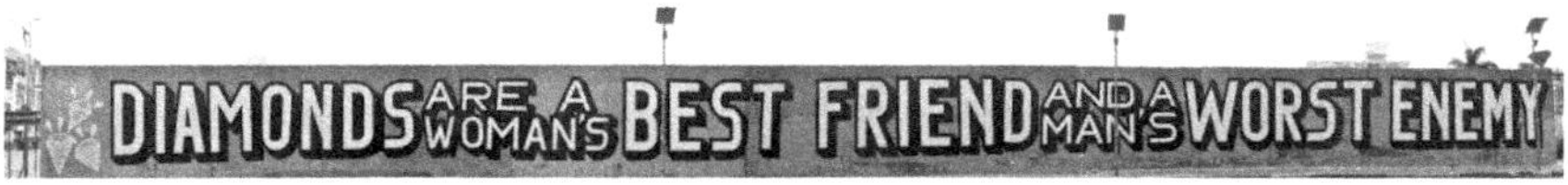

Fig. 13.2 *Diamonds Are a Woman's Best Friend and a Man's Worst Enemy* (2012), Jewel City, Johannesburg. *Photograph courtesy of Cale Waddacor.*

permission through commission while delivering a rhetorical pronouncement critical of Jewel City's corporate mandate and problematic social practices. At issue for ABOVE and other social rights and labor activists is the violent pursuit, sale, and circulation of conflict diamonds—otherwise known as "blood diamonds"—exploited by rebel organizations to finance wars and threaten the sovereignty of African nation-states.[8] Accordingly, ABOVE's wall piece not only affirms a penetrating critique of the conflict diamond industry in Johannesburg but also the encroachment of Euro-American hegemony on the natural resources and labor of South Africa.

Soon after *DIAMONDS ARE A WOMAN'S BEST FRIEND AND A MAN'S WORST ENEMY* was thrown up, authorities had it destroyed. Iain Nicol, asset manager at Redefine Properties, who owns the Jewel City vicinity, responded to the work by saying, "There's a place to do that and take on someone moving blood diamonds. We are not moving blood diamonds. There are probably more blood diamonds going through Antwerp, Israel and India" (Smith 2012). Though he discredits his argument by suggesting that blood diamonds "probably" exist in Johannesburg—but more are sold elsewhere—Nicol references the idea that there is a time and a place to "do" social activism. The strength of interventionist aesthetics lies precisely in its potential to surprise, provoke, and offend. By disrupting conventions of acceptable tropes of social activism, the work represents a powerful act of subterfuge—a condemnation of corporate denial and inactivity masquerading as cute street art. It paradoxically criminates itself as an act of vandalism while enmeshing property owners in critiquing their own corporate practices; this radical reversal of power relations delegitimizes the industry and officials who sanction conflict diamonds or choose to ignore their presence.

Likewise, Cape Town–based graffiti artist Faith47 also criticizes issues of economic disparity and class discrimination in post-apartheid Johannesburg through a series of sanctioned and unsanctioned graffiti and mural projects. Her work is strongly compelled by issues of empowerment—in the city, women continue to encounter abusive domestic environments, social inequality, and it is reported that approximately one in three women have been raped.[9] Arguably, she is best known for her 2010 series *Freedom Charter,* which reproduces particular words and phrases from the core principles of the controversial 1955 African National Congress's Freedom Charter document. The Freedom Charter was born out of South African anti-apartheid political organizations calling on citizens to submit their visions for a new democratic social order; however, outspoken critics of the charter maintain that the legacies of imperialism have exploited the labor force, natural resources, and financial capital of South Africa to the point where nationalization is a cold fallacy (see Peffer 2009). By inscribing texts from the charter in geographies where economic and sociopolitical change is exigent—low-income communities, high-crime locations, condemned buildings, and squatter's settlements—it is precisely this concept of intangible hope that Faith47 exposes. For instance, in *Rest, Leisure & Recreation: SHALL BE THE RIGHT OF ALL* (fig. 13.3), she takes issue with one of the ten demands listed in the charter: "There Shall Be Houses, Security and Comfort!" Affixed on a pillar under a bridge in the historical Newtown district of Johannesburg, the whimsical inscription of text contrasts sharply with what lies below—makeshift beds, various living supplies, and detritus. Against this climate of disillusionment, as manifested by the lack of affordable housing, the potential for radical social change lies in what might be considered an unobvious place. By marking the verisimilitudes of marginalization and poverty in and around Johannesburg, Faith47 politicizes overlooked topographies while emphasizing fractures in the social order. The almost-violent juxtaposition between these sites and its rhetoric of hope points to the charter's ineffectual promises and failure to introduce meaningful structural socioeconomic.

More recently, in late 2012, Faith47 returned to Johannesburg with the purpose of executing an unsanctioned project titled *The Long Wait* (fig. 13.4), the first installment of the series *Fragments of a Burnt History,* which demonstrated a concern with the structural and systemic consequences of idleness, a lack of employment, and self-fulfillment through labor. The twenty-four works appear in several areas of the city including Soweto, Newtown, Maboneng Precinct, Commissioner Street, Jan Smuts Avenue, Oxford Street, Louis Botha Avenue, Braamfontein, Yeoville, and Rosebank. Executed in black-and-white enamel, figures are seen hunched over and dejected with gaunt faces and sunken shoulders, her drip technique striving to conceptualize

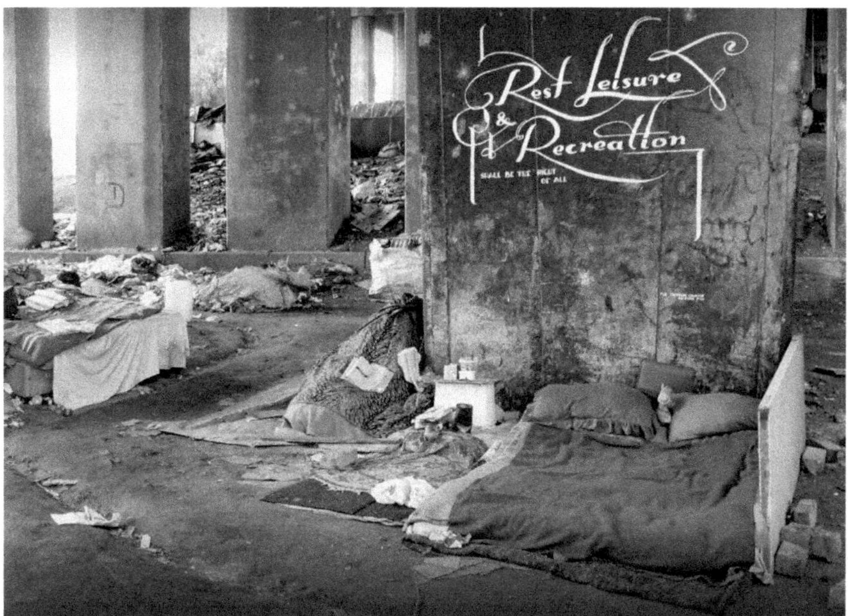

Fig. 13.3 Faith47, *The Freedom Charter* (series) (2010), Johannesburg. *Photograph courtesy of Faith47.*

how denizens of Johannesburg are threatened with the specters of inactivity and obscurity. For Faith47, the work makes a strong attempt to visualize "miners waiting for justice, workers waiting for a living wage, people waiting for service delivery, refugees waiting for assistance, we are all waiting for an honest politician. There has been so much waiting in this country that much time has been lost" (Krut 2014). She continues to expose these wounds much in the same way as ABOVE: by visualizing the perennial survival of its effects as they currently exist in reality and in the collective memory, and in this way, the work is heavily influenced by the earlier *The Freedom Charter* series in that it also draws attention to the structural and systemic imbalances in the city. In bringing attention to the vernacular, everyday proceedings of such topographies, she makes a conceded effort to snap individuals out of their passivity and into a more strategic oppositional politics. Finally, Faith 47 positions the physical body in spaces and sites where it was previously excluded under apartheid law, and where opportunities for gainful employment are difficult, in order to draw attention to the painfully sluggish socioeconomic progress of reformation policies following the fall of apartheid.

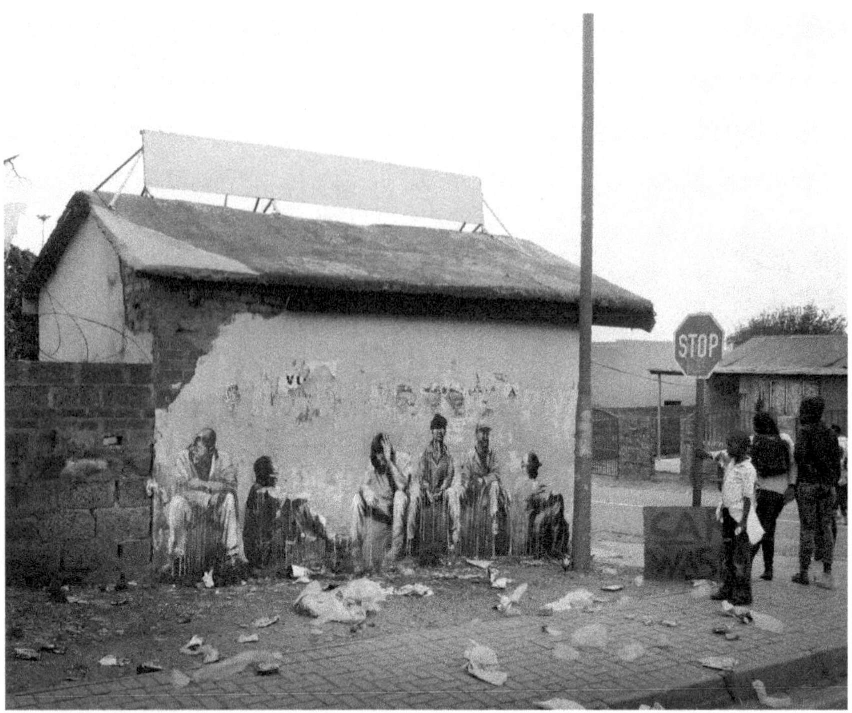

Fig. 13.4 Faith47, *The Long Wait* (series) (2012), Johannesburg. *Photograph courtesy of Faith47.*

CONCLUSION

In his examination of urban development in post-apartheid Johannesburg, Martin Murray (2011) argues that builders, developers, property owners, municipal authorities, and private security firms intended to model Johannesburg as a world-class city after the fall of apartheid. As a result of their quest to reshape the city under this rubric, they paradoxically succeeded in establishing new forms of spatial segregation between the upper classes and the black urban poor, effectively cutting them off from participating in the urban life of the city (Murray 2011; see also Gaule 2005). As Johannesburg and other cities in South Africa continue to structure and sanitize the urban landscape through the idealization of global capital, they also (see Bremner 2002, 171) "redraw" the boundaries of apartheid; however, it is the acts of everyday denizens that reinvigorate and renew the social life and topography of the modern city. The effort put forth by municipal officials to clean up particular areas and neighborhoods of Johannesburg, and therefore rid it of unsanctioned graffiti, tagging, culture jamming, and other unsightly markings, may suggest an effort to organize the city geographically based on ethnicity, class, and color. If this is so, then the boundaries for nonwhites and whites in and around Johannesburg are still being negotiated in ways similar to how they once were in 1897. At the present moment, municipal authorities are not drawing up spatial boundaries according to race, color, and ethnicity, it is where graffiti is destroyed and removed that may rightfully indicate the spatial boundaries between people.

Informed by the streets, it is fully possible for graffiti to represent a symbol of resistance to help forge a localized sense of community (see Lennon 2014). The heterogeneous images and texts created by graffiti writers are as important to understanding Johannesburg graffiti as are the body's participation in such acts. Unsanctioned graffiti involves a symbiotic relationship between the aesthetic and the political; the spray can, like the body itself, symbolize apparatuses for resistance because law, society, and unspoken rules often dictate where *they are not supposed to be*. The deconstruction of unsanctioned graffiti practices in Johannesburg serves to critique, delegitimize, and resist dominant ideologies embedded by colonialism and apartheid. This work is intended to prevent against the disappearance of traumatic historical events in the collective memory and in the minds of younger generations, which, in turn, help to forge a unified front against the violence and repression that the official city limits of Johannesburg is founded upon.

Matthew Ryan Smith, is a sessional professor of Visual Studies at the University of Toronto, Mississauga. His research explores the impact of colonialism on indigenous cultures and contemporary graffiti/street art practices.

Notes

1. For more information on the victimization of South Africa's poor and an analysis of crime rates in South Africa, see Naudé, Prinsloo and Ladikos (2006).
2. C. Waddacor, e-mail communication, December 10, 2014.
3. Ibid.
4. The idea of street-as-medium is derived from the author's reference to street-as -"material" "resource." See Riggle (2010, 245).

5. See also McCormick (2011).

6. Slavoj Žižek (2012, 281) interprets Hall's concept of delegitimation as a political struggle waged on the primacy of specific ideas and ideologies.

7. Waddacor, personal communication, December 10, 2014.

8. Though plagued with internal strife in recent years, the Kimberley Process has been a strong advocate for stemming the flow of conflict diamonds. For more information on the Kimberley Process, see http://www.kimberleyprocess.com/.

9. A 1999 survey of four thousand women, conducted by CIET Africa, a nongovernmental organization, reveals that one in three women were raped that same year in the city of Johannesburg, gaining the city a reputation of, according to the article, the world's "rape capital." See BBC News (1999).

References

Apartheid Museum. 2006. *Understanding Apartheid*. Johannesburg: Apartheid Museum.

Banksy. 2007. *Wall and Piece*. London: Century.

BBC News. 1999. "World: Africa, South Africa's Rape Shock." January 19. Accessed December 5, 2015. http://news.bbc.co.uk/2/hi/africa/258446.stm.

Bremner, Lindsay J. 2002. "Closure, Simulation, and 'Making Do' in the Contemporary Johannesburg Landscape." In *Under Siege: Four African Cities: Freetown, Johannesburg, Kinshasa, Lagos*, edited by Okwui Enwezor et al., 153–72. Ostfildern-Ruit, Germany: Hatje Cantz.

Brookings Institution. 2014. "Global MetroMonitor." Accessed March 30, 2015. http://www.brookings.edu/research/interactives/global-metro-monitor-3.

City of Johannesburg. 2014. "Report Graffiti Hotspots." Accessed December 5, 2015. http://www.joburg.org.za/index.php? option=com_content&view=article&id=8189:report-graffiti-hotspots&catid=88:news-update&itemid=266.

City of Johannesburg: Arts, Culture, and Heritage Services. 2005. "'Reclaiming Public Space': The Development of a Policy for Public Performance and Public Art." Accessed December 5, 2015. http://www.nyc.gov/html/ia/gp/downloads/pdf/art_johannesburg.pdf.

———. 2006. "Public Art Policy." Accessed December 4, 2015. http://www.joburg-archive.co.za/2006/pdfs/public_art_policy.pdf.

———. 2014. "Report Graffiti Hot-Spots." Accessed December 6, 2015. http://www.joburg.org.za/index.php?option=com_content&view=article&id=8189:report-graffiti-hotspots&catid=88:newsupdate &Itemid=266.

Cronin, J. Keri, and Kirsty Robertson, eds. 2011. *Imagining Resistance: Visual Culture and Activism in Canada*. Waterloo, ON: Wilfred Laurier University Press.

David Krut Projects. 2014. "Faith47—The Long Wait: Part II." Accessed March 30, 2015. http://davidkrutprojects.com/20700/faith47-the-long-wait-part-two.

Deitch, Jeffrey, Roger Gastman, Aaron Rose, and Ethel Seno. 2011. *Art in the Streets*. New York: Skira Rizzoli.

Dovey, Kim, Simon Wollan, and Ian Woodcock. 2012. "Placing Graffiti: Creating and Contesting Character in Inner-City Melbourne." *Journal of Urban Design* 17, no. 1 (February): 21–41.

Enwezor, Okwui. 2004. "The Enigma of the Rainbow Nation: Contemporary South African Art at the Crossroads of History." In *Personal Affects: Power and Poetics in Contemporary South African Art*, edited by David Brodie et al., 22–43. Cape Town: Spier.

Faith47. 2011. *Faith47*. Berlin: From Here to Fame Publishing.

Ganz, Nicholas. 2006. *Graffiti Women: Street Art from Five Continents*. New York: Abrams.

Gaule, Sally. 2005. "Alternating Currents of Power: From Colonial to Post-apartheid Spatial Patterns in Newtown, Johannesburg." *Urban Studies* 42, no. 13 (December): 2335–61.

Gerin, Annie. 2013. "A Second Look at Laughter: Humor in the Visual Arts." *Humor* 26, no. 1 (January): 155–76.

Heartney, Eleanor. 1994. "Ecopolitics/Ecopoetry: Helen and Newton Harrison's Environmental Talking Cure." In *But Is It Art? The Spirit of Art as Activism*, edited by Nina Felshin, 141–64. Seattle: Bay Press.

Heddon, Deidre. 2002. "Autotopographies: Graffiti, Landscapes & Selves." *Reconstruction: Journal of Contemporary Culture* 2, no. 3. Accessed December 5, 2015. http://reconstruction.eserver.org/ Issues/023/heddon.htm.

Holub, Robert C. 1991. *Jürgen Habermas: Critic in the Public Sphere*. New York: Routledge.

Johnston, Pauline. 2006. *Habermas: Rescuing the Public Sphere*. New York: Routledge.

Kanani, Bazi. 2012. "American Graffiti Artist Brags about Diamond Mural Prank." *ABC News*, April 24. Accessed December 29, 2015. http://abcnews.go.com/blogs /headlines/2012/04/american-graffiti-artist-boasts-prank-mural-south-africa/.

Klein, Naomi. 2002. *No Logo*. New York: Picador.

Klopper, Sandra. 2000. "Hip Hop Graffiti Art." In *Senses of Culture: South African Culture Studies*, edited by Sarah Nuttall and Cheryl-Ann Michael, 178–96. Oxford: Oxford University Press.

Kwon, Miwon. 2002. *One Place after Another: Site-Specific Art and Locational Identity* Cambridge, MA: MIT Press.

Landau, Paul S., and Deborah D. Kaspin. 2002. *Images and Empires: Visuality in Colonial and Postcolonial Africa*. Berkeley: University of California Press.

Lennon, John. 2014. "Assembling a Revolution: Graffiti, Cairo and the Arab Spring." *Cultural Studies Review* 20, no. 1 (March): 237–75.

Macdonald, Nancy. 2006. "The Feminine Touch: The Highs and Lows of the Female Graffiti Experience." In *Graffiti Women: Street Art from Five Continents*, edited by Nicholas Ganz, 12–13. New York: Abrams.

Marschall, Sabine. 2000. "A Postcolonial Reading of Mural Art in South Africa." *Critical Arts: South-North Cultural and Media Studies* 14, no. 2: 96–121.

———. 2002. "Sites of Identity and Resistance: Urban Community Murals and Rural Wall Decoration in South Africa." *African Arts* 35, no. 3 (Autumn): 40–53, 91–92.

McCormick, Carlo. 2011. "The Writing on the Wall." In *Art in the Streets*, edited by Jeffrey Deitch, Roger Gastman, Aaron Rose, and Ethel Seno, 19–24. New York: Skira Rizzoli.

Mosaka, Tumelo. 2004. "A Decade of Democracy: Witnessing South Africa." In *A Decade of Democracy: Witnessing South Africa*, edited by Gary van Wyk, 31–32. Boston: South African Development Fund.

Murray, Martin J. 2011. *Politics, History, and Culture: City of Extremes: The Spatial Politics of Johannesburg.* Durham, NC: Duke University Press.

Naudé, C. M. B., J. H. Prinsloo, and A. Ladikos. 2006. *Experiences of Crime in Thirteen African Countries: Results from the International Crime Victim Survey.* Turin: United Nations Crime and Justice Research Institute. http://www.unicri.it/services/library_documentation/publications/icvs/publications/ICVS_13_African_countries.pdf.

Ouzman, Sven. 2008. *Imprints: An Archaeology of Identity in Post-Apartheid Southern Africa.* Berkeley: University of California Press.

Peffer, John. 2009. *Art and the End of Apartheid.* Minneapolis: University of Minnesota Press.

Rabine, Leslie W. 2014. "'These Walls Belong to Everybody': The Graffiti Art Movement in Dakar." *African Studies Quarterly* 14, no. 3 (March): 89–112.

Riggle, Nicholas Alden. 2010. "Street Art: The Transfiguration of the Commonplaces." *The Journal of Aesthetics and Criticism* 68, no. 3 (Summer): 243–57.

Sassen, Saskia. 2011. "The Global Street: Making the Political." *Globalizations* 8, no. 5 (October): 573–79.

Schiller, Marc, and Sara Schiller. 2010. "City View." In Carlo McCormick, *Trespass: A History of Uncommissioned Street Art,* edited by Ethel Seno, 10–13. London: Taschen.

Seno, Ethel. 2010. "Rules of the Game." In Carlo McCormick, *Trespass: A History of Uncommissioned Street Art,* edited by Ethel Seno, 20–48. London: Taschen.

Smith, David. 2012. "US Graffiti Artist's Johannesburg Mural Takes Swipe at Diamond Trade." *The Guardian,* April 17. Accessed December 6, 2015. http://www.theguardian.com/world/2012/apr/17/us-graffiti-artist-johannesburg-diamond.

The Kimberley Process. 2014. "About." Accessed March 30, 2015. http://www.kimberleyprocess.com/.

Transvaal (South African Republic). 1922. Local Government Commission (Stallard). T.P. 1.

Waclawek, Anna. 2011. *Graffiti and Street Art.* London: Thames and Hudson.

Waddacor, Cale. 2014. *Graffiti South Africa.* Atglen, PA: Schiffer Publishing.

Warner, Michael. 2004. *Publics and Counterpublics.* New York: Zone Books.

Witherden, Amy. 2010. "Graffiti Devalues Communities." *Polity.org.za,* September 7. Accessed December 5, 2015. http://www.polity.org.za/article/graffiti-devalues-communities-2010-09-07.

Whitlock, Gillian, and Anna Poletti. 2008. "Self-Regarding Art." *Biography: An Interdisciplinary Quarterly* 31, no. 1 (Winter): v–xiii.

Žižek, Slavoj, ed. 2012. *Mapping Ideology.* New York: Verso.

INDEX

Page numbers in italics refer to illustrations.

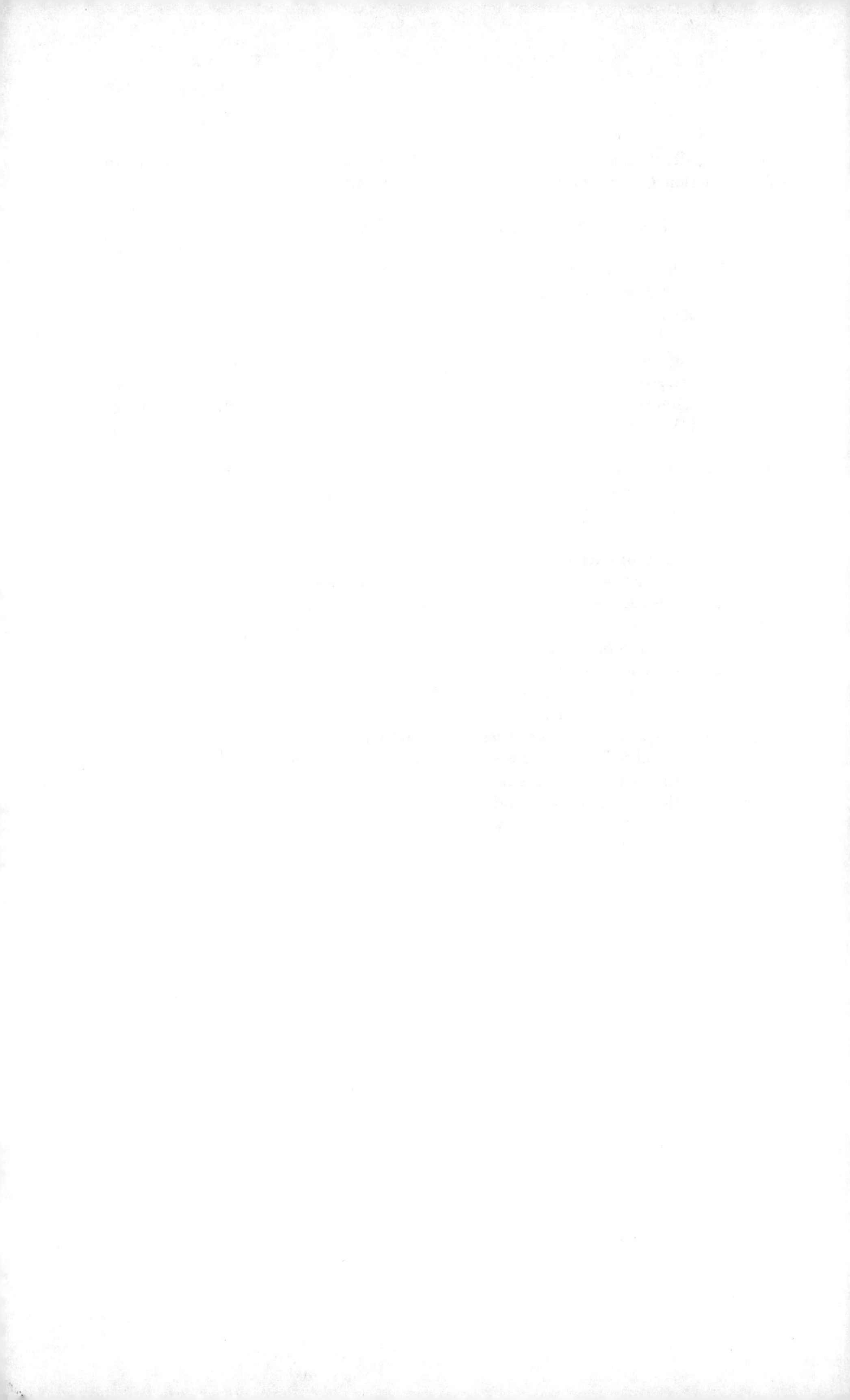

CPSIA information can be obtained
at www.ICGtesting.com
Printed in the USA
BVHW07s1104210818
525176BV00011B/310/P